POLITICAL
TOLERANCE

Contemporary American Politics

Series Editors

Richard G. Niemi, *University of Rochester*
Barbara Sinclair, *University of California, Los Angeles*

Editorial Board

John Aldrich, *Duke University*
Gregory Caldeira, *The Ohio State University*
Stanley Feldman, *SUNY Stony Brook*
Katherine Tate, *The Ohio State University*
Sue Thomas, *Georgetown University*

The **Contemporary American Politics** series is intended to assist students and faculty in the field of American politics by bridging the gap between advanced but oft-times impenetrable research on the one hand, and oversimplified presentations on the other. The volumes in this series represent the most exciting work in political science—cutting-edge research that focuses on major unresolved questions, contradicts conventional wisdom, or initiates new areas of investigation. Ideal as supplemental texts for undergraduate courses, these volumes will examine the institutions, processes, and policy questions that make up the American political landscape.

Books in This Series

DO CAMPAIGNS MATTER?
Thomas M. Holbrook

GENDER DYNAMICS IN CONGRESSIONAL ELECTIONS
Richard Logan Fox

THE CONGRESSIONAL BLACK CAUCUS: Racial Politics in the
U.S. Congress
Robert Singh

POLITICAL TOLERANCE: Balancing Community and Diversity
Robert Weissberg

POLITICAL TOLERANCE

Balancing Community and Diversity

Robert Weissberg

CONTEMPORARY
AMERICAN
POLITICS

SAGE Publications
International Educational and Professional Publisher
Thousand Oaks London New Delhi

For information:

 SAGE Publications, Inc.
2455 Teller Road
Thousand Oaks, California 91320
E-mail: order@sagepub.com

SAGE Publications Ltd.
6 Bonhill Street
London EC2A 4PU
United Kingdom

SAGE Publications India Pvt. Ltd.
M-32 Market
Greater Kailash I
New Delhi 110 048 India

Printed in the United States of America

Library of Congress Cataloging-in-Publication Data

Weissberg, Robert.
   Political tolerance: balancing community and diversity /
by Robert Weissberg.
      p. cm. -- (Contemporary American politics ; v. 4)
   Includes bibliographical references and index.
   ISBN 0-8039-7342-X (cloth)
   ISBN 0-8039-7343-8 (pbk.)
   1. Toleration. 2. Human rights. 3. Multiculturalism. 4. Political
correctness. I. Title. II. Series.
   JC571 .W385 1998
   323--ddc21
                                                                98-8983

This book is printed on acid-free paper.
98 99 00 01 02 03 04 10 9 8 7 6 5 4 3 2 1

Acquisition Editor:	Peter Labella
Production Editor:	Michèle Lingre
Production Assistant:	Lynn Miyata
Typesetter/Designer:	Rose Tylak
Cover Designer:	Candice Harman

Contents

Preface: A Personal Tale of Tolerance and Intolerance

Even the most crisply argued, finely etched explications undoubtedly began as a confused, vague, meandering idea. This book is no exception. *Political Tolerance* germinated some two decades ago at a conference seeking "international understanding." It was a distinguished, generously funded assembly in a spectacular physical setting topped off with fine food, live chamber music, and first-rate accommodations. Its motives—to promote harmony through mutual appreciation commencing with early education—were beyond reproach. All labored over the long weekend to invent fresh ways to make youngsters more receptive to "differences." Contrary to what might be anticipated, however, this experience hardly inspired my quest for "new and improved" tolerance; the very opposite ensued.

As the conference lumbered along, as loose discussions were transformed into written summaries and these synopses became expert recommendations, my uneasiness grew. Something was amiss, I sensed, despite an enthusiastic, almost gleeful atmosphere. I eventually detected the source of my unease—unquestionably prescribing "cultural relativism" to cure the world's ills. Our job as educators, we were reminded, is to persuade children that all is merely different, not better or worse, and imposing dogma is improper, even dangerous. Haughty intolerance, everyone assembled "knew," generated incessant hatreds, strife, and similar calamities. The task at hand, then, was to squeeze ingeniously this miraculous anti-absolutist message into an already overcluttered curriculum.

I quietly but openly demurred. I inquired of my fellow participants about cultures sanctioning mistreatment of women. Surely, I protested, this "difference" was unworthy of protection justified by multicultural tolerance. I further added that mere verbal acceptances of value distinctiveness seldom eliminates conflict. Close relatives routinely battle over mundane tangibles. I politely hinted that this wondrous but unverified cliché-like message might well drive perceptive students to cynicism. To me, promoting an "accept everything and everyone" was discernible nonsense.

Remarkable events followed. I was ostracized for questioning unrestricted "tolerance." I found myself eating lunch alone, idle social chatterers avoided me, and my comments were politely ignored. "Marginalized," is today's fashionable idiom. Thank goodness burning at the stake was illegal. My banishment was not, of course, a harsh punishment: The food, wine, and accommodations remained superb. Nevertheless, despite my isolation, I had learned a valuable lesson.

This message was deepened a decade later when I was asked to write an essay on public opinion. Until then, I had never engaged tolerance as a research topic though I occasionally lectured on the subject. Almost by chance, "tolerance" was chosen as the object of a case study. The long march through existent scholarship required in drafting this article again occasioned unease—this vast literature was incomplete, the world was not quite as depicted, and a familiar complacency prevailed regarding tolerance's virtues. This discomfiture soon found expression in additional papers plus a book review broaching my contrarian views. These writings did not denounce tolerance nor libel nor those cultivating the conventional survey-based approach. I was, at least in my own mind, merely calling for a more complex treatment of an over-simplified subject.

My qualms elicited some favorable response, particularly among those not yet professionally inducted into the scholarly "tolerance industry." Nevertheless, the reaction among my professional peers, the academic *nomenklatura* with a stake in the intellectual status quo, was hostility. I was committing heresy. Essays sent to fellow scholars for perusal, a common academic practice, received silence. An outsider would surmise that I was advocating some terrible unprofessional sin. Only friends paid attention. Those embracing a most generous tolerance, ironically, found my skeptical questioning insufferable.

"Real world" political shifts during the 1980s deepened my alarm. Like mobilizing society to combat an epidemic, a rush toward the imposition of tolerance through educational indoctrination seemed everywhere. The eradi-cation of racism, sexism, homophobia, and similar aversions is now "hot." Hundreds of thousands of students and workers find themselves involuntarily enrolled in sensitivity workshops and similar campaigns. To resist, even to gently raise doubts, only suggests bigotry, hatred, or worse, deep patholo-gies. Our new collective calamity is a form of psychological sickness.

This pernicious shift constitutes an easy first step in the march toward totalitarianism. This word *totalitarianism* is not used lightly; the business at hand is serious. The traditional focus on proper public behavior, not inner, private thoughts, is being repealed in the name of an unproved, unchallenged Utopian panorama. "Sticks and stones can break my bones, but names can never harm me" is judged antiquated, replaced by "the good society starts with good thinking, and who better to guarantee good thinking than the mighty benevolent government." Limited government for some is too obso-lete to solve "modern" problems. "Bad thinking" thus differs not at all from polluting the environment. Conjuring up visions of the well-funded, un-checked thought police industriously promoting "tolerance" is not a scare tactic. The shift from qualified behavioral tolerance to blank-check attitudi-nal tolerance should appall those cherishing individual liberty. *Political Tolerance* is, at least partially, a polemical book intended to expose the totalitarianism wolf parading around the barnyard as the ever-tolerant, good-deed dispensing sheep.

The understanding of tolerance present here is, I hope, far more compat-ible with individual liberty and a free society. The tolerance I embrace is reasonable acceptance within an entire society. Tolerance exists where eccentric political inclinations can exist without incapacitating interference, provided democratically determined law governs. Nothing here pertains to vague extra-legal "atmospheres" of intolerance though such factors may contribute. No standing enforceable obligation inheres to convert citizens into porous creatures to absorb yet one more novelty. The bottom line is freedom, not vague, ill-formed citizen musings about freedom.

As in all book projects, many others have contributed. Richard Niemi, the series co-editor for Sage, deserves special gratitude for the patient encour-agement and thoughtful commentary. A *mensch.* Thanks also go to William G. Jacoby, who carefully reviewed the manuscript. Assisting me was my ever-diligent, stealthy, and resourceful research assistant, Charles C. DeWitt. The library staff at the University of Illinois, Urbana-Champaign, deserves boun-tiful accolades. On numerous occasions, with speed, grace and charm, they unearthed the unfindable. Good friends Wayne Allen and Nino Langiulli read several chapters and supplied valuable ideas and corrections. The Earhart Foundation kindly provided the financial support necessary to complete the project. A special gratefulness goes to Erika Gilbert, my good Prussian "constant companion," who understands full well the trauma of nurturing complex ideas.

Unlike many scholarly books, *Political Tolerance* contains material a few might judge controversial, even inflammatory. Since these are "sensitive" times, let me declare that views expressed here are exclusively mine. I do not wish to embarrass or implicate anyone who might disagree. None of this material in the slightest detail reflects the contributions of my political science colleagues at the University of Illinois, Urbana-Champaign.

Tolerance

" "Tolerance" has become a commonplace, even over-used, word in contemporary politics. All political persuasions, from the liberal to the conservative, rush to embrace it: No sensible person favors "intolerance." The November 17-19, 1995 "USA Weekend," a mass circulation Sunday newspaper supplement, contained the heart-warming story by Mary Fisher recounting that while she and her husband have AIDS, her two AIDS-free young children are often ostracized by parents and playmates. She sadly concluded that AIDS "has become an American object lesson in intolerance" (5). The United Nations declared 1995 the "Year For Tolerance" and to celebrate this momentous event, it organized various international conferences, a motorcycle expedition from Denver to Panama City, and a sound and light show (Zaragoza, 1995). Both gays insisting on same-sex marriages and religious parents advocating prayers in public schools assert claims to "greater tolerance." Educators have made teaching respect for differences a sacred crusade. Buzz words such as "multiculturalism," "sensitivity," "diversity," "nonjudgmental," and "repression" all pertain to tolerance. The "political correctness" debate deeply involves tolerance with each side accusing the other of "true" intolerance. Tolerance, unfortunately, may be deteriorating into an empty, honorific slogan, a concept perhaps robbed of any meaning by relentless over-use.

Though tolerance has gained fresh notoriety, the underlying issue is hardly novel. Nearly sixty years ago, a group of distinguished Americans created

1

the "Council Against Intolerance in America" to inculcate tolerance among children as a bulwark against the hatreds then sweeping Europe. Their teacher's manual, *An American Answer to Intolerance* (1939), would fit unnoticed into today's curriculum. More fundamentally, friction over social and political acceptability is endemic; tolerance is intrinsic to politics. Only the modern vocabulary and incessant arguments are novel. Historical disputes over religious heresy, slavery, and socialism are at core about "what is to be tolerated?" Only the debate's content varies—we no longer debate religious tests for office, but skirmishes over homosexuality and abortion use now capture our attention.

The abiding character tolerance disputes cannot be over-emphasized. Insisting that everybody agree to "be tolerant" to ensure harmony is nonsensical, even delusional. A modern magical remedy for our collective ills has not been suddenly discovered. The specifics—religious doctrines, political views, appropriate sexual behavior, immigration, public decency—come and go, but this "What is to be accepted or banished?" controversy never ends. Resolutions, no matter how consensual or forceful, are inevitably temporary. Conflict over inclusionary principles is integral to our societal definition; antagonisms cannot be escaped by preaching a doctrine of unqualified acceptance of everything. High-sounding calls for ever expanding tolerance aside, no society can permit *everything* to flourish. The debate concerns what should be tolerated, not tolerance versus intolerance. Tolerance might profitably be thought of as a "window" separating what must be prohibited from what is laudatory. After all, who can demand that we tolerate the intolerable? Denial of this truism invites anarchy and chaos, not heaven on earth.

Today's widespread celebrations of tolerance typically flow from three barely articulated and rarely challenged premises. First, being highly tolerant as a general predisposition, apart from a specific situation, is a praiseworthy personal and civic virtue. It is integral to democracy's constellation of political virtues, coexisting with political attentiveness, voting, and obeying the law. As Ryszard Legutko (1994) put it, "Without much exaggeration, it can be said that the triumph of liberalism has elevated this category [tolerance] into the ultimate and almost only general litmus test of morality. At the very least, no single category—not justice, not equality, not even freedom— has won such wide moral support in the Western world" (610).

Second, this wondrous quality is presently in too short a supply, both individually and collectively. For this reason, no doubt, schools and mass media time should vigorously promote the acceptance of differences. Hatred and prejudice—virtual synonyms for intolerance—must be expelled. Finally, greater endorsement of personal and political diversity would help heal festering acrimonious divisions. Intolerance, thus understood, resembles a disease. If whites and blacks displayed greater tolerance of each other, or citizens display heightened sensitivity to the plight of recent immigrants, society would be more civil, harmonious and, ultimately, democratic.

Thus framed, the rush to embrace tolerance is seductively irresistible. No wonder, then, nearly everyone of repute compellingly endorses "more acceptance of differences." Who could possibly countenance bigotry and hate? Only those nostalgic for the Spanish Inquisition will confess to repressive urges or demands that government banish the unconventional. Tolerance has entered the Pantheon of self-evident virtue, a goodness akin to honesty, being informed, eating a healthy diet, and other nondebatable righteous qualities.

Political Tolerance takes a different and quite unfashionable path. We do not embrace intolerance; rather, we argue this topic is far more complicated, less one-sided, than initial appearances. Worse, the facile existent consensus regarding the need for more and more tolerance is misleading, if not dangerous. Unrestricted tolerance is an impossibility despite our infatuation with endless augmentation. If we truly wished unrestricted tolerance, we must dismantle the criminal code, not extend it. The fashionably reflexive embrace of tolerance as a magical cure for political and social disorders likewise betrays serious misunderstandings. Unthinkingly welcoming differences without a hard look at what these differences are, simply to escape being labeled intolerant, hardly engenders a better society, greater equanimity or happier individuals. Too many gladly received shades of opinion are possible. No logic connects a multiplicity of divergent inclinations with public happiness or social peace. Even worse, we shall argue, relentlessly discarding boundaries of acceptability may incite its own particular brand of misery and oppression. Raising up strong differences, and then compelling their acceptance, is not cost-free, however alluring this may be. If tolerance is to be pursued seriously, it must be rescued from becoming an empty cliché, a modern version of cure-all snake oil. Nor should it become little more than a rallying cry for unpopular or defeated causes. Endless invocation, in and of itself, with no serious understanding, accomplishes nothing positive.

Why Another Book About Tolerance?

The subject of tolerance may initially appear over-developed. Libraries of pertinent books and thoughtful articles already exist. Surely, it would seem, every point worthy of expression has been made, perchance a few times too many. Perhaps the word, or even the entire issue, should be rested or retired. The reality, however, is quite different. A great deal has been said but largely from one vantage point. A balance needs to be restored. *Political Tolerance* is an eclectic collection of arguments, empirical analyses, and prescriptions, all having something to do with our infatuation with greater acceptances of differences. Subsequent chapters are but disparate excursions, not a microscopic investigation of a narrow subject.

Our purposes are multiple. First, we assemble a variety of previous scholarly findings. Though not an exhaustive inventory, this tour provides useful high-altitude reconnaissance. This inventory also scrutinizes past investigations of tolerance. As we shall elucidate, this endeavor goes beyond typical social science methodological quibbling: The study of tolerance is hardly a politically neutral process. This summary of findings and approaches is not, however, our primary purpose. More important, we enlarge our comprehension of tolerance in some uncommon ways, not merely deepening prevailing approaches. Tolerance extends farther than what is typically presented in most contemporary explications. We portray the actual levels of tolerance in contemporary politics, not merely citizens' desires. Finally, *Political Tolerance* wrestles with a complex moral and prescriptive issue, particularly the balancing of political tolerance with a free and open society. We contend that unrestrictive tolerance is not the path to liberty and democracy.

Neglected Areas of Research

Selected facets of tolerance receive extensive scholarly attention. For example, the historical nature and philosophical evolution of tolerance are extensively documented. Chapter 4 briefly touches on this foundation, namely, the writings of John Locke and J. S. Mill. Similarly, modern research generously informs us regarding the distribution of attitudinal tolerance and its psychological correlates. Chapter 3 highlights many of these findings. Nevertheless, despite past research accumulations, the picture remains surprisingly incomplete. The knowledge map depicts a few explored continents, some intensely scrutinized islands, and sketchy reports on murky areas.

A conspicuously underscrutinized topic is deciding acceptability, how to delineate the "window," so to speak. Champions of modern tolerance remain embarrassingly silent here. Why, for example, do scholarly tolerance advocates routinely endorse permitting socialist views while rejecting a comparable graciousness toward fascism? Similarly, why is government containment of white racist militias generally commendable, but a free society is regarded subverted if the FBI infiltrates the Communist Party? Might a principle be found permitting us to demarcate government repression directed against, say, armed militias from an identical action against Louis Farrakhan's Nation of Islam? How do we choose? Do we probe written programs? Member actions? Can we distinguish abstract principles from heat-of-battle utterances? This is a critical subject, yet today's tolerance celebrations go shamefully mute when such dilemmas arise. To be sure, devising a simple discriminatory tool may be nearly impossible, but the quest for principles of assignment is a worthy one. Lines must be drawn, and to refuse to do so when demanding yet more tolerance is irresponsible escapism.

Analysis also challenges the all-too-common equation of public distaste with in-place forceful repression. Gardeners appreciate that it is one thing to try eradicating weeds, quite another to succeed. Surveys monotonously depict citizens' aversion to unpopular, controversial groups, but likening such repugnance to de facto banishment violates logic. Relatively little is known about the survival of hated groups despite inhospitable environments. Does vehement public opposition to Marxism necessarily incapacitate the Communist Party? Clearly not, says the historical record. Why do some outcast groups persevere while others quickly vanish? Does public intolerance guarantee these declines? Similarly, though intolerance seems ingrained in human beings, such tenacity is more likely to receive condemnation than explanation. Surely it is reasonable to ask why "wrong" views, opinions allegedly plainly subversive of democracy, resist unmerciful efforts at eradication. Might passions to banish be so deeply lodged in human nature, on a par with the need for family or the desire for order? Are anti-intolerance campaigns thus doomed to failure?

Our analysis restores balance to contemporary tolerance deliberations. Arguments for *in*tolerance are taken seriously. This contribution, undoubtedly, will be highly controversial and, for some, hopelessly misunderstood. With few exceptions, a sermonizing—almost proselytizing—quality surrounds public pronouncements and scholarly research. Books about tolerance ordinarily commence by informing the reader that subsequent findings will, it is hoped, further advance the frontiers of inclusiveness. A legitimate case for eliminating antagonisms, even forcefully if necessary, is rarely acknowledged, let alone developed. Even hinting at this possibility invites accusations of bigotry and hate-mongering. Nevertheless, given society's vast moral prohibitions, its innumerable criminal laws, and all the mounting pressures to forbid even more, advocating *in*tolerance is, in fact, the norm. In a sense, education itself, the teaching of right versus wrong, correct versus incorrect, is an exercise in repression though scarcely defined as such.

At a minimum, our analysis suggests criteria for intolerance, why some things must be assigned to the "not tolerated" list. What is usually implicit, hidden from public debate, will be made more open. Our goal cannot be definitive, easy-to-apply criteria—that is impossible, at least here. More germane is countering the emotional, simplistic admonitions. Distinctions are possible between coffeehouse groups play-acting revolution and

genuine subversive cabals. Those preaching novel moral orders do not have
to be accepted because "who can say what is right or wrong?" Defenses
against the objectionable can reach well beyond eventual rejection via a
marketplace of ideas; force and criminalization of heresy are not automatically undemocratic. Pleading that all dissenting opinion deserves equal
protection from harassment is fashionably painless, but such idealism is an
unaffordable, Utopian luxury. Some abominations *are* worthy of suppression, and determinations are not self-evident. Calls for tolerance cannot
escape this difficulty, though in practice they often do.

In taking up these under-scrutinized matters, we reintroduce a complexity
often expunged from inquests. Indeed, our style occasionally verges on
tedium. Modern social science inquiry is parsimonious, inclined toward neat,
precise analysis. Complex concepts are reduced to uncomplicated definitions
quickly transformed into simple numbers. Complexity is embodied in elaborate statistical techniques. The atmospheric level of tolerance in a community, even an entire state, might be indexed with a single digit. Here, however,
no easy escape from the messiness of reality is permitted. Simplicity is
necessary in scientific scholarship, but in grasping tolerance, this impulse
for black and white has become excessive. Given that much scholarship is
admittedly directed at providing slogans and ammunition for political improvement, this reductionistic inclination is perhaps understandable. It is not,
however, especially useful.

Such complexity is especially unavoidable when considering which unorthodox groups deserve exclusion. Decisions can be exasperating, and
unambiguous verdicts are all too rare. Arguing with two or three extreme
examples only superficially addresses this difficulty. Obviously, a violent
terrorist group clearly falls beyond the scope of democratic tolerance. At the
other extreme are the thousands of humdrum interest groups innocuously
plying their trade. Lying somewhere between are numerous organizations of
uncertain standing. Here the arduous decisions arise. Is the Ku Klux Klan a
"dangerous extremist group" worthy of oblivion, or is it a museum-piece,
harmless remnant of a once-dangerous entity? Is the Klan's behavior tolerable within certain specified legal boundaries, or is it wholly intolerable?
Innumerable subtle, unique factors and judgments are relevant here.

Unfortunately, when citizens are polled about tolerating Klan-like
groups—the commonplace modern path to assessing tolerance—questionnaires demand instant unadorned replies. Modern scientific political science
insists on such lack of embellishment. Perhaps citizens might tolerate some,
but not all, Klan behavior. Perhaps further knowledge is required before
rendering a judgment. The "real world" does not permit this facile simplicity.
Judges and public officials periodically agonize over ambiguities, trying to

balance competing principles. How might one respond, for example, if the Klan requests permission to participate in an "adopt a highway" program and, in full white-sheet uniform, hands out its literature while gathering roadside trash? (This actually happened.) What if the Klan sets up an Internet homepage? Such indeterminacy, at least in our estimation, has far more to do with deciding tolerance than easy-to-answer poll alternatives given to ordinary citizens.

The reintroduction of intricacy is particularly essential when considering the very meaning of tolerance. Though clear dictionary-like definitions are essential for scientific rigor, they often fall short in disentangling day-to-day politics. Forced to choose between the demands of precise empirical analysis and messy reality, we unashamedly opt for the latter. Delicate but critical nuances fade in the quest for punctilious social science. Tolerance as a mental inclination may be indistinguishable from, say, outward signs of indifference or oblivion, dispositions hardly judged to be tolerance. Even the individual, though perhaps not the disinterested investigator, may be hard pressed to say which disposition operates. This is not to say that finely etched abstractions have no place in our analysis. They abound, but their use is merely the analytical starting point, not the conclusion. There are no simple explanations, elegant theories, or cure-all prescriptions to be derived here; my promise is one of restoring needed realism to a subject usually made too plain.

Tolerance Scholarship

Rarely is the scholarly approach to a subject intertwined with the subject's explication. An investigation of ocean water temperature variation would not, for example, describe thermometers. Brief mention of the instrument suffices. Though the techniques of analysis might be depicted in detail, the reader would assume that the appropriate instruments had been employed, that these devices were accurate, and that substantive conclusions were independent of measurement. The separation of methodological critiques and exegesis of substance is likewise a well-honored social science convention—there are books devoted to each, but the topics are treated separately. We violate this convention.

Our reason is that tolerance instruments are not politically neutral; they sporadically serve as blunt weapons in cultural clashes. Though they may not intend to be political participants, researchers who venture into the area ultimately are political players, not disinterested observers. It is as if baseball umpires were covert team employees instructed both to keep score and silently assist their employer. Not necessarily conscious bias or deviously manipulating data; unthinking choices possess political reverberations. That nearly all researchers apparently share a common ideological perspective can easily obscure these political gestures.

Specifically, as Chapters 2 and 3 illustrate in detail, the overwhelming prevailing scholarly approach defines *tolerance* exclusively as an enduring individual attitude. Furthermore, this understanding lacks any explicit (or, for that matter, implicit) instruction constraining this tolerance when applied concretely. Tolerance is offered as an open-ended, purely psychological inclination to accept the disagreeable. As a short-handed name, we label this prevailing understanding "blank-check, hearts, and minds" tolerance. Proclaiming this approach not only constitutes a scientific research choice, it potentially alters the political landscape. Politics and the study of politics become joined. Now, definitionally, intolerance becomes a psychological, not a behavioral, problem. Deficiencies of acceptance thus require remediation via education, mass media campaigns and comparable techniques to modify thinking. In an instant wave of the scholarly wand, tolerance is no longer a problem of intolerant society correctable through laws or the physical separation of hostile factions. This shift toward an "inner" definition of tolerance, we shall argue at length, is a most pernicious alteration in its consequences.

To be sure, scholars following this choice are not consciously proselytizing naked ideology. Most would honestly deny any nefarious political motive. They are merely scientifically taking up a subject in the conventional manner. Nevertheless, the ceaseless repetition of this single blank-check, hearts and minds understanding, a view accompanied with all the prestigious trappings of modern social science, permits it to trump authoritatively all rivals. Older and more traditional alternatives gradually fall into neglect and soon become dim memories.

We directly confront this dominant paradigm. This is far more than a professional quibble with social science technique, more than just suggesting superior technique. The stakes are higher. Fundamentally, we argue that the transformation of tolerance into an individual attitudinal property opens the door excessively to risky state intervention to shape citizen thinking. The emphasis is on "excessive," not the state's influence on citizen thinking per se. Abandoning the "sticks and stones may break my bones, but names will never harm me" adage is momentous. Tolerance is now born by psychologically remolding citizens, not merely restraining aversion. Of course, it will be rejoined, such intrusion is hardly unique or inherently dangerous: state-controlled education shapes citizen thinking every which way, from instilling patriotism to encouraging voting.

Nevertheless, the promotion of the attitudinal tolerance celebrated in the dominant research literature is different and dangerous for two reasons. First, to the extent that intolerance as a psychological disposition becomes public policy, "bad *thinking*," independent of bad *behavior*, now changes into a communal problem. Moreover, since the scope of this hearts and minds tolerance is rarely fully delineated, the entertainment of "bad thoughts" becomes an offense potentially ensnaring virtually everyone. Who can pronounce authoritatively what thinking lies beyond acceptability? The implied norm is that, when uncertain, accept. Pushed to the limits, thinking badly about a group that maybe deserves "bad thoughts" becomes an offense against the creation of a harmonious, open society. Citizens perceptually live in a state of potential political sin. Or, so it would seem.

This is a shift of eventful importance within the American tradition of political separateness. An Orwellian flavor emanates from this displacement, shades of the *1984* neologism *thoughtcrime*. Certain religion-like definitions of transgression are likewise invoked—one sins not only by performing bad deeds but even by *thinking* evil. Even to sit passively while, say, unwanted Marxists parade about is deficient if one fleetingly craves to ban this procession. The emergence of *thoughtcrime* as part of our politics is not nearly as bizarre as it may appear. The situation in which proponents of better race relations insist that bad thinking about blacks ("white racism") is in and of itself a reprehensible act worthy of government intervention is a familiar one.

Second, and equally offensive to our traditional political standards, this conception of tolerance promoted by the research literature is boundless. *Thoughtcrimes* are easily created, and virtually inescapable. Polls, question after question, offer a menu limited only by the researcher's imagination of loathsome groups and activities. The "good democratic citizen," if he or she is to receive a passing grade, is expected to tolerate *everything*. This scholarly exercise implies that *nothing* lies beyond the pale. For an ordinary citizen to impose personal standards of inclusion and exclusion, to express intolerance toward anything, even if personally justifiable, constitutes the "wrong" response.

As studies multiply and their contributions permeate our collective self-definition, providing authoritative signposts for educators and policymakers, a subtle but critical understanding emerges: To express a repressive urge against the unpopular constitutes flawed citizenship. In a sense, scholarly inquiry teaches citizens that nothing is any better than anything else (see, for example, Noël, 1994, for an example of such unbounded tolerance). Relativism becomes, ironically, the new standard.[1] A parallel exists with studies exposing Americans as deficient in math and science—the decision to commission the inquiry and the message that "something needs correcting" are invisibly linked. Scholarship thus assists an educational function, imploring citizens to "be universally tolerant" without any clue on where to draw the line. Progress, as conveyed in this prevailing mode of erudition, is then merely a matter of judging how close Americans approximate this intolerance-free mentality.

It is perhaps no exaggeration to compare such pedantry with instruction manuals on breeding laboratory rats lacking an immune system. Confront citizens with lists of obnoxious, dangerous conspiracies. If they want to throttle a disliked group, this rejection becomes an act of undermining democratic politics. Accordingly, someone inclined to banish the Communist Party USA, an organization committed to destroying the constitutional order, is more injurious of democracy than the Party itself. We shall have much more to say about the pernicious effects of this type of blank-check attitudinal tolerance.

Plan of This Book

We have only highlighted complicated tolerance-related issues. Subsequent chapters will extend our understanding. Chapter 2 samples the complexities of defining tolerance and selecting among competing definitions. We show that what advances utility in empirical research typically fails to capture the untidy real world of political tolerance. A more realistic alternative, namely, that tolerance is better understood as a characteristic of a political system, not as a personal psychological trait, is suggested. Tolerance exists when many diverse views thrive, not necessarily when citizens would permit such noxious views. Our endeavor is expressly titled *Political Tolerance,* as distinct from *psychological* tolerance.

In explicating *political* tolerance as distinct from just "tolerance," we frankly confess a preference for a crude, plain-Jane concept serviceable for real-world assessments. Philosophical discussions of tolerance typically abound with intricate, finely crafted thoughtful distinctions and quarrels (see, for example, Halberstam, 1982-83; Heyd, 1996). We certainly offer no quarrel with highly nuanced meaning. Our concern, however, is acquiring some durable standard for communities less concerned about subtle distinctions and more attuned to coexistence despite sharp differences. We appreciate the plight of citizens and officials confronting an ever-expanding clamor for more and more differences to be admitted to the assembly. To them we offer some guidance.

Chapter 3 explores the emergence and scholarly domination of hearts and minds tolerance. Though this paradigm is troublesome, in our estimation, its domination of the field demands attention. We trace its development, the particular content of poll questions, and justifications for its popularity. Its political allure to researchers, apart from its asserted scientific utility, receives special attention.

Chapter 4 addresses a critical topic only hinted at in the habitual celebrations of tolerance: justifying *in*tolerance. We risk committing heresy. Two of the major theorists of modern tolerance—John Locke and J. S. Mill—are reviewed to uncover justifiable restrictions on repugnant, hated ideas. Despite their reputation as tolerance stalwarts, we argue that both accepted significant limits on actions today deemed eminently tolerable. How society as society *requires* intolerance will likewise be addressed. Try imagining a community whose lone principle was "nothing is forbidden." To illustrate the clash between abstract principles and humdrum reality, we examine the government's persecution of the Communist Party during the 1940s and 1950s. These actions, usually judged as classic intolerance, were democratically justified in our view. More generally, circumstances prevail in which forceful repression of unpopular, hated ideas sustains, not subverts, democracy.

Chapter 5 shifts analysis from theoretical consideration to unorthodox political opinion and action. Our expedition finally escapes the gravitational pull of "hearts and minds" tolerance to focus on what subsists concretely. Evidence comes not from polls but from the actuality of organizations, magazines, and other solid public manifestations of unorthodoxies appealing exclusively to small, deviant slivers of the population. Here we demonstrate that, despite widespread citizen reservations about matters far beyond the mainstream, unconventional, even bizarre, views flourish. The advancement of Marxism and homosexuality constitute case studies. If there is, as sometimes alleged, an widespread citizen inclination to rid ourselves of these two unwanted groups, it has come to naught. Judged from this perspective, America is a highly tolerant society for Marxists and gays, even too permissive according to some.

Chapter 6 continues this pursuit of "de facto tolerance" distinct from "tolerance as popularly desired." Here we calibrate intolerance. It would seem that distinguishing harsh, state-sanctioned repression from mere annoyance by local drunks is basic to determining the robustness of tolerance in our midst. A holocaust cannot be equated with petty harassment. Surprisingly, this delineation is all too rare. Crying wolf over innocuous annoyances must be distinguished from the genuine article. Gay organizations condemning America as an intensely homophobic society will draw careful scrutiny to render a jury-like verdict.

This theme of diversity despite public apprehension is central in Chapter 7. Here, possible survival mechanisms and strategies employed by disliked, controversial groups are explored. How is it possible, for example, for causes embracing the most friendless, perverse, and repulsive views to persevere?

Indeed, does public hostility of the sort revealed in opinion polls even affect group activities? We shall show that though hostile public sentiment may not facilitate group objectives, it need not be fatal, especially if group members behave prudently. We dwell on factors beyond "hearts and mind" tolerance that nourish political heterodoxy. Demonstrating the durability of nonconformity in the face of adverse public pressure is especially significant, given our fear of government intrusion into private thinking. After all, why risk possible brainwashing when the same goal can be accomplished without this dangerous strategy? Intellectually, our analysis is highly eclectic, exploring topics as diverse as modern military anti-racist programs to the survival of outlandish religious sects. We dwell on political arrangements—not a benevolent citizenry—to shelter political richness from powerful forces for homogeneity. A dependence on tolerant attitudes is both misguided and unnecessary: Better approaches can thwart the squelching of ideas worthy of inclusion.

Finally, we return to the theme initially raised in this chapter: The relentless imposition of general attitudinal tolerance to promote (allegedly) heaven on earth. Schemes will be examined in detail with an eye toward their unspoken assumptions and far-reaching ramifications. At best, such attempted indoctrination may be of marginal value in accomplishing the goal of a harmonious society. Not everyone can be a good student of tolerance. Time and energy spent on hectoring citizens to be ever more accepting of vague differences may be more productively employed elsewhere. Most important, it exposes citizen thinking to a type of governmental intrusion normally associated with totalitarian regimes. It is not enough to behave properly; one must also think the correct thoughts. Stamping out "bad thoughts" can be far worse than the thoughts themselves, particularly when the thoughts may be inconsequential. Such forceful intrusion, of course, is not the intent of most tolerance advocates, and they would, for the most part, recoil from such promotion if thought control were the inevitable result. Nevertheless, because noble intentions need not yield noble results, it is our responsibility to sound the alarm. Ours is a commitment to tolerance of views, a rich soup of competing positions and debates, not the compelling of citizens to embrace the objectionable.

NOTE

1. This connection between open-ended tolerance and relativism, though overwhelmingly common, is not fixed. Gray (1993) deduces the *reverse* connection in his analysis, namely, the act of tolerance, in and of itself, acknowledges that some things are "bad" though they must be accepted. Hence, a genuine relativist would oppose the very idea of tolerance on the grounds that it implied invidious distinctions. Though a logical and clever argument, it nevertheless seems to have limited applicability in the playing out of conflicts of tolerance.

Tolerance Deciphered

The unending public celebrations of tolerance barely reveal its underlying complexity. A restoration of needed realism now begins. Being weaned from superficial simplicity, especially when challenging a venerated cliché, is often painful. Our endeavor may also risk the appearance of medieval scholasticism insofar as we have a predilection for innumerable distinctions. Grains of truth, no doubt, lie in these accusations. Hopefully, however, the benefits of a deeper understanding outweigh the burdens of fresh nuances and exposed ambiguities. We take tolerance seriously, and if this idea is to escape its burgeoning enshrinement as a modern political slogan, careful study is required.

Our starting point is the definitional underpinnings dominating modern research, the so-called "hearts and minds" concept. This particular interpretation, a de facto investigatory gold standard, assumes a certain *weltanschauung* that is surely incomplete, if not misdirected. Furthermore, despite its scholarly popularity, it suffers from three grave flaws: the connection between attitudes and behavior is tenuous, it may not even exist in citizen thinking, and its measurement is typically perplexed with vagaries. Its current fashionableness derives more from convenience, less from demonstrated political relevance. Second, analysis explores various tolerance hybrids, distant and uncared-for relatives, usually neglected when the praises of acceptivity are powerfully proclaimed. Nevertheless, under certain circumstances these dimly recalled cousins and uncles may be indistinguishable, if not preferable, to the far more popular inner hearts and minds version.

Third, we address a troublesome but scarcely noticed problem afflicting the commonplace use of tolerance, namely deciding between subjective views and hard reality. Can we certify as "intolerant" individuals demanding the elimination of nonexistent groups? Conversely, how do we classify those who mistakenly believe themselves oppressed? Is suppression purely subjective? Analysis then attempts to disentangle intolerance from perfectly legitimate political opposition. Are distinctions even feasible in daily political conflict? Again, we interject a note of messy political realism to depictions in which, ostensibly, the virtuous tolerance battles the evils of bigotry and hate.

Finally, tolerance as a collective property (political tolerance), not an individual trait, will be investigated. This perspective, at least in principle, permits extensive citizen intolerance to coexist with a politics brimming with endless and irrepressible political diversity. This aggregate understanding, moreover, renders many of the citizen-based tolerance enhancement programs, agendas so popular with educators, largely unnecessary. Given their uncertain successes, rendering them obsolete is no small accomplishment. This shift in understanding has implications beyond educational tinkering, however. We hope to dislodge a theory of tolerance that contains the seeds of a potentially destructive totalitarianism. When government is authorized to insure "good thinking" among its citizens, we become extremely nervous. The infatuation with hearts and minds tolerance is not just misdirected, it may also be evil.

I. Defining Tolerance—The Preeminence of Hearts and Minds Tolerance

Understanding tolerance begins with definitions, for one's denotation of tolerance determines its existence. This is hardly irrelevant in a society where innumerable opposing viewpoints all advocate "true tolerance." Whether the United States smothers nonconformity or enjoys libertine permissiveness partially flows from definitions. Gestapo tactics to one observer are commendable maintenance of public safety to another. Indeed, controlling how tolerance is conceptualized is today's huge prize in the battle for the moral high ground.

A useful place to begin is the unabridged Oxford English Dictionary II (OED II), perhaps the most authoritative English dictionary ever assembled.

Several different meanings are offered, but the one most germane for our purposes is:

> 3. The action or practice of tolerating; toleration; the disposition to be patient with or indulgent to the opinions or practices of others; freedom from bigotry or undue severity in judging the conduct of others; forbearance; catholicity of spirit.

That is, a tolerant person is one who puts up with the objectionable, from pain to a political sect. It also means not be overly harsh in judging others or what is different. However, when we migrate to the domain of tolerance scholarship, this initial simplicity breaks down. Though a core definition exists, there are also many competing claims on the periphery. One overview characterized the field as being in "a state of disarray" (Ferrar, 1976).[1] The term's attractiveness, no doubt, encourages its extension into innumerable spheres, expropriated as an all-purpose synonym for untold praiseworthy attributes. Ferrar shows that tolerance is virtually equivalent to the absence of religious/racial/ethnic prejudice, a valuable flexibility of thought, a willingness to test scientifically competing ideas, and a receptivity to new visions. Susan Mendus, a leading writer on this subject, equates intolerance with "social disapproval" even if no legal sanctions are imposed. Perhaps, according to this understanding, even hatred of murder might constitute intolerance (Mendus, 1989, 5). Corbett (1982, 2) provides yet other meanings by appending support for political freedom and equality (including racial equality). Accordingly, an intolerant person resists minority group claims on economic equality. Tolerance is also commonly associated with championing civil liberties, particularly, but not necessarily exclusively, First Amendment protections.

Nevertheless, despite this melange of meanings, an emphasis on personally accepting differences found objectionable is central. In addition, this acceptance is generally agreed to pertain to social and political concerns, not personal taste. Thus, if former President Bush tolerated eating broccoli, a vegetable he loathed, this is irrelevant. But, his response to political enemies is pertinent to tolerance. A few examples from leading studies reveal this consensus. Nunn, Crockett, and Williams (1978) define it as "a straightforward attitude that allows people to have freedom of expression even when one may feel that their ideas are incorrect or even immoral. . . . it is an active process that reflects an appreciation of free flowing diversity of ideas and the recognition that one's own free expression is made possible by such a climate of opinion"(12). Sullivan, Piereson, and Marcus (1982, 2) propose a nearly identical interpretation: "Tolerance implies a willingness to 'put up with' those things one rejects or opposes." Thus, if one were opposed to, say, Communism, a lack of conscious opposition to this doctrine would display tolerance for Communist ideology. If, however, one were sympathetic to Communism, such acceptance cannot be tolerance. To Harvard philosopher T. M. Scanlon (1996), "Tolerance requires us to accept people and permit their practices even when we strongly disapprove of them" (226).

Sheer repetition of similar definitions might imply a term whose application is straightforward. Perhaps like physical science terminology—*mass, velocity*—this denotation of *tolerance* is the splendid outgrowth of decades of theoretical labor. Hardly the case, unfortunately, though the very core— accepting the disagreeable—is solid. A multitude of formidable application difficulties lurks below the surface. And these perplexities are politically consequential, not merely matters of etymology. Offering up "accepting the disagreeable" is only a first step in assessing tolerance, and a step that need not always lead in the right direction.

Tolerance as an Individual Attitude

This "accepting the disliked" concept is silent regarding what constitutes "putting up with." How precisely does one put up with something? Though permissible in dictionaries, this omission of details becomes troublesome in specific circumstances. What actions might potentially constitute this acceptance of the disagreeable? Our inquiry here may seem overly philosophical and nitpicky, but important, noteworthy issues are involved.

This conversion of a general "putting up with" into particulars follows a fairly uniform path involving two distinct choices, both of which are politically pertinent. First, *tolerance is conceived as a psychological or mental orientation.* To "live and let live," regardless of how technically measured, pertains to feelings, inclinations, attitudes, orientations, or beliefs. This psychological emphasis is not inherent in "putting up with"; it flows from more subtle, perhaps unthinking, interpretative habits. Actual *behavior* of citizens, the enforcement of protective laws or rushing to the defense of disliked groups and comparable actions, are all, implicitly or explicitly, excluded from this inner psychological rendering.

The second theme is equally important: *Tolerance is a property of individuals.* Only people are tolerant, not groups, organizations or societies. Tolerance is both democratic—one person, one unit of tolerance—and atomistic, a person's tolerance exists independently of what others think. Since a tolerant society consists definitionally of tolerant people, an implicit connection is assumed between the proportion of tolerant people and overall tolerance. Society-wide tolerance is, by implication, calibrated from 0 percent to 100 percent. This would be as if economists equated overall economic output by merely cumulating each worker's monetary productivity. The circulation of numerous unpopular unorthodoxies in an overwhelmingly hostile society becomes *definitionally* impossible. Conversely, this denotation, at least in principle, permits Nazi Germany to be a tolerant society had one uncovered extensive attitudinal permissiveness. In addition, the intensity of intolerance, its vigor and passion, is gauged from its pervasiveness: definitionally, the proportion of individuals expressing intolerant views. For example, if 80 percent of citizens insist that Socialism be banned, Socialism is in greater danger than if merely 40 percent embrace this view. Who holds what belief, their power and willingness to translate belief into action, conceptually lies beyond the scope of hearts and minds tolerance.

The authority of this dominant individual hearts and minds definition is neither philosophical or political. It is a modern, relatively recent invention of social science. In particular, and this point cannot be over-emphasized, it is highly *convenient* for research, given the ease of polling—the prevailing method of peeking into hearts and minds. Tolerance, thanks to the easy-to-execute survey, can be established as effortlessly as measuring water temperature with a household thermometer. Unfortunately, reality is far more complex. What is readily ascertained may not coincide with what ought to be carefully studied. Psychological dispositions capture only a small portion of the complete picture. It would be as if alcoholism were examined solely by collecting opinions regarding intoxication. Perplexing problems and ambiguities surrounding real-world disputes are severely masked by this alluring hearts and minds definition.

II. The Problems of Hearts and Minds Tolerance

Though hearts and minds tolerance resonates well with our intuitive understanding and enjoys an unquestioned research popularity, its allure resides only on the surface. When pushed and keenly probed, it proves quite troublesome. Three troubling features deserve special attention: (1) the uncertain connection between attitudes and behavior; (2) the meaningfulness of tolerant opinions; and (3) the inherent vague character of hearts and minds measuring instruments.

Attitudes Versus Behavior

The prevailing understanding directs attention exclusively toward *attitudes* or similar cognitions (belief, orientation, view, value). Though some studies briefly touch on actual behavior, actions themselves lie outside the very definition. Indeed, few scholarly inquiries ever escape the gravitational pull of the purely subjective. If, per chance, the Ku Klux Klan's Grand Dragon, incarcerated for racist mob action, were quizzed using the conventional questions, he could lie himself into certification as "tolerant." Unless the incarceration's cause were known, this fabrication would remain unchallenged if verbal data were the only information collected. It is assumed, typically with perfunctory discussion, that tolerant attitudes translate smoothly into corresponding behaviors. But, what if this assumption of consistency were unwarranted? Though potential attitude-behavior discrepancies are painlessly swept aside by pollsters, a realistic and full understanding of tolerance requires that they be addressed.

Can verbal responses be trusted to reveal likely behavior? As the specific affinity between tolerant attitudes and tolerant behavior have drawn scant attention, and much undoubtedly depends on critical details of circumstances and measurement, no absolutely conclusive answer exists. Nevertheless, our general understanding of these relationships powerfully argues *against* a close, one-to-one connection. Dozens of complicated findings and controversies surround this issue, but the scholarly consensus suggests only a very modest direct interconnection, at best (Deutscher, 1965; Fishbein & Ajzen, 1975). It is not that the two are randomly related; surely some people are perfectly consistent in word and deed. Moreover, under certain particular circumstances attitudes might shape behavior. Rather, attitudes and behavior on complex subjects such as tolerance are rarely—if ever—different indicators of the same thing. If one sought to predict one from the other, success would be dismal.

Before considering the detailed issues of this attitude-behavior relationship, briefly consider an early exploration of this connection, a sixty-year-old study with remarkable relevance to contemporary analysis. This is Richard T. LaPiere's (1934) straightforward field experiment on animosity toward Chinese among hotel and restaurant employees. Beginning in 1930, and for two years thereafter, LaPiere traveled across the U.S. with a young Chinese couple. Anti-Chinese, anti-foreigner sentiment was rampant and openly expressed. LaPiere and the couple attempted to check into some sixty-six places of lodging, ranging from "high class" to shabby. No effort was made to hide the Chinese couple at check-in time or otherwise obscure their ethnic identity. Only one lodging establishment refused service. Six months later, questionnaires were sent to these same establishments asking, "Would you accept members of the Chinese race as guests in your establishment?" (A second version of the questionnaire included other ethnic groups.) Overwhelmingly, among responding hotels and motels, the answer was "no." A similar pattern prevailed in restaurants—though intolerance was expressed in follow-up questionnaires, actual prior behavior was decidedly accepting. Supplemental studies employing different settings and people generally confirm the LaPiere results: What people do often conflicts with verbal intentions (see, for example, Deutscher, 1975, for an overview).

What lesson is to be gleaned from this sixty-year-old field study? That attitudes are *totally* irrelevant is perhaps an overstatement. Numerous factors determine behavior, and attitudes are undoubtedly part of this mix. Nevertheless, between acknowledging a role for attitudes and equating an attitude with a behavior, lies a huge chasm. This would be like saying that beef stew simply consisted of "meat" and then remaining silent. Without listing other ingredients and their blending, the recipe is far too unfinished to be useful. The real question is the usefulness of knowing only tolerant attitudes for predicting the more politically consequential tolerant behavior.

Knowing attitudinal tolerance, in and of itself, provides almost no clue for predicting action. To be sure, the applicable evidence is largely indirect and circumstantial, but it all points in the same direction. Reviews of attitude-behavior studies (for example, Crespi, 1971; Oskamp, 1977) suggest several commonsense conditions facilitating a close connection. First, if a verbally expressed inclination is measured with multiple and distinct indicators, behavior is better predicted. Numerous psychological forces shape action, and attitudinal predilections need not all point in the identical direction. In the LaPiere study, for example, anticipating the hotel clerk's response would have been safer if monetary desires, apprehensions over confrontation, and disposition toward politeness were combined with feelings toward Chinese. This richer, more detailed analysis of inclinations might well have demonstrated that an abstract dislike of Chinese was overcome by several opposing dispositions.[2]

A second factor promoting close association is the measured attitude's specificity. Narrow attitudes predict better than vague, general inclinations. Rather than abstractly inquire about all Chinese, one might specify a well-dressed, well-educated, and courteous young couple who happened to be Chinese. If attitudes and behaviors are to be connected, their content must be the same—apples to apples, not to fruits in general. Third, predictions improve with temporal proximity to behavior. Inquiring about some future behavior weakens prediction. A bigoted inn-keeper might receive our Chinese couple during the slow season only to turn them away six months later when customers abound. Furthermore, attitude can better forecast structured and routine behavior (as in daily consumer purchasing). Thus, if hotel clerks regularly dealt with well-mannered, polite Chinese seeking accommodations, attitudes and behaviors would probably eventually align.

Such factors hardly exhaust the possibilities disturbing neat relationships connecting word and deed (see Oskamp 1977, 231). Even defenders of collecting attitudes as valid dispositions of behavior frankly acknowledge the uncertainty of interchangeability. People can well reverse positions many times over, often justifiably. Someone proclaiming his or her tolerance in May, and who would act consistently on the basis of this disposition, might have a change of heart by December. Perhaps an event or experience intervened. Though technically not evidence of attitude-behavior inconsistency, a discrepancy over time thus manifests itself. Such shifting warns us against treating attitudes as a permanent trait. Also, if people cannot articulate their views correctly—a common situation for distant political matters like tolerance—a close attitude-behavior association is obscured. The measuring instrument's inability to tease out clear answers, not the underlying phenomena themselves, reduces predictability. Unavailability of behavioral options may likewise impede an easy translation. Imagine the frustration of an anti-Semite in a nation lacking Jews. Similarly, all sorts of unexpected events and situations can conspire to thwart attitude-driven behavior. Our anti-Semite might, for example, be unable to march in a Nazi parade due to illness, lack of transportation, or bad weather.

Clearly, it is easy to understand why the typical survey tolerance questions, such as, "Would you permit a Socialist to speak in your community?" scarcely predict future behavior. Lamentably, willingness to permit unpopular speakers is always ascertained with a single, all-purpose general inquiry. Other relevant features—the speaker's demeanor, surrounding political conditions, or the audience makeup—are not mentioned. As in the LaPiere situation, attitudes about well-dressed, courteous speakers versus unkempt fiery rabble-rousers, could well shape responses. What if the Communist speaker were a famous, distinguished world leader? What if the speaker were an invited guest of a sympathetic group holding a private meeting? These matters are surely pertinent to audience behavior.

The time framework, the need for proximity of thought and action, is also neglected in the typical survey. For the average citizen, decades may pass before an opportunity for politically intolerant behavior presents itself (if ever). Much can transpire during the interim—today's enemies become future allies, a once dangerous cause becomes harmless (or vice versa), or new information alters old opinion. A person may endlessly vacillate on good guys versus bad guys. The precise circumstances of this alluded-to incident can only be guessed at. A citizen generally expressing intense hostility to a homosexual speaking to school children may acquiesce if attendance is voluntary, the speech promotes religion, and homosexuality is off the agenda.

Finally, and perhaps most significantly, the events described in the typical tolerance question are exceptionally rare. Survey questions resemble the highly unrealistic dilemmas young children often pose: "Would you kill somebody for a million dollars if you could go undetected?" Some occupations—librarians, elected public officials, police officers, media executives, or educational administrators—might sporadically confront tolerance-laden situations depicted in surveys. Even among those "at risk" for addressing this quandary, the likelihood of having to make a choice is low.[3] Educational administrators probably complete their careers without facing unpopular groups requesting school facilities. Few police chiefs receive requests for marching permits from Nazi storm troopers. Among ordinary citizens, even more so, future tolerance situations are largely hypothetical. At best, even the most reflective survey respondent can supply only the roughest guess regarding future behavior.

The survey also assumes respondent honesty. Given the highly controversial character of many tolerance-related topics—Marxism, atheism, homosexuality, openly racist organizations—expecting perfect honesty may be unrealistic. Respondent misrepresentation is, of course, a general problem of the survey technique, but this potential flaw is especially appropriate here. Pressure to conform to social norms—for example, voting or following politics—is a common source of such misrepresentation. The "ought" becomes the "is." No doubt, more than a few respondents cover their true but "bad" (intolerant) opinions. Offering the "wrong" sentiment can be dangerous in a tolerance-obsessed society. A worker implored with on-the-job training to appreciate racial diversity will probably parrot this view, regardless of private doubts. After all, one never knows how this information will be used (future legal action? promotion reviews?) and trusting the official interrogator is risky. More generally, questioning about commonly understood "good" and "bad" behavior, regardless of disclaimers, simulates a "test" of officially proscribed knowledge. One "passes" by being tolerant. The situation here resembles that of citizens endorsing the 55 mph speed limit in the abstract and then frankly acknowledging that they regularly ignore it (see Murray, 1994, 147-148 on this point). The opposite is, of course, also possible: Individuals surrounded by intolerance may feel pressured to condemn unpopular views, despite contrary private sentiments.

The Meaningfulness of Tolerant Attitudes

The standard hearts and minds version suffers from a second serious and limiting flaw: equating questionnaire responses to an enduring, consequential predisposition. The attitude might not only be irrelevant to behavior, it may also be intrinsically meaningless. Research in this hearts and minds tradition assume that because tolerance is a serious democratic matter, the end product of an illustrious intellectual tradition, ordinary citizens ought to share this mindfulness. The unstated presupposition is that when citizens expression convictions about libraries stocking controversial Marxist books, this reply captures some underlying, enduring and personally central inclination. Unfortunately, this charitable assumption is often far too generous. Responses are more likely to be off-hand and superficial than "real."

Discerning the realness of hasty responses to survey questions, regardless of subject matter, is perplexing. Research into this topic overflows with debates far too complex to describe here (see, for example, Converse, 1970; Zaller, 1992, Chapters 4 and 5). The core problem is distinguishing real dispositions from those identical answers instigated by the survey itself. In other words, when asked a simple yes or no question, how do we separate a no reflecting a genuine disposition from a hollow reaction to an alluring phrase or word? Without unobtrusively peeking into people's brains, disentanglment is uncertain. Such partitioning rests on plausibility and indirect evidence, everything from the inherent character of the inquiries to interrelationships among various questionnaire items. The case can never be conclusive, only suggestive. Nevertheless, such cautions aside, when we inspect the usual tolerance questions and review our general comprehension of political thinking, the evidence plainly points in the direction of frequent "non-attitudes."

Consider the design format of these survey questions. In principle, like school examination queries that range from true/false to lengthy essays, pertinent poll questions could solicit various types of information. Typical tolerance inquiries, however, are especially *un*demanding. Indeed, the typical design makes it nearly impossible *not* to possess an opinion; its character is perfectly suited to disguising spontaneously offered empty guesses. Citizens need not provide well-reasoned arguments pro or con. A simple yes or no answers the question: "Would you permit a Socialist to give a public speech?" What deliberations underlay this reply, their seriousness or casualness, the depth of sophistication or superficiality, is unknown. Nor does the interviewer have any responsibility or motivation to push beyond this fleeting yes or no. Conceivably, the idea of a public socialist speech may never even have occurred to an erstwhile tyrant, but no matter. He or she may, in addition, possess only the foggiest grasp of Socialism, possible speech content, and the event's likely influence. The point is simple: These easy-to-answer tolerance questions, by their inherent nature, cannot distinguish between reasoned opinion and momentary whim.

Because the questions themselves cannot reveal authenticity, clues must be unearthed elsewhere. Our general knowledge of public opinion suggests that most—not all—responses to typical tolerance questions are unlikely to reflect deeply seated, well-developed thoughts. This is not to argue that citizens cannot, when pressed by specific events or a persistent interviewer, develop coherent, deeply felt opinions on the subject. Surely, an African American citizen will posses "real" thoughts if the Ku Klux Klan suddenly stages a neighborhood rally. Rather, when citizens are ordinarily polled on these matters, the circumstances are not ideal for eliciting well-developed thoughts on tolerance.

Several conditions strongly hint that most tolerance views should be deemed "non-attitudes." First, as numerous studies indicate, citizens express only modest concern about civic affairs in general. And when political concerns do surface, these protruding issues are unlikely to resemble those raised in the typical tolerance question. It is not that tolerance lies eternally beyond citizen mindfulness; rather, left to choose priorities, matters of this type are easily disdained. The average citizen is undoubtedly far more interested in non-political issues—family, job, sports—than obscure, distant matters regarding Communists giving radio talks (see, among others, Conway, 1991, Chapter 1). If and when citizens are drawn to political turmoil, their attention focuses on current personalities, dramatic events, and similar material prominently featured in the news media. Abstract issues, the very sort of controversies portrayed in tolerance questions, draw paltry popular fascination. Perhaps a local conflict regarding sexually explicit school textbook censorship or a Nazi march might momentarily invigorate public debate, but such events are both rare and transitory. Even if this type of conflict materializes, it likely becomes crudely transformed into personalities, not disputations over abstract principles.

Citizen information levels also caution us against assuming well-developed tolerance views. Put bluntly, most citizens do not know what they are talking about. As surveys themselves relentless demonstrate, once beyond the most obvious information, such as the president's name, knowledge declines sharply. Informational questions broadly resembling the subject matter of tolerance reveal dismal information levels. For example, less than half of the respondents in a 1989 survey correctly could identify the first ten amendments to the Constitution as the Bill of Rights. Less than one quarter in 1979 could explain the First Amendment. The proportion who, in 1973, could explain the Supreme Court's obscenity rule, a decision then attracting considerable publicity, was only 29 percent (Page & Shapiro, 1992, 10-11; also see Delli Carpini & Keeter, 1996, Chapter 2). Given comparable findings, it is reasonable to assume that many of those offering opinions about

Communists talking on the radio employ an inner-thought vocabulary based on an inadequate understanding of the subject.

Mueller's (1988) analysis of this dispute also points the finger in the direction of ephemeral answers to the conventional tolerance questions. He observes that relatively slight wording changes can shift support figures 20 to 25 percent. Changes of this magnitude are difficult to imagine for secure, well-developed preferences. Respondents also offer contradictory, illogical answers even for questions asked at nearly identical times (e.g., favoring a general principle and then contradicting it immediately with a specific application). Finally, Mueller observes that responses often reflect disengagement from daily politics. During the height of the McCarthy period, for example, when anti-Communist hysteria dominated the media, few citizens judged this issue important. During the 1970s, well before the gay rights movement emerged, many citizens would deny homosexuals the right to speak. These data, Mueller contends, reflect a degree of "casual caprice and amiable randomness," not confirmation of deep-seated genuine opinion.

Vagueness in Ascertaining Hearts and Minds Tolerance

Our final point regarding the insufficiency of the prevailing hearts and minds tolerance concerns the similarity between what citizens are asked about and "real world" politics. Polls taping citizen tolerance are almost always fleeting inquires about ill-defined groups and vague situations. The question inquires about "Socialists," not one of sundry organizations embracing some rendition of Socialism; the activity might be "give a speech" rather than give a speech to disinterested onlookers in Union Square in New York City at noon on April 15th. This tactic of inquiry is predictable—even necessary—given both the paucity of relevant incidents and the methodological convention of avoiding detail-laden questions. Nor do pollsters explain terms possessing elaborate historical meanings. Clearly, the convention reduces subtle and detailed matters to a few simple black and white choices.

Details are, alas, important in politics. Take as an example the oft-asked question, "Do you think the Socialist Party should be allowed to publish a newspaper in this country?" No doubt, questionnaire drafters assumed some citizen awareness of "the Socialist Party" and what "publishing a newspaper" implied. Though such assumptions are hardly eccentric, the resultant item leaves much to the imagination. Putting aside those clueless about Socialism (left undefined in the question) and equally oblivious to the precise meaning of "to publish," various problems still remain. For one, respondent and interviewer need not share common definitions.[4] What, for instance, does the term *Socialist Party* mean? Does it describe a devotee of a particular, articulated doctrine or merely a vague ideological inclination? Does it describe a member of a specific organization? If it refers to an organization, which one? The Socialist Party of America? The Socialist Labor Party? The Socialist Workers Party? Among the informed, these organizations possess unique histories and goals. There also may be a mental association drawn with European Socialist parties, mainstream parties such as the British Labour Party. Perhaps Socialism for some is closely identified with Communism which, in turn, was commonly equated with the former Soviet Union. Similarly, reasonable people can differently interpret "publish a newspaper." The range of alternatives here is expansive, and the question spells out nothing. Such a paper could, conceivably be blatant propaganda, perhaps the *Daily Worker* (the now defunct Community Party USA voice). Or, it might be indistinguishable from mundane dailies save an occasional Bolshevik slant. The tabloid could even be a small circulation obscure academic-style newsletter.

These gross simplifications are unappreciated until reality intercedes. Then, the vague generalities so serviceable in social science discourse become clumsy tools more likely to obscure than enlighten. The questionnaire's black and white breaks down as events become endless shades of gray, lines between talk and action vanish, and one person's cherished tolerance is another's abusive intolerance. Such situations of conflicting and confusing interpretations are common, not exceptional.

To appreciate this gap, consider events that occurred during 1995 in Saugatuck, Michigan, a small resort town west of Detroit. Most town residents are conservative people of Dutch background (*Wall Street Journal*, August 22, 1995). Though the town historically caters to families, it is now popular among gay vacationers. Both gays and nongays generally agree that Saugatuck offers an accepting atmosphere: Gays hold local elected office, own businesses, and easily mingle with town residents. On the surface, attitude and behavioral tolerance thrives.

Nevertheless, though anti-gay behavior is acknowledged to be minimal, some gays lobbied for an ordinance banning discrimination based on sexual orientation. Despite the physical reality of tolerance, and the ordinance's likely minimal effect, many residents objected. As Harry Van Single, a local city council member put it: "We laugh, drink, and play with [gays], why do we need an ordinance?" Many local gays concur, believing a low-keyed approach more effective. Essentially, opponents of the ordinance fear that public acknowledgment of the town's gay presence may scare off socially conservative family vacationers. Discrimination lawsuits could also burden a small frugal village with limited financial resources. Nevertheless, opposition to the proposal has drawn a strong rebuke from some gays. Jeff

Montgomery, a gay activist from Detroit, comments, "I guess we now know that it is folly to believe that there is this tiny oasis of tolerance out there." The prospect of an economic boycott has been raised if the ordinance is not passed.

Is Saugatuck tolerant? Are the citizens "really" intolerant despite their everyday putting up with gays? Are attitudes relevant here? What behaviors are most germane to a verdict—day-to-day behavior or legal confirmation of a principle with an unsure outcome? Perhaps the answer depends on what is being weighed. Saugatuck is both tolerant and intolerant in different senses of the word and from different people's vantage points. None of this is capturable by the conventional survey. More generally, Saugatuck illuminates a familiar phenomenon: People often draw distinctions between their specific, personal situations and their more global, abstract feelings. In a word, they are hypocrites or, to use a kinder word, inconsistent. They may denounce something in general but not exhibit hostility in the particular (or vice versa). Such confusion is prevalent, no doubt, and cautions us against drawing inferences about political life based on responses to a few uncomplicated survey items.

This prevailing hearts and minds approach to tolerance is, at best, incomplete. It reflects but one small sliver of tolerance—verbal reactions to simplistic propositions. Such pronouncements, moreover, are unlikely to predict behavior, may hardly even exist in the minds of respondents, and are poorly connected to real-world tolerance situations. The appeal of this dominating view, as we shall later explicate, has more to do with pragmatic research considerations than judging tolerance.

III. Forms of Tolerance

The notion of putting up with ideas and groups beyond the pale of acceptability lies at the center of tolerance. This holds whether tolerance is defined attitudinally or behaviorally, whether we are speaking of single individuals or entire societies. However, even within the unadorned definition of putting up with, yet other important ambiguities surface. Basically, conventional discussions embrace a dichotomous vision—a person either puts up or does not put up with, say, the town Communist. The reality, both conceptually and in practice, more closely resembles muddy thoughts and inclinations. Lines separating tolerance from intolerance can be fluid. Intensity of conviction—that is, how strongly one wants to suppress or accept that which is despised—is relevant here, but far more is involved. Innumerable other dispositions can combine with putting up with to create situations that, in some ways, are nearly identical to tolerance and yet simultaneously quite different. This blending of dispositions to create a tolerance-like compound is, unfortunately, obscured by the commonplace restrictive terminology. As in chemical isotopes, there are many tolerance-like substances that, for all intents and purposes, possess degrees of interchangeability.[5]

The form of tolerance embedded in prototypical dictionary-like definitions may be labeled "principled tolerance." This is the most commendable (and often only) form of tolerance visualized in contemporary exhortations. Here the conscious, explicit existence of a disliked group or idea is accepted, despite contrary inclinations. Reasoned principle—different views, even if obnoxious, deserve protection—intercedes and blocks natural inclinations to attack. In a sense, principled tolerance resembles a conscience: an "inner voice" instructing restraint despite temptation. Among those determined to build a tolerant citizenry through education, this understanding is often preeminent.

A related, and even more demanding, principled tolerance variant has been dubbed "positive tolerance" (Scarman, 1987). A *positive* intervention, whether by individuals or the state, to equalize disadvantages among the powerful and the weak is its distinguishing feature. Vigorous affirmative action for the friendless, in a sense. Drawing on this personal experience in the English legal system, Lord Scarman offers the example of a devout Muslim schoolteacher requesting Friday leave to observe the holy day of rest. A school administrator's non-objection is insufficient if Friday absenteeism brings dismissal. Here, tolerance demands positive steps—for example, legal protection—not mere principled acquiescence. When fully developed, positive tolerance might require government mandated reserved media time for heretical views and similar interventions resembling "affirmative action" for the unpopular.

A third distinguishable form of tolerance might be called "passive acceptance of the inevitable." In a word, fatalism. One dutifully puts up with a disliked group or value because no possible alternative exists. The urge to repress lies concealed, and may even find sporadic verbal expression, but passivity ultimately prevails. A belief in predestination substitutes for reasoned acceptance. Psychologically, this may resemble learning to live with an incurable medical condition. A more politically relevant example would be a racist resident of a city with a large African American population who "tolerated" annoying blacks since opposition was futile. In one sense, such tolerance is reasoned: The odds of successful repression, when calculated, are hopeless. Hence, rather than be upset over the inevitable, one might as well coexist with the enemy. Or, even if the odds of successful repression are tempting, the costs of fighting this disliked political behavior make the pay-off for hostility unrewarding. Publicly, this form of tolerance is probably indistinguishable from principled tolerance, though its underlying character is vastly different.

A distant relative of this conception, one sharing a surface resemblance, is the religious perspective that punishing hated views and groups, no matter how tempting, is not one's prerogative. Rather, these sinners, unless they repent, will receive God's wrath in the hereafter. It is less the indifference of obliviousness than disregard rooted in a division of the world into the secular and spiritual. The great Catholic theologians Augustine and Aquinas both shared this view (Conley, 1994). Intolerance may be unwavering; its earthly expression, however, is silent. Thus, for example, if one regards homosexuality as sinful, one need not be intolerant provided it is not personally threatening. Homosexuals will ultimately receive their harsh chastisement when standing before heavenly judgment. Earthly forbearance flows from patience and trust in the heavenly retribution, not genuine acceptance. Only God, not the police or an outraged citizenry, is authorized to punish.[6] Of course, the sinners may find this form of reproof perfectly acceptable.

Yet a fourth form of tolerance is what philosophers Fotion and Elfstrom (1992, 12; also Crick, 1971, 65-66) call "habitual tolerance." The disagreeable is sanctioned on the grounds that everything that transpires, perhaps for mysterious reasons, undoubtedly is purposeful. One might detest rain, yet grudgingly accept it as necessary for farming. There is neither an endorsement of principled tolerance or a passive embrace of inevitable evil. The tolerant person (in this sense) recognizes that what endures must serve some end, otherwise it would cease. Differences are appreciated, even enjoyed, manifestations of the variety of human existence. Justifying disliked oddities theoretically or practically is needless; actuality in and of itself vindicates existence. This form of tolerance resembles the inclination of those mystics suffering disease-carrying pests. Pests, too, have a place in the world's order. Thus, even if a disliked group could be vanquished, it is left undisturbed as an integral element of the world's natural and essential diversity.

Finally, there is the tolerance of indifference or even obliviousness—"out of sight, out of mind" tolerance. An activity may incite anger but, save perhaps the most life-threatening situation, denying its existence is usually possible. One puts up with a situation through self-imposed ignorance. Such disengagement is probably an especially common reaction to the disagreeable. For the spiritualist, having deliberately risen above worldly concerns, the fate of terrestrial dissidents and protesters must not hinder attaining inner salvation. Or, alternatively, self-absorption with immediate personal concerns—raising children, job, shopping, hedonistic pleasure—crowds out all else. Indeed, it is imaginable that many citizens strolling past a Communist demonstration might be oblivious, let alone a Marxist gathering demanding the government's violent overthrow. For them, it was merely just a bunch of barely noticed loiterers yelling nonsense.

For a portion of the population, impairment may dictate oblivion. Mental illness, both when left untreated and when heavily medicated, can produce zombie-like people. Similarly, those suffering from a debilitating addiction—drugs, alcohol, and various compulsions—can easily push aside reality. One might also add to this list the senile, the severely mentally retarded, and others unable to engage fully in worldly events. For such people, tolerance may be an involuntary way of life simply because "nothing happens out there." This obliviousness, at least on the surface, is indistinguishable from principled tolerance.

To appreciate the allure of this "tolerance via indifference," consider contemporary American tolerance of religious disputes. Historically, altercations over religious doctrine have been a source of innumerable cruel and murderous wars. Heresy was once a capital offense. Even today in Bosnia, India, Northern Ireland, and the Middle East, sectarian battles remain vicious. Fortunately, however, though the U.S. has had its share of bitter religious discord, strife between religious sects is today minimal, seldom more than rhetorical exchanges. Is this peacefulness a tribute to a deeply rooted religious tolerance? Have educators finally succeeded in vanquishing this pernicious antagonism? Has a treaty of doctrinal accord been ratified? Hardly. Rather, most American now fail to see spiritual dogma divisions as matters of concern. Religious warfare has been calmed by secularism, not tolerance. That a person is a Catholic rather than a Congregationalist (once a matter of the utmost importance in colonial times) barely matters any more.

A final relevant distinction concerns coerced versus voluntary tolerance. Discussions of accepting disliked differences implicitly assume a generosity freely given. Threatening force or punishment to accept a disliked group seems deeply antithetical to the very spirit of principled tolerance. As in the making of a moral choice, the election to accept must be voluntarily. A tolerant person should possess the option of intolerance.

In practice, the line dividing freely given and coerced tolerance may be imperceptible. The most self-consciously tolerant individual is undoubtedly constrained by threats of force, implicit and explicit, especially if tolerance is legally required. In fact, one might guess that of all the forms of tolerance, this legally coerced version predominates. It certainly seems to be embraced by civil rights leaders who have abandoned voluntary tolerance in favor of strict legal sanctions. Nontoleration of racial, ethnic, or religious groups may constitute a violation of state or federal law, punishable by fines or imprisonment. Attempting to shut-up a disliked speaker or excluding undesirables from one's neighborhood risks a civil suit. To the would-be intolerant, virtually everyone, sadly, now enjoys legal protection.

Law-based prohibitions ultimately become internalized, ingrained as unthinking dispositions. As the specter of punishment gradually becomes invisible, tolerance now appears deceptively volitional. Legal compulsion need not be state dictated: One's religious creed may also demand tolerance, and the sins of intolerance may be paid for with eternal damnation. Especially in intricate political situations, demarcating legal compliance based on punishment from voluntary obedience is impractical. Yet, despite their differing roots, these dissimilar forms of "putting up with" serve identical purposes.

Fear of forceful retaliation, not disinterested abstract tolerance, may likewise inspire acceptance. Intensely disliked groups are not always inoffensive, passive debating societies. Some, for example, the Black Panthers or the Ku Klux Klan, once flaunted their belligerence to intimidate enemies: One either tolerated them or faced possible physical retribution. Indeed, pariah groups may purposely adopt militaristic language and belligerent demeanors for self-protection. It is one thing to wish to silence the American Nazi party assembly, quite another to confront face-to-face a gang in full military regalia. Such putting up with, then, is rooted in fear, not principled tolerance.

The most common coerced acceptance is probably economic self-interest. Threats of boycotts or taking business elsewhere easily create the semblance of tolerance. To be sure, such tolerance may be willingly given, but its underlying motivation is avarice, not idealism. During the summer of 1994, for example, New York City hosted the Gay Games, a vast athletic competition drawing thousands of gays to New York's hotels, restaurants, shops, and theaters. The influx's huge economic benefits, at least on the surface, comfortably overwhelmed underlying anti-gay sentiments. Indeed, the games had the open support of two New York City mayors and the State Department temporarily lifted the ban against HIV-positive overseas visitors to facilitate international participation. Rudeness to gay customers made no sense—gays would simply patronize more accepting merchants, not flee the city. Economic self-interest similarly substituted for tolerance during the 1950s and 1960s when previously anti-black businesses suddenly learned to tolerate newly affluent black consumers.

Navigating these various tolerance denotations is challenging. More important for our purposes, however, is that these tolerance-like states are seldom judged interchangeable or even roughly comparable by tolerance scholars. Less-than-perfect relatives are simply air-brushed from the family portrait. Among those calling for instruction to appreciate diversity, indifference is hardly equated with principled resistance to suppression. An uncritical acceptance of life's great variety supposedly differs from a stoic capitulation to uncontrollable forces. Some might even argue that indifference and fatalism are wholly unrelated to tolerance. Advocates of positive tolerance may judge anything less unworthy of being designated tolerance. Applying the label *tolerance* to fanatic anti-Communists who suddenly treat visiting, big-spending, polite Marxists with great respect would probably be reckoned a linguistic corruption by those attached solely to principled tolerance.

Again, the critical point is whether these often imperceptible distinctions are readily discernible when probing hearts and minds tolerance. Or, even more fundamentally, does it make a difference? This futility of imposing minute discriminations is further compounded by the crudeness of the typical survey questions. Recall that key terms, such as *Socialism,* are left ill-defined and situations are overly simplistic. Moreover, are people themselves capable of the introspection necessary to discern the difference between, say, principled tolerance and passivity through intimidation? Probably not. When citizens are asked "Should a Socialist be permitted to make a public speech?" and they answer, "Yes," the underlying psychological basis for this response is indistinct. Even more important, any attempt to disentangle these feelings, even with probing follow-up questions, may be nearly impossible. The distinctions formulated here, though perhaps transparent to philosophers, remain cloudy to citizens. They also may shift with time, circumstances, and question details. Probing subtle differences of motive and understanding is as foolhardy as hunting microbes with a household magnifying glass.

IV. Tolerance and Reality

The prevailing hearts and minds concept of tolerance is fundamentally psychological, entirely subjective in character. It exists wholly as a mental state, beyond objective verification. As with all cognitions, distortions and errors may creep in. Given tolerance's distant nature for most citizens, the dearth of regular reality testing, inner psychological tolerance would seem an excellent candidate for ample misinformation. Creating subjective, purely personal realities is not a matter of personal predilection, as one might favor a color. Unless we willingly equate inner thoughts with real world politics, these discrepancies are troublesome. After all, if "reality" were purely opinion, government could manufacture paradise by brainwashing citizens. Two aspects of this "unreality" are particularly likely: (1) intolerance toward objects of minuscule political relevance, and (2) imagined feelings of intolerance where none probably exists.

Politically Irrelevant Intolerance

Surveys can inquire about almost anything. In scouring about for potential objects of intolerance, the possibilities are limitless. Neither researcher nor respondent need select genuine threats. What if hated objects are neither existent nor politically significant? In other words, intolerance, like some fantasy, dwells entirely "in one's head"? For example, suppose a recluse, when quizzed about what needs to be done about dissidents, announces, "I hate Know-Nothing Party members and they should be massacred immediately. Other than such treasonous creatures, all else is permissible." Technically, if this were the response to an inquiry, the respondent must be classified as "intolerant."

Is this inhospitality to nonexistent things that consequential? It depends. Conceivably, government may manipulate this hatred of inconsequential entities for its own purposes. It might, for example, suspend civil liberties generally until the Know-Nothings have been suppressed (which may be forever). Leaders may also conveniently blame this non-existent party for national calamities, thus escaping responsibility. Budgets may also swell to combat this "enemy." Citizens believing this falsehood may also feel freer to harass suspicious others who are, of course, completely innocent. Popular delusions may be real in their effect. But, there is another side to this story, one that is probably more common. Assuming that no threatening Know-Nothing Party members are alive (this organization vanished over 100 years ago), and innocent bystanders are not mistaken for the culprits, and government possesses no nefarious intent to manipulate to this mistaken belief, this intolerance is properly classified as an inoffensive delusion, hardly a political malady requiring remedy. Such a disturbed person or group can surely be disregarded despite "unhealthy" intolerance. When such intolerance is accepted on its face, independent of consequences, the survey misleadingly alarms.

This curious situation is not purely hypothetical. Americans periodically fall into intolerant frenzies over barely existent groups and conspiracies—anarchists, illuminati, international Jewish bankers, and Bolsheviks intent on conquering America by fluoridating the water supply. In the mid-1990s, popular targets of intolerance are anti-government armed militia groups, organizations of tiny followings and zero influence. Hatred of unseen, mysterious, diabolical forces may even dominate the lives of some. Disconcerting agitation aside, such intolerance is relatively harmless, at least for the objects of this hatred. Academic researchers can likewise share a fascination with nonthreatening nuisance groups. One major study (Sullivan et al., 1982) uncovered considerable intolerance, but the recipients of hatred were politically marginal. Some of the mentioned disliked groups—atheists, fascists—are barely organized entities of consequence (and how many citizens could define "fascist"?). Other groups—the John Birch Society, Ku Klux Klan, Black Panthers, Symbionese Liberation Army—were past fringe players in U.S. politics. The upshot, then, is that translating expressions of intolerance into actual intolerance may be impossible as the potential objects need not exist.

Intolerance as Paranoia

The subjective character of hearts and minds tolerance also permits illusionary beliefs about being the recipient of intolerance. That is, if people can display intolerance toward insignificant groups, the populace can likewise feel intolerance where none exists. Definitionally, only *perception* matters, not objective conditions. How, for example, do we regard those who sincerely tell interviewers (erroneously) that the CIA is out to "get them"? For them, the world is truly an inhospitable place. Must these mistaken people "prove" the existence of intolerance? Does objective evidence have any bearing, or is everything unchallengeable personal belief? What if the alleged objective "evidence" is unfalsifiable—vague allegations of dark, mysterious, conspiratorial forces? Going a step further, what if this paranoia is an epidemic? The result would be a society consumed with talk of oppression where none (objectively) prevails.

This possibility of grossly exaggerating intolerance is not idle speculation. One 1987 survey of people's beliefs about government repression found surprisingly large numbers of fearful Americans, especially among African Americans (Gibson, 1992a). Though we cannot say precisely, this disquietude is undoubtedly groundless. For example, well over three quarters of the respondents believed that the government would *not* permit them to organize a national strike. Sixty-four percent of the blacks and 40 percent of the whites conjectured that they would be denied permission to arrange a public meeting to protest the government's wrongful behavior. Even innocuously publishing a pamphlet was perceived as an impermissible activity by 53 percent of black respondents and 28 percent of whites.

To appreciate the paranoia here, compare responses to the same question from a 1990 poll conducted in the Soviet Union during the immediate post-Communism period (Gibson, 1992b). In a nation without a vigorous tradition of political liberty but rich with brutal political repression experience, the response patterns were comparable. Indeed, *fewer* Soviet citizens believed that the government would prohibit a nationwide workers' strike.

Whereas 57 percent of U.S. blacks believed that the government would ban speech criticizing government, the comparable figure in the former USSR was 39 percent. Overall, Soviet citizens fell between whites and blacks in their perceptions of enjoyed freedom. And in the USSR, unlike the U.S., these dissents are genuinely risky.

To argue that such perceptions of U.S. government inhospitality to organizing protest marches or holding public meetings accurately depicts reality is paranoid. The hard evidence contradicts this apprehensive vision. These political activities enjoy immense legal protection and, save for a nationwide strike of workers (a legal right), all are commonplace. College campuses abound with tolerated demonstrations by blacks and whites. Ordinary commercial bookstores surely offer innumerable revolutionary books and magazines. TV watchers during the 1960s and 1970s must surely remember coverage of anti-war demonstrations almost entirely unbothered by government crackdowns. From outside medical clinics to the White House itself, protest demonstrations are commonplace. Plainly, this fear of government-instigated intolerance is baseless.

Why are cries of intolerance so easily accepted as authoritative and genuine? Might not they be condemned for robbing the real article of meaning? Unfortunately, at least in our opinion, these exaggerations of intolerance may even be encouraged by government itself, and by schools and businesses. Increasingly, countless benefits, from preferential college admissions to advantages in government contracting, flow to those judged historically "oppressed." Group leaders may endlessly reiterate tales of intolerance to justify organizational existence. Self-interest thus encourages people to find evidence of past maltreatment, attempts at cultural extinction and other efforts of gross inhospitality, some of it political. Where clear evidence is lacking, especially of government mistreatment, it may have to be painstakingly rediscovered by experts (see, for example, LaNoue, 1993). Eventually, oft-repeated affirmations of (much exaggerated) intolerance become a permanent part of one's collective identity and a defended rationale for special treatment. In a phrase, I am not tolerated if only because I feel untolerated.

The reverse of mistaken intolerance is also possible, though perhaps less likely. Conceivably, particular citizens may live in grave danger, the object of intense intolerance, but consciously or unconsciously cannot acknowledge reality. This is not as odd as it may initially seem. For example, throughout the 1950s and 1960s, various national government police agencies secretly kept files on thousands of unsuspecting citizens, some of whom had unknowingly joined organizations with clandestine leftist views (see, for example, Goldstein, 1978, Chapter 10). Innocent attendance at a rally or subscribing to a controversial publication was enough to warrant being listed on a hidden government "enemies list." If denied a job due to this "unacceptable" political association, the real basis for this denial might remain unknown. Ignorance of hidden repression for both the affected individual and society more generally thus constituted misperceived political openness.

The problem, then, flows from the disjunction between tolerance denoted purely as an inner mental state and tolerance as an objective political condition. The two are quite distinguishable, may not even be related, and neither one can be dismissed as unauthentic. After all, if citizens feel persecuted or organize themselves to persecute non-existent or inconsequential groups, societal intolerance is, in one sense, unfeigned. Arguably, this intolerance is a collective delusion, not a bona fide reality. Still, if people trust something to be real, is it not genuine in its consequences? Forced to choose, we side with objective conditions, not mere perception for assessing tolerance. We shall return to this point in our concluding section.

V. Political Intolerance and Political Opposition

Accepting disagreeable differences, not applying politics to annihilate one's opponents, has a seductive allure among partisans of democratic politics. Indeed, the idea of tolerance permeates estimable democratic notions such as give and take, live and let live, agree to disagree and similar noble slogans associated with peaceful, civil politics. Nevertheless, when the virtue of tolerance is pushed, it soon collides with the inherent nature of political conflict, even the most humane democratic politics. Simply put, democratic politics is about defeating one's enemies—not killing them, of course, but still driving them from the field of play. That this is usually impractical, at least in the short run, does not obscure this as a motive. The Democrats "put up with" Republicans, but if the GOP were to be permanently vanquished, Democrats would not rescue it from oblivion. More likely, they would rejoice at their triumph.

A prominent incident occurring in France highlights this potential dilemma. In the July 13, 1993 issue of *Le Monde,* forty French intellectuals issued *"An Appeal to Vigilance"* to combat, in their estimation, the far Right's growing power in European intellectual life. This campaign of the Right, it was alleged, was a subtle seduction effort particularly waged against well-known democratic personalities and other intellectuals. To sound the alarm and stop the complicity, a committee—"Appeal to Vigilance"—was to be assembled "with the task of collecting and disseminating as widely as possible all information useful for understanding the networks of the far Right and their alliances in intellectual life (publishing houses, the press, universities), and taking public positions on all matters related to these concerns."

Had matters stopped here, this would have merely exemplified yet another group denouncing its enemies and threatening to expose alleged evils. However, these forty intellectuals took an additional step, a step illustrating the difficulty of separating intolerance from commonplace political action. The "Appeal to Vigilance" committee declared that its forty members "resolve to refuse all collaboration in journals, collective works, radio and television programs, as well as colloquia directed or organized by people whose connections with the Far Right have been demonstrated." In other words, a boycott to make ideas judged dangerous extinct. A newspaper that publishes an essay by a certified Far Rightist is thus denied all further writings by distinguished committee members and sympathizers. In light of group members' extraordinary position in France's intellectual life, this was not a trifling threat. The objective was not a call for op-ed refutations or clearly labeling "dangerous" ideology as such; the far Right's ideas themselves were to be, to the extent possible, wholly exterminated from public view.

Is this tactic properly judged an act of intolerance? To the extent that these forty intellectuals are unwilling to live and let live, this would appear so. If that is the case, then many similar intentions, all more or less integral to normal political conflict, are guilty of identical offenses. If a university refuses a white supremacist organization permission to disseminate literature on campus, are school administrators guilty of intolerance? Such attempt to shut up may be far more subtle. What if, for example, the established mass media never permitted certain political groups to express their views accurately and relentlessly portrayed sect members as "kooks" and "nut cases"? More generally, how are we to separate, especially under difficult real-world conditions, a legitimate and vigorous attempt to defeat one's opponents from intolerance of diversity? How is politics to operate if, in the name of tolerance, one's enemies cannot forever be silenced? Must the vanquished always receive yet one more chance to prevail? Politics is not a friendly sport. Political conflict means, by its very character, efforts to permanently subjugate adversaries.[7]

The answer, it would appear, is that discovering a clear, principled demarcation line is frustratingly difficult. Even if we could establish this instrument, it seems unlikely that this abstract standard could be universally imposed, particularly in the midst of bitter conflicts. The urge to hush enemies, criminalize their actions forever, is probably irrepressible. Totally leaving aside illegal and unethical political actions, how are citizens to know restraint? Can a civic version of the endangered species list be developed, a handy pamphlet that would, for example, say that groups advocating white racial superiority are now, like the snail darter, sufficiently rare to deserve official protection? Should these guidelines also distinguish among opponents that could be pushed hard toward abolition whereas others must be only gently nudged for fear of silencing delicate flimsy ideas worth preserving?

VI. Tolerance as Collective Property

As repeatedly observed, the conventional understanding of tolerance is individualistic in focus and psychological in character. Its prevalence is revealed by aggregating the opinions, perceptions, beliefs, and preferences of disconnected citizens. Hence, if nearly every citizen passionately sought to suppress something worthy of preservation, or everyone believed themselves not tolerated, one must count society intolerant. This habit of analysis is merely that: a habit. An intimate connection between individual traits and collective characteristics is neither logically necessary or empirically predetermined. Millions of intolerants need not bring forth an intolerant society. Or, conversely, the most oppressive society can survive a citizenry not otherwise inclined.

How are such apparent contradictions possible? The answers, surprisingly, are rather evident. Inequities in power and position can surely interfere with the easy cumulation of individual preferences into overall policy. An angry citizenry may intently yearn to lynch Communists or flog homosexuals, but those responsible—whether national leaders or the local police—may successfully defy popular passions. Such resistance, moreover, need not be rooted in any embrace of tolerance, love of democracy, respect for diversity, dutiful upholding of civil liberties, or comparable worthy intention. The clamor may be rejected on purely practical grounds—it is too costly, it overextends administrative capacity, it excessively disrupts, or it embarrasses those in power. Tolerance may be banal, not noble.

Ensuring the hated group's survival, despite public outcry, might even prove politically useful. It was once alleged, for example, that the FBI's total elimination of the Communist Party during the Cold War might disrupt agency funding and prestige. Protecting a modest number of ineffectual but outcast Communists constituted sound budgetary policy. Militant civil rights organizations likewise stand to gain in fund raising and recruiting by having the despised Klan around. Orwell's *1984* tells the tale of endless inconclusive wars propping up vast bureaucracies. Prolonging the struggle, not victory, served government propaganda far better.

Even if, in principle, pandering to citizen hatreds were feasible, this appeal may draw scant official interest, especially if potential pay-offs are modest. Save for the most desperate opportunist, better self-aggrandizing strategies may lie elsewhere. Historically, few (if any) American public officials, including the notorious demagogue Senator Joseph McCarthy (R-WI), have reaped sustained benefits from so-called Red baiting or witch hunts. It is not that such tactics are impermissible; rather, this strategy as a lifelong career seldom guarantees success. Perhaps the only politician of national reputation notable for translating strong anti-Communist campaigning into national prominence was Richard Nixon. Still, this strategy was relatively short-lived; it did not span an entire professional career. In short, pure narrow self-interest may well be insufficient to push leaders toward intolerance.

The nature of citizen intolerance, even when pervasive, could also render such inclinations inoperable. The sheer diversity and fragmentation of hated targets—sometimes called "pluralistic intolerance"—may preclude massive mobilizing (see, for example, Sullivan, et al., 1982, Chapter 4). Protection— or more accurately, apathy—is afforded by stalemate. Plans for future assaults on a multitude of heretics degenerate into endless ineffectual bickering. Invisible-hand "intolerance gridlock" prevails. Concomitantly, the ever-broadening of repressive campaigns can sow the seeds of its own destruction if a consensus is absent. For example, suppose that vehement anti-Communists added atheists to their hit list. This tactic might not only mobilize counter-reactions—those having no objections to atheism might now lose interest in the enterprise—but atheist anti-Communists might jump ship as well.

Conceivably, even if consensual intolerance prevails, it may well constitute a fairly low collective citizen priority. All impulses are inevitably constrained by time and resources, so momentary repressive urges conveniently drift toward the back burner. This is especially likely if despised groups are little more than out-of-sight pests. Indeed, several organizations singled out for hopeful extinction in polls—the Nazis, Socialists, the John Birch Society—are petty irritants, hardly the organizers of fear-provoking assaults (Sullivan, et al., 1982, Chapter 4). Given this irrelevance—the arcane character of such groups—almost any other activity, from the personal to the political, takes precedence. Expelling the loathed Marxists hidden away in some dingy part of town might soon resemble an endlessly delayed home project. Intolerance prevails, and prevails widely, but it is inconsequential for it never materializes. As Oscar Wilde said about Socialism—"It will never work. It takes too many evenings"—may equally be applied to intolerance.

We are not asserting that these factors forever thwart mass intolerance. Our analysis is abstract and hypothetical, not historical. These possibilities merely highlight complex connections between individual psychological dispositions and collective conditions. Ultimately, this linkage, regardless of plausibility, requires empirical proof. This central point is that portraits of popular preferences, no matter if accurate or detailed, cannot conclusively reveal political openness. Noxious weeds resist the most stout eradication efforts.

A Different Approach to Tolerance

The key to overcoming the limitations of hearts and minds tolerance requires that tolerance be analyzed from the perspective of what flourishes, not people's beliefs regarding permissibility. When we replace "inner tolerance" with "outer tolerance" we have *political tolerance.* Tolerance is objective and applies to the entire political community. We abandon those who mistakenly feel untolerated. Their views may be better treated as a psychological matter; private thoughts cannot be substituted for observable reality. From this vantage point, discovering that Socialists are hated outcasts or even that the government persecutes them is not the *ne plus ultra* of research. Such data are not necessarily irrelevant, but their applicability to the flourishing of Socialism demands demonstration. Far more critical is whether Socialist views are expressed, Socialist organizations survive, and citizens can embrace Socialist doctrines, if they so choose.

Does it really matter if ordinary citizens, deep in their hearts, are would-be tyrants if unorthodox opinions and persuasions thrive? No doubt, just as citizens discipline their lust and materialistic envy, hatred of eccentricities need not overwhelm society. A world of inept, bumbling despots hounding down crafty heretics is not inconceivable. The key question, then, is what transpires, not what citizens or government officials prefer to transpire.

As an alternative to hearts and minds tolerance, political tolerance offers numerous improvements. Both versions share the common core of putting up with the disliked, but the latter refers to society's inclination, not individual psychological proclivity. Much is to be gained in this shift. In an instant, the myriad problems of identifying fluid amorphous cerebral dispositions vanish. Delving into arcane debates regarding the existence of inner tolerance, the illusive relationship between opinions and action, the impact of questionnaire wording or similar survey research disorders no longer requires scholarly attention. Ditto for disentangling a fragile frame of mind from ever-present but conceptually distinct relatives, such as apathy or fatalism. Nor is there a need to agonize over intolerance versus legitimate political opposition. What matters, simply, is the manifest existence of wide-ranging political views and causes appealing to at least some citizens: not necessarily every imaginable view but an extended expanse. As in appraising a restaurant's menu, the question is one of satisfactory selection, not a compilation of every dish conjecturable. In a nutshell, the question is whether tolerance exists as a condition of society, not as a mental condition. Chapter 5 will address this question in detail after a detour into the rise of this ubiquitous hearts and minds tolerance and various arguments against too much tolerance.

NOTES

1. Our explication here is restricted to contemporary uses of tolerance. Historically, the Latin term *tolerabilis* (that which may be borne) well pre-dates current infatuations. When these earlier understandings are added to the discussion, the subject becomes even more complex. See, for example, Crick (1971, Chapter 3).

2. Howard Schuman (1972) offers an extended discussion on this point of multiple values shaping responses to complex situations. Several studies are summarized that show the proportion of people expressing support or opposition to racial discrimination can vary enormously if realistic situational factors are incorporated into the questions. For example, one study found that the number of people accepting discrimination against blacks in a restaurant doubled if the restaurant manager justified this exclusion on the grounds that it was necessary to keep white customers. In sum, tolerance or intolerance, as common sense would dictate, often "depends."

3. Stouffer (1955) in *Communism, Conformity and Civil Liberties* (Chapter 7) addresses this question directly in 1954, a time when sensitivity to Communism was relatively high. In the general population sample, 3 percent said that they knew somebody who admitted to being a Communist; another 10 percent said that they knew somebody who acted suspiciously enough that they *might* be a Communist (this varied by education with the college-educated having the most contact). Among community leaders, the average percentage saying that they knew a Communist leader was 11—the highest proportion (19 percent) was among newspaper publishers. Stouffer himself comments on this lack of contact, and further adds that contact is most likely among well-educated city-dwellers in the Northeast (182).

4. Research on the meanings attached to commonly employed political terms has been limited. Nevertheless, the results strongly suggest wide divergences of imputed content. For example, in one analysis of violence among men, acts such as burning a draft card are considered violent by some but not others (Blumenthal, Kahn, Andrews, & Head, 1972 Chapter 4). Comparable divergences of content have been found in the highly controversial slogan "black power" (Aberbach & Walker, 1970). Unfortunately, comparable analysis of terms often employed in tolerance studies—Communist, atheists—has not been conducted.

5. Several analyses of tolerance (for example, Corbett, 1982; Nunn, Crockett, & Williams, 1978) explicitly argue that genuine tolerance must be conceptually distinguished from look-alike dispositions. Similarly, Fletcher (1996) characterizes indifference as a "cheapening" of genuine tolerance and thus to be kept totally distinct. If constructing a dictionary were our objective, this strategy is commendable. Unfortunately, in the real world fine distinctions of meaning are not

always sustainable, even to those citizens thoughtful enough to reflect on their own motives. For us, if something closely resembles tolerance, regardless of some alleged violated pristine meaning, it will be construed as if it were tolerance.

6. Fletcher (1996) depicts a comparable theme in Jewish theology. Here the person intolerant of sin cannot force the state to impose morality, for such imposition removes ethical will from personal choice. To be truly moral, one must freely obey God's commands, not the magistrate's laws. Hence, for example, forbidding homosexuality (if that is judged immoral) subverts the very authority of God. Observing religious dictates, again, promotes passivity, though in Jewish theology each citizen is expected to inveigh his or her brethren to be moral.

7. Legutko's (1994) overview makes a more explicit connection between the expanding definition of tolerance and political struggle. For him, the relentless transformation from "negative tolerance" to "positive tolerance" constituted a campaign against specific ideologies and dogmas. Demanding "more tolerance" was the weapon of choice in subverting authoritarian philosophies, political absolutism and similar rigid orthodoxies. Tolerance is not value-neutral; it serves as a useful tactical tool, perhaps no different from populists insisting on elections as the best method of distributing political power.

3

Attitudinal
Tolerance Ascendant

Tolerance, both in popular discourse and among scholars, now denotes a psychological disposition. So dominating is this understanding that any alternative is virtually unthinkable, at least to those who preach the virtues of this passion for accepting disagreeable differences. Nevertheless, as Chapter 2 argued, this definitional consensus masks innumerable predicaments and ambiguities. It is also woefully incomplete. Clearly, a curious situation confronts us requiring explanation. On one hand, this comprehension of tolerance enjoys an almost unquestioned popularity. Simultaneously, this definition's multiple and serious blemishes are plainly evident. Why, then, this easy and unchallenged domination? Getting to the bottom of this paradox will be the task at hand. Appreciating this popularity in the face of countless inherent difficulties requires a historical excursion into modern social science. We shall trace out in greater detail this emergence of hearts and minds tolerance, its content and, to the extent possible, its theoretical and political justification. More important, we inquire into the sources of its popularity and the critical political ramifications of this one particular form of tolerance.

Reviewing a multitude of polls is more than a tour of scholarship, though it is that. If this literature was a matter solely of academic concern, its existence could be briefly acknowledged in a few citations. More, however, is at stake than dredging up fifty-year-old studies and surrounding disputes. These dimly remembered surveys shape our collective self-understanding; they have entered our cultural baggage, defined the existence of certain problems and pointed us toward specific prescriptions. Scholarship and politics are joined here. The dozens of polls on, say, Communist speakers proclaim more than cold, scientific facts; these data are images in the mirror of survey research, a way of gaining self-understanding with larger political ramifications.

What these poll data reveal is seldom flattering. Relying on attitude-based research, not the mundane substance of daily political conflict, investigators offer a portrait of extensive intolerance. Though all is not glum, the disturbing findings draw disproportionate attention. To argue otherwise doubts the revered authority of modern social science. It is not surprising, then, when contemporary educators and public officials urgently call for promoting tolerance, it is an invitation well-steeped in this hearts and minds tradition. Today's hard-headed practical businessman, it is sometimes said, often unconsciously slavishly adheres to some long-forgotten, long discredited abstract economic theory. The equivalent is true when it comes to promoting tolerance, though here the doctrine is much alive.

Before our review proceeds, a few comments regarding criteria for scrutiny. "Tolerance," as previously noted, is a broad term, applied to everything from supporting traditional civil liberties to endorsing programs assisting the disadvantaged. Hence, a casual sweep of polls all loosely connected to tolerance yields a disjointed harvest. We single out only polls inquiring about politically admitting controversial groups and ideas. For example, a question about permitting Marxists to express their ideas publicly is included. Inquiries regarding personal bigotry, prejudice, matters of individual morality, views on the rights of criminals and ethnocentrism, as well as those addressing political and/or economic equality are excluded. Thus, we skip over classics such as *The Authoritarian Personality* (Adorno, Franke-Brunswik, Levinson, & Sanford, 1950) that are entirely concerned with probing anti-Semitism's roots and similar hateful inclinations. Such treatment, though potentially insightful for understanding intolerance broadly, hardly ventures beyond inner psychological traits into larger political issues. No doubt a more comprehensive investigation of tolerance conditions might touch on citizen psychology, but such inquiry into the source of aversions must remain outside our scope. Our review is especially tilted toward major studies disproportionately shaping the overall direction of research addressing political issues. Finally, technical details will receive only modest regard. It may be that faulty samples or clumsy question wording invalidate the results, but these deficiencies are irrelevant here. The portrait painted by the attitudinal-based window into political tolerance is the task at hand.

The Rise of "Hearts and Minds" Tolerance Research

The Early Questions

Modern surveys began in the mid-1930s, and tolerance-related questions soon appeared on the pollster's agenda. Between 1938 and the onset of World War II, several questions asked about permitting controversial groups to voice their (presumed) unpopular views (Cantril, 1951, 244-245). These questions pertained to the events of the era. The late 1930s were politically tumultuous, controversial groups abounded, and political violence was frequent. One leading history of this period described it as "an eccentric decade of right-wing extremism in America" (Lipset & Raab, 1973, 150). Estimation of such groups ran into the hundreds, and such personalities as Father Charles Coughlin and Huey Long attracted huge followings. The Ku Klux Klan was a notable political presence. This right-wing liveliness was matched by similar vigor on the left. Communist and Socialist candidates for office, including presidential contenders, received millions of votes. Communist and sympathetic groups were tireless and figured prominently in the news, often attracting well-known intellectuals and union officials. Citizens were not being asked permission for the expression of unorthodoxy; it was a matter of accepting a *fait accompli.*

On the whole, poll results depicted a citizenry whose strong minorities and occasional majorities balked at permitting these controversial views. Put differently, many disliked political reality. The earliest poll inquiries were two May 1938 questions regarding Jersey City's Mayor Frank Hague's strong-armed anti-opposition tactics. Among those hearing of Hague and with opinions (a little more than half of the sample), the Mayor's policy of forbidding out-of-town radicals to hold meetings in Jersey City received a 3 to 2 endorsement. Three more polls shortly afterward (plus one in November 1940) posed the general question: Do you believe in free speech? Though free speech in general was nearly unanimously endorsed, majorities would deny radicals, Communists, or Fascists the right to hold meetings in their communities. A November 1939 survey confirmed this widespread intolerance: 68% said that a leader of the Communist Party should not be permitted to speak to a student group (only 8% offered "no opinion"). A September 1940 Gallup poll likewise reported that only about one third of those asked would permit a Communist Party candidate radio time. However, when questions vaguely referred to "those who oppose our form of government" rather than Communists, radicals or Fascists, support for free expression in two separate 1940 polls drew majority endorsement.

World War II era polls confirmed this earlier pattern. When questions referred to generalities (e.g., a 1943 National Opinion Research Center (NORC) poll on allowing people to "say anything they want in a public speech,"), a majority acquiesced. When queries became more detailed, support fell sharply. For example, in 1942 when questioned about permitting radicals to assemble in one's community, nearly two thirds opposed (Cantril, 1951, 245).

These early data depicted a clear pattern: As we move from broad, abstract endorsements for putting up with unpopular views to more specific applications, tolerance declines. Free speech is universally celebrated though it need not be extended to a known Communist addressing students or speaking on the radio. Whether, of course, such Communists and other equally hated groups did, in fact, enjoy such liberties is another matter entirely. As just mentioned, such dissent was common during the 1930s and 1940s. The germane point is the emerging twofold portrait. First, when attitudes on tolerance are assessed in some detail, Americans often gravitate toward intolerance. Second, that so-called controversial activities coexisted with these verbal inclinations was not integral to analysis. Future studies would endlessly confirm this depiction.

The 1954 Stouffer Study

These questions, and similar questions immediately following World War II, were akin to quick, disconnected snapshots of the public mood. The data were not singled out for special attention and were typically accompanied by polls on sundry topics, from religion to movie personalities. Well-developed theories, analyses, or ramifications were scant. This changed abruptly in 1955 with Samuel A. Stouffer's *Communism, Conformity and Civil Liberties.* It was not the first extended scholarly survey-based treatment of tolerance. Others had taken up the subject, but their focus was typically more concerned with psychological traits such as prejudice, not larger political matters. This book profoundly shaped ensuing understandings of tolerance and scholarly inquiry.

Part of the book's significance lay in timeliness. It spoke directly to a leading issue of the day. During the mid-1950s, the "what is permitted politically" debate was not just abstract philosophy. Strident anti-Communism and other repressive urges within and outside of government abounded. The Cold War with the Soviet Union was indisputable and ever threatened to explode into armed confrontation. Successful Communist takeovers of several European and Asian nations, often led by small but determined zealots, were fresh memories. Visions of the anti-Communist impulse encouraging a right-wing lead suppression of civil liberties were not fantasy. Prominent anti-Communists—Senator Joseph McCarthy (R-WI), J. Edgar Hoover, and General Douglas MacArthur—enjoyed wide popularity. Lurid, well-documented tales of Soviet spying abounded and might justify a police state. *Communism, Conformity and Civil Liberties,* like the police arriving at a trouble spot after a 911 call, sought to size up the situation.

Though rooted in events of its era, the book's significance transcended its historical setting. *Communism, Conformity and Civil Liberties* founded the tolerance research tradition. In the most authoritative manner possible, it supplied future scholars with a lucid model with which to investigate tolerance. As said in Latin, *facile est inventis addere*—it is easy to add to things already invented. To grasp how this occurred, both the author's credentials and the book's technical character must be more fully grasped.

Samuel Stouffer was among the most distinguished academics of the day, a Harvard sociologist with myriad landmark scholarly contributions already to his credit. The prestigious Fund for the Republic generously supported the project, and similarly distinguished scholars assisted Stouffer. Most consequential, the project's execution exemplified the highest possible standards of quality. Even today, despite technological and statistical advances, it remains an admirable classic. Two well-regarded polling organizations—Gallup and National Opinion Research Center of the University of Chicago—conducted independent national surveys; samples were carefully developed, and well-trained interviewers ferreted out reluctant respondents for face-to-face interviews. Questions were formulated by a distinguished expert panel and repeatedly pre-tested and costly, time-consuming but rich in meaning open-ended questions were used. Supplementing the mass survey was a special sample of 1,500 community leaders from cities of 100,000 to 150,000—mayors, heads of political parties, union officials, newspaper editors, veteran groups leaders, heads of women's organizations, school board presidents, and others. It is an impressive book, by any standards.

Communism, Conformity and Civil Liberties bequeathed several legacies. To its sponsors and others agonizing over the future erosion of liberty, it offered timely reassurances that, despite some disturbing findings, sounding the alarm was unnecessary. According to Stouffer, Americans were not suffering "a quivering fear or from an anxiety neurosis about the internal Communist threat" (220). Though question after question revealed a willingness to throttle unorthodoxy, this urge was neither over-powering nor ever-present. The problem, he speculated, was more akin to a temporary diet deficiency. Even better, the future looked promising. Long-term trends, especially increasing education, expanding mass communications, and social change, foretold greater future tolerance.

A second legacy was a general theory, frequently alluded to in subsequent research, regarding the preservation of freedom despite an unsure citizen commitment. In particular, community leaders, from elected officials to heads of fraternal clubs, clearly held more tolerant views than ordinary citizens, and given their influential positions, they potentially restrained citizen inclinations toward excesses. As bulwarks of democracy, civic leaders were, in effect, the "carriers of the creed." The paradox of reasonably accessible politics surviving amid intolerant citizens was thus resolved with an irony: A small elite would impose democratic values despite majority wishes. The precise dynamics of this process, and its testing with data drawn from actual events, was not, however, part of *Communism, Conformity and Civil Liberties.*

The most pertinent, at least for our purposes, legacy consists of techniques to assess tolerance. It was almost as if Stouffer bequeathed a social science version of the microscope or thermometer. To be sure, primitive tools already existed in the 1930s, but now the instrument was refined by top-notch prestigious scientists. Even the novice, someone lacking Stouffer's standing and resources, could now examine what was once reachable only with uncertain difficulty. The formula was simple and, possibly most critical, highly authoritative. Students of tolerance henceforth possessed a certified scientific technique employed by the very best in the business.

The Stouffer formula was straightforward. First, membership, or alleged or implied affiliation, in three controversial groups (occasionally collectively called "nonconformists")—Communists, socialists, and atheists—were combined with various activities—college teaching, having a book in the public library, speaking publicly on an unpopular theme, radio broadcasting, and so on. In short, a grid of groups and actions was assembled; questionnaire items occupied each intersection. For example, citizens were asked if an admitted Communist might be allowed to speak in one's community, have a book in the library, and so on. Second, these questions were asked of citizens in general or of those occupying potential positions of influence. As with employing a thermometer, the instrument could be put to use anywhere, anytime and still yield valid results. One did not have to find difficult-to-reach populations nor wait for opportune situations (e.g., citizens actually demanding a book be removed from the library) to assess tolerance.

The formula was adaptable, easily extended to evolving conditions, and offered an almost timeless, flexible, universal tool of inquiry. An update might inquire whether homosexuals should be permitted to rally on behalf of a gay rights ordinance. Stouffer's approach also provided the clear, easy-to-follow recipe for statistical analysis of tolerance. This was a remarkable contribution, paving the way for endless imitation. Basically, the response to specific tolerance questions now became numerical scores to be explained by a medley of personal, demographic, or psychological traits. A researcher might, for instance, ask how tolerance for Communists varied by age, education, sex, income, city size, ideology, or racial prejudice. Even as statistical analysis evolved into greater complexity, the Stouffer paradigm remained unchallenged: Tolerance was the dependent variable to be explained by other individual-level traits.

It is essential to recognize what this paradigm excluded, explicitly or implicitly. Proceeding from the pattern of individual opinion to overall political conditions was awkward and, ultimately, speculative. We might argue, for example, that widespread citizen intolerance explained the repressive government policies of the 1950s, but this connection lacked the scientific standing of, say, explaining individual-level tolerance scale scores by individual education levels. In the former assertion, in which the inference is from individuals to a collective property, argument rests exclusively on sheer plausibility. The thesis can never be conclusively confirmed statistically; it can only be plausibly asserted. When all the data pertain to individual-level traits (even for aggregate variables such as city size), a straightforward computational process exists, yielding a precise statistical product. Hence, to study tolerance easily and scientifically required relegating larger political phenomena to the analytical sidelines. Broader concepts, for example, "oppressive environment," might still appear in the text, but only as aggregations of isolated individual views or surrounding, contextual, or background material. What could not be precisely examined through this individual-based technique lay beyond the scientific analysis proper.

This paradigm also directed attention away from the unpopular object to the person being tolerant or intolerant. To investigate how Marxism managed during the 1950s, we would examine the fate of actual Marxists—were their views suppressed? Were their newspapers banned? Logically, no one-to-one connection need exist between the repressive impulse and its aftermath. An intently hostile public or government might prove ineffective in stamping out a determined, fanatical foe. Unfortunately, the inherent nature of the random sample-based opinion poll is ill-suited to study the objects of hatred. The most carefully conducted random sample-based national poll cannot round up significant numbers of political deviants, regardless of persuasion. Of 1500 respondents, a goodly number for a poll, those with controversial views will probably number less than a dozen. Moreover, these data would still be opinion data, not the hard experiences defining the meaning of intolerance. In sum, if the existence of repressive behavior is the object of scrutiny, the survey by its very nature is guilty of misdirection. Communism might be thriving—or on the verge of extinction—but the poll could never reveal this fact.

The Post-Stouffer Mini-Industry

Communism, Conformity and Civil Liberties is a classic, and deservedly so. Not surprisingly, its clarity of argument and technical explicitness inspired imitation from other prestigious scholars affiliated with top academic institutions. Foundations and government also continued their support. Like all classic first steps, it pointed in numerous directions regarding future investigation. One might ask, for example, what transpires when popular intolerance collides with more tolerant elite views? Similarly, what is the effect of citizen opinion on the day-to-day activities of outcast groups? On the whole, though Stouffer's work invigorated the field, future research largely deepened—not extended—this narrow attitudinal focus. This choice, as we shall see, had far more to do with the dictates of research than the emergence of worthy questions needing resolution. The larger political context, the issue of possible mass anti-Communist hysteria, the consequences of choking-off public debate, and the like gradually dwindled as elements of the tolerance research agenda. After several decades, the study of tolerance would shed nearly all its political application, evolving into little more than a psychological trait of unclear civic impact. With few exceptions, real-world political events faded into the deep background of this research tradition.

Two studies, both widely cited and admired, soon built on Stouffer's pioneering work (McClosky, 1964; Prothro & Grigg, 1960). Superficially, neither explicitly seemed to focus centrally on tolerance. Whereas *Communism, Conformity and Civil Liberties* principally addressed citizen anxiety over a possible Communist menace, Prothro-Grigg and McClosky searched instead for a consensus on political norms theorized as pre-conditions for democracy. In particular, both studies argued that democracy depended on extensive agreement regarding principles such as majority rule, minority rights, popular sovereignty, and respect for law. Nevertheless, in their actual design and questionnaire items, as well as the importance attributed to citizen attitudes, the similarities to Stouffer are apparent.

First, both the Prothro-Grigg and McClosky studies reflected Stouffer's elite-mass distinction in dealing with potentially undemocratic citizen opinion. The underlying and guiding theory was the "carriers of the creed" formulation—political openness disproportionately depended on the enlightened views of better educated, more politically involved elites. In the case of Prothro-Grigg, this was somewhat roughly done by stratifying responses by income and education. McClosky used two distinct samples—a 1957-58 national sample of 1,500 adults and an elite sample of 3,000 political activists drawn from delegates to the 1956 Democratic and Republican national presidential nominating conventions. The survey results clearly confirmed the earlier pattern: The better educated, more political activists showed a greater appreciation of democratic values (tolerance).

Second, questionnaire items in both studies closely resembled those employed in the 1954 Stouffer survey. For example, the Prothro-Grigg survey asked about putting up with speeches against religion, government ownership of industry, and an admitted Communist being allowed to speak, questions almost word-for-word from the Stouffer questionnaire. Other questions, for example, Communists and Negroes being permitted to run for public office, were obvious extensions of the groups and activities formula. McClosky's analysis used similar items to tap willingness to put up with unpopular views: "A book that contains wrong political views cannot be a good book and does not deserve to be published" (agree-disagree) or "Freedom does not give anyone the right to teach foreign ideas in our schools" (agree-disagree)(367). The overall results again corroborated the earlier Stouffer discoveries: Though abstract support for tolerance was common, enthusiasm fell off sharply as questions grew more specific.

What is important here is not the precise comparability of questionnaires across these studies or differences in findings, measures, or interpretations. More pertinent is the fast-developing scholarly consensus: Tolerance is a property of ordinary citizens as revealed in the general opinion poll. What transpires "outside" in the real world of politics is beyond the data. Each new study incorporating this standard helped to confirm this one particular perspective as *the* authoritative choice. Disputes among researchers over data or method eventually take place wholly within this framework, leaving the paradigm itself unchallenged.

By the 1970s the hearts and minds model had plainly become standard. *The Journal of Social Issues* in 1975 devoted an entire issue, some thirteen articles, to summarizing current civil liberties research suggesting opportunities for scholarly and civic progress. Articles covered varied topics, but the Stouffer conceptual and methodological legacy distinctly prevailed. Though authors might occasionally dwell on the uncertain connection between surveys and real-world political conflict, actual research ignored these qualms. Zellman (1975), for example, utilizing questions from Stouffer, Prothro-

Grigg, and McClosky, emphasized the sources of tolerant attitudes and their life-cycle dynamics. Hollander (1975) explored the association between nonconformity as a psychological trait and attitudinal support for civil liberties. W. Cody Wilson (1975) reported on a national sample of nearly 2,500 respondents utilizing questions nearly identical to Stouffer's. When the discussion turned to prescriptions to promote tolerance (Triandis, 1975), analysis focused almost exclusively on the hearts and minds of citizens. The implicit assumption was that tolerance or intolerance originated with citizens, and it was the responsibility of the researcher to promote the "right" attitudes.

McClosky and Brill's *Dimensions of Tolerance: What Americans Believe About Civil Liberties* (1983) further added to this growing literature. Data were drawn from two major national surveys conducted during the late 1970s plus a sample of nearly 1,900 community leaders ranging from local officials to school administrators. Like the Stouffer study, it represents a major financial commitment by a private foundation (Russell Sage) and involved dozens of other distinguished academics in its creation. Treatment of the subject was exhaustive and nearly encyclopedic. Almost every possible aspect of civil liberties is scrutinized, from the traditional-support for free speech and the protections of due process—to the more novel—the right to an odd lifestyle and privacy. Citizen views are systematically dissected over nearly 500 pages using a variety of social, psychological and ideological scales as possible determinants

The resulting portrait was the familiar one. Citizens are abstractly tolerant, but intolerance grows as inquiries become more specific. Better educated people are more tolerant, and tolerance is more prevalent among the "worldly." Young people and ideological liberals were especially generous in accepting differences. As before, community influentials, especially in occupations such as law and education, exhibited the most tolerance. Stouffer's optimism was confirmed: Rising education and exposure to new ideas seemingly encouraged greater accommodation of diversity and dissent. Only the observation that civil liberties norms may not be easily acquired by everyone lent a gloomy note.

The McClosky-Brill analysis represents a substantial corroboration of the Stouffer paradigm. As with similar past studies, however, this was a single effort that others could only admire (or reject). This soon changed. Beginning in 1972, the National Opinion Research Center (NORC) at the University of Chicago began to include several original Stouffer items (plus updated versions) on their annual General Social Survey (GSS). The format was simple. In the first survey, three groups were identified—anti-religionists, Socialists, Communists, the same groups originally used in *Communism,*

Conformity and Civil Liberties. Eventually, racists, militarists, and homosexuals were added. Each group member was placed in three situations—speaking in the community on a topic of group relevance, teaching in a college, and having a book in the library. A typical question was, "Now, I would like to ask you some questions about a man who admits he is a Communist. Suppose he is teaching in college. Should he be fired, or not?" Between 1972 and 1994, combinations of these questions were used in sixteen separate national polls.

This was more than yet another poll. NORC is a prestigious survey organization, is supported by the National Science Foundation, and enjoys an outstanding quality reputation. These tolerance items, moreover, were initially scrutinized by some 105 social scientists and have survived even more subsequent checking. The GSS data set is generally accepted as state-of-the-art by professionals in the field. Equally important, these data were designed to be an accessible public resource. Everything possible, from clear documentation to wide dissemination of machine-readable data, was done to ensure utilization. For the scholar concerned about the public's oppressive views, these NORC data afforded both an authoritative and a convenient way of attacking the problem.

Not surprisingly, a plethora of articles, reports, convention papers, and books soon emerged, heavily relying on these data. The richness of the GSS data permitted tolerance to be easily and creatively related to a multitude of subjects. Illustrations include examination of tolerance levels across religious denominations (Beatty & Oliver, 1984), the relationship between tolerance and age (Cutler & Kaufman, 1975), the changing content of tolerance attitudes (Davis, 1975, Mueller, 1988), the roots of working class intolerance (Grabb, 1979), tolerance among teenagers (Jones, 1980), and myriad others. Corbett (1982) employed the 1977 version of the Stouffer questions as a major data source in his undergraduate political behavior textbook. Nie, Junn, and Stehlik-Barry (1996) employed updated Stouffer items in a major analysis of American citizens and participation. If Stouffer had invented the approach, the NORC data democratized it.

Of the many analyses spawned by these data, perhaps the most well-developed and noteworthy was *Tolerance for Nonconformity* (Nunn, et al., 1978). Both its overall design—particularly combining the national surveys with a separate survey of community influentials—and analytical approach consciously replicated *Communism, Conformity and Civil Liberties.* Only details and examples were updated—for example, anti-war demonstrators joined other nonconformists and the effects of mobility received greater attention. Indeed, because the purpose of the analysis was to assess changes from the 1954 Stouffer baseline, continuity was accentuated. Its principal findings were predictable: tolerance was generally growing though it still varied by group, education remained its best predictor, and community activists still exceeded ordinary citizens' civil liberties in support. In short, though tolerance itself may have shifted since 1954, its understanding barely altered.

The Content-Controlled Alternative

The Stouffer approach, like nearly all social science techniques, was not without its critics. Of those expressing reservations, John Sullivan and his associates raised the most penetrating. They also proposed an alternative measurement strategy. Like *Communism, Conformity and Civil Liberties,* Sullivan's main work, *Political Tolerance and American Democracy* (1983), represents a landmark influential book on the subject. This alternative begins with a simple, common-sense observation anticipated by earlier research (for example, Lawrence, 1976): one's tolerance of a group is shaped by how one evaluates the group. Putting up with, say, Communists hardly constitutes genuine tolerance for a Communist sympathizer. The Stouffer and follow-up studies that focus on Communists, Socialists, atheists, or racists assume, not verify, the unpopularity of these groups. Perhaps tolerance is not really tolerance at all; responses merely reflect endorsing a collegial disposition. Definitionally, this is not authentic tolerance. Moreover, since public hatreds evolve over time, greater public tolerance of communism may reflect more on Marxism's irrelevance than on genuine increases in public acceptance.

To correct this flaw, Sullivan devised what he labeled a "content-controlled" measure of tolerance. First, survey respondents selected their own "least liked" group (two choices were allowed) from a list of ten groups, balanced from both ends of the political spectrum. Included were explicit political groups—fascists and Communists—to entities possessing a more moral flavor—pro- and anti-abortionists. Names not on the initial list could be added, if necessary. Respondents were then asked about political and personal activities available to the specified unpopular group member. In each instance, the name of the first and second least liked group was inserted when the statement was offered. Several activities were comparable to the original Stouffer situations: being banned from serving as president, teaching in public schools, having the organization outlawed, allowing the disliked person to live next door, and having one's son or daughter marry a group member. Thus, if the Ku Klux Klan was most disliked, the statement asked whether a Klan member should be permitted to teach in a college or university.

Political Tolerance and American Democracy is a complex book often relying on highly sophisticated statistical techniques. Nevertheless, its central conclusions are fairly plain and differ substantially from previous findings. First, the public's growing tolerance, as reflected in the traditional Stouffer-type questions, is an illusion, an artifact of inappropriate methodology. The intolerance objects have metamorphosed, they are more numerous and now often reside on the political right. This shift was obscured because the standard questions deal with a too limited array of ideologies and over-emphasized left-wing sentiments. Second, the content-controlled method also alters the familiar explanatory pattern. Past connections between tolerance, education, and levels of political participation were greatly weakened or disappeared altogether. In particular, the well-educated were only slightly more tolerant than the less educated; differences flowed from other factors, not education per se. Ditto for the often stated relationship between political activism and tolerance. The focus of intolerance is well predicted by one's ideology and personal characteristics. Blacks, for example, evidence the greatest dislike of the KKK; people on the left dislike those on the right. Finally, the best predictors of intolerance were perceived threats by those who were disliked and certain psychological factors, especially self-esteem and dogmatism.

Sullivan's substantive conclusions and inquiry stratagem constitute a major departure from past studies. Nevertheless, when observed from a larger perspective, in terms of implicit assumptions and habits of investigation, they fall well within the established tradition. Not only do they focus exclusively on attitudes, but as before, the questions are general, abstract, and unconnected to worldly political events. Authorizing John Birch Society members and comparable obscure listed groups to speak in one's community will undoubtedly strike most citizens as vague and hypothetical. These depicted situations were far removed from the civic agenda. In a nutshell, the exercise lacked realism. Furthermore, consistent with the conventional approach, the study's analytical focus is on sources of attitudinal intolerance, not on its political consequences. Whether any of these groups, or those spontaneously offered by respondents, are at risk politically due to citizen intolerance remains outside the study's scope. Whether Socialists are enjoying great freedom or are being hounded down are never investigated. Overall, then, though this research ostensibly challenges prevailing methodology, it nevertheless confirms its central features.

Situation-Specific Tolerance Studies

Stouffer's *Communism, Conformity and Civil Liberties* addressed the political pressures and fears of the mid-1950s. Virulent anti-communism was widely feared, and Stouffer sought to assess the likelihood of citizen hysteria. As studies multiplied and the Stouffer approach increasingly became the standard, the relationship between tolerance research and events weakened. With the exception of a few 1960s anti-war demonstrator questions, attitudinal analyses had a peripheral political character. Even Sullivan's more detailed and more varied methodological alternative largely dealt with matters that were barely a political sideshow.

Beginning in the mid-1980s and onward, notably in the work of James Gibson and his associates, a restoration of this pertinence occurred. Gibson's studies were scholarly landmarks, widely and approvingly cited, and often published in prestigious journals. Taken together, they constitute a substantial element in the evolving understanding of tolerance, a conscious attempt to move beyond the Stouffer paradigm. Here, citizen tolerance was to be firmly linked, theoretically and empirically, to larger political issues. The goal was to move beyond merely depicting what citizens thought about Communists holding meetings. Nonetheless, this effort, again largely utilizing surveys, fell well short of the mark despite claims to the contrary. In its own way, despite the struggle, these efforts confirmed the powerful gravitational pull of hearts and minds tolerance.

Civil Liberties and Nazis: The Skokie Free-Speech Controversy (Gibson & Bingham, 1985) is the major opus in this more realistic approach. The book dwells on well-publicized incidents occurring in Skokie, Illinois, a half-Jewish, middle class Chicago suburb. In 1977, Frank Collins, the National Socialist Party of America (Nazi Party) leader, sought the Skokie Park District's permission to hold what he promised would be a peaceful, inoffensive march. Numerous Skokie citizens, many of whom were Holocaust survivors, were outraged and vaguely intimated possible violence. City officials responded by insisting Collins post a $350,000 insurance bond as protection from possible damages and lawsuits. In effect, this heavy financial requirement stopped Collins, at least temporarily. A long, complex, highly emotional, and widely reported political and legal battle then followed. The situation attracted national attention; numerous suits and countersuits were filed. Collins eventually secured court permission for the parade, but he never did goose-step in Skokie, instead preferring in 1978 to hold two rather uneventful Chicago demonstrations.

The Skokie situation presents a near-perfect laboratory setting with all the essential ingredients for examining tolerance: a widely hated group, impassioned citizens demanding suppression, and public officials pulled every which way by complex legal principles and divergent pressures. Gibson and Bingham chose to investigate this situation by conducting a series of mailed questionnaire surveys of two well-known liberal groups: The American Civil Liberties Union (ACLU), a strongly pro-free speech group that had provided Collins free legal counsel, and Common Cause, a liberal organization mainly attentive to government openness. Well-educated, politically aware citizens, the types of people expected to be tolerant, dominate both organizations. In the case of the former group, the survey design was fairly complex. Several separate surveys of both regular members and those serving on state governing boards were conducted. Especially intriguing was a survey of ex-ACLU members who had resigned during the organization's contentious support of the Nazi march, a sizable number. The mailed questionnaire survey of Common Cause members was more straightforward.

Gibson and Bingham's questionnaire was far lengthier, more elaborate and probing than past tolerance instruments (Gibson & Bingham, 1985, Appendix B). Included were the traditional Stouffer-type questions: groups (anti-religionists, admitted Communists, the KKK, para-militarists, and Nazis) were combined with specific activities, the now familiar speak, teach, have a book in the library plus the new activity, march. A noteworthy aspect of this questionnaire, a feature that heightened its political relevance, was its focus on the *content* and possible *consequences* of these controversial organizations and their activities. Recall that past questions might mention "a speech," but the content and possible impact of this speech remained unspecified. For example, respondents were asked if the ideas advocated by Communists, the Klan, and Nazis, if implemented, would subvert our political system. Respondents could also assess a group's threat and offer advice on government reaction to group activities (e.g., outlaw the group or prevent it from fielding candidates for public office). Questions covered the First Amendment's desired scope regarding actions such as burning draft cards or using obscene language.

Perhaps most important, there were numerous detailed questions regarding preferred actions to be taken in specific, concrete situations. Other items inquired about the specific conditions under which police should be allowed to stop a rally, whether controversial action under difficult circumstances is allowable (e.g., the Klan marching in a Black area), whether a book challenging the Holocaust should be put in a nearby library, and what actions should be taken regarding this book. Several survey items addressed the Skokie situation directly—support for a law limiting such marches and beliefs about the First Amendment's applicability to the confrontation. Finally, respondents were solicited about tolerance-related behaviors: for example, whether they had resigned from ACLU membership over the Skokie controversy or if they ever engaged in demonstrations.

Civil Liberties and Nazis offers copious conclusions, many of them statistically complex and highly nuanced. Some, such as the relatively high levels of tolerance among ACLU and Common Cause group members compared to the general population, are predictable. The authors also demonstrate that attitudes regarding different types of controversial activity are far more complex than a simple "for" or "against" model. Details regarding content, perceived consequences, and one's own position are critical in shaping people's positions. Still, for our purposes here, the book's most important legacy is what was *not* examined. *Civil Liberties and Nazis* is a milestone in the study of tolerance, but less emerges here about tolerance dynamics than is implied.

Most critically, the most central analyses are exclusively built on questionnaire responses of ACLU members, people well distanced from the situation. Those directly participating in the confrontation—from city officials to private citizens—were never interviewed or directly observed. The enterprise is largely an exercise in psychology, regardless of the passionate feelings expressed. Save a tiny number of national ACLU board members responsible for Collins's legal bills, study participants were virtually all spectators. This remoteness is confirmed in the data themselves—only a minuscule number of those interviewed took actions such as demonstrating or contacting government (165). The overwhelming bulk of the situationly relevant behavior, for members of both organizations, was making a financial contribution, a condition identical to membership itself. Even ACLU state leaders were largely inactive. Resigning from the ACLU was perhaps the most forceful act that could be taken by these respondents, not a trivial act, but one of limited consequence.

Nevertheless, despite ample distance between the survey data and Skokie participants, connections regarding tolerance are still drawn. This analysis, however, takes place wholly within the questionnaire responses. Details of the Skokie incident, the threats and legal actions, serve largely as accompanying background narrative. Reports of ACLU member behavior, though at a physical distance from daily circumstance, are cumulated and then statistically associated with a variety of attitudinal measures of tolerance—for example, support for freedom of speech, support for freedom of assembly, views of the Skokie anti-Nazi ordinance, opinion of the ACLU actions, and religious affiliation. When all is said and done, with the appropriate qualifications regarding the association between attitudes and behavior, the authors conclude that "attitudes concerning tolerance have behavioral consequences" (178). A more accurate conclusion might have been that observers *react* to publicized events in foreseeable ways.

This research, apart from its findings, thus conveys a simple message about grappling with tolerance: it remains possible to render conclusions, even in specific, concrete situations, without escaping the confines of surveys. The nature of the questionnaire, not the events themselves, is what is critical. This is not to say that Gibson's findings are irrelevant for they do inform us about how citizens assess controversy; how Nazis come to express their views escapes notice. Far more important are how abstract legal principles become concrete, how Nazi opponents eventually abandoned their opposition, and what eventually encouraged Collins to fade into oblivion.

Civil Liberties and Nazis was followed by a second and similar study, "Homosexuals and The Ku Klux Klan: A Contextual Analysis of Political Tolerance" (Gibson, 1987), seeking to connect the views of citizens to a specific, highly contentious event. In June of 1984, a small group of KKK members marched through a largely gay section of Houston, Texas protected by some 800 police officers. Though the local gay organization had not opposed the march—indeed, they called for its boycott to deprive the Klan of publicity. Nevertheless, it was met by about 2,000 jeering counter-demonstrators. As in the Skokie situation, the resolution of a highly controversial issue turned out, eventually, to be relatively uneventful in practice.

A mailed questionnaire was sent to Gay Political Caucus members, the most prominent local gay organization. This was the core data of the overall analysis. Questions were specific and included details about parade circumstances drawn from past legal disputes (e.g., how should the disruptive efforts of procession opponents be treated?) In general, endorsement for the Klan's right to express their views, even when these views displayed extreme anti-gay sentiments, was extensive (71%). Among opponents, the principle objection was the fear of possible violence; the cost of police protection was also worrisome. Only a handful based their objection on the hateful character of the Klan's views.

As before, the object of explanation was a person's attitude toward tolerance. Psychological dispositions, social status, levels of information, political activism and political ideology are all brought to bear in accounting for differences in supporting the Klan's march. Statistical associations tended to be modest or close to zero but, consistent with studies using the Stouffer-type questions, education was moderately and positively related to tolerance. In general, those most understanding of tolerance, those possessing adequate psychological security, and those more political active were most tolerant.

A second element of the research concerned behavior. Again, as in the Skokie study, few survey respondents took any action; they were spectators. Donating money to the anti-Klan cause was the most common activity. Not unexpectedly, the best predictor of involvement here was past political activism. Education was not associated with taking action. An especially novel finding, one with interesting implications, is that among those expressing intolerant views, the most dogmatic were disproportionately apathetic (445). Gibson speculates that this association may help explain the paradox of widespread tolerance at the political system level in the face of extensive popular intolerance.

Our comments about the Skokie study are equally relevant here. The survey, as a tool of inquiry, reveals only a partial story. We know that the Klan did parade, its message was proclaimed, and this venting received the full protection of the Houston police. It is plausible, no doubt, that the permissive views of local gays and their political groups, documented in the survey, facilitated this event. The contribution of other circumstances— Houston's political environment, past experiences with similar demonstrations, police policy, the Klan's reputation for violence, and its immediate objectives, among a host of potential factors—lies outside the survey. The views of gay bystanders may or may not be decisive, but this falls beyond statistical analysis. For our larger purposes, what is central is that analysis, again, reinforces the claim that tolerance is explainable via scrutinizing attitudes. Though Gibson certainly makes no claim that attitudes are the beginning and end of fully grappling with tolerance, the analysis itself surely suggests their overriding pertinence.

The Skokie and Houston studies represent one form of this event-specific design. Different tactics followed in two separate studies added a new element to the analytical mix: the actions of government. Recall that previous studies treated citizen attitudes as the phenomena to be explained; attitudinal differences among citizens, not tolerance itself, was to be accounted for. Now, the openness of the political system itself, as reflected in politically restrictive statutes, was to be incorporated. Technically, of course, this statutory effort is only an *effort* at repression. It is entirely possible that attempts at political repression, like campaigns to eliminate alcohol and drug use, become largely ineffectual gestures. Yet, this focus nevertheless serves as a closer approximation of openness to divergent views. Citizens views were now an independent, not a dependent, variable.

"Political Intolerance and Political Repression During the McCarthy Red Scare" (Gibson, 1988) seeks to disentangle the effects of citizen and elite views on political repression during the mid-1950s. To combat Communism, states passed various anti-Communist measures, banning Communists from state employment, denying them ballot access or banning the party outright. These and related legal actions are combined into an overall index reflecting each state's repressive effort. This intolerance score is then correlated with both the general public and community leader opinion data from the original 1954 Stouffer study on a state-by-state basis. Again, it should be noted that respondents were spectators, not participants, in the era's battles. This is critical—what these respondents did in the way of political behavior remains totally unknown. Gibson finds a positive relationship for both ordinary citizens and elites: The least tolerant tended to live in states governed by the harshest laws. But, after complex statistical analysis of these relationships, he concludes that elites had a more powerful voice in shaping this anti-Communist response.

"The Policy Consequences of Political Intolerance: Political Repression During the Vietnam War Era" (Gibson, 1989) is similar. How states during the 1960s legally dealt with university campus disruption, especially outsiders who instigated anti-Vietnam war protests, is scrutinized. States were classified by the vigor of their anti-dissent laws; state-by-state mass and elite opinion is revealed by the 1973 NORC Stouffer replication. Were there correspondences between mass opinion and attempts at restricting dissent on campuses? Surprisingly, and contrary to the earlier McCarthy era pattern, in those states that have enacted the strongest anti-dissent laws, both ordinary citizens and community leaders display the greatest tolerance. Closer to expectations, however, is the positive link between citizen tolerance and university dissent. Gibson suggests a complex relationship between mass opinion and legal restriction of protest activity: Generally tolerant states are conducive to student protests and these, in turn, set the stage for severe legislative reaction. A paradox prevails: Tolerance eventually breeds an intolerant counterreaction. Overall, Gibson concludes that whereas many of the connections between citizen views and repression are murky, it seems clear that ordinary citizens during the 1960s were not responsible for the repressive impulses of government.

These situation-specific studies are generally judged to be state of the art for deciphering political tolerance. They not only inform us on the health of contemporary tolerance (defined as hearts and minds tolerance) but they instruct on its proper measurement. Typically, the findings—who is tolerant or what explains this disposition—draw the reader's attention. If, however, we look beyond the substantive conclusions, we discern a more subtle but ultimately more weighty message: Ordinary citizens' views are integral, even essential, to the complete illumination of tolerance. This is true when such attitudes correlate positively with intolerance (the 1950s) or relate negatively (the 1960s). Put differently, to discern tolerance in America, conducting a poll is obligatory. Just how this intimate connection between mass sentiment and tolerance precisely operates, if it operates at all, rarely elicits much concern in this literature. Overwhelmingly, attention concentrates on attitudes themselves, their distribution and inter-relationships. It is to this assumed conjunction, the relevance of mass attitudes to societal conditions, that we now turn.

Justifying the Study of Tolerant Attitudes

Our overview of polls on tolerance has spanned sixty years, from the 1930s to the 1990s. Dozens of surveys, commissioned at considerable expense, are explicated in numerous books and articles. And, our review has been selective, limited to major research projects and providing only fleeting summaries. This endeavor has occupied the attention of the most talented, skilled social science practitioners. We know a great deal about how citizens think about tolerance and the correlates of this belief. The critical question here concerns the *consequences* of these views. Put bluntly, are citizen opinions on permitting Communists to teach college any more politically pertinent than, say, citizen opinions on life on other planets? What do these data reveal about tolerance beyond what citizens opine on the subject?

Considering the prodigious effort poured into assessing public views, establishing their relevance draws far less attention. Indeed, possible relevance is sometimes skipped entirely or superficially covered; relevance is easily assumed. One major study (McClosky & Brill, 1983, 4) confines analysis solely to mass dispositions, totally evading the laborious task of fashioning linkages. When connections are sketched, they often rest on loose, amorphous arguments whose validity draws more on faith than on empirical verification. Only recently, decades after assembling these attitudinal data, have scholars sought to assess their theoretical and empirical significance. Still, far more is known about citizen attitudes composition than their effect. Associations remain tentative, partial, and speculative. It is not that citizen attitudes remain irrelevant to tolerance; this may or may not be true. Rather, this connection, despite the mountains of data, remains a largely untested hypothesis.

How have citizen attitudes and tolerance been linked? Though connections are often vague and elusive, and theorizing and rhapsodizing are often indistinguishable, several distinctive potential relationships can be teased out. The simplest argument focuses on something called "democratic consensus." This reasoning, particularly explicit in Prothro and Grigg (1960) and McClosky (1964) described earlier, merely holds that (1) democracy is impossible if most citizens reject democratic principles, (2) support for democratic openness (tolerance) is a democratic principle, so that (3) democracy requires tolerant citizens. This consensus is measured simply by examining the proportion of tolerant people, with special attention to a net percentage endorsing tolerance of disapproved opinion. A slightly more sophisticated version emphasizes tolerance in facilitating an open politics, particularly accessible electoral competition (for example, Gibson & Anderson, 1985; Nie et al., 1996; Sullivan et al., 1982, 51). Democracy necessitates an often disorderly give-and-take, a marketplace of ideas, and this rests on citizen willingness to stomach the obnoxious.[1] As Nunn et al. (1978) commented, "A healthy commitment to the Bill of Rights is becoming more important not less. . . . The Founding Fathers of this country prescribed tolerance in the marketplace of freely flowing ideas as the key to democratic process and the necessary condition for orderly change and innovation in a democratic society" (7).

This "a collectivity of tolerant citizens facilitates democratic politics" contention offers an easy plausibility and flatters ordinary citizens as democracy's bulwark. Alas, as a theory to justify the intensive scrutiny of citizen views, it falls short. Two serious problems present themselves. As already intimated, it is a hopelessly imprecise thesis, almost mysterious in form, unable to define key terms and silent on critical details, such as essential tolerance levels, the limits of tolerance, and the explicit makeup of these requisite tolerant dispositions. Imprecision likewise besets how popular sentiments sustain democracy—do citizens electorally reject intolerant office seekers? Do democratic stalwarts refuse to obey repressive laws? Are would-be dictators ostracized socially? Establishing such details is a critical precondition for testing this relationship, but thus far this indispensable elaboration is lacking.

The second flaw is empirical: Democracies such as the U.S. and Great Britain evidently flourish *despite* modest consensus on admittance for unpopular groups (see, for example, Barnum & Sullivan, 1989; 1990). Wide-open elections occurred even during periods when citizens expressed strong intolerance. The public may wish to exclude books by Communists or homosexuals in their libraries, but such books abound.[2] Public aversion might be likened more to a potential nuisance than to a powerful force of oppression. This disjuncture between theoretical prediction and empirical reality appears to be true, regardless of how tolerance is assessed precisely, and perseveres over many decades. That mass sentiment is largely irrelevant or, more likely, operates in ways not yet understood is an equally plausible contention. In sum, the verdict regarding the pertinence of "the democratic consensus" to the study of tolerance attitudes is: "not proven."

An influential and often mentioned variant of this "mass-consensus-essential-to-democracy" argument concentrates on the critical role of political elites. In a nutshell, the more active, more politically sophisticated and more tolerant citizens impede the autocratic impulses of their compatriots. An open political process is owed to elites. If, for example, the masses sought to incarcerate Communists, atheists, and other nonconformists, community leaders, being more tolerant, would resist. Again, as was true for the theory's simpler version, it is an assertion more often stated than rigorously scrutinized. Two problems are notable. First, if this formulation were true, it argues *against* the study of mass views. After all, why study ordinary folk if their opinions are ignored or subverted by influentials?

Second, investigations of this hypothesis are insufficiently direct. Empirical analysis, from Stouffer to Gibson's more recent work exclusively probe elite-mass differences in *attitudes,* not how elites specifically perform their democratic service. Beliefs about tolerance, no matter how carefully drawn, cannot by themselves tell us how political openness is perpetuated. Though the term *behavior* might occasionally be interjected, the actual behavior is far removed from events. Much more information is essential: We have to catch the elite "in the act." Where elite views co-vary with larger tolerance-related events, as in Gibson's McCarthy and Vietnam war era studies, analysis excludes pertinent elite behavior. Just how these elite attitudes, regardless of content, shape policy again remains mysterious. After all, community leaders may vehemently oppose myriad dangers, from crime to sexual immorality, but these psychological dispositions, in and of themselves, hardly determine what transpires. In sum, this elite version of the democratic consensus theory remains an untested conjecture.

A second general linkage argument concentrates on ordinary citizens and stresses people's actions flowing from tolerant attitudes: Intolerant citizens, afforded opportunities, will act accordingly. Attitudes are critical because they foretell behavior. This relationship was initially expressed by Stouffer (1955, 48) who, ironically, simultaneously observed the difficulty of easily predicting behavior from attitudes. Though recognizing the intermediary role of specific circumstances, he nevertheless insisted that attitudes provide a *latent tendency* (italics in original) for future action. Though intolerant citizens themselves might not initiate action, they nevertheless might be easily stirred up by demagogues. Attitudes are the inflammatory substance awaiting the spark. This latent tendency argument is never fully developed theoretically or tested empirically by Stouffer. Conceivably, the inflammatory material can lie dormant for decades, if not forever, while remaining potentially dangerous. This linkage, alas, merely stands as yet another plausible, though unproved, contention.

Stouffer's latent tendency argument, despite its speculative nature, nevertheless easily legitimized the avalanche of future research. Monitoring public tolerance attitudes was to political repression what recording barometric pressure was to weather forecasting—a convenient and inexpensive predictive tool. This reliance persisted despite growing evidence from attitude-behavior consistency studies strongly suggesting the riskiness of prediction. These consistency studies, as Chapter 2 depicted, did not invalidate all relationships; rather, associations were complex, dependent on complex circumstances. That banning Communism as an opinion might eventually translate into relevant action is a hypothesis, not a fact.

The ill-defined, undemonstrated connection did not, however, deter the accumulation of "suggestive" attitude data. This intricate relationship between words and deeds was conveniently pushed off to the side, typically finessed by acknowledging the problem. Sullivan, Piereson, and Marcus (1982), who undertook one of the more sophisticated, careful treatments of the subject, exemplify this evasion via fancy linguistic footwork. The subject occupies about one page (50-51), and they frankly acknowledge that attitude analysis sheds little light on behavior. This absence of connective tissue is lamentable, declare the authors, but the neglect is nevertheless within the mainstream of tolerance research. The consensus may be faulty but it still remains the authoritative consensus. Having implicated others for support, they now boldly assert that public's thinking is not totally unrelated to behavior. Attitudes "set the stage by creating a range of potential behaviors and by making some behaviors more likely than others" (50). A study is then cited (Oskamp, 1977) confirming the complex attitudes and behavior bond.[3] This discussion concludes with: "Thus an understanding of attitudinal tolerance is critical to an understanding of behavioral tolerance" (51). The mechanics of this linkage are not, however, explored since actual behavior is beyond *Political Tolerance and American Democracy.*

The most direct and detailed discussion of this attitude-behavior connection is offered by Gibson and Anderson (1985). After reviewing several analyses of this linkage, they note that "the behavioral consequences of tolerance attitudes are far from obvious, simple, and direct" (129). Multiple factors—cost of actions, intervening circumstances, the nature of the behavior, and many contingent conditions—all make this relationship painfully perplexing. To illustrate this complexity, they note that in the Skokie study, intolerant Jews were more likely to act than intolerant non-Jews, but religion had no discernible impact among those who were tolerant. In sum, attitudes sometimes predict behavior, sometimes not, it all depends—a most reasonable, and undoubtedly correct assessment, but one not very useful in applying the mounds of attitude data to political conflict.

Resolving the relationship between attitudes and behavior is not germane here. Suffice it to say that on the specific issue of tolerance, despite all the research, our knowledge is almost nonexistent. Studies of racial prejudice, violence, or cheating on exams, topics addressed in this consistency literature, can only *suggest* tolerance-related possibilities. Direct analyses of linkages with tolerance attitudes are very limited and few in number. Recall that the Gibson studies of Skokie and Houston, in which behavior was present, did not include direct participants. Only interested observers were interviewed about their actions and, not surprisingly, few respondents reported serious personal involvement. Again, we can only conclude that a clear theoretical and empirical justification for the examination of tolerance attitudes is only weakly made.

A different and more plausible linking of tolerant attitudes to tolerance as a general condition would treat these sentiments as ordinary policy preferences. That is, when citizens express a desire to prevent Communists from speaking, this preference is no different from, say, expressing a desire for lower taxes or more government defense spending. Conceivably, these desires are translated into policy via elections—candidates expressing anti-Communist positions gain election, a situation no different from the success of anti-tax candidates if this policy were popular. Or, alternatively, various groups lobby government to ban communism. There is no requirement that individual-level attitudes translate accurately into behavior other than via voting or lobbying. Simply put, intolerance among ordinary citizens matters because opportunistic candidates and/or group leaders will seek to capitalize on it.

This linkage is straightforward, yet it is surprisingly absent from the tolerance literature. Gibson and Anderson (1985) briefly touch on this relationship in their overview of connecting possibilities but only to lament the paucity of research here. An approximation of this "opinion generates policy" association is offered by Page and Shapiro (1992). Here nine civil liberties issues among some 357 cases of opinion-policy congruence are examined. In eight of the nine cases, government moved in the direction of public sentiment within one year. Unfortunately, as was true in the Gibson studies of the McCarthy and Vietnam war eras, these juxtapositions are vague in specifying just how popular sentiment shapes government policy. That tolerance (or intolerance) exists as a result of citizen demand is merely one of several outcomes. Conceivably, as is occasionally acknowledged, government officials or the mass media could disproportionately determine public tolerance levels. History provides numerous examples of citizen views on unorthodox views being manipulated by elites (see, for example, Levin, 1971). In sum, our assessment of this "citizen tolerance affects government policy" argument is now familiar: "not demonstrated."

The final possible connection between tolerant attitudes and tolerance at the societal level is Gibson's novel "atmospheric" formulation (1992a). Interestingly, Gibson begins by frankly acknowledging "a growing concern about whether these research findings [on attitudinal tolerance] have any real political implications" (338). An involved argument then follows, suggesting that they do but not in the most obvious way. His principal concern is citizens' *beliefs* about freedom to express their views. Is subjective political freedom shaped by tolerance attitudes? Whether or not political diversity flourishes, whether or not efforts are made to repress unorthodox views and, the role of attitudes in maintaining this condition, are beyond the research design. What is to be explained is what citizens think, not conditions or events.

Relying on the 1987 NORC GSS survey, Gibson finds that large numbers of Americans, especially African Americans, think their liberties are severely constrained. These convictions and related data are the study's dependent variable. For example, 55.6 percent of blacks and 29.6 percent of whites believe that government would *not* allow them to make a speech critical of government; 53.0 percent of blacks and 28.1 percent of whites believe that government would *not* permit them to publish a pamphlet criticizing government. Moreover, even higher proportions—both white and black—avoid commonplace political actions such as putting a bumper sticker on a car, wear a political button in public, or even write a letter to an elected representative. Many citizens also avoid politics for personal reasons, such as fear of arguments or negative social reactions. In short, sizable numbers of citizens, majorities in some instances, would fear exercising basic freedoms.

These beliefs are then joined with tolerance, as measured with Stouffer-like items, under diverse contextual conditions. The question is whether a person's environment—family, friends, or neighborhood—shapes the connection between perceptions of perceived freedom and tolerant attitudes. Gibson answers a resounding "yes." Less tolerant people feel more politically constrained, and those living in less tolerant, less diverse environments, feel especially constrained. More generally, attitudinal tolerance matters because it creates a political culture, a psychological atmosphere that deepens and reinforces citizen willingness to express political views. Political openness is difficult when people are intolerant because the social milieu's repressive character inhibits. Tolerant attitudes shape culture, and culture molds beliefs about political expression.

Leaving aside the argument's technical limitations, frankly admitted by Gibson, what can we say about this connective theory? As the analysis of "subjective tolerance" in Chapter 2 argued, substituting subjective perceptions for objective reality opens the door to endless mischief and hardly elucidates tolerance. These data might more accurately be characterized as revealing the public's distance from political reality, evidence that mass opinion on such matters is dismissible. Subjectivity has been recast as objective conditions. Activities such as organizing public meetings or publishing pamphlets are dully routine. Further recall from Chapter 2 that if one were to examine these data minus identifying labels, one might surmise that the poll was conducted in the Soviet Union, not in the U.S. in the late 1980s. Indeed, in a different study (Gibson, 1992) the same questions are asked in the Soviet Union, and levels of fear there are occasionally *lower* than in the U.S.

A second pitfall is the absence of any behavioral connections, individually or collectively, to larger events pertaining to political openness. As is typical with studies based on NORC data, analysis exclusively deals with intra-survey relationships. The exterior world exists only as perceptions. We are presented with "beliefs about tolerance in America," not a portrait of "tolerance in America." Surely perceptions play a role in political action, but they constitute only one element, and of uncertain weight. It is entirely possible, for example, that many of those fearful of organizing a public meeting, talking politics with friends, or participating in a demonstration have taken, or would gladly take, these steps. Unease expressed in idle conversation is hardly identical to facing enforced government prohibitions. Stories of once politically shy citizens forcefully mobilizing under the right circumstances are commonplace. Even the most repressive environment (e.g., the South of the 1950s) did not deter black dissenters from marching despite grave threats. At its core, this formulation derives from perceptions whose connection to reality is uncertain.

The Lure of Attitudinal Tolerance

The few unadorned poll results of the 1930s have been replaced by analyses of intimidating statistical complexity. Intellectual progress, however, has not been commensurate. The consequences of these attitudinal data have, lamentably, remained underexamined. The enterprise resembles gathering rocks, sorting them by color and shape, piling them into heaps, arguing about their nature, but refusing to dwell on their ultimate purpose. Research

is, apparently, governed by a simple syllogism: Democracy requires tolerance: citizens' attitudes are integral to tolerance; therefore, investigating
citizen views assists in maintaining democratic survival. The reviewed scholarship rests entirely on this unchallenged, even unexamined, syllogism. We
now consider the roots of this intensive scrutiny, given the less-than-clear
consequences of this accumulation.

At the outset we should acknowledge the uncertainty of probing motives
for conducting research. No doubt, much tolerance scholarship was driven
by a commendable desire to combat anti-democratic, authoritarian tendencies. It was sincerely assumed that the hearts and minds of citizens were
surely pertinent to a free and open society. Inquiry would not only shed light
on this connection, but offer useful advice to those worried that the U.S.
might, like pre-World War II Germany or Italy, slide into tyranny. Though
we submit that this reasoning was not as self-evident as imagined, we can
hardly impugn the impulse to defend democracy from potential adversaries.
Nevertheless, we shall argue that this motive was joined with other, and quite
different, objectives. This is especially true as this research tradition matured
and the weak link between citizen opinion and real-world events became
increasingly evident. After a point, scholarship took on an intellectual life of
its own, ever more divorced from shoring up democracy.

The vocational character of contemporary academic life has much to do
with attitude data accumulation. Copious publication of works employing
complex statistical techniques is today the coin of academic success. Disciplinary attainment is further enhanced if the techniques are novel, and for
decades survey methodology was "innovative." Independent of our insight
into the workings of democracy, statistically dissecting poll data secured
professional accomplishment. This is especially true given the quality-
certified NORC data and for-hire organizations to collect survey data. Attitudinal tolerance can easily be examined—no need for contacting dissident
groups or observing infrequent, distant, unpredictable situations. The professional norms of modern political science also facilitated this poll data
focus. Interviewing Communists or Klansmen to explain their survival yields
anecdotal findings only publishable in less prestigious nonscientific journalistic outlets. Scientifically minded colleagues might even label that endeavor
"unscientific" given its reliance on qualitative data. In short, disciplinary
incentives, the need to advance professionally, greatly favor the treatment of
tolerance as hearts and minds tolerance.

The vocational incentive structure is only partly explained, however.
Raising up hearts and minds tolerance as the preeminent form of live and let
live also conforms with the profession's underlying liberal political dispositions. Our contentions here must be somewhat speculative; we have not

peeked into the minds of tolerance researchers. Evidence is indirect and partial, and our case rests on plausibilities. Essentially, this focus on psychological dispositions, apart from either individual behavior or larger societal conditions, fits well with the prevailing citizen-centered, energetic, benevolent, state liberalism. Researchers are not necessarily guilty of propaganda or unscrupulously exploiting their prestige to advance a specific agenda. Matters are more subtle, even less conscious. Rather, there is a gentle slide toward analysis easily compatible with underlying ideological views. Easy habits of thinking, not devious manipulation, are the culprits.

Appreciating this conjunction between political ideology and the embrace of attitudinal tolerance first requires recognizing the poll's malleability. Though nobody, not even powerful public officials, can dictate events, this scarcely applies to the more manageable world of the survey instrument (see Ginsberg, 1986 on this point). The questionnaire comfortably serves as a virtual political reality. It is the investigator's prerogative, subject only to technical guidelines, to decide what should be examined, when, whose opinion will be ascertained, the language to be employed, and how these data become cold, hard, statistical reality. Respondents can only express themselves in the researcher-provided world. Information furnished outside the framework will simply not be recorded or, if recorded, can be ignored in the final product. This investigatory process, powerfully supported by the mantle of prestigious science, authorizes the researcher to decide questions of political significance. To use a now popular term, the survey *empowers* the investigator.

This power is most unmistakable in determining what groups and/or activities deserve public tolerance. The potential menu of groups that might not be tolerated is huge, everything from the Catholic Church to Trotskyites, from obscure peaceful demonstrations to openly subversive terrorists. From this varied array, the god-like analyst designates the chosen few: atheists, but not Christian fundamentalists, Socialists but not libertarians.[4] Periodically, perhaps like a capricious pagan god, groups are mysteriously added and dropped. For example, the NORC GSS survey deleted questions about Socialists in 1976, substituting militarists and racists. The inquiries about Communists and atheists, however, were continued. That these choices imply what should or should not be accepted cannot be over-emphasized. Who is to say that Americans should tolerate the Klan or homosexuals? For better or worse, experts designing the questionnaire decide. Surely a case can be advanced that such authority is better lodged in citizens or their elected leaders.

Equally noteworthy, the selection criteria are rarely—if ever—articulated and integrated into a larger theory of necessary democratic political heterogeneity. Choices are relegated to technical discussions, presented without much debate. We might even surmise that researchers unthinkingly assume that mere unpopularity qualifies a group or idea for tolerance. To be sure, the project may derive from particular events (a recent Nazis or Klan march, for example), but confrontations are endemic to politics and cannot, in and of themselves, certify a group for inclusion. Surely, rigorous and explicit criteria justifying the need for tolerance are necessary. Awkward, perplexing, theoretical decisions are painlessly evaded through the choice of exemplars; criteria for separating out, say, child pornographers from Marxists are not self-evident. Researchers have unreflectively assumed that tolerating Communists served only to harmlessly enrich the range of public debate. That repressing them *might* be justifiable is never contemplated.

Nor can this ad hoc approach be conveniently covered with a vague and simplistic "domino theory." That is, throttling any one disapproved sentiment must inevitably spill over to all controversial inclinations, no matter how innocuous, so studying the fate of one heretical tendency unveils the future of all dissent. Today the Nazis, tomorrow the gays, next week the Republicans. As Nie et al. (1996) boldly declare, "In the absence of this freedom [tolerance protected free expression], the system is weakened, for intolerance of the expression of political interests by one group of citizens means that the interests of *any* citizen may be deemed inappropriate and thus silenced (1996, 29-30, italics added). If accurate, if the repressive impulse were akin to an unstoppable deadly virus, the U.S. would have long ago become totalitarian. At best, a contagious choking of heterogeneity theory is a tentative hypothesis lacking verification; at worst it is a cliché serviceable for public speeches and avoidance of thorny theoretical issues.

Holding this power of selection is not inconsequential. Even in the most permissive environment, not every idea, group, or action is acceptable. Society's very nature demands limits. This shaping of the agenda by the academic investigator contrasts with either direct popular authority or political rules issued by public officials. Ordinary people, their representatives or judges, might not wish to have Marxists in their midst. They may even hold valid, plausible reasons for this exclusionary inclination. But, through the research process, this prevalent rejection of an ideology can be certified, with all the trappings of science, as "a problem threatening democracy" and requiring remediation. These now-certified intolerants will not even be permitted to make their case to the interviewer, and even if they were, their side of the story will not be engaged. No exchange occurs between academic and citizen, no decisions based on evidence or argument, only summary expert verdicts. And, it might be added, this analyst rarely has a responsible connection to events portrayed in the questionnaire—it is not the question-writers who confront neighborhood demonstrations or have children reading provocative library books.

This playing of God via the survey is especially consequential given the relative political homogeneity within the political science profession. Evidence (Carnegie Foundation, 1989; Ladd & Lipset, 1973) depicts the social sciences heavily tilted toward the political spectrum's liberal end, especially at major research-oriented schools. Unconsciously or consciously, outcroppings of the political landscape receive selective attention. Predictably, then, tolerance studies have been more agitated over repressive inclination toward Communists or Socialists than, say, traditional Christian evangelical organizations or "extremists" rejecting the modern welfare state. After all, despite their neglect by tolerance researchers, the political landscape abounds with prominent right-wing, religious-oriented "extremists" who could easily have been placed on the "to be tolerated list" (see, for example Lipset & Raab, 1973, especially Chapters 3-5). Imagine, for the moment, that tolerance investigators were disproportionately conservative business and military people. They might very well discover a "disturbing" number of intolerant academics, otherwise well-educated souls, anxious to restrict the freedom of those advocating traditional gender roles, silence those infatuated with militarism, or ban books acknowledging racial differences in intelligence. Even citizen aversion to right-wing militant militias might be deemed a "dangerous anti-democratic tendency."

Question content is not the debate here. If investigators suddenly asked citizens solely about conservative groups, our basic position remains unaltered. The critical issue is, *who has the power to control this selection of what is to be tolerated?* Adjusting questionnaires to reflect fluid political conditions (adding racists, dropping Socialists, for example) does not redistribute authority to decide inclusion. The locus of authority is key, not the wisdom of selection. Matters would be far different if social scientists acceded to decisions rendered by legislatures rather than drawing on their own, often unarticulated, ideological predispositions.

Indeed, to speculate further, this exclusive reliance on the survey serves, at least potentially, a more radical, corrosive purpose as well. In every society, no matter how open or permissive, some ideas reside totally and justifiably beyond the pale. This is the essence of society—delineations of acceptability and unacceptability. In the U.S., these "unthinkables" might be state suppression of religion or abolishing private property. Suppose, furthermore, that despite widespread citizen loathing of these unorthodoxies, the hated ideas still persevered. A researcher with a radical agenda now possesses an opportunity to advance these popularly rejected notions: Legitimize unwelcome views by transforming the issue into one of accepting a process of openness. Via the tolerance survey and the invoking of "democratic tolerance," assert that citizen abhorrence—deftly leaving aside the ideas themselves—now constitutes a "problem of democracy." Rejected substance is made acceptable under the guise of democratic procedural tolerance. Refusing to admit a widely forsaken philosophy to public debate, no matter how well reasoned, commits sinful intolerance. In principle, of course, ideological bias is not inherent—questions could inquire about tolerance for slavery or "ethnic cleansing." Should we condemn as intolerant those who steadfastly refuse to even consider the virtues of slavery? Given disciplinary ideological predispositons, however, this is highly unlikely.

Finally, the attraction to attitudes conforms with modern liberalism's commitment to vigorous state intervention in people's lives. If, as all the research intimates, the problem lies in citizen hearts and minds, these hearts and minds require fixing. After all, who yearns for a society seething with hatred and bigotry? And, who better to repair this predicament than modern government, ably assisted by certified professionals familiar with the intricacies of intolerance? In one sense, this fixing of harmful intolerance is yet another helpful government intrusion no different from, say, the obligation to drive bias from the workplace.

This rationale for state intrusion is clear-cut. Given both the nature of citizen opinion and research flexibility, *some* intolerance will inevitably be uncovered. This discovery need not be a credible demand; any hint of intolerance is usually sufficient to instigate "concern." Detecting the hated groups or controversial activities is just a technical matter in formulating penetrating questions. Even if an incredible zoo of political diversity prevailed, some inclinations would undoubtedly attract repressive calls. The revelation of democratically "defective" views, even if trifling, now authorizes and legitimizes a *general* program of corrective educational intrusion. After all, today's civic disorder may seem frivolous or the hated group may be truly loathsome, but who can foresee where repressive impulse may lead? To contend otherwise, given intolerance's pernicious character, endangers democracy.

By education or public indoctrination, the state remolds citizens to cure the defect, in principle superficially no different from public health informational anti-smoking programs. Teachers, administrators, publishers, program developers, and additional components of "the therapeutic state," guided by government bureaucracies, assist in eradicating this undemocratic flaw. Researchers are not the ones who demand vigorous state action; that would be inappropriate by disciplinary standards. Rather, scholarship reinforces the rationale for such intervention by scientifically depicting the problem's definition.

This government intrusion pushes beyond ridding ourselves of unhealthy inclinations. Promoting hearts and minds tolerance is *un*like the ill-fated prohibition campaign or plugging teenage condom use. It is a *dangerous* intrusion, despite the claim of rescuing democracy from would-be repressive citizens. Let us be precise in our claim: It is not these intolerant attitudes themselves that pose an impending danger; it is the state intervention to "fix" them that is far more menacing. This counterintuitive argument rests on two somewhat different aspects of this intrusion. First, to the extent that government is now authorized to mold political thinking, *totally apart from behavior,* such invasiveness subverts limited government. Traditionally, behavior, not thought, was the primary object of state intervention. Our penal system does not recognize *thoughtcrimes.* One might fantasize about being a Nazi storm trooper, but so long as this remained a fantasy, it existed beyond state control.

This is not to argue that *thoughtcrimes* have always escaped punishment. Innumerable citizens have paid heavy prices for thinking "bad thoughts," but—and this is critical—such reproof is widely understood as an unfortunate lapse in an otherwise free society. Indeed, historic civil libertarian aversions to "Red scares," "witch hunts," and the like were rooted in the belief that such officious policies attacked unpopular *thought* apart from illegal behavior. Merely "thinking Communist" should *not* receive rebuke. This division into private thinking and public expression or action is fundamental. Surely a legislative chastisement for "evil thoughts" would be immediately rejected by citizens and courts. Hearts and minds tolerance, in a highly benign appearing manner, brings back bad thoughts as an offense against the political order.

Second, the insistence that ideological exclusion, independent of content or reason, constitutes a "problem of democracy" assails the very foundations of political community. To contend that any aversion to doctrinal promiscuity is a deficiency disables our collective immunity system. Faced with never-ending calls for extending attitudinal tolerance to ever new claimants, a prudent citizen might ask: "How are we to pronounce good from bad and follow the good when denied the option of exclusion?" Such a citizen will forever subsist in a state of boundless hodgepodge; everything must be kept on the political menu. Refusing to tolerate the reprehensible Klan or violence-prone Black Panthers now becomes a defect, not a virtue. Insisting on choices regarding communal definition itself becomes reprehensible, an affront to democratic openness. The inner logic of hearts and minds tolerance research, unqualified by firm rules of closure, is an anathema to the notion of a well-defined sense of political commonwealth. Chapters 4 and 6 will further explore this difficult issue.

Conclusions

Our analysis has spanned a vast territory, depicting how one aspect of tolerance—citizen attitudes—has grown from a few disjoined poll items in the late 1930s into a thriving scholarly industry. This endeavor has generously rewarded its practitioners. And, to its credit, it has shed ample light on select features of public thinking. It has, however, also had its costs, though these are hardly obvious or personally painful. Easily examining hearts and minds tolerance has encouraged the neglect of other tolerance-related issues. The combination of scholarly incentives and modern technology distorts and misdirects.

If such flaws were simply a waste of academic resources, the situation, though lamentable, would hardly alarm. After all, society hardly suffers calamity when academics publish endless seldom-read Shakespeare studies. The situation here is seriously different. Disregarding tolerance as a general condition of society in favor of citizen attitudes of unclear relevance ignores matters of consequence. To fashion rules of admittance, to uncover ways of preserving necessary openness, to formulate principles of closure are formidable, essential tasks of democratic scholarship. When such labors are eschewed in the race to document, yet one more time, the character of public tolerance views, opportunities are missed and responsibilities disregarded.

This abandonment is not, obviously, a crisis compelling urgent public response. Few worry about the direction of tolerance research save those academics paid to mill data. Nevertheless, intellectual opportunity cost payments will eventually come due. If recent trends continue, an ever greater number of ideas, causes, and movements will plead entry into public debate. Partial success at admittance will soon be followed by clamoring for full acceptance. This liberationist process is evident in sexuality, family arrangements, drug use, and other traits once conventionally labeled "deviant." Everyone, it seems, wants full, unrestricted acceptance as "normal." Pluralism's great tent grows larger and larger and, conceivably, the very concept of a tent—a demarcation between insiders and outsiders—may founder. Ultimately, "anything goes" may be a respectable philosophy.

How this crush for inclusion is to be resolved remains unclear. Eventually, the push toward universal, unqualified acceptance of "differences" may be harshly challenged. Advance tremors are perhaps already discernible. Not everyone welcomes the swelling culture mosaic via immigration or multicultural education. Specters of tribalistic strife abound. Some critics of uncontrolled inclusion will object to the particulars such as language; others will protest the very principle of open admission. There can be no escape:

Choices are inescapable, criteria need to be delineated and wearisome battles fought. The hearts and minds research literature will offer but slight contribution to such disputation. When solicited for sage advice on the consequences of repressive inclinations or preserving openness, the response will be far closer to intuitive guesses than empirically based generalizations. Only then will the cost of the unreflected infatuation come due.

NOTES

1. This alleged intimate connection between tolerance and an open society via the marketplace of ideas is deceptively complex, more often repeated as axiomatic than empirically substantiated. There need not be a tight connection (see, for example, Weissberg, 1996).

2. The tension between public desires and reality is clearly displayed if we simply examine one tidbit of data: The prevalence of Karl Marx's *Communist Manifesto* in public and university libraries versus people's desire to remove it. Stouffer's benchmark 1954 surveys found that about two thirds of the public would want a book written by an admitted Communist removed from their public library (the corresponding figure for community leaders was 54%). According to *The National Union Catalogue Pre-1956 Imprints,* some 355 versions of Marx's *Manifesto* could be found in dozens of libraries in all sections of the nation. As this compilation does excludes small, local public libraries, it is possible that Marx's writings cannot be found there. But, anyone wishing to read the *Manifesto* could either visit one of these libraries or, more conveniently, order it from one of several publishers issuing it. It is inconceivable that a citizen in 1954 would be unable to obtain almost any of Marx's polemics with a modest effort.

3. Neither the Oskamp (1977) nor any cited other study specifically addresses tolerance or similar dispositions. Assigning tolerance to the class of attitudes that might be associated with behavior is pure speculation. Recall the assessment in Chapter 2: The distant, amorphous character of tolerance makes it a poor candidate for a close attitude-behavior association.

4. The researcher's power over the agenda is also true in the "content-controlled" formula, though the respondent does have substantially more leeway. Increasing the number of groups from, say, four to a dozen is not much of an increase when one realizes that the potential number of candidates may be several dozen.

4

Tolerance Balanced

Contemporary political tolerance scholarship, especially those studies focusing on popular attitudes, is typically partial and unbalanced. Occasional hedge aside, an unashamed infatuation with accepting the disagreeable predominates. No political idea or cause, from the Klan to the Communist Party USA, is judged worthy of banishment, let alone criminalization. Citizen aversion toward the politically unorthodox is relentlessly ferreted out and roundly criticized as antidemocratic. To be sure, a few take a perfunctory stab at establishing limits but are all-too brief or inconclusive. For example, Gibson and Bingham (1985, 9-12) briefly acknowledge that excessive tolerance might disrupt democracy, but they remain absolutely mute on rules for drawing this dividing line or its precise location. A few paragraphs later they boldly assert that, in the context of (some unspecified) democratic theory, *all groups* (italics in the original) but not all activities, especially violent activities, deserve protection. Sullivan, Piereson, and Marcus (1982, 7-23) essentially avoid a demarcation. After marshaling a medley of quotations, from Supreme Court judges to political theorists, they cautiously conclude that sensible, thoughtful opinion exists on all sides, and one's ultimate position rests on one's preferred theory of democracy.

This neglect is unfortunate, even if the problem is perplexing, if not insolvable. Surely these scholars must realize that civil society is unworkable without extensive *in*tolerance. Anarchy is not tolerance; surely some "extremists" and fringe ideologies are excludable. Repealing the criminal code or welcoming terrorism hardly engenders an open society, the primary object of greater tolerance. Nor are these scholarly advocates covertly embracing libertarian doctrines of minimal state control. Though a few philosophers occasionally wrestle with the tensions between maintaining community and permissive tolerance (for example, d'Entreves, 1990), the promotion of tolerance is almost always one-sidedly incomplete. Openness to virtually everything receives an unqualified embrace, yet this unqualified acceptance cannot possibly be valid.[1]

Such evasion is predictable. Determining the balance might be an exasperating exercise for scholars who eschew moralizing. Nor is concocting a modern "index of the forbidden" popular in a world in which unambiguous, unreflective tolerance is both intellectually easy and politically seductive; few wish to be labeled a "McCarthyite." At best, an aberrant group might be disdained as "extremist." Nor does the statistical analysis of attitudinal tolerance, the form of tolerance dominating research, require explicit attention to its limits. Recall that the choice of groups and activities deserving acceptance is privately made by the researcher. If the pollster deems Nazis welcome, the respondent cannot object. Boundaries are authoritatively, privately, and quietly decided prior to the research, not openly discussed within the questionnaire.

Our analysis restores balance to the discussion, gives voice to the other, often hushed, side. We embark on a general excursion, a dusting-off of important and perhaps forgotten justifications seldom explicated in defense of greater acceptance of noxious views. The search is for rules and principles to guide acceptability. Our point is simple: The forceful repression of political ideas and groups, even if not an immediate physical threat or a clear violation of criminal law, can be reasonably defended, even in a democracy. Let us be clear. We are not talking of mere rebuke or condemnation, we are vindicating state *coercion*. To proclaim, even apart from the usual libel and free speech guidelines, "This should not be expressed and if you do, you will be severely punished!" is not automatic self-certification as a congenitally authoritarian antidemocrat. We are not for restoring narrow tyranny unless one (erroneously) assumes that the prohibition of one idea inevitably gives rise to the suppression of all. Future chapters reveal the opposite inclinations. Rather, there *are* arguments for limiting access, and these do not deserve their customary facile consignment to oblivion.

The writings of Locke and J. S. Mill and their classic, frequently cited defenses of tolerance are our points of departure. Though many important theorists have likewise dwelt on tolerance, notably Milton, Hobbes, and Macchiavelli, we focus exclusively on Locke and Mill for they loom large in contemporary discussions of tolerance. Given that we defend *in*tolerance, to begin with hallowed defenses of openness may appear ironic, misdirected. Nevertheless, as will become clear, even these saints of inclusiveness accept approbations severe by today's standards. The modern, blank check tolerance literature may routinely invoke Locke and Mill as Founders, but this invocation is incomplete. Their writings are not the starting gun for the race toward unrestrained openness. A second exploration brings into focus the notion of how societies define and defend themselves. Kai Erikson (1968), in particular, contends that vigorous intolerance of outsiders, not gracious permeability, allow societies to function *qua* societies. Unadulterated tolerance is a dangerous illusion. To embrace all fanciful notions as worthy of protection can be as subversive of democratic life as permitting zero deviation. Finally, this theoretical analysis will be made concrete by examining the worthiness of tolerating the Cold War American Communist Party. Questions regarding Communists were poll staples. With Soviet Marxism defunct, and cries of McCarthyism more distant, a fresh look is possible regarding whether these oft-condemned repressive urges were, indeed, justifiable. Put sharply, was all the scholarly condemnation of citizen intolerance warranted?

I. The Classic Defenses of Tolerance

John Locke

Few thinkers enjoy a more prestigious place in our liberal tradition than John Locke (1632-1704). Like other late seventeenth century philosophers— for example, Milton, Spinoza, and Pufendorf—the issue of tolerance of religious differences (or "toleration" as it was then known) occupied a central place in his work. Though his writings are now judged timeless, an abstractly universal theory was not his goal. Locke was personally embroiled in a fierce political battle over religious freedom; he was not a disinterested philosopher. The brutal suppression of religious heresy, especially Protestantism, widely afflicted Europe, including Locke's England. The Thirty Years War in which Catholics battled Protestants and Germany lost a third of its population was still a fresh memory. Slight doctrinal divergences routinely brought torture, execution, property confiscation, or exile. Though modern-day tolerance adherents fret over ordinary citizens as dangerous hate mongers, government was the culprit here. Indeed, Locke himself was a casualty of government-inspired intolerance, living a portion of his life as an Amsterdam refugee.

His *A Letter Concerning Toleration,* written in 1685 and published in 1689 in both Holland and England, constitutes one of the most important, enduring endorsements of religious tolerance. Though mild by today's calls, the very opposite was true then. Locke could well have been judged guilty of seditious libel, maligning government officials, and could have been executed. In fact, Locke's *Letter* was initially published in Gouda, Holland, written in Latin, with an impossible-to-decipher encoded authorship. When an English version appeared, the secretive Locke initially denied authorship and then, after being inadvertently exposed as the writer, prudentially distanced himself from the Latin-to-English translation. These were controversial opinions in their day, even in relatively open-minded England.

Compared to other writers of the era (e.g., Pierre Bayle (1647-1706) the French Calvinist professor of philosophy), Locke's case for freedom of intellect and faith was mild. The English *Preface* translation insisted on absolute freedom, but this was the translator's view, not Locke's. Nevertheless, given both his standing as a political theorist and contribution to American political thought, he has been inducted into tolerance's modern Pantheon. In spirit, though not necessarily in precise detail, Locke is customarily invoked to assist modern defenses of openness. Sullivan, Piereson, and Marcus, for example, in *Political Tolerance and American Democracy* depict *A Letter* as an early step in tolerance's evolutionary development (3-4). McClosky and Brill (1983, 38-39) frequently evoke Locke's name. Colloquially speaking, Locke is "a good guy" when sagacious authority is conveniently marshaled to justify admitting unsavory views. The reality, however, is less straightforward and more nuanced. Locke offers much to caution us against treating it as a sweeping manifesto.

Locke unambiguously separates secular and religious spheres. These two domains are not merely territorial, as one might divide a land into two sovereign nations, but of a fundamental character. When men join to form a state, they surrender a portion of their natural rights, thus agreeing to obey the civil magistrate's will. By its intrinsic character, within the bounds of inalienable natural rights, the state can forcefully compel. By contrast, when men voluntarily elect to assemble as a church to worship and seek salvation, they surrender no natural rights. Thus, churches can coerce neither members nor outsiders by force; they can only expel heretics. Distinctiveness and exclusivity of domains are critical: The state, despite its civil authority, lacks religious supremacy whereas religion, notwithstanding its spiritual authority, possesses no civil command.

Nevertheless, though a constituted religious body is harmless to the state, what prevents tyrannical state imposition of religion? Why should a Catholic monarch refrain from commanding Catholicism on his subjects? Surely this cannot be the dissenting religion's countervailing might. At least in Locke's Protestant world, nonconforming sects were militarily defenseless. Locke's answer is twofold. First, and most important, civil restraint proceeds from the true nature of religious faith. Profession of belief must be, by its inherent nature, an inner, exclusively private, personal matter beyond state intervention. As Locke put it, "All the life and power of true religion consists in the inward and full persuasion of the mind; and faith is not faith without believing" (17). The king may compel outward observances, but no sovereign can impose, by force or confiscation of property, inner belief. Hence, state religious imposition "is altogether useless and unprofitable."

Tolerance's second defense is the sheer unlikelihood of the emergence of a single faith. People naturally and perpetually disagree on doctrinal matters. The one true religion is, ultimately, unknowable to mortals. And, given that churches only possess the power to excommunicate, not compel, religious bodies must proliferate. Each sect will possess its own revelations of divine truth, and such revelations can only be known, not proven or disproven. Again, marshaling state might to impose uniformity of creed in a world of countless variety is futile and violates the magistrate's proper authority.

In general, Locke offers a limited defense of one aspect of human existence—religion—and even then, it is of modest reach. Fundamentally, toleration is but a shield against unwarranted state intrusion into matters of slight or no real-world consequences. Only "errors in speculative opinion and ways of worship," in Locke's words, are beyond the magistrate. Toleration's philosophical foundations are likewise narrow. There are no grand buttressing principles generalizable to a larger, more encompassing tolerance conception. Not the slightest trace of "democracy" or government's obligation to guarantee openness of opinion emanates. As with terrible weather, religious diversity must be accepted because, given the impossibility of discovering the one true religion, neither government nor citizens can justifiably impose uniformity.

The limits of Locke's defense become even more plain if we delve into what lies unprotected. By contemporary standards, Locke's beliefs are notably restrictive. First, even within religious life, some check is necessary. Churches cannot suppress both heretics and each other; nevertheless, civil government, by virtue of its contractual identity and power, is empowered to suppress religion when it collides with civil law (Kamen, 1967, xxxv). The civil magistrate cannot interfere with matters of doctrine or rituals, for these are strictly matters of creed. However, if the church ventured into civil matters, civil law, guided by the limitations imposed by natural rights, prevails. As King (1976, 88) observes, beliefs on matters of little civic concern are to be tolerated; behavior, except if equally inconsequential, can be forcefully controlled. Locke uses the example of child sacrifice versus sacrificing a calf. In the latter, public law permits the slaughter of animals; the former is contrary to statute and thus also forbidden in religious ceremonies (65). People cannot thus ". . . lustfully pollute themselves in promiscuous uncleanliness" and claim protection under the guise of religious tolerance.

Second, the state reserves the power to ban certain religions altogether if members are, doctrinally, beholden to a foreign power. In his era's politics, this especially applied to Catholics, for Locke held English Catholics to be French agents. The Catholic Church was also governed by a Roman Pope asserting both spiritual and temporal authority. Thus, suppressing Catholicism legitimately falls within the magistrate's domain. More generally, this dictum withdraws religious tolerance from sect followers fusing religious and political power once adherents left their homeland. In present-day England this might well include certain Moslems who, as members of the Ismaili Shiite Moslem sect, technically owe allegiance to non-English leaders.

Furthermore, tolerance was denied to atheists and sects, such as Unitarians, that rejected the Trinity's existence. As Locke said, "Those are not at all to be tolerated who deny the being of God. Promises, covenants, and oaths, which are the bonds of human society, can have no hold upon an atheist." Again, this exclusion is pragmatic—civil society's functioning requires a trust rooted in binding oaths, and non-believers will surely feel no compulsion to honor them. Who would trust an atheist's oath who swore on a Bible to tell the truth at a trial? What about a public official who privately denied authority to his or her oath of office? Atheism subverts society, and the civil magistrate is charged with the protection of civil society.

Finally, though Locke was chiefly concerned with removing Protestant sects from state intrusion, his *Letter* and other writings also comments on the relationship between civil authority and private morality. It is not, by today's yardstick of personal liberation, a very permissive vision. To understand this outlook, it is first necessary to grasp a view of freedom espoused in his *Two Treatises of Government* already hinted at. Here, in the context of the period, Locke makes a strong case for personal freedom, his "liberty to dispose, and order, as he lists, his Person, Actions, Possessions, and his whole Property, within the Allowance of those Laws under which he is; and therein not to be subject to the arbitrary Will of another, but freely follow his own" (quoted in Baldwin, 1985, 38). Yet, as generous as this freedom may initially appear, it is not "licence," and is strictly conditioned by the morality of natural law. Society, properly understood, is not a collection of people freely acting unrestrained. The great protector of freedom—natural law—also gravely constrains. True freedom is only possible within the confinement of immutable higher morality.

The state's absolute responsibility for enforcing natural law both bridles and liberates. Tolerance is subservient to natural law, and unless belief or action is defensible under such law, it can be rightly prohibited. To be sure, for some religious moral failings—uncharitableness, idleness and lying, for example—Locke would absolve from civil punishment. More serious sins, however, warrant magisterial intrusion. In a contemporary context, Locke's views would place him far closer to Moral Majority religious fundamentalists than liberationists. For example, when imploring the magistrate to remove himself from matters of harmless religious doctrine, he chides civil authority for ignoring the more weighty offenses of adultery, fornication, uncleanliness, lasciviousness, idolatry, and like things, which cannot be denied to be works of the flesh. To be "sincerely solicitous about the kingdom of God," the magistrate should apply himself to the rooting out of immoralities, not "the extirpation of sects" (11). As Wolfson (1996) argues, civil society for Locke required morality and rationality among citizens, and the indoctrination of these virtues was proper government activity.

If a single lesson is to be gleaned from Locke, his teaching affirms government's authority to protect civil society. Locke plainly places the requirement of lawful civil society ahead of the obligation of unconditional tolerance. When religion and state clash, the state prevails. Provided the civil laws accord with higher natural law, the magistrate has no obligation to accept subversive practices, doctrines and sects. Those who refuse to be bound by public authority, cannot be trusted, engage in subversion, or owe their allegiance elsewhere forgo legitimate claims for tolerance and may be put down. Equally relevant, those disobeying legitimate moral law, as rightfully incorporated into civil law, similarly relinquish claims to tolerance. Moral wrongs, from adultery to pornography, for Locke are outside the true Christian faith and thus cannot be defended with petitions for tolerance.

In short, though Locke may reside in our modern tolerance Pantheon, dutifully cited in defense of expanding the scope of political freedom, he hardly prefigures this modern generosity. He was among the most tolerant of his era but this cannot be taken to mean that he would be among the most tolerant today. His prescriptions address religion, and cannot possibly be extended to the political or the social. His message is modest: tolerate only when the distasteful is unavoidable and does not subvert civil society.

John Stuart Mill

No intellectual ancestors of modern tolerance literature receives greater veneration than John Stuart Mill (1806 -1873). Above all others, he is its patron saint, and passages from *On Liberty* (1859/1947) are proudly quoted as defending ever more acceptance. Gibson and Bingham's *Civil Liberties and Nazis* quotes Mill's "rigorous formulation" (7) at length to justify a virtually unchecked absolution. Far more than Locke, Mill proffers a detailed and comprehensive, carefully argued plea for extensive personal liberty. His stand is encompassing, questioning everything from private morality to society's ultimate purpose. Not surprisingly, a robust literature today celebrates Mill's contribution; less prominent are those dwelling on their ambiguities, contradictions, omissions, and alleged deficiencies. Our purpose here, however, is not to settle these debates; we examine Mill to seek guidance in deciding what is to be permitted and excluded.

Understanding Mill begins by examining his most basic, boldly stated defense of personal liberty. Early in *On Liberty* he boldly states an oft-quoted axiomatic first principle:

> That principle is, that the sole end for which mankind are warranted, individually or collectively, in interfering with the liberty of action of any of their member, is self-protection. That the only purpose for which power can be rightfully exercised over any member of a civilized community, against his will, is to prevent harm to others. His own good, either physical or moral, is not a sufficient warrant. He cannot rightfully be compelled to do or forebear because it will be better for him to do so, because it will make him happier, because, in the opinion of others, to do so would be wise, or even right. There are good reasons for remonstrating with him, or reasoning with him, or persuading him, or entreating him, but not for compelling him, or visiting him with any evil in case he do otherwise. (9-10)

This is a revolutionary, radically uncomplicated argument, even by today's indulgent standards. Though unrestricted permissiveness is not demanded, the principle gravely restricts prohibitions. The burden of forbiddance, furthermore, is squarely placed on those asserting larger social harm. To appreciate this view's revolutionary character, consider the principle's scope. Recall that Locke, and other tolerance advocates of his day, exclusively addressed religious tolerance. Morality and politics submitted to civil law without special protection. Mill, by contrast, extends tolerance to all human endeavor—religion, morals, economics, education and, particularly important here, politics. The principle does not distinguish between, say, a minor matter of faith, a major government policy, and the practice of homosexuality.

Similarly, though his examples draw from the controversies of mid-nineteenth century England, his contentions apply universally, regardless of national boundaries, time, or circumstances. No authority, whether a democratically elected government, a dictatorship, or a church claiming absolute control of its members, has the right, according to Mill, to deprive citizens of their liberty unless behavior is socially harmful. The application of utilitarianism—actions are to be judged exclusively by their contribution to the greatest good for the greatest number—is raised up to an eternal, immutable, universal law. For a government to chastise socially unharmful behavior is akin to repealing a law of physics.

Mill's dictum also does not distinguish the intolerance of government from the suppressive urges of ordinary citizens. To Mill, "Protection, therefore against the tyranny of the magistrate is not enough; there needs to be protection also against the tyranny of prevailing opinion and feeling; against the tendency of society to impose, by other means than civil penalties, its own ideas and practices as rules of conduct on those who dissent from them. . . ." (4-5). Again, this proclaims a significant shift from the Lockean view of government as the dangerous foe of tolerance. Mill anticipates the modern scholarly research underscoring the potential dangers of mass sentiments.

Clearly, this most generous understanding of tolerance no doubt helps explain its present-day popularity. If strictly obeyed, laws banning prostitution, gambling, alcohol consumption, deviant sexuality and other "victimless crimes" might not survive. This view, moreover, is seemingly hospitable to all but the most violently aggressive political organizations, and even then, tolerance extends provided words, not action, prevail. Nevertheless, a more extended reading of Mill, and attention to the implications of this principle, expose a less charitable position. *On Liberty* furnishes numerous exceptions and reservations and, though they may initially appear as modest asides often deemed inconsequential by Mill himself, their totality is considerable. Despite all the quotations, the Millian vision is not the blank-check tolerance invocation commonly implied. There is certainly no linking of openness with political democracy. Not surprisingly, this side of *On Liberty,* this making of black and white into numerous shades of gray, is seldom acknowledged by those who cited Mill to champion a near absolute tolerance.

Let us begin with some simple, almost mundane, exceptions to this grand principle of liberty. Who warrants exclusion from enjoying such liberty? Exclusionary fine print appears scarcely a few paragraphs following this vigorous inveighing against imposed constraints, and concerns capacity for rational thought. By today's egalitarian standards, it appears almost anachronistic, rarely drawing scholarly attention, and Mill seems hardly concerned, but the exclusion is noteworthy in exposing Mill's larger view. It is also a criterion applicable to the concrete administration of tolerance rules. To Mill, the grand principle of liberty only applies to those who possess sufficient rationality, those with the capacity to weigh alternatives, exercise judgment, and debate matters intelligently. Obviously, Mill notes, this excludes children. Less obvious are what he calls "those backward states of society in which the race itself may be considered as in its nonage" (10). Under such conditions, the principle of liberty has no application; such people are to be despotically governed.

Mill only touches on who might be excused, but disparate candidates abound, people who would not qualify as "human beings in the maturity of their faculties." In other words, those not proficient in intelligent, adult thought. One would surmise that the actions and views expressed by severely mentally ill (the "delirious," in Mill's language), the retarded, the senile, those incapacitated by addictions or physical injury, and people otherwise "in some state of excitement or absorption incompatible with the full use of the reflecting faculty" (98) would not qualify automatically for acceptance. A larger, and admittedly difficult to delineate, category that Mill would likely exclude are those lacking in rudimentary education, hermits, people highly susceptible to intemperate judgment and individuals enduring desperate physical conditions. Taken together, these classes comprise a significant portion of the population. It is *not* that the opinions of incompetents require suppression and, conceivably, raving lunatics may enjoy total liberty. Rather, in Mill's scheme of things, those not in possession of their faculties cannot insist on equal evaluation of their views and actions. Their views are dismissible though not necessarily repressible. As one paternalistically protects juveniles, for example, not heeding all requests, a similar response is appropriate for those unable to act.

Equally unnoticed in modern celebrations of *On Liberty* is Mill's sensitivity for the quality of public life. He acknowledges (99) that certain private behaviors harm only the person involved or nobody, but when performed in public "are offenses against decency." Classic examples are public intoxication and rowdiness. While Mill facilely dismisses these nuisance behaviors as only tangentially related to his explication, they are hardly nonexistent in contemporary tolerance controversies. Battles over panhandling, the homeless sleeping in public, open displays of sexuality, boisterous loitering, and similar seemingly harmless crimes against civility are a staple in many urban areas. Equally familiar are controversies regarding artistic decency, for example, public homoerotic art and theatrical presentations, all defended in the name of "tolerance." Though we can only speculate here, Mill's exceptions betray an underlying constraining "old fashioned" morality undergirding pure utilitarianism. Quite possibly, Mill (like Locke) would be quite agreeable to banishing morally offensive behaviors even if no demonstrable social harm were demonstrated.

Moreover, despite his relentless inveighing against the "tyranny of opinion," Mill apparently acknowledged the legitimacy, even necessity, of private, morally based social pressure apart from legal proscriptions (Himmelfarb, 1990, 93-98). Here, Mill significantly diverges from notable contemporary tolerance treatments whereby government acquires a positive responsibility to restrain privately imposed sanctions. Mill admits that certain dispositions, for example, vices such as cruelty, malice, dishonesty in dealing with others, and love of domination adversely affect others. Such inclinations, to the extent that they are social, are not to be excused by invoking tolerance; they are properly punishable, though not governmentally. Present-day fundamentalist Christian denunciations of licentiousness, dissoluteness, and other immoralities or socially harmful actions would conform with Mill's dictum. More generally, social pressure—ostracism, ridicule, disdain, humiliation—in and of itself, is not definitionally intolerance. Much depends on the nature of the behavior. To reiterate, such condemnations, for Mill, would not constitute intolerance for they are extra-legal and concern public, not purely private, harm. Government bares no obligation to shield the unorthodox from the communal scoldings.

Mill also reveals a sensitivity to preemptive state intrusion to avert injury, even if no immediate social harm is evident. Consider the example of selling poisons (97-98). If poisons were only used for illegal purposes such as murder, their outright ban is self-evident. However, as they also possess legitimate uses, total prohibition is unwarranted. How, then, does one navigate the predicament? The answer is both simple and, today, commonplace: Extensive regulation, which may require that all toxins be properly labeled or purchase records kept. More generally, for Mill no inherent principle pits liberty against preemptive state coercive intervention provided, of course, the possible harm is documented. The magistrate need not passively anticipate a crime if intervention is possible.

Nor is Mill's well-known and elaborate defense of free expression as starkly one-sided as is often implied. To be sure, the questioning of sacred doctrine or the challenging of honored traditions is fully sheltered by the principle of protected liberty. Indeed, such challenging is not only permitted, it may well be essential to society's intellectual life, invigorating both our capacities and the doctrines themselves. Nevertheless, because mere words can shade into actions and actions may have preventable injurious consequences, the right to express one's views is not unbounded. By a half-century, Mill anticipates modern Supreme Court doctrines when he acknowledges that a rabble-rouser inflaming an angry mob can be legally suppressed. Nor does freedom of expression repeal slander and libel law.

The final tolerance-related constraint is the most consequential, namely, the utilitarian limitation of social aftermath. Recall that intolerance *was* justified if social harm transpired. This element of Mill's position, and for good reason, has attracted considerable reproach, the gist of which is that the

distinction between a purely individual detriment and a social evil is insus-
tainable, both in principle and in practice. As Fitzjames Stephens (1991, 28),
one of his most severe critics, put it, "the attempt to distinguish between
self-regarding acts and acts which regard to others, is like attempts to
distinguish between acts which happen in time and acts which happen in
space. Every act happens at some time and in some place, and in like manner
every act we do either does or may affect both our selves and others . . . the
distinction is altogether fallacious and unfounded." At best, even if such a
distinction could be abstractly defended, so much depends on circumstances
that principles collapse into squabbling chaos in actual practice. Mill furnishes only a transcendent philosophical argument, not serviceable guidelines. The utilitarian principle of unlimited tolerance of personal eccentricity
may be comparable to a law of nature sans a precise mathematical expression.

Consider intoxication, a frequent topic in *On Liberty*. Obviously, the
principle of personal autonomy is perfectly serviceable for private drunkenness. Suppose, unfortunately, that this drunk supported a family, and as a
result of intemperance, the family became destitute and requested public
assistance. Further suppose that others, witnessing the joys of immoderation,
imitated this behavior with similar harmful consequences. Soon, tens of
thousands drew public financial support while inebriation became rampant.
In contemporary life this intoxication example can easily be replaced with
those drawn from illegitimacy, promiscuous sexuality, drug abuse, a disdain
for work, and other conduct now designated as social pathologies. Personal
problems, multiplied, soon become public tribulations.

Mill wrestles mightily with the problem. Unless such drunkenness inter-
fered with a clear legal obligation (guard duty, for example), Mill believed
that it could only be controlled through "moral disapprobation," not law.
Perhaps others, on seeing the personally harmful consequences of intoxication, would reform. Nevertheless, in the final analysis, coercive state intervention cannot be justified beyond the enforcement of a purely legal obligation. Non-support of family might be legally punishable, but the cause of this
action—excessive drinking—escapes legal reach. To wit, remedies like dis-
couraging alcohol use through higher taxes or limiting its sale is "suited only
to a state of society where the laboring classes are avowedly treated as
savages" (103). Needless to say, whether moral pressure or education can be
effective is debatable. And, if such efforts fall short, as is too often the case,
it is unclear what further remedies exist. Is civil society wholly dependent
on moral exhortations and hoped-for social pressure?

The more general problem of deciding these societal choices still remains
unsolved. Even if Mill were a philosopher-king rendering perfect judgments,
he is long gone and, as he himself frankly acknowledges, abstract principles

do not easily convert to exact guidelines. Daily governance is hardly facilitated by invoking grand principle. Because they ultimately rest on complex judgments, not hard and fast categories, utilitarian invocations are a potentially indeterminate, even porous, defense against intolerance. Arguments of a vague social harm are facile, especially likely on matters of great complexity and partial evidence.

At core, Mill's arguments, no matter how detailed or cogent, venture no further than highly developed and dogmatic admonitions for the sanctity of the socially harmless. *On Liberty's* protestations against the "despotism of custom" and the crushing philistine atmosphere of conformity and mediocrity remain more personal than political. Individual eccentricities, not political causes, reside at the argument's heart. Providing a large-scale, practical blueprint specifying clear substantive constraints on authority comes up short, despite the opposite intent. Though Mill's *Liberty* may initially appear to afford greater autonomy than Locke's *Letter,* the inevitable specter of "social harm" looms everywhere as a potential plea for intolerance. Mill's modern defenders may profitably conjure up his spirit, but the full vision is conveniently ignored.

This unwillingness, perhaps incapacity, to transform the general principle of personal liberty into a useful, openly stated form is understandable if one peers beyond *On Liberty's* manifest content. His proposed solutions rest on arrangements undoubtedly unwelcomed by modern admirers. Mill was vehemently not a populist and harbors no illusions about democracy's virtue; *On Liberty* vitriolicly attacks suffocating popular pressures and the public's unfortunate susceptibility to sensuous pleasures and deceits. Public opinion, Mill knew, was often wrong and lacked expertise. Hence, recourse to democratic, majoritarian mechanisms—mechanisms so beloved in today's democratic tolerance literature—is unthinkable. Nor could Mill philosophically invoke natural rights or social contract theory to legitimize individual liberty. Such justifications, for Mill, constitute foolish fictions and superstitions.

The reality, as Cowling's (1990) analysis of Mill notes, was that choices of inclusion were delegated to the enlightened intellectual class, people like Mill himself. To be sure, these "higher minds" would not dictatorially supplant, at least formally, an elected representative government. Nevertheless, by their superior mental ability, by their capacity to sculpt society's intellectual and moral character, these men and women, not ordinary people or even government officials, would decide complex particulars. In a nutshell, it is rule by an enlightened erudite aristocracy. Let us be clear, it is not some immutable, abstract tolerance *per se* that is being enshrined; it is tolerance as best understood and carefully decided by a self-anointed, cultivated elite.

Overall, Mill's advice is a deceptively generous slogan. Even then, when all the exceptions and potential loopholes are accounted for, it is not nearly as absolute or firm as is portrayed in modern invocations. More important, even without violating the spirit of the principle, personal liberty can be substantially constrained. Intolerance is hardly forbidden. All depends on the outcomes of reasoned discourse, not the formal application of immutable principles. Save purely personal eccentricities and private matters, almost anything, including speech, can be judged socially harmful and thus prohibited. Conceivably, rational, educated, and reasonable officials might conclude that Communism or any other "dangerously attractive" idea was excessively harmful. Indeed, some today contend that pornography, racist literature, and homophobic tracts, even if read clandestinely, subvert the common good by fostering hatred and violence.

What, then, can we learn from this brief excursion? Modern tolerance writers eagerly adopt both Locke and Mill as forerunners of their own, highly permissive views. The *Letter* and *On Liberty* thus become, with the select quotations, early prototypes of today's expansive democratic theory, the first inklings of a venerated and binding tradition. Clearly, our analysis demonstrates this inference to be a difficult stretch. A contrarily inclined scholar could well conclude the opposite: Locke and Mill, for different reasons, provide ample justification for what today would be judged intolerance.

Nevertheless, leaving aside possible charges of intellectual kidnapping, what can be said? Most obviously, Locke and Mill both share a deep affection for civil society. In today's cultural wars, they would favor propriety, public decency, and a respect for traditional virtues. Not endorsed, no doubt, would be offering tolerance to those wishing to undermine family, the authority of teachers and, more generally, those assaulting "the traditional Western value system." To be sure, the mere thinking of the controversial, unorthodox views, even their private expression, need not be suppressed, but once thoughts become actions, no matter how innocuous or seemingly inconsequential, civil society must be protected, and such protection involves far more than lively intellectual rejoinder.

Defending civil society goes beyond an aversion to the repulsive. Locke and Mill, notwithstanding disagreeing in their reasons, believed that civil society, provided it conforms to proper principles, cannot be left unprotected from radical challenges. Society must not indulge its mortal enemies. The desire for tolerance, no matter how pressing, is not a prescription for political paralysis. The magistrate need not be idle until the seditious army arrives. That enemies have declared their intentions and attempted to enlist adherents is sufficient. Reasonable men and women can disagree on the threat's seriousness, but sworn adversaries cannot seek protection in the name of tolerance.

II. Tolerance and the Defense of Community

Contemporary attitudinal-based tolerance research avers all signs of intolerance. Scholars, unfortunately, seldom venture into the relationship between tolerance and other values. Analysis, no matter how conceptually or statistically complex, merely inquires about tolerance levels, its sources or social distribution. As a distinct political value, tolerance exists isolated from possibly competing, political objectives. In a nutshell, a reading of the tolerance literature tells us that tolerance stands detached.

This view is misguided, or at least an inadvertent exaggeration. Tolerance, even in the most open, permissive democratic society, can be only one of various esteemed values. Permitting political heterogeneity to flourish must be balanced against other values, and it cannot be assumed *a priori* that tolerance will—or must—subordinate all else. In particular, advancing tolerance almost inevitably must remain secondary to maintaining political community. This political commonwealth, the organization of people sharing a mutual loyalty into a common decision-making body, from city to nation, does not compete with the principle of political tolerance; it is, more fundamentally, *a precondition*. Tolerance might inhere within a community, but tolerance is impossible in anarchy. Thus, to the extent that encouraging tolerance subverts a community, such promotion ultimately becomes self-destructive.

This argument does not portray open-mindedness to the unorthodox, however paltry, as the first step on the path to hellish anarchy. The Spanish Inquisition and some alluring *Gemeinschaft* are not the only alternatives. Rather, increments of acceptance must be counter-weighted against upholding civil society. To repeat, this is a matter of equilibrium, not the collision of exclusive principles. An analogy might be made with the body's need for trace metals such as zinc and potassium—a certain level is essential, but too much is lethal. Make no mistake, tolerance is worthy of celebration, but this celebration, like all jubilations, can sometimes get out of hand.

Tolerance and the Necessity of Deviancy

Tolerance means putting up with the disliked. Conversely, demanding suppression or even criminalization of an idea or cause—not just vigorous disputation—proclaims intolerance, an activity generally deemed undemocratic. Such polarity is not inherent; it merely rests on contemporary convention. An entirely different perspective exists. Kai Erikson's (1968) analysis of the early decades of New England Puritanism draws on sociological theories of deviance to suggest that disapprobation, even expulsion or incarceration, of heretics can help sustain political community. *Intolerance,* the active effort to destroy an idea or a group, not merely to object to it, is *integral* to community. Though Erikson's analysis concerned a theocracy, the argument is a general one, applying to all communities, even those embracing openness. We are talking of severe suppression, not merely protecting the status quo from belligerent dissenters. Two arguments are involved: (1) approbation defines communal boundaries, and (2) punishing enemies, harmless or not, affirms and invigorates collective identity.

Setting Boundaries

All communities, by definition, maintain boundaries of acceptable beliefs and behavior. These frontiers are frequently imprecise—the domain of permissible activity may defy exactitude, quarrels occur on where gray becomes black, or borders fluctuate. Judges are forever wrestling with establishing clear divisions—for example, the line separating unacceptable public obscenity from strong but nevertheless permissible language. What exactly is a "peaceful" protest or "marriage"? Moreover, how is this line to be conveyed to those yet unacquainted with society's boundaries, people such as children, or immigrants?

For Erikson, periodic public condemnations and punishments of the violator serve to locate publicly essential demarcation lines. Approbation may occur formally—trials, expulsion, deportations, incarceration—or informally—ostracism, malicious gossip, humiliation, or economic chastisement. The process may be directed against actual people or impersonally revealed in the common culture, from serious books to comic plays with a moral message. This castigation dramatically punishes the particular transgression, but more important, it broadly serves as a teaching lesson. Indeed, lurid, sensationalistic newspaper and TV accounts of outrages and accompanying retribution, even if exaggerated or fictional, may be more effective in defining community boundaries than the dry technical language of statutes or dimly remembered school lessons.

This didactic function may be especially critical as fresh attacks emerge and the division between the acceptable and unacceptable remains unclear. Erikson (70) provides the example of the difference between U.S. reaction to fascism versus Communism following World War II. Though wartime propaganda distinguished between democracy and fascism, this demarcation was less legible for Communism versus American democracy, especially considering the Soviet Union's status as wartime ally. Many Americans, no doubt, only dimly grasped the goal of expansionistic post-war Communism or its subversive methods. Thus, the widespread government and private Cold War anti-Communism campaigns, from well-publicized congressional investigation and media coverage of infamous spy trials to fictional documentary-style TV shows, helped the American public define this new threat.[2]

Strengthening Communal Identity

The identification and punishment of deviance also strengthens the existing bonds of communal solidarity (Erikson, 1968, 4). The meaning of "us" is deepened by the visibility of an antagonistic "them." The despicable outrage becomes the subject of conversations and media reports, which, in turn, permit people to reaffirm personally and collectively seldom articulated deep premises of the social order. Cohesion, as Coser notes (1964, 35) requires conflicts with collective enemies. Protecting the realm not only means employing the traditional means of defense, such as a strong military, but also invigorating the immunity system, our patriotic spirit and will to resist. Quietly ferreting out traitors and secretly punishing them is insufficient. It is also necessary to mobilize ordinary citizens, to loudly and emotionally publicize enemies as "highly dangerous un-Americans."

This process was especially apparent during the 1940s and 1950s when anti-Communism generated strident communal affirmation, everything from American Legion-sponsored hyper-patriotic essay contests to nationalistic, anti-Soviet election campaign rhetoric. Though not all schools formally instituted anti-Communist political instruction, openly defending Russia was done at considerable risk. Bowman gum company, in addition to producing baseball cards, issued collectible "Fight the Red Menace" trading cards picturing the likes of Stalin and "visit by Red police." *The National Police Gazette,* the forerunner of today's supermarket tabloid ran stories, such as "Terrifying Story the Rosenbergs Wouldn't Tell" (Barson, 1992). The FBI consciously promoted its media image—the relentless, incorruptible "G-man" tracking down dreaded Red spies. Between 1953 and 1957, for example, the FBI assisted in 117 episodes of the TV drama *I Led Three Lives* featuring undercover agent Herbert A. Philbrick. *I Was a Communist for the FBI, My Son John,* and similar movies further highlighted evil communism (Powers, 1995, Chapter 9).

Communal ties can also be strengthened through scapegoating—blaming opponents for one's own deficiencies (Coser, 1964, 45). Though scapegoating is ordinarily dismissed as pointless, even dangerous, it nevertheless may perform a useful purpose in strengthening ties during stress. For example, during the late 1940s, the Soviet Union gained unexpected victories in Poland, Hungary, Czechoslovakia, and, most important, China. The USSR also quickly reached nuclear parity with the U.S. At least for some, the Soviet Union was gaining compared to a demoralized, directionless America. Predictably, diplomatic and scientific setbacks were quickly blamed on Communist sympathizers in government and lax security. Highly publicized congressional investigations were periodically conducted. Though such high-profile confrontations had modest impact on the USSR's activities, they therapeutically confirmed America's damage by despicable foreign agents, not ineptitude.

This heightened assault on un-Americanism, this delineation of "us" from "them," involved far more than patriotic speeches and G-man movies. What is germane here, conceivably more important than scope of punishment, is the action's *public nature*. In 1948, the federal government charged more than 100 top leaders of the U.S. Communist Party with violating the Smith Act, a law making it a crime to advocate the government's violent overthrow. In two highly publicized and lengthy New York City trials, complete with a parade of surprise undercover witnesses and attention-getting allegations, virtually the party's entire leadership were convicted or fled underground. Following the trial, J. Edgar Hoover, head of the FBI, made it unequivocal that the trial's major purpose was public education on the grave dangers of Soviet subversion (Powers, 1995, 227). In March of 1951, the federal government tried Julius and Ethel Rosenberg for passing atomic secrets to the Soviets. Again, an almost circus-like character surrounded the prosecution. The trial, subsequent appeals and eventual execution, attracted intense publicity and debate. The "Americans versus the evil Russians" vision was now deeply etched in the public's mind.

This necessity for public assault on deviance says nothing about precise content. The object of intolerance must vary by historical circumstances and its menace to communal ties. In ancient times communal sins might be publicly imputed to a sacrificial animal. Today's conventionality may be demonized and hunted down tomorrow. Schur (1980, 23-24) suggests that targets for loathing depend on both the hated object's gravity and perceived threat. Each historical era and community fashions its own intolerance. While U.S. cold warriors were busily denouncing the Communist menace, Soviet officials were likely brow-beating their citizens on the dangers of American capitalism. By the late 1960s, with the Marxist threat well understood by Americans, anti-Communism grew increasingly irrelevant. Public affirmation of community values now became more cultural. Those embracing an "alternative lifestyle," the use of mind-altering drugs, acceptance of sexual promiscuity, a disdain for conventional employment, a disheveled style of dress, and a general loathing of established authority attracted public approbation.

An unexpected insight relevant to our understanding of tolerance emerges here: sustaining community does *not* require the total suppression of deviancy. The conventional and the aberrant enjoy a symbiotic relationship. In fact, the hated apostasy may be usefully sustained to prove the threat's seriousness. The heresy's popularity and power may even be exaggerated by its ostensible opponents. For example, though the Ku Klux Klan by the 1980s had greatly deteriorated and its remnants lived under government surveillance, civil rights groups routinely invoked the image of a vigorous, expanding, dangerous, and resourceful Klan (D'Souza, 1995, 293). Civil rights leaders are thus of a divided mind: though the Klan is evil and thus ought to be forcefully suppressed, they exploit the Klan's persistence in energizing its followers. Put more generally, public denunciation, even harsh criminalization, cannot automatically be equated with the desire for total suppression.

Similarly, masses of heretics do not have to be gruesomely punished to accomplish this didactic purpose. It is the punishment's ostentatious character, the visibility of the sins, the clear explication of the reasons for the outrage, and the mobilization of communal sentiment that define boundaries and orates. A few celebrated cases dispensing only minor punishment may be far more consequential than hundreds of secret draconian retributions. Criticizing a contentious congressional investigations of "un-Americanism" as a failure because of the minuscule number of convictions gained misses its educational purpose. Dragging a reluctant witness before a hostile congressional committee for a few hours and making him or her squirm before a national TV audience may accomplish far more than lengthy incarceration.

Overall, our analysis alerts us to how *in*tolerance assists community. Though he reaches his conclusions differently, Erikson's discussion of early Puritan society echoes the sentiments of Locke and Mill—communal continuation inevitably conflicts with the demands of unchecked tolerance. Civil society must, by its intrinsic character, impose limits, and may demand incarceration or death. What precisely is condemned, and by what instrumentality, cannot be deduced logically or historically. It all depends on historical circumstances, and the inherent murkiness of dividing lines makes implementation controversial. But such dilemmas, imprecisions, and hazy boundaries are not an invitation to the blank-check type of tolerance routinely invoked in the modern tolerance literature.

III. Anti-Communism and the Cold War

The zeal for tolerance, no matter how abstractly alluring, must be counterweighted with maintaining community. Here, we explore this balancing process more concretely by examining tolerance of Communism in the United States, especially during the Cold War. The key question is: Can the public's anti-Red urges, from banning newspapers to firing Communist teachers, be justified to protect community. Past scholarship generally suggests a question long resolved—these suppressive urges were not defensible. We take the matter to be less settled. This resolution is not easy, and controversies over guilt linger on even today. Offering a definitive conclusion is not, however, our objective. We illustrate the balancing of tolerance and community and, despite the inconclusiveness of all the evidence, come down on the side of justified repression to protect community. We contend that citizen intolerance of Communism was justified and was not a "problem of democracy."

Cold War Anti-Communism

The American public's anti-Communist aversion is unmistakable. From the late 1930s onward, polls painted a picture of an unambiguous desire to expel Marxism from public life (Adler, 1991; Erskine, 1970). For example, about two thirds of Gallup Poll respondents in 1947 and 1949 wanted to outlaw the U.S. Community Party (cited in Belknap, 1977, 43). Several National Opinion Research Center (NORC) questions from 1953 to 1964 inquired whether Communists should be allowed to speak on the radio. Overwhelming majorities, even among college graduates, were opposed. Similarly, only about a quarter of those asked in 1954 would permit Communist-authored books in the library. Not until the early 1970s did a majority relent to accept this modest—and, of course, inevitable—reality. The public's willingness to permit Communist teachers remained unpopular even after the Cold War thawed during the 1970s (GSS, 1972-1994: Cumulative Codebook). All in all, these poll data plus the allure of anti-Communist rhetoric, TV programs, films, books, and similar cultural artifacts depict a deep and, at least according to one perspective, unwavering intolerance.

This repressive urge was not universal, especially among tolerance scholars. Though most academics personally abhorred Marxism, the harsh form expressed in populist revulsion was roundly condemned. Scholars typically distinguished between bad ideas (here, Marxism) and forcefully expelling them. The former was tolerable; the latter was impermissible and greatly distressed scholars. Some like Samuel Stouffer (1954), found this anti-Communist impulse to be "a disturbing situation" (9) but were reluctant to sound the alert to action given its low salience. Others, however, found anti-Communism far more threatening, even portraying an aversion to the Soviet Union as revealing troublesome dysfunctional mental illness, paranoia, and similar disorders (for example Adorno, 1950; Hofstadter, 1964). Experts assembled in *The Journal of Social Issues* 1975 symposia took a tougher and openly political stand regarding intolerance of Marxism as undermining our civil liberties. Scholars, it was asserted, must vigorously join with The American Civil Liberties Union, Common Cause Legal Aid, and similar liberal groups combating intolerance (Triandis, 1975; Zalkind, 1975).

This outspoken scholarly reproach was reasonable. Though most citizens took no action based on this hatred, popular sentiment, it was asserted, might provided a fertile breeding ground for periodic bursts of frenzied witch-hunting and authoritarianism. That anti-Communism often combined with fascism, anti-Semitism, neo-Nazism, blatant racism, and other politically unsavory predilections further alarmed. Anti-Communist impulses also often possessed a scary, nutty quality. When citizens cried "Communist menace," they frequently struck the news media as dangerous lunatic asylum escapees. Though these "crazies" were tiny in number, their ceaseless talk of conspiracies, secret plots, and support among military retirees often exaggerated their threatening character. Predictably, journalists and researchers had a field day flagellating these "nuts." Crude, bombastic military types (as portrayed in the movie *Dr. Stangelove*) and "little old lady in tennis shoes" became convenient anti-Red crusader stereotypes. Bizarre hallucinations and hare-brained plots provided attractive copy, and a mini-industry of extremism books soon emerged—*The Strange Tactics of Extremism* (Overstreet, 1964) and *The American Ultras: The Extreme Right and the Military Industrial Complex* (Suall, 1962). That responsible scholars and reporters depicted anti-Communism, not Communism, as the authentic American danger is understandable. Nevertheless, the story has another side.

A Communist Menace?

Communism's domestic threat is mired in historical controversy. Many Americans, together with conservative government officials, long asserted that U.S. Communism was fundamentally a well-controlled extension of Soviet foreign policy. The party's purpose, despite contrary claims, was to destroy America and impose Soviet domination. By contrast, scholars and liberal journalists frequently interpreted U.S. Communism as consistent with

America's long history of indigenous democratic, populist and radical politics. To be sure, it was admitted, the Soviets often attempted to manipulate domestic Communist activities, but U.S. Marxism remained outside Soviet control. At worst, a few Americans were unwittingly deceived. Pejorative terms like "Soviet agent" were no more than a right-wing smear tactic against American progressives.

This debate remained largely unsettled for decades, with lurid accusations from one side followed with equally strident denials. Documentary proof was insufficient. Even court-admitted legal evidence was occasionally greeted with claims of fraud. With Communism's collapse, however, scholars have gained entrance to the former Soviet Union's extensive archives. These documents remain to be fully analyzed, but they nevertheless provide detailed documentation only speculated about Communist activities. They often confirm clandestine organizations and connections only dimly suspected. More important, these revelations settle critical debates about who was lying. One recent examination of this Soviet treasure concludes that the evidence overwhelmingly supports the anti-Communist position that the U.S. Communist movement was, from day one, under the complete domination of the Soviet Union and, when feasible, engaged in subversion and espionage on behalf of a hostile foreign power (Klehr, Haynes, & Firsov, 1995, 18). The CPUSA (Communist Party USA) may not have been the all-powerful peril imagined by alarmist anti-Communists, but this was not the CPUSA's intent.

This subversive effort is clear-cut in relentless military spying. It is not spying per se that is the issue. Many nations gather covert intelligence, often with paid informants pilfering secrets. Though intelligence work is occasionally unsavory, catching spies normally cannot justify widespread political repression. What is critical is that U.S. Communists conducted this decades-long espionage activity *under the guise of being a legitimate political party or social movement.* The party's claim that it was no different from the Democrats was a blatant lie. Communists such as Harry Gold, David Greenglass, Julius Rosenberg, Morris Cohen, and others who pilfered atomic bomb secrets were not radically inclined political activists. They were paid Soviet agents impersonating political activists. Democratic politics was the cover story.

A critical party function was recruiting American sympathizers for "informational work," the party's euphemism for spying (Klehr, et al., 1995, 232-234). These sympathizers were often unaware that they were supplying sensitive information to agents of a hostile foreign government. This was an enduring, central party activity and makes a critical point, one seldom fully appreciated when examining what appear as harmlessly democratic CPUSA activities. A line divides free association and conspiracy to commit a crime, and this line was routinely and consciously crossed. Front organizations with high-minded appellations such as "The Friends of the Soviet Union," "The League for Peace and Democracy," and the "Committee of Struggle Against War and Fascism" (which attracted distinguished American intellectuals during the 1930s) provided Soviet intelligence agents opportunities to befriend future spies and propagandists. Bookstores specializing in leftist tracts were also convenient recruiting grounds and sites to coordinate espionage activities (Koch, 1994, 18). When the Spanish Civil War erupted in 1936, thousands of Americans enlisted in Communist-controlled voluntary military units to fight fascism. Some of these veterans were eventually transformed into party-controlled agents.

Government agencies processing highly sensitive information received special attention. During World War II, the Office of Strategic Services (OSS), the forerunner of the CIA, employed numerous undercover Communist agents. Though the OSS recognized the Communist ties of some, the import of this association was generally minimized. Agents usually hid their connection, and only recently has the penetration's extent been documented (Klehr, et al., 1995, Chapter 7). An infamous example of a recruited spy was Judith Coplon, an employee of the counterintelligence unit of the Department of Justice's Foreign Agents Registration Division. As a Barnard College undergraduate, she joined the Young Communist League and was soon recruited by Soviet intelligence (Klehr, et al., 1995, 295). In 1949, the FBI became suspicious and placed her under surveillance. Coplon was eventually apprehended while turning over secret information to a UN-employed Soviet citizen (on a legal technicality, her espionage conviction was ultimately overturned).

The most spectacular alleged Soviet infiltration involved Alger Hiss, a high-ranking State Department employee. Hiss had been involved in creating the UN and had accompanied President Roosevelt to Yalta. According to Whittaker Chambers, an ex-Communist turned government informer, since the 1930s Hiss and his wife, Priscilla had been Soviet agents within a federal employee spy ring. Chambers initially revealed this information in 1939 but it was corroborated only in 1945. In 1948, Hiss publicly vehemently denied the accusations before a House investigating committee, and both the press and President Truman generally accepted his denial. Nevertheless, thanks to the persistence of then Congressman Richard M. Nixon, Chambers produced hundreds of sensitive microfilmed documents and papers that Hiss had entrusted to Chambers for delivery to Soviet agents. Laboratory analysis confirmed Hiss' connection to the material. As the statute of limitations on this particular crime had expired, Hiss was only convicted of perjury.

Communist subversion extended beyond planting agents in government. Significant efforts were made to insert a pro-Soviet bias into the media and mass entertainment. Evidence from Soviet archives now demonstrates what was once only suspected—pro-Soviet writers and journalists were guilty of more than misguided idealism. Some, like *New York Times* Soviet correspondent Walter Duranty, who systematically refused to report Soviet atrocities during the 1930s while praising Stalin, were probably victims of self-imposed horrendous misjudgment, though the Soviets certainly cooperated. Soviet agents ran press agencies that channeled legitimate stories, salted with Marxist propaganda, to the news media (Koch, 1994, 18). More commonly, Moscow carefully fed willing accomplices straight propaganda to be published as "objective" news. One such accessory was Edmund Stevens, a *Christian Science Monitor* war correspondent, advisor to high government officials on USSR policy, and author of several books on Russia, including the Pulitzer Prize winning *This is Russia—Un-Censored.* Throughout his career, Stevens denied that his generally pro-Soviet reporting flowed from Soviet government generosity, namely the lush personal housing while in Russia or freely leaving Russia with his Soviet citizen wife. Records definitely indicate, however, that Stevens was a lifelong Soviet agent (Klehr, et al., 1995, 301-302). Earl Browder, head of the CPUSA, even explicitly praised Stevens's work in a 1942 memo to Russian intelligence.

Far more common than overt control were Communist-dominated front organizations enlisting prominent artistic and communications personalities. Here, well-meaning but often politically naive public figures were guided toward the pro-Soviet position under the pretense of promoting world peace or fighting fascism (hidden Soviet operatives cynically called these "Innocents' Clubs"). Such organizations were less concerned about narrow political tasks than about the general delegitimization of American culture while flattering Soviet views. The war here was fought at the cultural level (Koch 1994, 31).[3] This was a regular feature of the party's subversive efforts, zigging and zagging with current issues and personalities. For example, when the pro-Soviet Union Henry Wallace launched his 1948 presidential campaign, intellectuals were attracted to the campaign's Independent Citizens Committee of the Arts, Sciences, and Professions. In 1949 this organization held a New York conference to help soften U.S. resistance to Soviet Eastern European expansion. Notable attendees included Charlie Chaplin, Albert Einstein, Paul Robeson, and Leonard Bernstein (Powers, 1995, 200-208). The CPUSA was particularly active in Hollywood, where it created for actors and scriptwriters the Hollywood Independent Citizens Committee of the Arts, Sciences, and Professions. The party also attempted to control Hollywood through the labor force, namely the Conference of Studio Unions (Powers, 1995, 218).

Another major thrust of the CPUSA, especially given its claim as the workers' party, was attempted labor unions domination. Early party efforts sought favorable publicity by organizing high-profile strikes—for example, the early 1930s coal miners' strike in West Virginia, Kentucky and Pennsylvania that reaped both good press and the support of acclaimed intellectuals such as Theodore Dreiser. But, the internal control of unions and membership was the enduring objective. The Party achieved several initial victories. During the 1920s the New York City Furriers Union fell under Communist control. By 1934, the CPUSA could claim control of 135 American Federation of Labor (AF of L) locals and was a sizable presence in another five hundred locals (Powers, 1995, 121). The emergence of the Congress of Industrial Organizations (CIO), the industry-based rival of the trade-based AF of L, during the late 1930s greatly strengthened Communist labor union influence. By 1937, top CIO officers were CPUSA members, and unions in key American industries—steel, automobiles, docks, and transportation—were Communist dominated.

Our sketch of Communist infiltration, spying, and attempts to manipulate American opinion is limited. Additional examples could be marshaled and, no doubt, Soviet archives may soon provide even more damaging information. Nevertheless, the point should be clear: The CPUSA was a genuine, though ultimately unsuccessful, threat. It was a deceitful, conspiratorial organization under Soviet domination irrevocably committed to political subversion. The party's public side, its prattle of protected political dissent, its convenient invocation of First Amendment privilege, was always a charade. Though many bought the deception, it was hardly convincing, especially given the character of overseas Soviet aggression. It was never, as was occasionally claimed, just another radical organization, albeit one with overseas branches. To be sure, this damaging evidence is not 100% conclusive, and skeptics may never be converted, but the evidence is sufficient to sound serious alarm.

What do these data tell us regarding popular aversion to Marxism? Can the familiar verdict of "insufficiently tolerant" so confidently rendered in the tolerance literature be appealed, given fresh evidence? The answer, I believe, is yes. Equally important, the judgment was plain four decades ago. The fresh documentation only confirms what was already legally proven (as in the case of the spying) or what was strongly suspected (CPUSA membership denied by many Communist sympathizers). When citizens expressed their strong aversion to Marxism, this was not exclusively an irrational, right-wing induced hysteria or paranoid response. Such approbation was based on well-publicized evidence. The threat had been well-documented during the 1950s in books and articles by former Communists like Louis Budenz, Eugene Lyons, Granville Hicks, Max Eastman, Elizabeth Bentley, Whittaker Chambers, Isaac Don Levine, and others. Mass circulation magazines like *The Saturday Evening Post* and *Colliers* regularly printed exposes by these ex-Communists. McCarthyite abuses, and they were abuses, or the odd antics of little old ladies in tennis shoes cannot invalidate mountains of evidence.

The CPUSA, an organization totally dominated by a hostile foreign power, *was* a genuine threat to America, and its failure does not diminish the threat's seriousness. After all, and this point cannot be over-emphasized, this strategy of subversion, infiltration, and manipulation did succeed in several Eastern European nations and came close elsewhere, including Greece and Italy. The post World War I Nazis also began as an "insignificant" German conspiracy. Political generosity cannot be imposed retroactively to faded threats. Nor was the Communist Party's slide into irrelevancy preordained; it occurred because citizens, labor unions, schools, private companies, and government made sure it happened.

In judging these arguments, three points deserve attention. When we align survey questions employed in tolerance studies, we employ instruments devised by researchers probably not taking the CPUSA's threat seriously. No doubt, Stouffer, McClosky, and others following in this research tradition viewed international Communism on the same frightening level as, say, atheism. Perhaps the kooky character of the domestic anti-Communist movement, its frequent association with unsavory fringe causes, reduced its credibility. That the CPUSA had over 75,000 members at the end of World War II, had elected local office holders, and had captured substantial unions made no difference, obviously (Goldstein, 1978, 298, 306). Subsequent investigators (for example, Gibson & Bingham, 1985; Sullivan, Piereson, & Marcus, 1982) would lump Communists together with neo-Nazis, John Birchers, the Klan and other insignificant entities, though the party still existed, recruited agents, and maintained its Soviet ties. In a nutshell, the questionnaire content reflected scholarly views possessing little inkling of Communism's true subversive nature. For them, it would appear, talking genuine threat was utter nonsense.[4] In the light of history, lumping the CPUSA together with anti-religionists and Socialists reflects an odd political sophistication. Certainly atheists—or any other group mentioned in the surveys—were not bent on overthrowing the government nor receiving covert financial support from an expansionistic, hostile, foreign nuclear power.

Imagine tolerance questions drafted by scholars taking CPUSA subversive plans seriously. Topics such as banning books from libraries, expelling

Marxist-inclined professors from universities, or permitting radio speeches would probably be dismissed as a side-show. Surely no reputable, experienced anti-Communist took public library books and radio broadcasts as the principal battlefield. Thus, anti-Communist citizens not only were asked to address peripheral controversies but were asked only questions in which anti-Marxism could take on a decidedly anti-civil libertarian cast. The questions should have addressed CPUSA members (not just radicals) holding sensitive government jobs, spying, the control of labor unions, disinformation propaganda campaigns, Communist domination of the media and education and other topics more germane to the ideological and international conflict.[5]

To inquire about book-banning is almost guaranteed to reinforce the "nutty" images typically associated with extremist right-wing anti-Communism. Moreover, one can only picture the conclusions if sophisticated, committed anti-Communists were in charge. Rather than the results being condemned as evidence of an anti-civil liberty disorder, this loathing of Marxism would be welcomed as reassuring proof of citizen virtue.

A second point is a rejoinder to a common argument, namely, that though the CPUSA might have been dangerous, even influenced by a hostile foreign power, it still was technically legal and thus deserving of democratic protection. Furthermore, as a practical matter, stamping out Marxism could well rage out of control, inviting indiscriminate anti-Left assault. Tolerating the CPUSA, despite its abuses of democracy, was freedom's price. This argument rests on the spirit of democratic openness and celebrates a marketplace of ideas, including even noxious views. This is the position of the ACLU and the tolerance literature.

This position makes excellent Fourth of July rhetoric, but surely even an open democratic society cannot be compelled to be defenseless. The Constitution hardly authorizes a safe haven for groups espousing violence bent on revolution. The crimes of treason and sedition are an integral and legitimate element of our history. The standard for noninterference cannot be perfect evidence. As Robert H. Jackson, former chief prosecutor at the Nuremberg International Tribunal and liberal Supreme Court Judge said when upholding the constitutionality of the Smith Act: "There is no constitutional right to 'gang up' on the Government" (*Dennis et al. v. United States of America,* 341 U. S. 494-592). If the national government wished to outlaw the Communist Party, as it largely did in the Smith Act, this does not in a single stroke create a dictatorship.[6] The outlawing of an organization like the CPUSA is the prudent protection of the community from subversion.

Third, and finally, let us be clear regarding the true nature of this anti-Red campaign. Though words like "McCarthyite" or "Red baiter" may conjure up strong unpleasant reactions, visions of the demonic J. Edgar Hoover's FBI on rampages, the punishment dealt to members of the CPUSA and sympathizers was hardly severe or cruel. Even in the heyday of the excessive "Red scares" during the 1920s, when "Red squads" freely ignored basic civil liberties, the penalties for dissent—mainly deportation of aliens—never remotely compared to brutalities carried out in the Soviet Union, Nazi Germany, or Communist China. Surely Cold War anti-Red tactics—compulsory loyalty oaths, FBI infiltration of leftish groups, deportation, lists of subversive organizations, refusal to grant passports, blacklisting, firings, hostile questioning before an investigating committee—are minor inconveniences compared to years of forced labor, incarceration in mental hospitals, or execution. Constitutional abuses did occur, but if flaws are the sole criterion to render government action misguided, few anti-criminal campaigns pass muster. It is an undertaking of balance and circumstances. Not even the most vehement anti-Communist official called for slave labor camps for suspected Marxists.

The relatively mild character of this legal assault against the CPUSA is equally noteworthy. Within government, including the Justice Department and the FBI, great restraint was often shown despite intense public clamor for harsh action. The government typically moved cautiously, sometimes reluctantly, with ever an eye to constitutional principles of free speech and free association. Arrests occurred only after extensive documentation and full scrutiny of all the legal ramifications (Belknap, 1977, Chapter 2). When accused Communists did come to trial as in 1948 with the Smith Act prosecutions, the accused were immediately released on relatively low bail, were allowed an extensive team of defense lawyers, and were granted innumerable accommodations to defend themselves (Belknap, 1977, Chapters 3, 4). Trials were public, time-consuming, and often attracted endless courthouse rallies to free the accused.

The numbers prosecuted, by government itself or by institutions such as universities, let alone convicted, were relatively small, even as a portion of the active far-left. At the national level, exactly 140 Communists or Communist sympathizers spent time in jail for violating the Smith Act or for contempt of Congress (cited in Roche, 1989). And, such incarcerations were all accomplished legally, with due process, not secretly in star chambers. Most jail terms, moreover, were relatively brief. The maximum jail term given to members of the CPUSA convicted under the Smith Act was five years plus a $10,000 fine (Belknap, 1977, 115). Many guilty Soviet agents never served time. Ellen W. Schrecker's *No Ivory Tower: McCarthyism and the Universities* (1986) provides a highly sympathetic account of those persecuted, but she concludes that only about one hundred university faculty members were fired or did not have their contracts renewed due to anti-Communist pressure.[7] John P. Roche, who taught at various universities during this Cold War period and was an active Socialist and ACLU official, personally recounts that this alleged "Red terror" was a distant side-show on apathetic college campuses (Roche, 1989).[8]

These facts are all too easily obscured by current infatuation with McCarthyism that takes the anti-Communist impulse of the 1950s and raises it up to the era's defining and catastrophic feature. An entire literary industry, from PBS specials ("Seeing Red") to books like David Caute's *The Great Fear* (1978), convey the vague impression that tens of thousands of perfectly respectable liberals, like the 112,000 people of Japanese ancestry interned during World War II, were ruthlessly hunted down by crazed right wingers. The evidence, however, offers a contrary picture. Intense commotion, dramatic confrontations on national TV, vocal cries of "injustice" and the like need not reflect a barbaric political pogrom. Though excesses undoubtedly transpired and innocent people were harmed, a perspective must be maintained. Let us not equate ceaseless oratory of repression with the transformation of the US into a totalitarian state.

Conclusions: A Lesson in Democratic Repression

Our analysis reveals an odd paradox. On the one hand, investigators who study attitude-based tolerance are reluctant to discuss its restriction. Though almost all cite Locke and Mill, these scholars, unlike Locke and Mill, apparently avoid balancing attempts. Developing a framework to weigh tolerance against community seems, perhaps, too formidable or even unnecessary. But, where scholars fear to tread, ordinary citizens and public officials comfortably proceed. Unburdened by esoteric academic notions of democratic theory, judgments are quickly passed. That these choices may contravene arcane theoretical democratic requirements hardly inhibits. Perhaps non-scholars must bend theory to accommodate an uncertain, sometimes dangerous reality. Obviously, there is some joining to be done here.

How, then, is this reconciling to be accomplished? Let us offer one possibility: Derive lessons from the history of intolerance. By examining records of repression, we can judge when such intolerance was *democratically* justified. This process assumes that forceful repression of dissidence is periodically permissible. As Andrew R. Cecil, one of the few scholars to acknowledge this difficult weighing, put it, "The democratic State has the duty to protect its primary and essential right of preservation and has the authority to judge regulations required in the interest of public safety and welfare (Cecil, 1990, 148). The question is *when,* not *if.* This strategy is, of course, familiar to constitutional scholars teasing out First Amendment guiding principles. Our focus, however, extends beyond translating a single principle. We probe the circumstances surrounding citizen-inspired action when it passes through elected representatives. We search for evidence of democratic repression. For example, was harsh intolerance a rash, impetuous, undebated act made under emotional strain? Did documented circumstances warrant the potential risks to free expression? Were measures lawful? Though instances of legally sanctioned repressive force are rare in U.S. history, they are consequential and offer a superb opportunity to explore a difficult question.

On the eve of the Second World War, Congress enacted The Alien Registration Act of 1940, better known as the Smith Act. As the first peacetime sedition act passed in more than 140 years, civil libertarians have long condemned this statute as the essence of unjustified political repression. McClosky and Brill's (1983, 12) exhaustive study of tolerance offers a view typical in this literature, characterizing the Smith Act a "legislative abuse of civil liberties." This Act sought multiple objectives, but the critical portion (Section 2) made it unlawful to knowingly advocate or teach the overthrow of the government of the United States by force or violence, print or distribute writings of this advocacy, and organize or knowingly become a member of a group advocating such violent overthrow. Though the Communist Party is not mentioned by name, little doubt exists that outlawing the CPUSA was the statute's principal intent (Pritchett, 1977, 375). Let us be clear on what this statute did not do. Criticizing the government or seeking change through elections, lobbying, and so on remained untouched. Nor was there any reference to ideological content—it applied equally to neo-Nazis and the Klan. The legislation was aimed at conspiracy to promote active, violent subversion, not the marketplace of ideas and peaceful democratic action.

Evaluating the Smith Act requires attention to the cumulation of several legal ventures and specific historical circumstances. Efforts to produce a national sedition law dealing with Marxist radicals date to the immediate post-World War I period. Indeed, some seventy bills to accomplish this task were introduced in Congress during 1919 and 1920, but widespread public opposition doomed them all (Belknap, 1977, 16). A similar barrage of proposed sedition legislation appeared in the 1930 Congress, but again public outcry brought its defeat. In 1935, yet a third effort to stamp out anti-government subversion emerged. Despite strong military backing and the efforts of untold patriotic and business groups, vocal opposition, especially from law professors and publishers, prevailed. A comparable 1936 measure received even less support and quickly died. In 1938, opponents of Communism and other such movements would try again, and more than 100 bills were introduced, one of which, H.R. 5138, eventually became the Smith Act.

Times had changed by 1939 and objection to a national sedition bill weakened. Opposition mail disproportionately originated from New York and bore the not-so-subtle stamp of CPUSA instigation. Labor unions, past enemies of such measures, largely stood silent. Only the ACLU plus a few left-leaning members of Congress intensely objected. Particularly quiet were newspapers and publishers, past doubters worried over restricting public debate. Support, however, was widespread. Congress and its committees deliberated for a year, debated language, negotiated compromises, and listened to innumerable appeals. In June of 1940, the Smith Act passed and was soon signed by President Roosevelt.

Historical details are important in understanding this statute. Until August of 1939 and the signing of the Hitler-Stalin non-aggression pact, the CPUSA was very much in an accommodationist mood with government policy. It was the era of Popular Fronts, broad-based alliances of anti-fascists, and working within a democratic framework. In fact, it was not unusual for Communist sympathizers to enter Roosevelt's New Deal and the newly emergent CIO. To be sure, individual states had legally prosecuted a small number of Communists and calls for repression existed, but the U.S. and USSR were not at war and the foreign domination of the CPUSA was murky. The position that Communists were just another radical political group, perhaps no different from indigenous radical organizations, was at least plausible.

The Hitler-Stalin non-aggression pact dramatically altered political reality. Moscow gave the orders and the U.S. party jumped immediately. Now the CPUSA abruptly joined forces with anti-Roosevelt isolationists proclaiming, "The Yanks Are Not Coming." It was evident that if American Communists were not under direct Soviet control, they were performing a convincing imitation. Numerous party members and sympathizers abandoned ship in disgust. Finally, the outbreak of a European war in September of 1939, and the realization that the U.S. might well be drawn into it, heightened the need for laws addressing espionage and subversion. After all, World War I subversive activities and actual homefront sabotage were still remembered.

This historical sketch reveals that the Smith Act did not unexpectedly erupt as a Red-scare hysteria. Previous legislative versions had been pondered by Congress and rejected, after vocal public pressure. If uncontrollable national paranoia were sufficient to instigate a national sedition law, this would have transpired twenty years earlier when such sentiment was more strident. Moreover, legislative drafting received considerable care, as would be expected given the potential legal challenge. It did not single out organizations by name or confine itself ideologically (and future prosecutions were not one-sided). Nor did the Act spark an immediate attack on the CPUSA. In fact, an eight-year period elapsed between passage and the first anti-Communist prosecution (ironically, the CPUSA supported the Act when directed against their Trotskyite enemy). As already described, the prosecution was scrupulous: an enormous amount of evidence was collected, the public trial (lasting nine months and costing the government one million dollars) fully honored due process. The conviction of eleven people, moreover, is hardly a nationwide roundup. In fact, when the convictions were announced, public and newspaper support was overwhelmingly positive across the political spectrum. Even magazines critical of the Smith Act commended the government for its legal fairness and patience (Belknap, 1977, 114-116).[9]

Finally, in 1951 when it first came before the Supreme Court as *Dennis v. United States,* the Smith Act survived constitutional scrutiny by a six-to-two vote. Several distinct judicial opinions supported this constitutionality. Writing on behalf of four of the majority, Chief Justice Vinson argued that surely the government possessed the right to safeguard itself against violent force. As for the mere expression of dissent, apart from violent action, Vinson invoked the "clear and present danger" doctrine—the government is not compelled to wait "until the *putsch* is about to be executed, the plans have been laid and the signal is awaited" (cited in Pritchett, 1977, 375). Justices Frankfurter and Jackson concurred separately in Vinson's opinion. Jackson's conclusion is especially noteworthy for it went beyond depicting the CPUSA as a mere contemporary danger. Jackson stressed the ideology's modern nature, its infatuation with secrecy, its capacity for well-organized subversion, its totalitarian temper, its complete domination by a hostile foreign power, and its international successes. Communists are not insignificant street-corner orators. Frankfurter paid homage to the importance of free and open debate, but similarly acknowledged the grim political reality of fighting organized subversion. He concluded that Congress, not the judicial branch, is best suited to untangle this problem (Greenawalt, 1989, 203).

The 1957 Supreme Court case of *Yates v. United States* again raised the constitutionality issue. *Yates* resulted from federal prosecution and conviction of fourteen Communists under the Smith Act. Though acknowledging the Smith Act's constitutionality, convictions of five of the fourteen convicted Communists were nevertheless overturned. The decision sharply restricted the Smith Act's implementation. In particular, CPUSA membership, in and of itself, did not constitute proof of violent subversion; one had to be personally guilty of a subversive act, not guilty solely by association. The sentences of the remaining nine were upheld, though the Justice Department eventually requested that the original indictments against these Communists be dropped for insufficient evidence. In sum, though the Smith Act served as an important anti-Communist weapon in the late 1940s and early 1950s, by the decade's end judicial reinterpretation had made it largely obsolete. The threat had been addressed.

What do all these accounts inform us about intolerance? Most evidently, there are occasions when democratic government can legitimately repress forcefully, provided it is done deliberately, cautiously and in accordance with democratic procedures. Midnight raids against lawful but hated dissenters is not permitted intolerance. Nor is firing a teacher because he or she writes controversial magazine stories. Nevertheless, enacting a sedition law and enforcing it against those who will, if at all possible, subvert a democratically constituted government is authorized. Tolerance in a democracy may be generous but it is not a blank-check invitation.

This is an unadorned admonition, but it is exceedingly perplexing in application. There is no neat formula, nor can one be furnished. Searching for an effortless, logical, abstract way to establish the point at which a democratic group crosses the line and transforms itself into a subversive conspiracy is foolhardy. No scrutiny of democratic theory can supply this convenient standard. Equally relevant, citizens, no doubt, cannot render such decisions unaided. Thus, it would be senseless to ask them about obscure organizations engaged in indistinct activities. It is the evidence of wrongdoing that matters, not the embrace of slogans. Providing this documentation is the job of the police, the FBI, other law enforcement professionals, the mass media, and citizens themselves. Over time, reasonable proof of such subversive activity may surface. Perhaps not conclusive, airtight evidence, but proof enough to sound the alarm.

Much remains to be done to fashion distinguishing criteria. Tolerance research, unfortunately, continues to be fixed on unreflective celebration of tolerance or ferreting out the latest suppressive urges of citizens. Surely, resolving when abhorrence is justified, even commendable, is a worthy task. To argue that all intolerance, regardless of object and circumstances, is politically equal ignores reality. Condemning the CPUSA in 1948 differs greatly from condemning it in 1998, though both actions display intolerance. Tolerance is not an abstraction always in too short supply; it depends on circumstances.

NOTES

1. It is worth mentioning that the education literature on tolerance (to be explored in Chapter 8) seemingly "solves" this contradiction between maintaining order and promoting tolerance by substituting the term *zero tolerance* for intolerance. Hence, Whereas a sweeping tolerance for things different is celebrated, there will be zero tolerance for "bad" things such as sexual harassment. Perhaps there exists the fear that simply endorsing intolerance as a legitimate behavior unleashes some evil spirit. This resembles the practices of certain religions where the names of powerful demons cannot be uttered in public without grave consequences.

2. An interesting oddity of this anti-Communist campaign was that the momentum for legally requiring anti-Communist indoctrination in the schools picked up only in the late 1950s, well after the most highly publicized incidents of Communist subversion. Until that time, civic education treated the subject rather informally, often leaving it up to individual teachers or school boards. Perhaps the creeping acceptance of the USSR coupled with its sudden emergence as a technological power rekindled fears (see Zellman, 1965, for the details of this rush to explicitly attack Communism in the schools).

3. Koch (1994, 231) also makes the important, but seldom realized, point that the support of well-known Hollywood, Broadway, and literary personalities was an important source of party funds. Money raised for a variety of idealistic campaigns plus dues usually found its way to far "dirtier" activities.

4. An interesting example of how scholars misperceived the true nature of the Soviet Union is revealed in Walsh (1944). Walsh stratified his sample by political knowledge using three questions. One of the questions deals with the objectives of the Soviet Union; the alternative indicating the Soviet's goal of worldwide expansion is scored as "an error" in this knowledge quiz.

5. A small number of such questions were asked in the very early days of the Cold War. For example, a July 1946 AIPO poll asked if U.S. Communists should be allowed to hold civil service jobs; 69% said no compared to 17% yes. The same poll asked if CPUSA members are loyal to the USSR or the USA. Twice as many answered "the Soviet Union" (cited in Cantril, 1951).

6. Ironically, when the Smith Act was first employed during World War II, it was used against the Trotskyites, the arch enemy of the CPUSA. It was also used against those suspected of working on behalf on the Nazis. In both instances, this government repression was cheered on by the CPUSA. Only when the Smith Act was turned on them did they discover all its anti-civil libertarian features (See Belknap, 1977, 38-40).

7. Schrecker's assessment of the McCarthyite effect on academic life is very revealing. She frankly admits that no firm numbers exist on who was mistakenly punished though it must have been "in the hundreds" (10). It is tacitly assumed, moreover, that all those harmed did not deserve harm. To appreciate her view, consider the following statement: "McCarthyism was amazingly effective. It produced one of the most severe episodes of political repression the United States has ever experienced. Only two people were killed; only a few hundred when to jail. *Its mildness may have well contributed to its efficacy* (9, italics added).

8. Roche also compares the campus anti-Red atmosphere of the 1950s with the turmoil of the 1960s and beyond. In his view, the more recent "political correctness" atmosphere, from affecting Vietnam war positions to discussing affirmative action, is far more oppressive than McCarthyism.

9. One interesting historical note concerns the jury's composition. Initially, the defense argued that Communists could never receive a fair trial because the jury would be dominated by the oppressors of workers. The jury actually selected, however, was truly proletarian in composition and included three blacks. Seven of the twelve were women. Not a single capitalist served. The jury's foreman was a black housewife and part-time dressmaker (Belknap, 1977, 78).

5

Political Diversity

A ttitudinal tolerance, as the existent research literature conceives it, is but a means to an end—facilitating a multiplicity of ideas and sects. It is assumed that if attitudinal intolerance grew, unorthodox predilections would similarly diminish. Chapter 3 argued that this theoretical connective linkage, the *leitmotiv* of a burgeoning scholarly literature, remains largely an undocumented supposition. Here, we demonstrate empirically the faintness of this connection. A virtual zoo of heresies, unpopular causes, and loathsome groups can easily coexist with inhospitable atmospheres. It would be as if a visiting Martian concluded that no weeds and insects could possibly thrive given the immense industry dedicated to their eradication. Deep aversion and successful extermination are hardly identical.

Fleshing out the detailed linkage between mass opinion and would-be suffocating campaigns is not our task. Such an endeavor, though obligatory for those who traffic in attitude-based tolerance research, is unnecessary here. We instead work backwards, starting with the critical end product—unhampered political diversity. After all, if there is no smothering of nonconformity, no offense against democratic vitality, why delve into the murky waters of citizen sentiment hunting for intolerance? In social science terminology, we begin with the dependent variable and then, having established its nature, we can search out explanatory independent variables. As Chapter 3 lamented, the study of tolerance now exists largely as a devotion to a potentially powerful independent variable—citizen views—inattentive to what might be explained.

This survey of heresies is more than a snapshot of current political proclivities; it endeavors to reorient tolerance inquiries away from individual psychology and toward assessments of society at large. Our substantive argument coexists with advancing an alternative research paradigm. This should be judged independently of any marshaled empirical evidence regarding the authenticity of contemporary tolerance. That is, even if one were to dispute our substantive conclusions, to wit, to believe that our claim of tolerance is exaggerated, this disagreement should not invalidate our alternative conceptual framework. Evidence and theoretical structure necessitate distinct evaluations.

Demonstrating this proliferating jumble of fringe sentiments is ironic given that our era abounds with cries of suppression, repression, and forceful stifling of "diversity." Any hint of opposition to the unconventional surely elicits howls of "McCarthyism." For adherents of off-center views, it has almost become axiomatic that they confront powerful hostile forces. Seldom is this apprehensive vision challenged; even fewer dare hint self-serving paranoia-like delusion. Intolerance, proclaim those living outside the doctrinal mainstream, is an inescapable societal pathology. This odd paradox of the tolerated wailing intolerance is especially prominent among university academics, those disproportionally molding public discourse. This irony is only compounded when self-depicted victims of confinement enjoy intellectual prestige while comfortably expanding their supposedly "harassed" unorthodoxies. We hope to bring some much need reality to this apocalyptic apparition.

Two Complexities

Our core argument is that unpopular, even loathsome, groups manage survival despite substantial citizen intolerance. This contrasting of robustness with the lingering legacy of citizen attitudinal intolerance constitutes plausible evidence for our argument, but it is not a scientific demonstration of independence. It is still possible that citizen views do shape what survives politically, though this relationship may be beyond our inquiry. The limitations of our investigation should be kept handy; we do not wish to exceed our evidence. Far more is required to elevate our contention to scientific status. To make this incompleteness crystal clear, let us take two brief side-tours, one conceptual, the other concerning evidence.

Conceptual Uncertainty

To tease out this complicated relationship between citizen sentiment and repression, precise over-time data on both citizen attitudes and heretical vigor requires alignment. If this task were accomplished and if those researchers who stress attitudinal tolerance's political influence are correct, political diversity would mimic shifting public opinion. During the early 1950s, for example, when anti-Communism hysteria reached its apogee, Marxism would practically have vanished from the landscape. However, in the 1960s, as Cold War worries gave way to apprehension over a self-indulgent counterculture, black nationalism and violent anti-Vietnam war protests, Marxists could return from hiding, so to speak. In this scenario, a credible case exists that public intolerance causally determines the presence of once-hated sentiment.

Yet, almost identical data might sustain the opposite conclusion: The emergence of vigorous though friendless ideas helped reduce public aversion. A possible sequence might be (1) public hostility erupts, (2) hated organizations respond with energetic protective propaganda, and (3) these organizations battle back public antagonism. This conclusion assigns public sentiment a vastly different role than in the first argument—it is a *consequence* of unorthodox vigor, not a cause. It all depends on which came first, public attitudes or multiplying of the unpopular. It is also conceivable that attitudinal intolerance results from the emergence of a once repressed viewpoint: Openness breeds intolerance. Indeed, the National Gay and Lesbian Task Force, a group monitoring anti-gay violence, even suggests that recent gay boldness has instigated a backlash (NGLTF fact sheet, July 1996). A further wrinkle is also possible: Mass intolerance is but the result of elite manipulation. The connection between attitudinal tolerance and what exists is spurious. To wit, to advance their own agendas, political leaders whip up and turn off mass hysteria. It might be argued, for example, that the popular anti-Communism of the 1950s merely reflected the government's anti-Soviet policy. When conditions altered, "Red-baiting" was cooled down by those in power.

Unraveling these multiple chicken and egg relationships is critical. Moreover, all casual relationships can coexist simultaneously—the public independently softens its hostility, which encourages once-hated tendencies to surface, which, in turn, nurtures approving sentiment for some and heightened hostility for others. Similarly, government inspires intolerance, but these views take on a life of their own and ultimately independently influence elite policy making. Unfortunately, lacking the necessary over-time data and insight into elite machinations, we are limited to juxtaposing attitudes and diversity of view during one historical moment.

Insufficient Evidence

The second complexity disturbing the juxtaposition of attitudes and diversity also entails inadequate information, though here the obstacle is knowledge of repression. Specifically, concentrating on public attitudinal intolerance may miss the real culprit in a repressive campaign. There *really* is intolerance but it cannot be discovered via the survey. Chapter 2, it will be recalled, submitted that "objective" and "subjective" intolerance may diverge widely. An extensive but almost entirely invisible crusade can be waged against the unpopular. Its casualties may even be oblivious, imputing their unfortunate fates to luck or personal shortcomings. Hence, the hidden character of repression makes the impression of genuine openness an illusion. And, what does ultimately emerge, despite its abundance, may only be a small portion of sought expression.

The government's assault against the so-called alternative press in the mid-1960s and early 1970s illustrates this possibility. The "alternatives" were rambunctious newspapers with colorful names—*Quicksilver Times, Berkeley Barb* and *Queen City Express*—run by young radicals mixing anti-war messages with hedonistic liberation (see Rips, 1981 for the details). Unknown to editors and writers, the national government waged a systematic battle to discredit and eventually destroy their operations. It was wholly undercover and devious. Among other tactics, government infiltrators instigated personal jealousies, promoted dissension, and committed outrageous, discrediting, and embarrassing acts. Anonymous letters from federal agents were mailed to school officials. Parents received disturbing information stories of drug use and sexual peccadilloes (letters were often signed "A concerned citizen"). Local police departments cooperated with highly disruptive drug raids. Advertisers under pressure removed ads. The government also leaked outrageous and sometimes fabricated stories of illicit behavior to the conventional media where it surfaced as "objective" news. Only years later, thanks to diligent legal work plus the Freedom of Information Act, did the true nature of this subversive harassment surface. If not for a few persistent individuals, the sudden demise of the alternative press would have appeared perfectly natural.

This tale alerts us to the possibility that depicting thriving unorthodoxy cannot demonstrate conclusively the absence of repressive intolerance. Nor would poll data reveal it. It could be energetically employed though barely recognized. It may also exist purely psychologically but very realistically, not physically—lingering vivid memories of unpleasant fates once suffered by the politically disagreeable. Despite our effort to uncover intolerance, we cannot probe the FBI's clandestine workings, the local police's secret "Red

Squad," or any other potential instrument of repression to provide the authentic account. Our canvass only portrays existent diversity, implicitly contending that if powerful repressive forces continue, they appear ineffectual. Those insisting otherwise, that stifling antagonism is everywhere, may be correct, though our evidence suggests otherwise.

Plan of Analysis

Demonstrating tolerance at the systemic level involves two tasks. First, depicting heterogeneity and, second (addressed in the following chapter), calibrating the effect of intolerance on this diversity. Each is a daunting task. The ever-evolving political life-forms vary from untold highly organized groups to some unknowable number of ill-formed nebulous "tendencies." An exhaustive enumeration would resemble an inquiry into all politics. Similarly, assembling oppositional urges, from unverified allegation from the self-certified oppressed to more concrete legal documentation, would be even more monumental. Nevertheless, it is insufficient to proclaim "a lot thrives despite malice" and retire from the field. To balance the obligation for both rich detail and practical constraints, we limit ourselves to two general segments of the political spectrum often raised in scholarly tolerance studies, namely, socialism/Marxism and the promotion of homosexuality.

Chapter 3 revealed that survey questions mentioning socialists, Communists, and homosexuals were staples central to the attitude-based tolerance literature. The poll results, moreover, often painted a troubling picture of ideas worthy of protection being at risk. In 1972, for example, the NORC GSS survey revealed only a bare majority of those interviewed would allow admitted Communists to speak in public or have a Marxist book in a library. A clear majority would deny a college teaching position to this person. Identical questions asked during the early 1990s, after the Soviet Union collapse, still showed strong domestic antipathy to Marxism—about 30 percent still refused an admitted Communist permission to speak publicly, and nearly 40 prcent rejected his or her right to teach college.[1]

Survey data on gay rights depict a parallel softening between the 1970s and the early '90s though significant aversion remains. Assessing the true level of this antipathy depends on which poll questions are scrutinized. On the side suggesting tolerance is a 1994 General Social Survey question showing that "only" 26 percent would withhold a college teaching position to an admitted homosexual and a "mere" 28 percent are inclined to remove a library book advancing homosexuality (GSS Surveys, 1972-1994, 102-

104). But not all is so rosy for gays, at least according to other attitudinal data. Between 1973 and 1998 NORC questions regularly inquired into whether same-sex relations were morally wrong. The proportion saying "not wrong" never exceed 15 percent (Smith, 1990). When this question was asked again in 1994, the proportion saying that homosexuality was not immoral had risen to 23 percent. Even in 1996, when the issue of gay rights had long been on the public agenda and was afforded favorable publicity, some 61 percent opined that homosexuality was morally wrong. NORC/ Gallup data during the same period never found a majority accepting the legalization of homosexuality. A 1992 *Newsweek/*Gallup poll reports that 57 percent do not consider homosexuality an acceptable lifestyle; only 54 percent believe that gays should be hired as high school teachers (the figure for grade school teachers is 51 percent). Forty-four percent in the same survey believe that gay rights are a threat to the American family and its values.

Marxists and gays are also important for illustrative purposes because these advocates—in contrast to atheists, another once-mentioned heretical view—continue to persevere politically, frequently prominently. Their disputatious doctrinal nature, their periodic public challenge to political convention, makes them unambiguously controversial for intolerant-minded citizens. If Americans are committed to translating their intolerant views into forceful repression, these two contentious collections of sentiments are superb candidates. Surely society has not yet welcomed Marxism and nontraditional sexual orientation into the sociopolitical mainstream.

From the onset, we confess to a necessarily unsystematic and inexact canvass. Readers may periodically complain—perhaps rightfully—that it lapses into tedium and microscopic detail. This excess is intentional; no alternate procedure commends itself for convincingly documenting our overriding point. We likewise concede that some misclassification is inevitable while political content may be murky or disguised. Our sweep of Marxist/ Socialists is broad, ranging from the traditional, well-defined Communist Party USA to obscure sects whose espousal of socialistic principles is barely audible. Some preach a rhetoric of political violence; others are little more than lethargic employee-run bookstores more agitated with paying the rent than with world revolution. Estimating group size or probing actual behavior is a formidable enterprise. In assembling an overview, mere existence is what is to be established, not precise scientific depictions.

Ditto for our treatment of sexual orientation tendencies, inclinations, and affinity groups. Enormous variety inheres in doctrine and activism; some shade off into therapy activities minimally attending the political. Militant high-profile gay activist organizations coexist with quiet academic-style discussion seminars. Groups also mutate over time; yesterday's militant provocateurs may be today's moribund mailing list. Finally, we occasionally rely heavily on classification decisions and compilations executed by others. An exhaustive, accurate encyclopedia with a common definitional framework is a scholarly army's life work, no doubt out-of-date when finally issued.

The Landscape—A Quick Overview

We commence our high altitude, albeit somewhat eclectic, reconnaissance with the closest approximation of an inventory of functioning radical and leftist political penchants, Laird Wilcox's *Guide to the American Left: Directory and Bibliography* (1988). Wilcox has spent three decades scrutinizing this immense disparate phenomenon. Though he plainly admits he is unable to depict each group's precise personality, mountains of germane evidence come from massive collections of newspapers and pamphlets now assembled at the University of Kansas Library. The 1988 version, compiled at the end of the Reagan presidency, offers thirty-two pages of tiny typescript for U.S. left-oriented groups and covers several different political inclinations, from environmentalists to broad-based liberal organizations (a companion volume covers the spectrum's right side). This collection is routinely updated—all groups cited existed in 1988. His label "Marxist-Socialist" focuses on the revolutionary, radical character of a group; these are not "good government" reform groups. "Feminist-gay" groups are avowedly political, not innocuous psychological self-help entities.

If one hypothesizes that loathsome Marxists and sexual politics groups are on the endangered species list—a supposition occasionally endorsed by those proclaiming the need for greater tolerance—Wilcox's compilation advertises otherwise. A simple count reveals 1,122 separate Marxist-Socialist groups and 495 Feminist-Gay organizations of one type or another in 1988. A few are instantly recognizable to students of American political history as familiar old-line, traditional, radical groups. Still functioning, for example, are the Industrial Workers of the World, The Communist Party USA and the Socialist Workers Party. By contrast, many have adopted more novel, creative names, perhaps to reflect their idiosyncratic approach—for example, the Old Wives Tales Lesbian Bookshop of San Francisco, California and the Fort Hill Fagots for Freedom of Roxbury, Massachusetts.

A cursory overview of this listing suggests that joining a widely untolerated controversial Marxist or sexual politics group would be relatively convenient. Organizations seldom disguise their authentic purpose, there is no hiding behind innocuous-sounding euphemism as was once common for controversial "front organizations." Truth in labeling prevails. To wit, there is the American-Soviet Friendship Committee, the Center for Marxist Education and the Lesbian/Gay Labor Alliance. Moreover, most purveyors of unorthodoxy are not seeking to elude government or mobs of enraged citizens or otherwise cover their tracks to escape persecution. The United States is not Soviet-era Eastern Europe in which dissidents survived by encoded names and secret headquarters. Nearly all, even the most outlandish, list easy-to-find addresses. The Communist Party, for those who wish to enroll, is centrally located at 239 West 23rd Street in Manhattan; the International Workers of the World, the so-called Wobblies who once enjoyed a reputation for violence, can be found at 3435 North Sheffield, Chicago, Illinois.

Nor are these groups safely concentrated in large urban areas traditionally associated with renowned radicalism. To be sure, there is an expected geographical pattern—New York City predictably harbors numerous leftish groups—but even the hinterland possesses its share of groups guaranteed to outrage the intolerantly inclined. The Alliance of Lesbian Activists resides in Luttell, Tennessee; Jackson, Mississippi is home to the Workers of the World Party. Silicon Valley's homosexuals have High Tech Gays located in San Jose. At least in 1988, when these data were current, virtually all Americans lived in proximity to a wide variety of Marxist-Socialist and sexual politics organizations. Bookstores catering to those with unorthodox political tastes are nearly everywhere. A Philadelphia Marxist might find a cornucopia of materials, from the writing of Lenin to announcements of meetings, at Wooden Shoe Books and the W. E. B. DuBois Bookstore. It is hard to argue that citizens interested in these political causes must wander around the wilderness to find cobelievers.[2]

The Landscape: A Closer Inspection of Gay Political Expression

To demonstrate the sheer variety of tendencies allegedly on the political endangered list, this multiplicity demands depiction in near-exhausting detail. We do not wish to be accused of deceptively offering up a few choice examples or empty numbers to aver (falsely) widespread tolerance. Let us begin with a simple but crucial point: Nonconformists need not be diligent researchers to ferret out compatriots. Lists are hardly hidden away under lock and key. Compilations of sexual orientation assemblages involving political relevance are openly listed in miscellaneous commercial resources, most of which are financially subsidized by paid advertising. Consider, for example, a would-be gay activist living in the Chicago area seeking greater involvement. Presently, three newspapers serve this gay citizenry and occasionally list gay-oriented associations with political overtones. The October 26, 1995 *Windy City Times: Chicago's Gay and Lesbian Newsweekly* offers a typical community service bulletin board inventorying hotlines, entertainment, counseling, religious congregations, sports clubs, medical services, and politics (among other resources). Under the political heading are the affiliates of well-known organizations, such as ACT-UP! and Queer Nation, plus a variety of less familiar names: Coalition for Positive Sexuality, Bisexual Political Action Coalition, and the Chicago Area Republican Organization, to enumerate but a few possibilities.

If this compilation proves insufficient, a more comprehensive selection of possibilities appears in *Out,* a regularly published Chicago-based handbook for services and businesses with a gay clientele. The Summer/Fall 1995 issue is typical in its offerings. For Blacks in or near Chicago, for example, organizations include Active Proud Black Lesbians and Gays, African American Womyn's Alliance, Chicago Black Lesbians and Gays, and Image Plus (for young Blacks). Abundant other affinity associations exist, some based on a common heritage such as Irish Queers others sharing a hobby or occupation, such as the Illinois Gay Rodeo Association. If this compilation were insufficient, *Out* provides a register of twenty-three gay-lesbian related newspapers, magazines, and resource guides just in Illinois, complete with phone numbers and addresses.

The gay newspaper industry's expanse is seldom appreciated by outsiders. James Sorrells' 1993 compilation of gay community newspapers in the United States does, however, offer a glimpse. Excluded were erotic theme periodicals, a staple of the gay-oriented print market.Though this listing is not claimed to be exhaustive, some 300 U.S. newspapers did circulate. Not unexpectedly, a familiar geographical concentration in large coastal urban areas emerges, but only Wyoming, North Dakota, and Montana lack a paper. Several flourish in localities not usually associated with a gay presence—the *Lesbian World Newsletter* in Euclid, Ohio and *The Klondyke Kontact* in Anchorage, Alaska, for example. A few claim notable circulation for newspapers of this type—the *Gayly Oklahoman* in Oklahoma City, Oklahoma had a circulation of 10,000 in 1993 (Sorrells, 1993, 47). To be sure, many such newspapers have uncertain survival rates and modest circulations. But what is important for our purposes is concrete documentation of communication channels that facilitate mobilization. These are real papers, not possibilities;

no doubt, anti-gay activities will receive prompt attention in places like Reno, Nevada, Omaha, Nebraska and Concord, New Hampshire thanks to these newspapers. This network also has the assistance of two gay journalistic organizations, the Gay & Lesbian Press Association of Universal City, California and the National Lesbian and Gay Journalism Association in Oakland, California.

If we direct our tour away from the above-board gay media outlets and venture into the more underground portion of the gay scene, the number of print outlets explodes. Indeed, most citizens, even those who might claim some familiarity with unconventional lifestyles, cannot possibly imagine what transpires beyond what is displayed at ordinary newsstands. *Factsheet5* is a periodical that regularly catalogues and briefly summarizes underground magazines (denoted as " 'zines" in this industry). In the mid-1990s, thousands of such zines circulated, ranging from the humorous to home-made poetry reviews. Many zines are one-person, unfocused, amateurish efforts, but many more cater to well-defined though below-the-surface unconventional groups. One of the largest and fastest growing specialties is a category called "Queer."

Factsheet5 lists at least *seventy* magazines devoted exclusively to homosexual or "Queer" topics (others mingle homosexuality and heterosexuality but these are excluded). Several would give credence to homophobic nightmares of what contemporary homosexuality is "really" like. Most conspicuously, there is the *Nambla Bulletin, Voice of the North American Man/Boy Love Association.* Let us be explicit here: This is an organization promoting (illegal) sexual relationships between adult men and boys. Articles in other magazines also acknowledge illegality—for example, sex in public toilets. *Pornorama* celebrates a life of unbridled hedonistic sexual pursuit for lesbians. For cross-dressers there is *Dragazine*; fanciers of unconventional sexual practices can read *Fetish Times.* Among the more provocative titles are *Rampaging Teenage Pervert, Bitch, Shoot People at Random, Something Queer is Going On,* and *Naked Teenagers that Fight Crime.* There are serious magazines dealing with AIDS, gay literature, discrimination among gays themselves, and censorship; others are comic books trying to offend with the outrageous. More than a handful proffer graphic, unrestrained visions of gay life that most citizens would judge to be lewd or pornographic.

To repeat what has become an *idée fixe,* there exists a lot "out here" for gays, regardless of how unconventional their views or tastes. And, somewhat less obvious, though not all declare explicit political content, their inherent nature resists the political status quo. This is tolerance in being, over and above tolerance in principle. Complaints of censorship and repression must be judged alongside these seventy-plus freely circulated magazines (none of which hides its address) that explicitly challenge conventional sexual morality.

Returning to more mainstream publication outlets, various national reference-like compendiums provide would-be sexual orientation politics participants instant access to expansive informational networks. One exemplar is the *Gayellow Pages* which, like its Yellow Pages namesake, furnishes an encyclopedic catalogue of services and organizations. Under the general heading of "Organization Resources" are sundry subheadings that would seemingly satisfy almost any specialized concern. Entries occasionally include publications and electronic network addresses. A brief sampling must suffice to capture this variety: Bisexual Resource Center, American Federation of Teachers National Gay and Lesbian Caucus, Gay & Lesbian Press Association, Gay/Lesbian Postal Employee Network, National Gay Pilots Association, Campaign to End Homophobia, Gay & Lesbian Advocacy Research Project, Overlooked Opinions (covers public opinion polling of gays and lesbians), Gay & Lesbian Labor Activist Network, Human Rights Campaign Fund, National Center for Lesbian Rights, National Gay and Lesbian Task Force, Pro-Life Alliance of Gays & Lesbians, and Republicans for Individual Freedoms, among the many dozen listings.

This depiction of materials sympathetic to the gay political agenda expands yet further when specialized journals, magazines, and mainstream publishers printing openly gay tracts are included. Though the radical alternative press of the 1970s may have gained uninvited government suppression, gay-oriented materials today flourish, often readily available, even in many national chain bookstores, or by mail. If a repression campaign is underway, it must be judged a pathetic failure. Our *tour d'horizon* includes the widely distributed *Advocate (*circulation 76,000), which, like many gay-oriented periodicals, combines intermittent political espousal and reporting gay-related events with entertainment. A similar mass circulation gay magazine is *Out.* For African American gays there is *BLK,* and books of interest to gays are noted in the *Lambda Book Report* and *The Lesbian Review of Books.* Gay-oriented magazines catering to more specialized markets periodically slip in political material (such as government funding on AIDS research) between features on fashion, travel, and entertainment. *I O: The Essential Queer Youth Magazine* exemplifies this category. Lesbian-oriented fiction (which can be implicitly political) appears in *Common Lives/Lesbian Lives.* Blends of the political and nonpolitical are also found in gay magazines appealing to local or regional audiences—for example, *Metrosource: The Gay Guide to Metropolitan New York* and *Q San Francisco.* Additional magazine-like publications episodically touching on gay-relevant political matters include *Lavender Culture, Outweek, Curve: The Lesbian Magazine, RFD:Country Journal for Gay Men Everywhere,* and *Inside/Out.*

Scholarly journals and more serious magazines similarly abound. There is *The Journal of Homosexuality, Masculinities, Lesbian and Gay Studies Newsletter, The Harvard Gay and Lesbian Review, Gay Books Bulletin, Lesbian Ethics,* and *Law and Sexuality: A Review of Gay and Lesbian Legal Issues.* In addition to those scholarly outlets that are almost exclusively gay-oriented, several others regularly have a conspicuous gay presence, such as *Feminist Studies, Law and Sexuality, Journal of the History of Sexuality, Women Studies Quarterly, Feminist Teacher, Signs, Discourse: Journal for Theoretical Studies in Media Culture* and *Hypatia: A Journal of Feminist Philosophy.* To this compilation might be appended various decidedly liberal popular publications, both popular and scholarly and catering to educated audiences, that often carry gay-friendly political news and commentary, such as New York City's *Village Voice, Mother Jones,* and *Radical America.* And we are limiting ourselves to domestic publications—many foreign gay-oriented publications enjoy wide U.S. distribution.

The presentation of these pro-gay messages is not something assigned to poor quality, secretive, amateurish made-in-the-basement mimeographed newsletters *à la* the 1960s alternative press shipped only to the trusted. Many receive wide distribution beyond specialized gay bookstores. Their acceptance is confirmed when they often share shelf space with respectable magazines, such as *The New Republic* or *The Economist.* This openness of purpose and widespread distribution are important when considering claims of far-reaching deeply ingrained intolerance. Advertising content is one revealing clue to their established character. A fleeting glance demonstrates that many are light years from the anti-war, liberationist, coarse newsprint shoestring alternatives of the 1960s and 1970s, dependent on local record stores, organic restaurants, and head shops for advertising revenue. *Out,* for example, hawks Ralph Lauren, American Express, The Gap, Aetna Insurance, Budweiser beer, and Aiwa Electronics, to mention but a few mainstream businesses. These handsome ads when combined with those of businesses appealing strictly to gays—vacation resorts, travel agencies, jewelry, fashion accessories, sexual paraphernalia, homoerotic books, and the like—provide a substantial revenue base for continued publication.[3]

Perhaps the strongest case for the argument that gay voices are heard comes from a survey of "serious" books with candidly pro-gay postures. It is no exaggeration to declare that these books might stock an entire bookstore, or at least an ample section, and more issue daily. The September 30, 1996 *Publishers Weekly* offers an *incomplete* listing of some 123 *new* Fall books on gay and lesbian topics. A cursory overview of this publishing undertaking reveals important realities. First, many publishers are high-profile, prestigious commercial houses possessing ample resources to market these books aggressively. This is no small advantage in today's highly crowded marketplace of ideas. To be sure, innumerable books bare the small press imprint, such as Diana, Alyson, Arte Publico, Naiad, Pandora, Fire-brand, Fletcher, Sister Vision among a myriad others. Indeed, one compilation of small presses in 1995-96 listed some 58 separate publishers devoted merely to publishing lesbian-orientated titles (Fulton, 1996). Far more consequential, however, are the likes of Harper and Row, Knopf, Viking, Random House, Free Press, Vintage, Oxford, St. Martin's, Dutton, Basic Books, and nearly every other consequential publishing house. One venerable publisher in particular—Routledge—has made a specialty of publishing for the gay market.

Equally notable, numerous eminent university presses are currently issuing gay-oriented works, often having a separate distinctive series devoted to homosexual issues and politics. Columbia University has "Between Men-Between Women: Lesbian and Gay Studies." The University of Chicago Press has two series concerned with homosexuality: "Chicago Series on Sexuality, History, and Society" and "World of Desire: The Chicago Series on Sexuality, Gender and Culture." University press books, both in design and explicitly of title, often target audiences well beyond those scholars concerned with homosexuality. Among the presses offering books avowedly pro-gay are Princeton, NYU, Columbia, Duke, Cornell, University of California, University of Chicago, Wisconsin, Indiana, Minnesota, Massachusetts, Tennessee, and Georgia. Clearly, for those desiring to publish books celebrating gayness, there is no shortage of both commercial and prestige university presses.

These multitudinous treatises have repercussions well beyond the sudden physical existence of books exposing a once taboo topic. Even if they remained unbought and unread, their significance is tremendous. After all, they still remain a small portion of the total market; volumes on gardening, dogs, or even graphic "how to" books for heterosexuals are more numerous by a factor of 100+. What is critical is not just the aggregate but how these treatments both legitimize the vivid, open character of contemporary gay life and the shaping of today's university. Let us consider first the mainstreaming effect.

Books on contemporary homosexuality are rarely tedious, scholarly tomes in secured library rare-book rooms directed toward cloistered medical specialists in human sexuality. No hiding explicit sexuality or intimidating nonexperts with obscure technical jargon. Titles are frequently candidly sexual in character, unashamedly erotic, sporadically hinting at the sexually bizarre, and often well-promoted. A sampling of this openness includes

Queer Science (MIT); *Out of the Closets* (NYU Press); *Camp Grounds: Style and Homosexuality* (Massachusetts); *Boots of Leather, Slippers of Gold: The History of a Lesbian Community* (Routledge); *The Homoerotic Photograph: Male Images from Durieu/Delacroix to Mapplethorpe* (Columbia); *The Geography of Perversion* (NYU), and *Wolf Girls and Vassar: Lesbian and Gay Experiences, 1930-1990* (St. Martin's). Ideas and practices once confined to the far fringes of public acceptability—transsexuality, transvestitism, sadomasochism, pedophillia, anonymous public sex, explicitly homosexual art, arcane fetishes, and other once-marginalized practices are now openly discussed, often celebrated, in treatises issued by America's most established publishers. Victorian-era standards where chicken parts hinting at sexuality (breast, legs) were dubbed asexual white and dark meat are long forgotten.

Let us be unmistakable regarding our contention, for the point of our excursion might readily be misunderstood. We do not condemn public discussions of homosexuality, nor admonish publishers peddling books titled *Fear of a Queer Planet: Queer Politics and Social Theory* (University of Minnesota Press) or those merchants energetically marketing these adulations to ordinary, unsuspecting Americans; the issue of "has open homosexuality gotten out-of-hand?" is best resolved elsewhere. Our critical point is that an ordinary citizen who ventures into a bookstore, scans publishers' catalogues, or picks up *The New York Times Book Review* section or *The New York Review of Books* must reasonably conclude that books with openly gay themes or advocating gay political views flourish. Obviously, this proliferation is not universal, gay books are not top sellers like quickie diet books, and a few hanker to put the genie back in the bottle, if possible. We cannot equate a few hundred once scandalous books finding their way into Barnes and Noble as absolute certified mainstream acceptability. But, to argue that "American society is intolerant of gays," that millions of ordinary citizens are waging an effective war against the public side of homosexuality, grossly avoids this just-documented reality.

The publication of hundreds of gay-sympathetic books plus the proliferating specialized journals and magazines, has a second, and more subtle, consequence for our tolerance portraiture, namely, it invigorates academic propagation of the gay perspective. Some brief background. In sustaining academic enterprises, from physics to physical education, publications are the essential currency of scholarly standing, the intellectual building blocks for disciplinary legitimization. Books and articles also provide needed teaching materials. Try imagining an academic unit, even at an undistinguished college, in which instructors lack classroom materials because disciplinary members wrote nothing. A department without a corpus of literature, a body of certified experts, and a scholarly association built on learned contributions, would quickly vanish as academically irrelevant. Thus, when a university press underwrites journals on gay themes or a publisher contracts books on lesbian sexuality, these deeds breathe life into academic units committed to conveying gay and lesbian viewpoints. And this, in turn, impels even more books, essays, lectures, and symposia to enter the public arena.

One indicator of this growing academic legitimacy is the formation of separate gay and lesbian groups within general disciplinary associations. By the mid-1990s, these appear in nearly all academic fields, plus professions such as health care, psychological counseling, and law. Examples include the Society of Gay and Lesbian Anthropologists, Gay and Lesbian Section of the American Folklore Association, Committee on Lesbian and Gay History (part of the American Historical Association), Society for the Psychological Study of Lesbian and Gay Issues (affiliated with the American Psychological Association), Society for Gay & Lesbian Philosophy, and Lesbians in Science, to provide just a few from the many (for the full listing, see *Gay and Lesbian Professional Groups,* Gay and Lesbian Task Force, American Library Association). Most of these associations also issue regular newsletters.

This organization activity has consequences well beyond mere public recognition that, indeed, homosexual scholars exist and openly proclaim this existence. Like traditional group-based interest organizations—for example, the NAACP for African Americans—unions of like-minded scholars serve as scholastic guardians and informational conduits in matters relating to job protection, access to benefits such as health care, and scholarly activities. Consider, for illustrative purposes, the role performed by the Gay & Lesbian Caucus for Political Science for gays in this academic profession. Not only does it monitor member concerns, such as possible discrimination in hiring, but it sponsors scholarly activities whose involvement assists in professional advancement and status. In 1995, the Caucus claimed only 161 members, but the profession's 1996 annual national convention included eight scholarly panels with names such as "Theorizing a Queer Constitution" and "Queering Citizenship: Membership, Visibility and Equality" (*PS,* June 1996). Without getting into statistical details, the ratio of Caucus members to convention participatory opportunities is exceptional compared to, say, more traditional fields like legislative politics. Thanks to the Gay & Lesbian Caucus, gays and lesbians within political science easily explicate their views and simultaneously advance their careers. This process of rewarded expression of a viewpoint once ignored is happening in nearly all the social sciences and humanities.

Added to this disciplinary exposition is the emergence of academic organizations exclusively devoted to expanding the gay perspective. There is the Lesbian and Gay Studies Association founded in 1991. An especially active group is The Center for Lesbian and Gay Studies (CLAGS) at the Graduate School of the City University of New York. CLAGS publishes a variety of materials and provides a clearinghouse for those promoting gay and lesbian academic causes. That CLAGS has received $500,000 from the Rockefeller Foundation is one indication of its respectability (*CLAGS News,* Summer 1996). In fact, bringing gay scholars together to share views and give speeches is a growth industry. Conventions exclusively devoted to gay themes have grown quite popular, and sponsorship by universities such as Yale, Harvard, Rutgers, and CUNY provides them with considerable respectability (Muller, 1993).

Not surprisingly, given the openness of academic life to gays and gay-friendly ideas, the university curriculum increasingly reflects a gay presence. Some of this influence resides in the fast-growing area of Women's Studies, as lesbianism is often intertwined with feminism. In 1993, there were an estimated five hundred separate college-level programs in Women's Studies, fifty feminists' institutes and some *thirty thousand* courses (Muller, 1993). Innumerable courses with conventional, traditional titles, from psychology departments to English departments, now contain some treatment (almost always favorable) of the homosexual experience.

The Center for Lesbian and Gay Studies, located at the Graduate School and University Center of the City University of New York, has collected some eighty-five syllabi from courses with a predominant gay-lesbian theme. A cursory overview confirms by now predictable patterns. Most notably, academic offerings are not limited to trendy avant-garde schools or those situated in urban areas. Among those institutions represented in this collection are Knox College (Galesburg, Illinois), Samaritan College (Huntsville, Alabama), University of Wisconsin-River Falls (River Falls, Wisconsin), University of Delaware (Newark, Delaware), Santa Monica College (Santa Monica, California), Metropolitan State College (Denver, Colorado), and the University of Nebraska (Lincoln, Nebraska). And, whether the courses are in English departments, History, Political Science, Social Work schools or departments of Religion, syllabi typically offer page after page of field-specific readings. The University of California at Riverside has even recently established an interdisciplinary undergraduate minor in gay and lesbian studies. No doubt, this modest compilation is merely the beginning of an avalanche of future courses.

The gay presence also now extends into cyberspace. The Internet currently abounds with a huge variety—over a thousand, I would estimate—of sites catering to gays. These range from the overtly political to ones providing information useful in combating discrimination. As was true in our tour of publications, only the tip of this considerable and quickly expanding iceberg can be exhibited here. For example, at the QRD: Politics, Political News, and Activism (http://www.qrd//www/qpolis.html) site one could find information about the enemy (here the religious right), data on same sex marriages, survey data regarding homosexuality, facts on gays in the military, information about civil rights and anti-gay initiatives, how to contact federal government officials, plus a list of openly gay elected and appointed U.S. government officials. Another gateway site to gay and lesbian topics is: http://ezinfor.ucs.indiana.edu/sanderss/gaylespolguide.html. A general net search employing AltaVista on gay politics turned up a staggering list of entries. The range was enormous—data bases, bibliographies, histories, political alerts, exposes of enemies, invitations to join campaigns, and interviews with prominent gays.

At http://www.luc.edu/orgs/glaba/resources.html one finds a typical assortment of gay-relevant resources. Among those with a political flavor are Amnesty International Members for Lesbian & Gay Concerns, The Queer Resource Center: Information=Power, Servicemembers Legal Defense Network, plus information about upcoming events, parades and political rallies. A similar collection of links is to be found on the Gay/Lesbian/Bisexual Advocacy page. Here one can make contact with And Justice for All, Cristo Press (a religious publisher combating homophobia), GLAAD (Gay & Lesbian Alliance Against Defamation), Gay Rights in Puerto Rico and even Dyke TV, a half-hour weekly lesbian-theme TV program produced by lesbians. The most comprehensive listing—literally dozens of distinct groups reflecting a mammoth array of concerns—is situated at http://www. qrd.org/qrd/org/. Here one finds the Freedom to Marry Coalition, Gay & Lesbian Atheists and Humanists, Gays in Boy Scouts and Girl Scouts, Law Enforcement Gays & Lesbians International, Gay, Lesbian and Bisexual Veterans of America, Jewish Activist Gays and Lesbians, Lesbian Avengers, Lesbian & Gay Immigration Rights Task Force, Old Lesbians Organizing for Change, National Lesbian & Gay Law Association, Stonewall Democratic Club, Deaf Queer Resource Center, and the Wall Street Project, among innumerable others. Again, to emphasize our oft-repeated theme, a search for involvement in gays activism encounters a seemingly unending collection of specialized groups, resource centers, and open invitations. Even the most diligent could not read it all, let alone respond.

Equally important, though predictably far less numerous than websites, are the gay/lesbian political advocacy groups lobbying government, promoting public education, and contributing to political campaigns. These organizations are outwardly identical to the legions of commonplace groups that collect information, issue press releases, testify before Congress, solicit funds, and otherwise attend to the details of ordinary politics. In a sense, the existence of these gay lobbyists with a full-time, paid professional staff, often in Washington, D.C. physically amid a plethora of similar pressure groups, confirms the mainstreaming of the gay political presence.

For Republican gays, the Log Cabin Republicans in Washington offer seminars and publications within the Republican party to promote gay-related issues. Dignity USA, also in Washington, D.C., works with homosexual Catholics, their friends and families to urge spiritual development and social integration. Parents, Families, and Friends of Lesbians and Gays is a third Washington-based organization monitoring proposed legislation and regulation. The National Gay and Lesbian Task Force and Policy Institute engages in a multitude of tasks, educating the media on gay matters, tracking legislation, and collecting data on anti-gay violence. The National Organization for Women (NOW) also makes a major effort to protect gay political interests in addition to a more general concern for women's rights. Beyond Washington are other advocacy groups espousing a political agenda: The Astraea National Lesbian Foundation, Gay and Lesbian Community Action, the International Gay and Lesbian Human Rights Commission, the Lambda Legal Defense and Education Defense Fund, the Lavender Family Resources Network, the Lesbian and Gay Public Awareness Project, the Lesbian Herstory Educational Foundation, and the National Center for Lesbian Rights, among others.

An especially important type of lobbying group for gays is those pressuring government for greater vigor in AIDS research. Perhaps the most famous is AIDS Coalition to Unleash Power (better known as ACT-UP!) noted for its direct action confrontational tactics to influence government and pharmaceutical companies. Less visible to the public are several other national and state organizations performing a similar role. Among these are AIDS Action Council, AIDS Action League, the American Federation for AIDS Research (which in 1994 allocated some $25.5 million), Gay Men's Health Crisis, Triangle AIDS Network, and the Barbra Streisand Foundation.

There are two national, Washington-based avowedly gay-friendly political groups deeply involved in electoral politics:

The Human Rights Campaign (HRC), which counts 175,000 members, supports candidates, gay and nongay, Democrats and Republicans, who endorse the HRC's understanding of human rights (i.e., ending discrimination against gays, increased funding for gay-related health matters, and comprehensive civil rights protections for gays). Through its Political Action Committee it raised a million dollars during the 1996 election cycle and provides an array of electoral services to favored candidates: money, media consulting, volunteers, coordinated fund raising, and voter guides (Human Rights Campaign, *A Manual for Candidates,* 1996). The HRC is also important for our tour, because it demonstrates how e-mail and the World Wide Web can be fully exploited to link physically distant people into a grassroots political organization. Its homepage (http://www.hrcusa.org) lists the names of government officials to contact (based on one's zip code) plus voting records and issue stand information. A user can also send the government officials messages, either spontaneous or one suggested by HRC. Several specialized e-mails also provide political updates and membership news, and list future events. This complex electronic system was assembled with the acknowledged donations of people in high-profile computer companies (Sun, Lotus, and Cisco).

The Gay and Lesbian Victory Fund shares the HRC's concerns but limits itself exclusively to recruiting and helping openly gay or lesbian candidates. With some 3,500 members nationwide, it claims the fifteenth largest U.S. PAC, dispensing some $1.3 million in funds since its inception. Most of the openly gay state legislators have received its assistance. It also helps novice gay candidates through its Leadership Training Institute and supplies a variety of professional campaign services. The Victory Fund predictably has taken a strong role in opposing (successfully) anti-gay ballot initiatives.

Beyond the high-profile national associations are countless state and local groups agitating on behalf of gay political issues. Again, to reiterate a repetitious point, there exists a wide geographical dispersion despite the clustering in urban areas. Mobile, Alabama is home to the Gulf Alliance for Equality, there are the Alaskans for Civil Rights, the Gay and Lesbian Action Delegation in Fayetteville, Arkansas, the Des Moines Gay and Lesbian Democratic Club, the Gay and Lesbian Utah Democrats in Salt Lake City, Pride Montana in Helena, and the Tennessee Gay and Lesbian Alliance in Nashville, to acknowledge but a few. *Out for Office: Campaigning in the Gay 90s,* published by the Gay and Lesbian Victory Fund offers an extensive list of professional campaign consultants marketing vital services, such as media use, polling, direct mail, fund raising, event planning, and overall strategy. If this compilation were insufficient to would-be gay office seekers, the International Network of Lesbian and Gay Officials, founded in 1985 (htt://www.geocities.com/WestHollywood/2663/inlgo.htm) sponsors conferences and links to specialists in electoral politics for gays. Its regional conferences also pair up political novices with more experienced gay political professionals. Clearly, a gay political activist has considerable resources to draw on to meet potential hostility.

Finally, there exists a small but seemingly growing list of openly gay officeholders who, we can safely assume, overwhelmingly draw their votes from nongay citizens. The most notable in recent years have been three

House of Representatives members—Barney Frank, Steve Gunderson, and Gerry Studds. Less prominent are state and local officials, such as Judy Abdo, Mayor of Santa Monica, California; Bill Crews, Mayor of Melborne, Iowa; Gerald E. Ulrich, Mayor of Bunceton, Missouri, plus many state representatives, state judges, and high-ranking appointed officials (these are 1996 listings from *Out for Office;* there is also a netsite at —http://www.qrd.org/qrd/usa/national/glb.elected.officials tracking this information). The message here is not that gays are a voting bloc capable of tipping electoral outcomes (thought this may be true in some cities) but that hundreds of office seekers no longer see being "outed" as a career-ending liability at election time.

Cataloguing financial contributions, proliferation of gay political clubs, and rising numbers of gay officeholders only tells part of the story. To be sure, closeted gay office-seekers may still be common, but surely it cannot be claimed that being openly gay when appealing to nongays is the kiss of death. This was amply illustrated in the 1996 congressional race in Oklahoma's Sixth Congressional district, a rural "Bible Belt" district largely populated by conservative Southern Baptists. The Democratic nominee, Paul Barby, sent his fellow Democrats a letter openly admitting his homosexuality (Barby lost, as did all Democratic House candidates in Oklahoma). As of October 1996, nobody, including his Republican opponent, has made an issue of this sexual preference (*New York Times,* cited in Podhoretz, 1996). A similar story pertains to six-term congressman Jim Kolbe, a Republican in a staunchly conservative Arizona district—silence greeted his declaration of being gay. Kolbe did gain re-election. When Congressman Steve Gunderson (R-WI) openly declared his homosexuality, he received the warm support of Newt Gingrich. Newt even provided a blurb for the book Gunderson and his lover wrote about their lives (Podhoretz, 1996).[4]

The Landscape: Contemporary Marxism

Though the tolerance literature typically treats homosexuality and Marxism as two sentiments more or less equally at risk, they obviously differ fundamentally in core political character and histories. The current gay political movement is of recent origin and spreading at a frenzied pace. The founding organizations—the Mattachine Society, the Daughters of Bilitis—originated only in the 1950s and by the 1970s had been replaced by more flamboyant, energetic groups. By contrast, Marxism is more established, tracing its roots back to the 1852 Proletarian League and the Workingman's Party of America created shortly thereafter. Marxism has also been constantly transforming itself into thousands of diverse organizations, from the reform-minded Socialist Party of America to underground violent anarchism-like conspiracies. An incredibly diverse saga of tolerance and hatred has unraveled. Prior to the Russian Revolution, socialism was often commonplace in U.S. politics, even blending with Christian reform sentiment or flourishing in immigrant communities importing ideology from Europe. Marxism experienced a revival of acceptance during the 1930s Great Depression and the 1940s wartime Soviet alliance. Nevertheless, our most energetic, high-profile repressive undertakings—the mass deportations of the 1920s, Smith Act trials of the 1940s, the congressional investigations of the 1950s—have repeatedly selected Communism and allied ideologies as targets.

Gay politics cannot be paralleled with Marxist politics in terms of tolerance acceptance standards. Specifically, gay political groups, even the most outrageous and intemperate, do not challenge the constitutional order. Attacks on public decency and morality, perhaps, but not sweeping political revolution. Gay demands, fundamentally, are for social acceptance, a "piece of the action" in matters such as same-sex marriage, immigration, health care benefits, government funding of AIDS research, and civil rights protection. Marxists, by contrast, ultimately seek total transformation of American life though practicality imposes tactical caution and moderation. Queer Nation is hardly Communist Party USA. As such, it is extreme to insist that Marxist groups by right, in the name of democratic tolerance, automatically deserve an honorable place at the table of permitted organizations. It depends. The lessons of Chapter 4 should not be forgotten: Marxists *were* frequently genuinely subversive and therefore deserved government's assault. Espionage is not tolerable. Our more detailed *tour d'horizon* of Marxism that we now launch should not be taken as conclusive certification that what exists is somehow healthy for democratic tolerance.

Given that documentation of anti-Marxism efforts is a robust industry of multitudinous books, one would guess that this heretical sentiment has all but atrophied. Or, perhaps like some soon-to-be extinct species of toad, the collapse of the Soviet Union now propels domestic Marxism toward becoming a rare antique ready for the political museum. Hardly the case. Though the 1980s and '90s are not the boom times of the mid-1930s, like the Energizer Bunny, the message of Karl Marx just keeps on going and going. As was true for gay organizations, lurking below the surface of ordinary, pedestrian politics is immense activity apparently barely noticed by those bemoaning America's stifling intolerance.

The continued actuality of openly Marxist political parties makes this plain. The Communist Party USA, the most famed of all Marxist parties, is, as noted earlier, still functioning at its headquarters on 23rd Street in New York City. It claims affiliates in nearly all fifty states and, like the Democrats and Republicans, holds a national convention every four years. It continues to print a newspaper—*People's Weekly World,* plus the monthly *Political Affairs*—and run candidates for public office. It also makes its public presence felt, albeit on a modest scale via rallies and street-corner information tables. Equally venerable, though less well-known to ordinary citizens, is the Socialist Labor Party of America founded in 1876. Though its mid-1980s membership was minuscule, its weekly paper, *The People,* claimed a readership of some 10,000. A third surviving notable Marxist faction with long U.S. historical roots is the Trotskyite-oriented Socialist Workers Party (its newspaper is *The Militant*). Finally, no cataloguing of Marxist-rooted political parties would be complete without paying homage to Social Democrats USA, the successor to the Socialist Party. Under the reform-minded leadership of Norman Thomas, this party received millions of votes during the 1930s but today is only a remnant of its former self.

Surrounding these established Marxist political organizations are factions and party-like entities whose names and programs perpetually evolve. Their very existence, no matter how fleeting and inconsequential for the larger political scene, nevertheless reveals something profound about our politics: Founding a *public* revolutionary organization is no big deal. For example, not to be confused with the Communist Party USA is the Los Angeles-based pro-Chinese U.S. Communist Party. This, in turn, is not to be mixed up with the Revolutionary Communist Party (RCP) that rejects even Chinese Communism as too mild and longs for Maoism. The RCP publishes *Revolutionary Worker* and *Revolution* to promote this strictly orthodox Marxist view. A second Maoist party is the Maoist Internationalist Movement, home to the monthly tabloid *MIM Notes* and *Maoist Sojourner.* A rather mild-sounding party is the New Union Party, which, despite its innocuous name, calls for the complete worker ownership of all means of production. Another group hardly sheepish about its strident revolutionary character is the Sparticist League, a Trotskyist party candidly committed to leading a working-class revolution. Its publications include *Women and Revolution, Workers Vanguard* and a yearly *Sparticist and Workers Vanguard.* The Sparticist Youth Club is active on several campuses advancing "the formation of a revolutionary vanguard party of the working class to lead the struggle here and internationally for a successful communist revolution."

If one Trotskyite group were insufficient for America's needs, additional groups are standing by. These include the Worker's League and the Worker's World Party (the publisher of *Liberation and Marxism).* The latter party—

which, in 1996, had the distinction of running two women of color for U.S. president and vice-president—has adapted well to the electronic age. Though tiny in membership and influence, it nevertheless runs a handsome, well-organized website broadcasting updates on its activities and offering access to its publications (http://www.workers.org/).

Several less revolutionary parties within this Marxist tradition also have a presence. The World Socialist Party of the United States, an affiliate of the British Socialist Party, is located in Watertown, Massachusetts, and, despite its emphasis on democratic means, it still advocates the core principle of government ownership of all means of economic production. It publishes *The World Socialist Review,* a quarterly. A similarly mild-mannered variant of Marxism is the Democratic Socialists of America, which strives to build a peaceful society serving human needs in which all key means of production and distribution will be government owned. Together with its youth-oriented section, it is especially energetic on college campuses, organizing itself into anti-racist, feminist, Latino, and even religious subcommittees. Feminist-oriented socialists can enlist in the Freedom Socialist Party. The FSP targets people of color, gays, women and indigenous peoples to create an independent labor party to end exploitation. Though small, its publication list is abundant—*Socialist: Voice of Revolutionary Feminism, AIDS Hysteria: A Marxist Analysis, The War on the Disabled* and *Women of Color: Frontrunners for Freedom,* among others.

Various listings of Marxist political party headquarter locations cannot fully capture the continued proliferation of this sentiment. Many have less visible "branch offices," often combined with a retail bookstore, widely scattered about, thereby providing local Marxist revolutionaries ample opportunities to meet and review the impending demise of capitalism. The Revolutionary Communist Party, for example, in 1989 had seven branches in separate locations such as New York City, Cincinnati, Chicago, St. Louis, Houston, San Diego, and Portland. The Socialist Labor Party, an entity invisible in U.S. political life, had twenty-one affiliates sprinkled all across the country, from coast to coast. In 1989, the Spartacist League, an outspoken, energetic group, had twelve local organizations in divergent cities representing the national party (Laird, 1989). This far-reaching presence of revolutionary groups is hardly exceptional. From the perspective of a rabid anti-Communist, America must appear to be crawling with would-be Marxist revolutionary leagues, though the absolute number of members must be tiny.

Given that Marxist political parties seldom achieve much electoral success, many predictably eventually shade off into more educational or direct-action focused groups. Again, even a fleeting expedition reveals appreciable below-the-surface vigor. For youngsters of an anti-imperialist persuasion, those opposing U.S. invention in third world nations and those endorsing the rights of gays, African Americans and other oppressed people, there is Youth Against War and Fascism, located in New York City. Meanwhile, the Young Social Democrats of Washington, D.C. advances an eclectic program of greater democratic control over daily decision making, plus enhanced public investment in mass transit, health care, education, housing, and other social services. Its publications include *Socialist Currents, The Social Democratic Prospect,* and periodic policy statements. The Young Communist League of the United States claims some 50 local groups dedicated to ending the arms race, cleaning up the environment, ending sexism, and analogous programs to promote social equality. More academically inclined is the Center for Social Research in San Francisco that sponsors conferences and lectures advancing democratic socialism. It publishes *Socialist Review* quarterly. Also in the Bay Area is Socialist Action, dedicated to the creation of a workers' government through the abolishment of capitalism. The academically inclined might find The Institute for Democratic Socialism attractive with its offering of conferences, speakers bureaus, educational programs and miscellaneous publications. For Marxists with a humanist orientation, there is the News and Letters Committee working to promote unity among various minority groups and maintaining a library and collecting bibliographic information.

As with gay groups, the Internet has infused fresh vigor into groups pushing unorthodox "fringe" views. It is no longer necessary to rent space, print stationery, or even pay for promulgating a manifesto—a phone line plus modest technical savvy creates an instant presence in the world of Marxist politics. Sympathizers can simply type in "Marxism" on AltaVista and be rewarded with several *thousand* potential information sites. For example, the venerable Industrial Workers of the World (the "Wobblies") maintains a homepage—http://iww.org/gnat/9508/p/politic-i.html—that offers access to a bewildering assortment of broadly interpreted left-oriented groups and activities. Again, a highlight must suffice: Anarchism and Revolution (in Salt Lake City), the Noam Chomsky Archive, Democratic Socialists of America website, the Marx/Engels Archive, Refuse and Resist, Russian Anarchism (Anarcho-Syndicalism from the late 1980s to the present), and Lumpen (a collection of news stories). Additional abundant resources for the curious can be explored on the Marxist homepage-http://jefferson.village.virginia.edu/ spoons/marxism_html/marxis m.html that features everything from links to academic and direct action organizations to more personally eccentric sites such as Little Red Web Page, the Labor Cartoon web site and Haymarket Web Page. The adventurous can click on Fidel Castro's homepage, Che's homepage, and the one for the Sandinistas (among others).

The Marxist homepage is perhaps most serviceable (especially for fresh recruits to the tangled world of left politics) in offering links to the established Marxist political parties and publications. Among the linked parties are the Communist Party USA, Democratic Socialists of America, Workers World Party, the New Communist Party of Great Britain, the Portuguese Communist Party, and the Communist Party of Peru. Over and above the more commonplace Marxist print sources are such exotic publications as *Regards* (from France), *Red Pepper, Red Orange, Living Marxism* and *The Left Business Observer.* This survey is hardly exhausting; other home pages cater to more esoteric interests, often blending Marxism with environmentalism, racial politics, women's liberation, insurgent movements, and whatever else attracts political attention at the moment. Yet a third Socialist homepage at http:www.eye.net/Netizen/Progressive/list/left.html?resources= 50&pass=++ proffers an even more extended assortment of left-leaning causes, parties, and newsgroups. Here we find access to the All-African People's Revolutionary Party page, the Irish Republican Socialist Committee-North America, League of Revolutionaries of a New America, Leftist Leon, Leftlink, the Maoist International Movement, the Progressive Labor Party, Red Cell (an anti-capitalist clandestine movement), and the Socialist Party of Cyberspace, to cite but a sampling.

Our excursion has periodically referred to miscellaneous Marxist-centered publications, but this important landscape is even more populated than hinted at thus far. This stunning number of print outlets constantly churns out almost every thinkable bent within the Marxist portion of the political spectrum. Almost no idea, no matter how obscure, goes unexpressed. A parallel exists with the expression of gay perspectives: Outsiders scarcely grasp what flourishes beyond conventional publication outlets. All Marxist factions, even the smallest, issue newspapers to proclaim the word. Several have already been noted, others include *Sparticist, Workers Vanguard, Women and Revolution, Communist Voice, Industrial Worker, The Militant,* and *People's Weekly World.*

Far more numerous are journal-type outlets mixing political rhetoric with more abstract theoretical-historical analyses. The *Alternative Press Index* monitors these off-the-beaten-path journals and, in 1995, listed some twenty-six magazines self-identified as Marxist in orientation. Several—*Dissent, Socialist Review, Monthly Review,* and *The Progressive*— are well-known and often found in magazine sections of stores catering to an educated clientele. Less familiar are the likes of *Against the Current, Antipote, Crossroads, Democratic Left, Capitalism, Nature and Socialism, Forward Motion, Rethinking Marxism, Struggle: A Magazine of Proletarian Revolutionary Literature,* and *Radical History Review.* Journals also exist for more specialized interests—*Left Curve* combines art and Marxism; *Nature, Society and Thought* blends the study of nature with radical politics.

Marxist publications reside even further afield from the journalistic mainstream, periodically surfacing only to eventually vanish. Though an infinitesimal part of the discernible political scene, they nevertheless well illustrate our contention that odd, radical ideas can flourish amid general contemptuousness. These may be thought of as print versions of personalized websites. For example, there once was the *Wage Slave World News,* a Madison, Wisconsin-based irreverent, humorous, self-described "trashy journalism of the working class," radical newspaper (it was eventually incorporated into *Industrial Worker*). For those in Pennsylvania, there is the *Keystone Socialist;* if you are wondering about post-Cold War Marxism, read *The New Socialist.* In some instances one part Marxism is mixed in with ten parts off-beat notions to concoct a unique product. The *Discussion Bulletin,* for example, somehow manages to combine Marxism with libertarianism, ecology, anarchism, and various other less-than-wildly-popular philosophies.

Standing notably apart from this Marxism of small revolutionary political organizations and street-corner tabloid publications is academic Marxism. Recall that questions regarding admitted Communist teachers and Communist library books were poll staples. These surveys reveal sizable aversion to youngsters being exposed to those who reject capitalism. Even in 1994, for example, the National Opinion Research Center (NORC) found that a bare majority of those interviewed (55 percent) would permit an admitted Communist to teach in a college. As was true in the gay and lesbian presence in university, the numbers of adherents, courses offered, or other purely physical manifestations reveal only part of the story. The actuality of vigorous academic-based Marxism bestows a powerful legitimacy on these ideas and permits, if not encourages, its continuance across generations. There is also the issue of who is exposed to Marxism. The Revolutionary Socialist League, populated by citizens of meager resources who preach to the indifferent bystanders, cannot be compared to an academic department of tenured Marxist faculty instilling their lessons to ever-attentive students, many of whom will become influential citizens. To demonstrate a vital Marxist presence in academic life surely confirms America's tolerance of an ideology rejected by nearly all citizens.

Touring academic Marxism is hardly straightforward. No prominent organizations abound with self-identifying names, no Bolshevik Workers Party, Physics Department section. The congealing of political sentiment, as with scholarly views, is decentralized and idiosyncratic. Endless varying perspectives thrive, not a few dozen tight, discernible groups. Even more perplexing, much deemed Marxist in the contemporary academy has only the faintest connection with Marxism as designated outside the academy. Professors applying Marxism analysis in fields such as English, literary theory, and, indeed, politics would likely be incomprehensible to earthy Communist labor organizers. Even to suggest that the professor and party official share the common label "Marxist" may be a stretch. Communist Party USA adherents might judge these professors as inauthentic, mere pretenders to revolutionary tradition. Conversely, some academic fields, such as "Peace Studies," eschew the Marxist label, yet may be judged as Marxist fellow-travelers by outsiders.

To complicate matters yet further, only a blurry line may separate the dyed-in-the-wool, hard-core Marxist academic champion from the unbeliever who just happens to find the relentless application of Marxism intellectually useful. Teaching Marxism does not certify one as a Communist. An instructor may assign *The Communist Manifesto,* depict the harsh exploitation of workers by capitalists, and even speak highly of a revolution but demur when asked if he or she is a Marxist. Finally, the landscape can shift dramatically from decade to decade as fashions change and professors retire. Today's ferment can be tomorrow's languor; yesterday's radical party line may be today's rejected ideological error.

A convenient place to begin our overview is to ask just how many Marxists and possible sympathizers populate the academy. Data on this point are provided by an extensive faculty survey conducted by the Carnegie Foundation for the Advancement of Teaching. Let us stress the approximate nature of this census and its already dated character (though we suspect that Marxism's vigor would not be found to be diminishing if the survey were conducted today).[5] Nevertheless, limitations aside, the statistics are informative. The 1984 survey reports that 5.8 percent of the 5,000 professors at various schools interviewed politically self-classified themselves as "left" (not just "liberal"). Numerically, this would roughly be 35,000 professors of the 600,000 in American universities. In other words, would-be McCarthyites seeking to rid American universities of leftists face a formidable task.

More significantly, however, the proportion of self-designated leftists increases as we move to more prestigious, research-oriented schools, especially in the social sciences. Younger faculty also disproportionately tend leftward. Among philosophers at four-year institutions, for example, 21.7 percent classify themselves as politically "left." For sociologists, the corresponding figure is 37.0 percent; among political scientists, 19.8 percent. These numbers far exceed "strongly conservative" figures. Over-representation within the social sciences is especially significant, for the opportunity exists here to color one's classroom teaching with ideology. A physics professor, no matter how Marxist, would still be virtually indistinguishable in the classroom from his or her conservative colleague. This is less likely in political science, anthropology, sociology, history, and economics where subjects often involve real-world politics and Marxist scholarship can be assigned without violating professional norms.

An excellent overview is provided by Bertell Ollman and Edward Vernoff's two-volume compilation, *The Left Academy: Marxist Scholarship on American Campuses* (1982, 1984). This anthology covers a wide range of academic departments, and all entries are written by prominent academic Marxists well-acquainted with their respective disciplines. How do these Marxists judge the vitality of Marxism in the 1980s? Was Marxism being hounded out of the academy by mobs of intolerant adversaries? Volume I of Ollman and Vernoff's opus is upbeat about a reawakening after decades of slumber. The Introduction declares: "A Marxist cultural revolution is taking place today in American universities. More and more students and faculty are being introduced to Marx's interpretation of how capitalism works (for whom it works better, for whom worse), how it arose and where it is leading" (1). The authors then pridefully review recent accomplishments of academic Marxism—electing presidents of scholarly associations, the proliferation of courses (nearly 400 at the time of this analysis), and the issuing of countless Marxist books by prestigious publishers. In volume II, published a mere two years later, even greater optimism and excitement gushes forth—Marxism has now spread to "all corners of the academy" (ix).

Marxist contributors confirm this growing academic influence and acceptance. Richard Flacks, a sociologist, traces the reemergence of Marxism's prestige and popularity to the post-1970s period when mainstream approaches failed to predict upheavals in U.S. society. Flacks argues that his radical perspective no longer lives "underground," and parades numerous highly regarded Marxist scholarly works and other accomplishments for all to admire. He concludes (44) that Marx has been "restored" to sociology. Herbert Gintis concurs in his overview of academic economics. During the 1960s, Marxism lay dormant professionally, but by the late 1970s, as the U.S. experienced fresh economic problems such as stagflation, it resurfaced as a disciplinary force. Books and essays proliferated on the labor process, economic crises, the capitalism-gender connection, poverty, and discrimination. Marxist academics became sufficiently numerous to justify a separate organization (The Union for Radical Political Economics) and publish their own journal (*Review of Radical Political Economics*). College students can now even learn economics from several widely adopted Marxist textbooks and readers. By the late 1980s, Marxist economists had expanded into building institutes (the Center for Popular Economics) and even serving the radical movement more broadly by publishing *Dollars and Sense* magazine (Miller, 1992).

Marching from one discipline depiction to another in Ollman and Vernoff's expedition tells a repetitious tale: Academic Marxism is alive, hardly under attack, though some places more (history, political science, anthropology), some places less (psychology, art history). A contemporary update would unlikely depict academic Marxism as retreating. Even where Marxist professors comprise but a slender share of the discipline, such as art history, there is sufficient activity here to produce pages of recent Marxist bibliographic citations. This vitality, or at least professional capitulation to this perspective, is even true in fields not usually associated with academic Marxism. In biology, Martha R. Herbert observes that Marxism has provided multitudinous contributions in diverse domains such as agriculture and public health. Especially important is Marxism's feat in alerting people to the intimate connection between science and the exercise of political power, and how Marxists have helped recapture science for the people.

A complementary strategy to appraise the vitality of academic Marxism is to scan the list of professional journals and books colored by a pro-Marxist orientation. To reiterate our review of gay-oriented scholarly publications: Even if nothing ever gets read or bought, publishing opportunities are critical for sustaining academic legitimacy. There can be no distinguished Marxist professors, no classes, no well-publicized visiting lectures if Marxist interpretations remain unpublished. Publications esteemed "serious" by fellow academics provide legitimacy and intellectual authority to ideological perspectives beyond their indoctrinational effects. If one wished to expel Marxism from the academy, harsh classroom censorship is unnecessary. A more effective, less visible technique is making Marxist writings unpublishable or devaluing the intellectual worthiness of outlets. With no respectable scholarly literature, no academic field survives.

The cursory overview of pro-Marxist academic writings would overwhelm the most ardent revolutionary. Academic journals with a clear radical/Marxist perspective offer a convenient starting point. Many began as associational newsletters demanding direct action during the 1960s anti-war movement and ultimately evolved into more "respectable" scholarly journals. Indeed, the late 1960s constitutes the "big bang" of leftist academic publications. *Insurgent Sociologist,* for example, originated in 1969 at Berkeley and called for resisting bourgeois hegemony and expanding welfare programs. It eventually softened its radicalism and renamed itself *Critical Sociology.* Similar evolutionary paths were taken by *Radical Religion,* the *Radical History Review*, and *NACLA:Report on the Americas* (an anthropology journal covering Latin America). Other journals tracing their origins back to this "big bang" include *Radical History, Radical Teacher,* the *Insurgent Sociologist,* and the *Radical Philosopher's Newsjournal,* among others (Shore, 1992).

Complementing these "insurgent" journals are others, often issued by mainstream publishers or sponsored by university departments, indistinguishable in style and format from non-Marxist scholarly periodicals. One relevant 1986 survey estimated the number of Marxist and left-leaning professional journals at more than thirty (Balch & London, 1986). Included are *Dialectical Anthropology, Diacritics, Politics and Society, New Political Science, Science and Society, Social Praxis, Social Theory and Practice, Behavioralists for Social Action, Human Development, Psych Critique, History Workshop: A Journal of Socialist Historians, International Labor and Working Class History, Social History, Journal of Peasant Studies, Science for People, Radical Science Journal, Crime and Social Justice, Law and Society Review,* and *Art History* (Ollman & Vernoff, 1982; 1984). Marxist-oriented journals catering to more general audiences would include *Dissent* and *The New Left Review.* Moreover, and this is critical, Marxist scholars are by no means forbidden to publish their analyses in abundant mainstream, non-Marxist academic journals (Balch & London 1986). These professional channels may have specialized and demanding criteria for scholarship, but seldom does an ideological point of view automatically invite rejection.

If the periodicals landscape appears highly evolved and copious, the world of books is even more extensive. As with gay publications, there exists an entire universe of specialized publishers catering to this market. *The International Directory of Little Magazines and Small Presses* (1996) catalogues twenty-one separate presses issuing books dealing with Socialism, Communism, Marxism, and Leninism. Some appear to be tiny, obscure, hole-in-the-wall operations, such as Star Rover Press and See Sharp Press. Others, such as the South End Press are quite consequential, despite their offbeat name and occasional taste for the bizarre (one of their books draws connections between the Nazi *Waffen SS* and recent GOP ethnic outreach programs). Recent South End titles include *Socialist Visions, Unorthodox Marxism, Social and Sexual Revolution, Marxism and Socialist Theory,* and innumerable other radical indictments of U.S. politics and society. A very different printer of Marxist material is International Publishers. Despite all the anti-Red censorship campaigns, this company has churned out revolutionary classics since 1924. It currently has more than 200 titles in print, largely cheaply priced "classics" of Communist ideologues often sold in left-wing bookstores. This is the publisher to contact when searching for the fifty-volume set of the *Collected Works of Karl Marx and Frederick Engels.*

Needless to say, as any book fancier will attest, those seeking pro-Marxist tomes need not rely on obscure publishers or hard-to-find bookstores. Commercial publishers and for-profit bookstores have long catered to Marxism devotees. Almost all mass market presses together with prestige university presses have brought revolutionary thinking to the American public. Volume I of Ollman and Vernoff's (1982) celebration of Marxist academic success was issued by McGraw-Hill, hardly a Bolshevik subversive tool. Indeed, a few presses devote entire series to sympathetic treatments. Oxford University Press, for example, has its "Marxist Introductions" series that includes ten separate book titles covering ecology, the city, international relations, and literature. Not to be outdone is Cambridge University Press with its "Studies in Marxism and Social Theory," also with ten titles. Other prestige publishers with comparable series include Princeton, Rowman and Littlefield, Routledge Kegan Paul, and Humanities Press.

Ultimately more important than a mechanical listing of Marxist publications is the ease of painless dissemination. After all, it counts for little if thousands of Marxist books are published and then shipped to locked warehouses, never to be read. Though publishers' circulation figures on each and every Marxist tome would statistically demonstrate the permeability of U.S. society to these revolutionary views, such documentation is superfluous. A perfunctory visit to middling bookstores, from subsidized college-run bookstores to commercial giants such as Barnes and Noble, displays a modest welcoming of radicalism. The *Communist Manifesto* even appears to be an always-to-be-kept-in-stock item at decent bookstores. To be sure, the Marxist books sitting on shelves pale in comparison to diet and self-help books, but would-be Bolsheviks can always gain instruction. If recipes for anti-capitalist revolution are unavailable, nearly every bookstore would happily special order it to secure their profit. Moreover, modern technology facilitates this task. On the Internet access, www.amazon.com will produce an online bookstore with over a million titles, 430 of which are about Marxism (though a few seem to be anti-Marx). These cover nearly every possible dimension of Marxism. The most isolated radical-in-the-making can privately browse and order even the most inflammatory Marxist books, most discounted from suggested retail.

Conclusions

When our *tour d'horizon* commenced, our initial contention that "there's a lot out there" appeared eminently reasonable. Hopefully, this assertion has now been demonstrated through what must occasionally seem like a too-tedious recitation of never-before-heard-of journals, marginal book publishers, obscure foundations, Lilliputian political clubs, eccentric magazines, and other novel outcroppings of an expansive political landscape. And, we have not committed every item to paper; quite likely sundry political life-forms remain undetected. Political diversity aficionados should also be pleased that as technology widens, this spectacle will become increasingly over-grown. Self-publishing and electronic distribution are now an unchallenged reality and can only extend as the technologically adept multiply. Our Martian mythical visitor observing American tolerance surely has concluded that "everything is permitted and wildly germinates."

Though our portrait is likely to draw widespread praise, especially from those celebrating intellectual diversity, not everyone will be delighted. A few will be offended, angered. Some of this animus will flow from aversion to the particulars—for example, the prospect of Marxists teaching college may inflame strident anti-Communists. There is, however, another—almost perverse—source of unhappiness with our compilation. Here, most surprisingly, it is the very proclamation of this plethora that occasions unease. They need not welcome repression, yet denoting nearly unlimited opportunities for expressing dissent is hardly greeted with joy. In particular, a vested interest can exist in proclaiming the mantra of an ever-present smothering intolerance. A few academics find a dismal portrayal a useful peg on which to hang their studies of attitudinal intolerance. For them, the "unsettling" intolerance data—independent of evidence showing actual curbing—conveniently sounds the alarm for yet more inquiry into an alleged anti-democratic threat. Documenting abundant tolerance thus undermines a professional livelihood.

More noticeable are activists whose discoveries of public loathing validate tickets to lucrative government and corporate entitlement benefits. The unchallenged assumption of massive intolerance becomes the *raison d'être* for autonomous academic departments, conferences. subsidies for new-sprung journals, and similar fresh benefits accorded those who, allegedly, suffer. More will be said about such crying wolf later.

Yet others will reject our assessment by disputing the evidence. This evidence-based rejection can take different forms. For the conspiratorial-minded, believers in unseen powerful forces despite contrary appearances, our richly detailed account is illusionary. All the Marxist revolutionary parties and gay liberation convocations exist only at the pleasure of those stealthily in charge. They persevere—even the most outlandish revolutionaries—only because they are harmless. Should the signal be given, the instruments of oppression would quickly grind them into dimly remembered nothingness. Perhaps under the flimsy excuses of combating domestic terrorism or protecting public morality, prominent dissenting oddballs would be rounded up and punished on trumped-up charges. Repression ever darkly lurks below the surface. Nobody is really safe ultimately, even tenured Marxist professors. In short, a counterrevolution against our version of tolerance would be quick and easy, if decided on.[6]

No convincing rejoinder against this argument, at least when applied to contemporary politics, is possible. Its advocates will surely point to the "spontaneous" anti-Communist passions of the 1920s as historical evidence for this possibility. No doubt, examples of similar quickly mounted assaults against civil liberties can also be demonstrated. This apprehension that our portrait of robust diversity is superficial cannot be completely dismissed. To the extent that "anything is possible" politically, we confess that our narrative may falsely characterize a passing sham, misconstruing manipulation for a golden historical moment. Nevertheless, let us not equate "might happen" with "will happen."

A seemingly more credible version of this argument is that our inspection covers only the smallest portion of the civic terrain. Our inventory, it might be contested, only catalogues the marginal and minor league. What difference does it make if untold petty Marxist and gay political tendencies flourish if these sentiments are relegated to obscurity? We have just exposed isolated ghettos for the politically unconventional. Put in positive language, true political tolerance exists only when those marginalized ideas are mainstreamed, abound in common discourse, not confined to peewee urban bookstores. Even worse, the existence of all these curiosities reinforces the dangerous myth that "real" political diversity prevails. Malcontents can always be placated by acknowledging all the inconsequential, and therefore fraudulent, diversity.

Nonsense. The restricted, even infinitesimal, nature of what we depict cannot invalidate genuine tolerance. Robust accommodation is not the true measure of tolerance. To solicit Marxists and gays weekly for school "show and tells" would not therefore create "authentic tolerance." There is no requirement that unsavory causes be promoted to qualify ourselves as a genuinely accepting society. The Communist Party USA surely desires more members; few people, however, wish to join. The gay political movement is not constrained only by resistance from nongays; there are just too few activist-oriented gays. Unpopularity of things deemed wondrous by some is not proof of repression of desirable change. As Chapter 2 noted, political resistance and intolerance may be behaviorally identical but they are fundamentally different entities. To ignore the Communist recruiter is not to display undemocratic aversion to important ideas deserving a hearing. Tofu may have marvelous nutritional properties, and everyone may benefit from eating a pound a day, but its unpopularity has more to do with taste and texture than insensitivity to foreign foods. Those who like tofu can buy all they want, and this is sufficient.

The bottom line is simple. Though polls monotonously unveil public hostility to Marxism and gays, both now survive rather nicely, even thrive, in contemporary society. A reasonably competent citizen wishing to join a Marxist organization or promote gay candidates faces no serious obstacles. Nor, judging by the number of people engaging in such activity, is this person at risk. To be sure, this was not always true, and may be less correct in some places than others, but it is true generally. This is what counts when assessing tolerance accurately. This is not to claim that gays and Marxists are welcomed with open arms by all citizens and share equally in society's generosity. If this were true, many of the organizations depicted here would soon vanish. No doubt Marxist adherents and gays have legitimate complaints with treatment received, and perhaps things need improvement. But to acknowledge points regarding fair and equitable treatment cannot diminish our evidence: To claim that gays and Marxists are not tolerated in our political life is a vast overreach. Members of these less-than-welcome entities experience few problems making their voices heard, though not everyone wishes to listen.

NOTES

1. It may be argued, of course, that the collapse of the Soviet Union in 1989 makes the entire issue of domestic (and international) Communism moot. Both experts and ordinary citizens are apparently of a mixed mind, according to a 1991 *Washington Post*-sponsored survey. On the one hand, only about 28 percent of the responders felt that the Soviet Union might return to its old Communist system; 76 percent believed that Communism was dying out as an ideology. Yet, at the same time, some 91% said is was not yet dead and 34 percent were still willing to use force to stop the spread of Marxism. In short, one might describe the public's view as limited apprehension (*Washington Post* Soviet Attitude Poll, 1991).

2. We might speculate that if such unorthodox organizations decline, such a decline will more than likely mirror the far more general decline of smallness in American life than any campaign of oppression. Just as small-town, locally owned businesses are vanishing, the hole-in-the-wall Marxist bookstore or neighborhood lesbian action group may be swallowed up by the nationally based groups better able to avail themselves of media and technology. This might even be called the "WalMart-ization" of radical politics.

3. This unguarded embrace of gays by mainstream business has become so commonplace that it is hardly noticed. The 1997 New York City Gay & Lesbian Business and Consumer Expo

conspicuously acknowledged the sponsorship of, among others, IBM, American Airlines, Holiday Inn, American Express, and the United States Postal Service.

4. Our tour of mainstream acceptance of being gay has skipped over perhaps one of its most visible features—the openly gay characters on popular TV programs. The highly publicized April 30, 1997 "coming out" of Ellen DeGeneres, star of ABC-TV's *Ellen,* in real life and in the program is just one of many notable such incidents. Other highly rated TV shows with gay characters have included *Frasier, The Larry Sanders Show* and *Married . . . With Children.* To be sure, some mainstream sponsors have avoided the *Ellen's* coming-out episode, but other sponsors have filled the void. These media events can be further followed on GLADD'S homepage: GLADD @glad.org.

5. The reader unfamiliar with academic Marxism might wonder how this ideology could survive the collapse of the Soviet Union. There is no contradiction as few academic Marxists would consider themselves supporters of the former USSR. Indeed, more than a few might contend that the Soviet Union was a corruption of Marxism, not a manifestation. Hence, insofar as their own stands are concerned, the demise of the USSR is of no consequence.

6. An even more extreme version of this view is that existent tolerance, by its intrinsic nature, is repressive because it promotes the dangerous illusion of a free and open society. The harsh reality, the argument continues, is one of stifling challenges to a conservative status quo. When the powerful permit a few harmless eccentrics to parade in public, this gesture masks the consequential and structural instruments of oppression—a biased educational system, capitalism, standing armies, and the like. Tolerance thus misleads just as a magician might distract the audience. This contention is more fully developed by Marcuse in his famous "Repressive Tolerance" (1968).

6

Intolerance Calibrated

D ocumenting oppression, both as historical scholarship and as a contemporary political cry, is a robust industry (see, for example, Schrecker, 1994). A similar passion informs the study of political tolerance; it is this industry's *raison d'être.* Lurking behind virtually every analysis of citizen tolerance is the assumption that worthy unorthodoxies suffer relentless onslaught. One recent study began by asserting that "the challenge of sustaining a politically tolerant society is enduring . . . while intolerance is an ever-present danger, it need not simply be accepted" (Marcus, Sullivan, Theiss-Morse, & Wood, 1995, 3). This omnipresence of tenacious intolerance is the analytical, axiomatic starting point of research, not the evidence-supported conclusion.

Our inquiry here takes a closer theoretical and substantive look at the intolerance indictment. We continue with one of the two previously depicted groups, namely, gays. This analytical choice reflects the ceaseless charges of widespread homophobia leveled by gays themselves and their sympathizers. By contrast, at least for the present, comparable cries of social or government-inflicted repression do not emanate from Marxists, though their vision of repressive capitalism remains intact. We conduct a scholarly trial regarding societal intolerance against gays. Examination begins, however, with evidentiary rules, divergent meanings of "intolerance." We shall then summon the evidence, call the witnesses, and otherwise form a judgment regarding unwarranted homophobic repression.

Calibrating Intolerance

If *intolerance* and *repression* are to be useful terms, calibration beyond simplistic binary division is essential. Cleaving the world into *free* and *oppressed,* where *free* is the complete absence of *any* unjustifiable stifling and *oppression* means *some* repressive attack would be as practicable as abolishing the felony-misdemeanor distinction.[1] Worse, such indiscriminate lumping together dulls our moral sensibilities, rendering us incapable of distinguishing colossal wickedness from minor inconveniences. Unfortunately, contemporary politics, with competing cries of victimization, encourages crude, binary usage. To follow this facile convention abandons scholarly analysis to cliché-mongering.

Hypothesize an intolerance continuum ranging from "the most imaginable" at the left to none on the right. At the scale's extreme left would lie Hitler's Holocaust against Jews. Innumerable other historical crusades of genocide, mass starvations, ethnic cleansings, enslavement, and similar grievous atrocities likewise deserve placement here. The contemporary scene, most unfortunately, further provides us with shocking examples from Bosnia and Rwanda. Stalin's 1930s "Great Terror" in which more than a million political foes were executed, usually on trumped-up charges also comes to mind. Only slightly less oppressive might be the August 1572 Massacre of St. Bartholomew's Day in which some 80,000 Protestant Huguenots were slaughtered in Protestant-Catholic strife. Closer to some hypothetical middle might be the U.S. deportations of suspected revolutionaries during the early 1920s or the harsh internment of more than 100,000 Japanese Americans during World War II. Yet, further along this imaginary line are various federal government anti-Marxist operations. During the 1950s heyday of anti-Communism, for example, states banned Communists from public employment though suspects were seldom, if ever, interrogated by some secret political police.

As the Garden of Eden-like "zero intolerance" draws closer, intolerance becomes less systematic, more idiosyncratic, and more extra-legal individualistic. So-called "hate crimes," in which individuals are physically battered principally due to their appearance, or their religion or their sexual preferences, would lie here. Suffering is genuine but hardly systematic, brutal Soviet-style Great Terror. Beyond such encounters in which a genuine harm is suffered, we might place actions captured by terms like *annoyance* or *harassment.* The intolerance casualty might be demonstrably insulting or humiliating, but no serious physical damage occurs, no loss of job, status, or other harsh punishment for being "different." A world of difference separates death camps and abuse by intoxicated rowdies. These distinctions are obvious but often overlooked when howls of intolerance emanate from the outraged.

A recent *Wall Street Journal* story of Martha Grevatt, a gay Chrysler factory worker, usefully illustrates these distinctions. According to Ms. Grevatt, an openly lesbian employee with nine years of factory service, fellow employees have repeatedly tormented her, from leaving hate messages at her workstation to gluing pornographic pictures to her toolbox. Though Chrysler has a clear anti-harassment policy and has instituted training to eliminate harassment, the company's labor contract fails to contain an official anti-gay harassment policy. This refusal, in turn, has resulted in picketing by gay employees and a threat of a national boycott of Chrysler by homosexuals (*WSJ*, October 28, 1996, B1, B5). Is Chrysler guilty of "intolerance" toward Ms. Grevatt? In some ways, yes, other ways, no. Though Ms. Grevatt has suffered psychological distress, no claims are made that this distress has undermined her work performance or otherwise damaged her life. Certainly this harassment is not Chrysler instigated and the company seeks to stop it, but it does occur on Chrysler-owned property by Chrysler-paid workers.

We can also imagine a situation in which tolerance is almost— but not quite—perfect. Here a gay person a thousand miles away reads this *Wall Street Journal* story and feels outraged, even alienated from American society, because of corporate indifference to a fellow gay's plight. No personal harm is experienced; yet it is all psychologically "real." He or she might identify with the harassed worker and easily imagines similar experiences. Even if attacks never materialize, the very possibility, never discountable, encourages a belief that unchecked intolerance toward homosexuals prevails. And when government denies protective legislation, even if such inaction is justifiable, this unease intensifies.

This rough and ready delineation raises important questions rarely addressed when all intolerance, no matter how grievous or slight, premeditated or unintentional, is clumsily though conveniently aggregated. Indifference to distinctions is costly. Most evident, though nearly everyone pushes higher and higher tolerance standards, some compromise with the dictates of reality requires accepting imperfection. As with pollution, though everyone longs for an absolutely clean environment, people acknowledge limits. The key question, then, is how much perfection is sufficiently acceptable? At what point is pursuit of the ideal replaced by "we have achieved about as much tolerance as is feasible." To return to Martha Grevatt's situation, even draconian Chrysler anti-gay harassment efforts need not extinguish an occasional thinly veiled insult or minor social ostracism. If coercive effort were invariably successful, crime would be long gone.

Ruthlessly seeking zero intolerance can be costly, even engendering police state totalitarianism, albeit under the guise of a kinder, gentler social order. For example, to fully protect Ms. Grevatt by providing a totally unhostile working environment, we might insist that Chrysler go beyond tough-sounding decrees with stern punishments. Harm must be fully prevented before it occurs; deterrence via punishment is insufficient. The company might install hidden closed circuit TV monitors, hire undercover spies, or institute intrusive psychological tests to weed out homophobes—all potential unsavory invasions of privacy. Life for everyone, not only Ms. Grevatt, would ultimately resemble *1984*.

Chrysler might simply segregate all workers by sex, race, sexual preferences, or whatever to minimize future conflictual incidents or hire only a homogeneous workforce. Factories might have "gay only" sections. The preservation of differences, ironically, would be maintained by eliminating them. Chrysler could close the plant or ship jobs oversees to a country indifferent to homophobic behavior. Ms. Grevatt would, unfortunately, lose her position but on the plus side, she would totally escape abuse. Clearly, practicality and compromise may oblige tolerating minor intolerance. Workers might willingly suffer modest harassment to preserve well-paying employment.

What about virtually pure tolerance, the 99.99 percent point on our continuum? One possibility, recall from Chapter 2, is "affirmative tolerance." Here, the powerful—government, corporation, school—must anticipate all possible intolerance and prevent oppressive intrusions before they materialize. In addition, heretical views or unorthodox lifestyles must actively be made comfortable. Perhaps the holder of unorthodox views deserves "respect" for challenging the conventional. A few might further assert that government must vigorously interject nonconformist views into public discourse (Sunstein, 1993). Thus understood, when pushed to the *reductio ad absurdum* logic, even the visible absence of bigotry, hatred, and malice would not qualify as authentic tolerance if the preventive mechanisms were absent. Perhaps Chrysler should institute periodic "Gay Pride" days or corporate anti-AIDS contributions with mandated employee participation. The upshot of this understanding is, of course, a potential paradox: On-the-surface acceptance simultaneously coexists with *perceived* intolerance. Demonstrating a peaceable, all-accepting world, it might be said, merely hides subterranean intolerance.

When viewing the plight of self-identified intolerance victims, even if such hostility is real and calculated, one should not forget that annoyance and hostility are endemic to life. Human survival begets interpersonal friction. Mortality means occasional insults, slights, insensitivities, discriminations, outrages, and harms as people with different views clash. Diversity itself encourages conflict. Only in cemeteries does perfect tolerance of human differences prevail. This inevitability cannot justify illegal behavior, but insisting on harm-free life is fantasy. Others at Ms. Grevatt's Chrysler plant may well suffer humiliation for being obese, exhibiting eccentric appearances, speaking with odd accents, neglecting personal hygiene, being exceptionally short, or possessing amusing names. Absolute animosity-free existence cannot be imposed as the standard for judging tolerance.

A calibration of intolerance must address self-imposed or highly exaggerated intolerance. Initially, the idea of actively seeking humiliation, insults, or physical harm due to bigotry seems alien. Nevertheless, though such incidents may be statistically rare, their often outrageous character generates intense media coverage which, in turn, promotes the widespread, though misleading, public perception of intolerance. Being provocative to draw hostility is a time-honored political tactic. Intolerance is also contrivable. Recall when a black girl in New York City—Tawana Brawly—alleged to have been sexually assaulted by a gang of white men, smeared with feces and left beaten in a trash can. The public was, justifiably, outraged and cries of vicious racist intolerance proliferated. This event proved to be a series of self-inflicted hoaxes.

Even documentation need not settle problems of interpretation. One notable example of exaggerated intolerance concerned the rash of southern Black church burnings drawing intense national attention during 1995 (Fumento, 1996; Tooley, 1996). These arsons received front-page attention, together with strong condemnation from elected leaders. The House Judiciary Committee conducted public hearings; Congress voted for higher prison sentences for the culprits and funded an extensive investigation. Deval Patrick, the Assistant Attorney General for Civil Rights, called these conflagrations an "epidemic of terror." Representative Maxine Waters (D-CA) spoke of "outright tyranny" while Jesse Jackson intoned "an anti-black mania" and "white riot." A prominent black minister attributed the burnings to racism, homophobia, talk of crime, and the nation's anti-welfare, anti-crime mood. President Clinton drew a parallel with grim genocide events in Bosnia and Rwanda. Hillary Clinton, when touring Auschwitz, compared the burnings (which, significantly, did not involve fatalities) to the Holocaust, in which six million died. Prestige newspaper pundits easily invoked apocalyptic images of a widespread rampaging racist conspiracy. The U.S. Commission on Civil Rights opined that these arsons were even more dangerous than mere conspiracy.

The facts, apart from grossly invalid human life comparisons, expose a contrary story. Of the 148 fires since 1995, a little more than half affected white churches. Moreover, according to official state and federal records, no evidence exists that the 73 fires at black churches resulted from a white racist conspiracy (ironically, fires at Southern Black churches had *decreased* overall since 1980). Many blazes were set by blacks themselves or by the mentally unbalanced, intoxicated teenagers, burglars, and pyromaniacs. Not uncommon were "copy-cat" arsons subsequent to the national publicity. Zero evidence of a white conspiracy has been uncovered by a small army of federal investigators. Given the actuarial odds of thousands of Southern Black churches catching fire accidentally, a Holocaust comparison is unwarranted. In fact, the Insurance Information Institute judges black church fires well within the "expected" range, given church numbers, age, isolated locations, flimsy wooden construction, and other relevant features.

Further investigation offers a lesson for treating intolerance allegations. This misleading outrage is largely the work of the Center for Democratic Renewal (CDR), an anti-racism political group. Together with its ideological allies, it released numerous stories to the news media, some ultimately proven false, that successfully galvanized public opinion. It skillfully organized news conferences and arranged meetings of high public officials. A once non-issue suddenly became "hot" (no pun intended). These exaggerated allegations brought massive contributions—as of mid-1996, some *$9 million* has been raised by the CDR, a third of which has been allocated for purposes other than rebuilding churches. Indeed, with the insurance money plus all the donations, each black church could be rebuilt *three* times over (Fumento 1996). Though only the deranged wish to see churches destroyed, crying the wolf of intolerance has its benefits.

The critical issue of *who* is intolerant also deserves examination in this calibration. Whether the repression is governmental or private is critical. And, contrary to what some tolerance scholars argue (for example, McClosky & Brill, 1983, 15), government-organized repression is far more consequential. The state enjoys a monopoly of legitimate force—its agents can confiscate your property, exile you, shut newspapers down, and execute you, all lawfully. Not every harassment is identical intolerance. Unarmed, unorganized citizens can hardly resist a despotic, well-armed government. To be sure, one's neighbors might attempt similar actions, may even enjoy greater initial tyrannical success than inept officials, but their actions are not official state conduct. If a mob threatens violence, the police can intervene. This is far, far different if the police themselves incarcerate you for unorthodox opinion. The Klan can never be the Gestapo unless it captures the government.

Intolerance also differs in its escapability. Jews caught up in Hitler's final solution could flee only with enormous difficulty, some six million could not. Ditto for those victims of the Soviet Great Terror. During the so-called McCarthy anti-Communist campaigns, reasonable options were open to those at risk—one might, for example, simply abandon politics, change one's name, switch jobs, recant previous statements, or be hypercautious. Not the best alternatives, surely, but hardly the most gruesome either. As we will show, contemporary politics affords an ample escapability without necessarily compromising principles or embracing apathy. This is hardly trivial. An outspoken Marxist with a taste for violent rhetoric unquestionably does not enjoy the same employment opportunities as an apolitical, convention-heeding citizen. Nevertheless, he or she is hardly doomed to apolitical despair. Prudent choices regarding residence, employment, and one's associations shape encountered intolerance. "Democratic tolerance" does not require an outspoken Marxist to move to Los Alamos, New Mexico, live among conservative Republicans, and seek employment at the local nuclear weapons laboratory. "Persecution" under these circumstances is to be expected.

The *consequences* of intolerance also demand consideration. Our hypothetical continuum of intolerance's left side is defined by repression whose consequences is death or grievous harm. When we move rightward, however, the aftereffects lessen. Unemployment due to anti-Communist hysteria is not a pleasant prospect, but this harm is mitigated somewhat if a comparable new position is quickly found or if dismissal brings a sizable cash settlement. We do not submit that intolerance may be routinely self-inflicted to gain rewards, nor that petty intolerance is inevitably inconsequential. Instead, intolerance per se cannot be automatically equated with immense suffering, especially if ample protection is afforded the injured, victims may eventually gain. This is an empirical matter determined on a case-by-case basis, not definitionally settled.

In assessing intolerance's scope, separate *acts* of hostility must be distinguished from intolerant *people*. Consider, for example, the statement: Intolerant acts doubled from the past year. What might this mean? One common, almost reflexive interpretation, is that tolerance has declined, that is to say, more people expressed intolerance than previously. Not necessarily. Obviously, this increase might simply be due to shifting public understanding of intolerance. The shift might also reflect new laws criminalizing once-permitted behaviors, more diligent record keeping, or altered data classification schemes (for example, attacking two people at once now counts as two crimes, not one crime involving two people). This statement is also imprecise regarding how many intolerant *people* are involved. Perhaps a few bigots committed multiple misdeeds. After all, local crime waves can be generated by a single energetic criminal—infractions are up though not the population's criminality. We cannot unreflectively treat all heightened intolerance claims as proof of ever-growing hostility to the unpopular.

Homophobic Intolerance:
A Case Study in Calibrating Intolerance

Public opinion poll data show substantial aversion to homosexuality. How much *behavioral* repugnance, how expressed, with what consequences now becomes the critical question. Simply pronouncing "intolerant opinion abounds and gays and lesbians feel oppressed" is insufficient to condemn our society as sternly homophobic. To repeat our warning, any departure from absolute tolerance, especially if merely perceptual, cannot be equated with massive collective intolerance. Today's homophobia cannot, definitionally or simply by accusation, be made commensurate to Nazi anti-Semitism.

Sounding the Alarm

Overall, what collective judgment is offered by reports from private and public organizations monitoring homophobia? Whereas no single gay organization speaks for all gays here, among those that do pronounce, a judgmental consensus exists. It is a harsh indictment; gay-friendly organizations endlessly proclaim that conditions are deplorable and, though exceptions occur, matters are deteriorating. Reports convey an alarmist, frightening flavor of citizens under siege. Comparisons of the violent, systematic oppression of German Jews during the 1930s are easily invoked. Indeed, one report by a gay organization depicts a multiplying national epidemic of hate crimes sweeping America, with its victims being as diverse as Blacks, gays, Asian Americans, and Jews (NGTLF Policy Institute, 1992 Report). The 1995 Report of the National Anti-Violence Programs puts it tersely:

> Anti-lesbian and anti-gay violence remains a pervasive problem throughout the United States. Over the last two decades, dozens of prevalence surveys, academic studies, government funded reports, and community based analyses of gay and lesbian victim information have been conducted. Without exception, each has found that gay men and lesbians are disproportionately the victims of hate motivated violence. . . . Even if complete statistics of anti-gay/lesbian violence were available, the numbers alone would not convey the terrible impact this violence on both individual victims, our communities, and the social fabric of this country. (6)

Consider, for example, the vision offered by *Hostile Climate 1995,* an extensive overview produced by People for the American Way, the premier anti-hate association. The report begins by noting that, as a consequence of the Republicans' 1994 election landslide, innumerable Religious Right groups have stepped up "the vitriolic anti-gay rhetoric that creates and nurtures the divisive atmosphere across the country and too often results in public policy that targets and demonizes lesbians and gay men solely on the basis of their sexual orientation" (5). Furthermore, forthcoming evidence will show that "the hatred and contempt that many individuals feel for lesbians and gay men has been institutionalized at the highest levels of government, in corporations, organizations, and even religious denominations. Sadly, those entities that should be setting the example, by standing firm for the principles of justice and fairness and working to bring our nation and communities together, are the very sources of disdain and discrimination" (5).

The severity of this hostility is expressed afresh. Our nation has "an anti-gay climate" or "a climate that is fundamentally hostile to lesbians and gay men" and "anti-gay forces have . . . narrow(ed) the circle of who is welcome as a participant in the American community" (5). To be sure, some progress has occurred, but "the overall climate in this country continues to be shockingly hostile to lesbians and gay men" (5). That massive amounts of overt hostility, discrimination, and violence exist unseen and unreported is self-evident.

Though might be dismissed as overblown rhetoric intended to mobilize the troops and solicit contributions, these reports reveal a pervasive under-lying interpretative political framework. Since this *Weltanschauung* is criti-cal to judging the claims of rampant homophobia, let us briefly interrupt our excursion to dwell on this oft-repeated vision. First, it is presupposed that gays are singled out for hatred *solely because of their private sexual prefer-ences*. The very first paragraph of *Hostile Climate* makes this explicit: "many thousands of our citizens are finding this nation an unwelcoming and hostile place solely because they are gay or lesbian" (3). Other possibilities—gays' advancement of an odious nonsexual, leftist, political agenda, their uncon-ventional exhibitionistic public behavior, the public financial burden of AIDS, the subversion of civic morality, and other possibilities—remain automatically outside consideration. Thus, if a gay teacher were criticized by religious fundamentalists, this *could only be due to the teacher's private sexual activities.*

A second recurring motif is that the mighty, whether government officials or corporation, mold climates of mass opinion by conspicuous example and, in turn, this climate of opinion prods ordinary citizens to homophobia. Prominent officials "signal" an open hunting season on gays. And what might these examples be, these policies favored by the mighty instigating "hateful and irrational judgment"? Often this is *proposed* legislation, such as a congressional bill limiting the amount of AIDS/HIV training received by federal employees. The Colorado and Oregon ballot initiatives limiting sexual preference in anti-discrimination legislation also qualify here. An example of an *enacted* anti-gay measure was a New Hampshire school board's rule that schools are forbidden to teach homosexuality as a positive alternative lifestyle (Berrill, 1992, 7). When Republican candidates for the presidential nomination attend a Christian Coalition rally against same-sex marriages, this act is interpreted with great consternation as "hateful elite signaling" to a receptive homophobic public.

This "blame the establishment" attitude is well-illustrated in the outrage over several apparently homophobic Texas murders. Local gay activists effortlessly attributed the blame to conservative Republicans. Dianne Hardy-Garcia, Executive Director of the Lesbian/Gay Rights Lobby of Austin, Texas, put it boldly: "There is no doubt in my mind that there is a connection between these murders and the incredibly harsh, hateful, anti-gay and anti-lesbian rhetoric out of the far Republican Right." That the actual murders were done by teenagers, not party officers, was dismissed as irrelevant. Prominent gay activists, authors, ministers, and columnists all joined the choir in being absolutely positive that the GOP was the unindicted accomplice. The teenage culprits are, apparently, zombies under conservative control (Boulard, 1994)

In propositional form, the argument goes as follows. Some official expresses hostility to the gay agenda—for example, increased federal funding for AIDS research. Specific content of the disapproval is largely irrelevant. Nor is the ratio of favorable to unfavorable utterances pertinent: If 100 legislators comment favorably regarding gays, this is overshadowed by a single unfriendly reference. Citizens then pick this aversion out of the immense flow of daily jumble and exploit this on-high pronouncement to legitimize their own hatreds and aggression..

Third, those resisting gays are guilty of promoting injustice, intolerance, and unfairness. Aversion to *any* gay demand, for whatever reason, is *totally* unjustified intolerance. As hateful intolerance is the *only* motivation, definitionally, no valid reason exists for excluding gays from the military or bestowing health care benefits on same-sex partners. The call for rightful inclusion axiomatically presupposes that gays are indistinguishable from everyone save in their sexual attraction. Ostracizers are "impugning the moral character of people who are good neighbors, attend church and pay taxes like other citizens—and who also happen to be lesbian or gay or support gay rights" (Berrill, 1992, 8-9). To select gays for exclusion is wholly inappropriate.

Again, a complex accusation *sans* documentation. Obviously, numerous gays and lesbians are indistinguishable from their heterosexual neighbors. Yet, as we shall eventually discuss, a growing number of gays vehemently reject being "closeted" into invisibility and conventionality. Indeed, a dominating themes of the modern gay movement is "pride," the open celebration of homosexuality's *distinctiveness* (Muller, 1993). Added to this less visible dissimilarity are more overt divergences—often hedonistic, indulgent lifestyles, cross-dressing, transsexuality, sado-masochism, exhibitionism, and other sex-related activities well beyond inclinations customarily judged "normal" in most communities.

Alarmist indictments are not limited to excitable political organizations. Consider, for example, the allegations emanating from *Hate Crimes: Confronting Violence and Lesbians and Gay Men,* a scholarly investigation of homophobia conducted by respectable scholars (Berrill, 1992). Again, the axiomatic, repetitive point of departure is that anti-gay violence is exploding. In only a few short years, it is argued, from the mid-1980s to the early 1990s, the frequency of attacks on gays has skyrocketed as hate groups, notably the Klan and neo-Nazis, discover gays to be tempting targets. Berrill's introductory essay concludes that "there is ample evidence to show that the problem is severe. Indeed, the quantitative and qualitative data gathered thus far are frightening testament to the human cost of anti-gay bigotry" (40). One analysis insinuates that the violence faced by gays is deeply built-in to the character of modern America (Herek, 1992). To quote: "Anti-gay violence is a logical, albeit extreme, extension of the heterosexism that pervades American society. *Heterosexism* is defined here as an ideological system that denies, denigrates and stigmatizes any nonheterosexual for a behavior, identity, relationship or community" (89).

The Character of Alleged Homophobia: Crime

The allegations made by gays vary from cold-blooded murder to commercial censorship to hounding teachers from the classroom. Our analysis cannot accept undocumented charges, no matter how impassioned, on their face. It would be as if a trial concluded with the prosecution's opening speech minus the defense's detailed rebuttal. Crying wolf is not unknown in politics; we must venture beyond nebulous inflammatory declarations. We begin with accusations of extensive anti-gay criminal disorder and then move to the purported campaign against gay and lesbian teachers.

Creating A Hostile Climate

"Hostile actions" supposedly create the venomous foundation promoting more serious illegal physical assaults against gays. What are some of these detestable, anti-gay occurrences promoting this "frightening" climate of hostility? *Hostile Climate* (People for the American Way, 1995) offers a rich and authoritative compilation. We skip over legislative battles—the Colorado and Oregon propositions, for example—already mentioned. Though each incident possesses its own flavor, they nevertheless fall into distinctive categories. One such homophobic action, according to gay-defense groups, offensively characterizes homosexuals. To wit:

U.S. House Majority Leader Dick Armey (R-TX) during a radio interview referred to openly gay Representative Barney Frank (D-MA) as "Barney Fag." Armey later apologized to Frank and said that he would not condone using this term. At a subsequent press conference, a spokesperson for the Human Rights Campaign Fund referred to Armey's speech as hateful and dehumanizing. (Berrill, 1992, 19).

Republican Randy Cunningham on the floor of the House of Representatives referred to gays as "homos" during a speech discussing the Clean Water Act. Cunningham said there was no bigotry behind this usage. (Berrill, 1992, 19-20)

When the Rev. Fred Phelps of the Westboro Baptist Church in Kansas announced plans to picket San Diego's gay pride parade, he referred to the parade as "the filthy fag parade" and claimed that "fags are dead while they are alive." One Phelps supporter wore a T-shirt proclaiming "Intolerance is a Beautiful Thing." (Berrill, 1992, 34)

At an Albuquerque, NM convention of the National Federation of Republican Women somebody put on sale anti-gay bumper stickers with slogans such as "The Miracle of AIDS: Its Turned Fruits into Vegetables." These bumper stickers were not sold or approved by the National Federation, and when a Federation member requested that they not be sold, they were removed from the convention grounds, (Berrill, 1992, 80)

Insensitivity to gay sensibilities also abounds. Intended hostility is immaterial; rather, the perpetrators react to gays in ways judged inappropriate by gays themselves. For example:

When forty openly gay elected officials attended a White House meeting with members of the Clinton Administration, uniformed Secret Service members wore rubber gloves. When asked the reason for wearing gloves, the officers said protection from possible HIV infection. Though wearing gloves is a permissible option for these officers, President Clinton afterwards offered an apology. An investigation was also launched and additional special training was implemented. (Berrill, 1992, 21-22)

In 1994 a group calling itself "Normal People" filed a lawsuit attempting to force organizers of San Diego's gay pride parade to allow them to march as heterosexuals. "Normal People" eventually abandoned its lawsuit. (Berrill, 1992, 35)

The Bay Area Christian News in San Mateo, California published an article by John McTevnan claiming that "a careful study of . . . disasters, especially the stock market crash and major earth quakes . . . reveal that they occur in connection with abortion and/or homosexual related events." McTevnan also explained the extensive 1993 flooding of the Missouri and Mississippi rivers in terms of the Gay Pride Day of that year. (Berrill, 1992, 37)

A book, *The Pink Swastika: Homosexuality in the Nazi Party,* was published by Scott Lively and Keven Abrams that claims that homosexuality played a prominent role in the German Nazi Party. The book claims that Hitler could well have been gay, and many of his top aids were certainly gay. A video based on this book has appeared on cable television. (Berrill, 1992)

Resistance from teachers, parents, school board officials, and community groups in exposing schoolchildren to gay-sympathetic educational material is particularly common. The conflict is not one of inserting anti-gay material in the classroom; it is over whether material sympathetic to gays should be presented with the pedagogical alternative being silence. From the gay perspective, resistance to pro-gay material—even if this involves first graders—is anti-gay behavior. Consider the following:

Two San Francisco teachers were criticized and had their teaching certificates challenged for inviting Community United Against Violence (CUAV) to speak to their sixth grade classes regarding hate-crimes against gays and lesbians. CUAV speakers acknowledged that in addition to discussing hate crimes, they also spoke of anal and oral sex plus the use of dildos (a sex toy). A parent of one of the school children objected. The campaign by parents against the teachers has been characterized as "a witch hunt" and "McCarthyism." (*HC, 35-36*)

Numerous school boards across the country complained when Apple Computer distributed a CD-ROM with its bundled software called *Who Built America.* The material was intended for grade schoolers and included several references to homosexuality, including a poem written by a gay cowboy about his dead lover and how Oscar Wilde was imprisoned for homosexuality. Apple responded to objections by requesting that the producer of *Who Built America* remove the homosexual material as a matter of customer preference. When the company refused, Apple discontinued distributing *Who Built America* to elementary schools but not to high schools. (Berrill, 1992, 27-28)

A West Covina, California teachers' workshop "Out of the Closet and Into the Classroom" intended to promote sensitivity to lesbian, gay and bisexual students was canceled after the school board decided that this was an inappropriate topic for 12 and 13 year old students. Thirty-three of the teachers are suing the School Board for violating the Constitution's First and Fourteenth Amendment. (*HC, 37-38*)

The "offensive climate" assaults on gays also involve private, not public, censorship of materials exhibiting gay themes. For example:

> The October 1995 issue of *Guitar* magazine was removed by many newsstands and music stores because its covered depicted two male rock musicians kissing on the lips. (Berrill, 1992, 27)
>
> The publicly funded Public Broadcast Service sent its member stations the documentary *Coming Out Under Fire,* a film about gays in the military. The showing of this film was made optional with member stations. Originally, the film was scheduled as a "hard feed" meaning that stations would have no option but to show the film, The creator of the film believes that this shift was a result of catering to the Religious Right. *(HC 26)*
>
> Television station WAFF-TV in Huntsville, Alabama blanked out a kissing scene between two women in the film *Serving In Silence: The Margarethe Cammermeyer Story* (the story depicted the release from the military of a lesbian). *(HC 29)*
>
> When the Durham, North Carolina Pride Celebration scheduled a gay film festival, fifty residents organized a demonstration calling the films obscene. The films included *Boys Short's: The New Queer Cinema,* and *Dyke Dramas.* The films were eventually shown despite the objections of two of Durham's five council members. (Berrill, 1992, 85)

Physical Assaults and Abuse

No physical harm occurred in the preceding incidents. We now turn to circumstances involving possible legal violations, from verbal harassment to homicide. Are homosexuals, as homosexuals, the object of criminal attacks and, given the nature of these violations, are today's gays and lesbians seriously at risk physically?

The FBI now compiles hate-crime statistics, though these data are only voluntarily supplied by local police departments. These official compilations, however, have been condemned for underreporting the incidence of crimes against gays. For example, in 1992 the FBI recorded 4,558 national hate episodes of which 422 were gay-related. By contrast, the major gay organization taking on this responsibility found 1,001 episodes in just five cities (NGLTF, 1992, 4). In 1995, 392 homophobic hate crimes were acknowledged by the FBI versus 1,212 forwarded to the gay anti-violence project (54). Given these discrepancies, data collected by gay groups are used to avoid accusations of relying on misleading information.

These figures are face-value *reports* of homophobic attacks by the victims themselves or police record interpretations. No independent official corroborating organization exists, so all personal accounts are given credence. Be advised, however, that these gay organizations, in contrast to local police departments, are highly motivated to uncover violations. This attentiveness probably minimizes, but does not eliminate systematic underreporting.

Since the 1980s, multiple studies have depicted anti-gay violence. Do these statistics proclaim a rampaging national plague? The answer depends on how the data are collected and interpreted. An especially grim picture of widespread homophobic aggression emerges from Berrill's overview of some twenty-four self-reporting multi-city studies conducted during the late 1980s under the auspices of the National Gay and Lesbian Task Force, community groups, and various government agencies (1992). These are "first wave" studies. Regardless of location, the tale told is of widespread, serious victimization for being gay. Consider, for instance, a 1984 study of 2,074 respondents in eight major cities. Here 86 percent reported verbal abuse; 44 percent were the object of violent threats; 19 percent had their property vandalized; 20 percent reported police victimization; and 62 percent worried about personal safety (Berrill, 1992, 22). Studies from other localities, including college campuses, reveal roughly comparable results. Overall, at least in the eyes of gay organizations, these raw numbers proclaim that gays nearly everywhere live at risk.

This appalling picture becomes less convincing, however, when data collection techniques are examined. The deck is stacked in favor of malice in these reports. First, as Berrill frankly acknowledges, nearly all statistics derive from questionnaires distributed at gay events, sites where gays congregate (including bars), and through gay publications and mailing lists. Study participants are thus self-selected with White well-educated males being overrepresented. Just how this atypically shapes the overall results is unclear. Nevertheless, it is quite reasonable to suppose that study participants share an "activist mentality," are more visibly gay, and likely reside in high profile gay areas. Since homophobic hate crimes are disproportionately common here, distributing surveys exaggerates encountered hostility.

Furthermore, shifting from harassment to more serious offenses reduces the proportions. Indeed, some included "offense" categories are technically unlikely to be crimes—for example, family verbal abuse. Or, if they are crimes, they are relatively minor, such as being spat on. The incident's true nature—for example, who provoked whom?—also remains murky. Turning to serious matters, we find that across diverse studies the proportion of gays assaulted with a weapon (of all assaults) is 10 percent or less. Sexual assault numbers were generally slightly lower. These raw numbers can mask a time frame problem. Surveys may include an open-ended time perspective (see, for example, von Schulthess in Berrill (1992) on this issue). That is, when asked if they were the victims of attack, the question concerned a person's entire life. A single incident years back was counted as "a gay person threatened." This differs sharply from conventional victimization studies in which crimes are compiled on a time-specific basis. No doubt, in many crime-charged urban areas where diverse people collide, a life without hostile incidents—homophobic or otherwise—would be remarkably rare.

We can also guess that because gay organizations often seek to show widespread anti-gay violence, respondents err on the side of homophobia in ambiguous situations. One person's verbal abuse from a parent may be lively discussion to another. Moreover, even a nonthreatening situation can, via the fixed poll question, easily be interpreted as something sinister. A silly slur expressed by a harmless drunk can become a cold number depicting homophobic verbal abuse. Let us be clear here: We are *not* facilely discarding all homophobia reports as trivial or paranoia. They are often real and profoundly harmful to recipients. That gray, murky areas surround "threatening harassment" is easily forgotten when scanning the cold numbers.

An altered picture of homophobic crime emerges from studies conducted in the mid-1990s. Federal and state hate crime laws have revised the compilation ground rules. A "homophobic incident" has become more precise though still somewhat ambiguous. Questionnaires distributed at events have been replaced by intake procedures that resemble police-collected data. Relying on official FBI criteria, gay organizations have defined a homophobic crime as an incident in which a reasonable person would conclude that the action was motivated wholly, or in part, by bias against gays, lesbians, bisexuals, or transgendered persons (National Coalition of Anti-Violence Programs (NCAVP), 1995, 8). Irreducibly, a judgmental element remains, though matters are not based entirely on personal perception. Motivation is established if the offense is associated with any one of the following :

1. The offender uses anti-gay language or makes reference to AIDS.
2. A history of hate crimes exists in the area of the incident.
3. A perception exists among the immediate gay/lesbian community that the crime was bias motivated.
4. The crime coincides with a gay event such as National Coming Out Day.
5. Evidence exists that the victim was selected due to appearances (e.g., wearing of gay pride T-shirt) or some behavior (e.g., a gay couple holding hands).
6. The offender is a member of a group with a history of anti-gay behavior.
7. The victim was active in promoting some gay cause.

Though homophobic motivation is a bit narrower than before, extensive categories of hostility remain covered. The NCAVP reporting guidelines

Table 6.1   Reported Anti-Lesbian/Gay Hate Crimes in Selected Cities, Selected
Years

City	Number of Incidents and Year		
	1992	1994	1995
Boston	238	234	173
Chicago	252	177	83
Columbus	*	149	181
Detroit	*	96	90
El Paso	*	92	131
Los Angeles	*	332	256
Minneapolis/St. Paul	311	190	218
New York City	662	632	625
Phoenix	*	69	84
Portland	*	106	47
San Francisco	435	324	324
Total	1998	2401	2212

*No reporting program at time.

offer twenty separate divisions, from harassment (using offensive language or other distress-causing communications) to criminal breaches (assaults, intimidation, rape, extortion, bomb threats, arson, vandalism, robbery, and murder). Police harassment is included (entrapment, unjustified arrest, or raids by law enforcement agencies serving no discernible purpose other than to harass gays and lesbians).[2]

Let us begin with the total incidents from the cities with established hate-crime tracking programs. An "incident" is any number of offenses comprising a single encounter. If a gay person is assaulted and robbed, this counts as a single incident though two distinct crimes have been committed (in fact, two separate alleged crimes per incident is about average). No distinction is made here between which of twenty types of hate crime was perpetrated; a verbal assault is equal to a bomb threat.

When overall totals are divided into specifics, a more varied, less alarming, and familiar picture emerges. First, and perhaps most substantially, many of the offenses, though undoubtedly disturbing to victims, hardly indicate brutal violent homophobic terror as intimated in publications such as *Hostile Climates 1995*. Of all national offenses in 1995, not merely incidents, actual physical assaults constituted 22.4 percent of all offenses. In turn, about half involved weapons and, among the weapons employed, a firearm was used in about one out of eight instances. More common were violent assaults using rocks, bricks, bottles, knives, and other sharp objects. Attempted, but not consummated, assaults constituted 3.8 percent of the total (NCAVP, 1995, 23). More commonplace were intimidation (20.7 percent) and harassment (41.7 percent). Property crimes, including vandalism, were of minor consequence. Police harassment—an offense inherently highly subjective—is a separate category and constitutes merely 3 percent of all reports. The most dangerous crimes in these compilations, those likely to generate an official investigation-based statistic—arson, sexual assault, bomb threats, murder, and extortion—are less prominent overall. In short, hate crimes are predominantly unpleasant, abusive personal confrontations; physical assaults constitute a sizable but still minority portion of offenses and seldom involve deadly weapons.

It might be rejoined, predictably, that these data expose only the iceberg's tip, for many anti-gay crimes go unreported. Data collected by gay organizations suggest that only about a third of all incidents in 1995 were incorporated into the official record (NCAVP, 1995, 49). Fear of retribution and anticipated hostility from the police were probably to blame here. Yet, it is also acknowledged that some uncomfortable encounters—obscene gestures and sexual epithets—are technically not illegal yet become statistics. Other abhorrent behaviors—for example, verbal intimidation—are no doubt generally perceived as low police priorities though perhaps technically misdemeanors. Even if reported, the results would be minimal as the likelihood of apprehending the culprits is about zero. We might guess that underreporting is more likely for less serious infractions.

What about murder, the most frightful of all homophobic crimes? In 1995, the eleven gay-administered national tracking programs reported twenty-five murders deemed gay-related. Other programs counted an additional fourteen deadly assaults. Excluded are murders of homosexuals appearing to be drug related, domestic violence, or disputes among friends and lovers. Of these twenty-five homophobic homicides, a third were excessively brutal—mutilation, dismemberment and far more force than necessary to kill. Once again, the alarm is sounded loudly; and once again, matters are less clear-cut if inquiries venture beyond initial raw numbers.

What specifically makes these terrible lethal crimes homophobic? According to the National Coalition of Anti-Violence Programs' standards, any one of several elements: anti-gay statements by the perpetrator, the viciousness of the crime, location in an area known for anti-gay attacks, absence of signs of forced entry to victim's living quarters, and commentary by witnesses, friends, and community leaders. There is no possibility of rejoinder by attackers or, if a defense is offered, it is immediately disbelieved; labeling is one-sided and unappealable. It is axiomatic that the victim is totally innocent of action engendering the crime. Such explicit or implicit criteria, not unsurprisingly, generously expanded the list of homophobic attacks. Hypothetically, a gay's brutal murder in Manhattan's West Village, a popular gay neighborhood and thus the scene of anti-gay violence, will be calculated as committed by a homophobic assailant. Without any hard evidence, perception translates into reality, and the murder becomes of grim statistic of anti-gay savagery.

Of these 1995 murders, 40 percent (10 of 25) were admittedly associated with sexual pick-ups. The perpetrator and victim met publicly to facilitate an erotic liaison—in bars, parks, street corners or even public toilets—and the slaying occurred after leaving to consummate the arrangement. Assessing the nature of pick-up violence is complicated, especially since not all the pertinent details are known or, if known, gay defense organizations are mute.[3] A third of these cases involved robbery, so it is conceivable that some murders resulted from muggings or burglaries "going wrong," i.e., the puny take outraged the assailant. A transgendered person—a man pretending to be a woman—was involved in four cases. In three of these, the murderer claimed that he acted only after uncovering the deception.

Our final point on gay murders is critical: The available evidence points to full-fledged prosecutions. Or at least the gay organizations compilations do not relate any prosecutional indifference. Police may ignore taunting, but not barbaric crimes. There is no officially sanctioned "open season" on killing gays, courts do not buy a justifiable homicide defense for killing gays, nor do they mitigate assailant punishments as "gays have it coming to them." Unfortunately, statistical evidence is partial and comparison with nongay murders is uncertain. Nevertheless, the picture is reassuring to those dreading judicial indifference. In Comstock's review of cases receiving newspaper attention, the lightest punishments in which a death was involved were received by juveniles or young males whose assault involved just fists or kicking. Among adults, gun use drew rather severe sentences—two fifteen-year terms and one forty-year sentence. Acquittal was rare (Comstock, 1991, 80-81). Where non-juvenile perpetrators committed the attack, of the ten cases in which the sentencing outcome is presented, two outright acquittals and one due to the insanity defense were received. All others were punished, with sentences ranging from 5-7 years to the death penalty (Comstock, 1991, 83-84).

To repeat, we are *not* belittling the traumatic or deadly anti-gay violence; it clearly exists and deserves full prosecution. Rather, these murders are infrequent acts commonly associated with practices such as picking up strangers for sexual relations or congregating in districts with known reputations for anti-gay violence. Others result from young toughs harassing gays "for sport" and the situation escalating; violence, but not necessarily murder, was intended. Some of these criminal episodes, as with all crimes, are prudently avoidable. Unsafe neighborhoods, parks, streets, and business places are generally well known. This surely does not make these misdeeds permissible or authorize trifling punishment. Nevertheless, we must be cautious about accepting a terrifying vision of hapless gays unable to escape execution due to their sexuality.

Two further observations placing alarmist accusations into perspective are necessary. First, who generally inflicts this harm? The answer is unambiguous. Despite all declarations of well-organized violence, right-wing homophobic conspiracies, and institutionalized anti-gay campaigns, almost without exception these infractions, from harassments to injurious assaults, are committed by disparate individuals acting autonomously. Prominent Christian fundamentalists may loudly condemn homosexuality, but instances of armed, well-directed congregations marching off to thrash gays are exceedingly rare, if they occur at all. Never stated yet of great importance in this entire analysis is that homophobia is *not* official government policy. It is *all* extra-legal. To be sure, an occasional public official—probably a police officer—might treat gays disrespectfully, even abusively, but this is not government policy and it is seldom systematic. The era when accused homosexuals were executed or publicly pelted with rotten fruits and vegetables is long gone.

The 1995 NCAVP report notes that nationwide, a total of thirty-three serious reported incidents occurred in which the evildoer acknowledged association with an identifiable hate group, for example, neo-Nazi skinheads or the KKK (37). Surely, neo-Nazis and the KKK are hardly well-organized, mainstream organizations. Church organizations and other "established" opponents of homosexuality are "guilty" of rhetoric and proposing anti-gay legislation and little else. Moreover, though theoretically possible, neo-Nazi skinheads and Klansmen are unlikely to be secret agents of respectable religious assemblies, pro-family groups, political conservatives, and other alleged hostile environment perpetrators.

This atomistic, unorganized character of aggressive homophobia has been well-documented. The typical attacker acts alone or in a small band (two or three) against a stranger (see Berrill, 1992, 29, for a summary on this point). Mob action, (i.e., attacks by groups larger than ten) is virtually nonexistent (NCAVP, 1995, 32). Furthermore, as one might predict from overall comparable crime statistics, perpetrators were disproportionally young, overwhelmingly male. Most surprisingly, given claims that anti-gay activity comes from "the establishment," in 1995, 51 percent of all offenders nationally were either African American or Latino, though this racial/ethnic mix varies considerably by locality (NCAVP, 1995, 36; see Berrill, 1992, 29-30 for this variability). In short, the quintessential narrative of homophobic incidents depicts young male rowdyism, frequently pushed via peer group pressure or alcohol, into illegality, occurring in localities where gays openly congregate.[4]

The second important truth regarding these allegations concerns its statistical baseline. Alarms regarding criminality must not be based on absolute numbers. A city might experience a hundred murders a year, but this says little regarding the dangers citizens face. Twenty murders is grim in a small village; the identical number in Detroit makes the city virtually "murder free." Equally important, raw numbers are useless for comparative purposes—the initially alarming figure of one hundred becomes quite comforting when other urban areas have a murder rate several times that.

Though comparing crime figures using alternative collection methods is risky business, even the most imperfect rough-and-ready sketch is revealing. Recall that in eleven cities with tracking programs in 1995, twenty-five homophobic homicides were recorded by gay organizations. By contrast, in 1995 the FBI's *Uniform Crime Report* for the same cities had 4,012 murders. New York City, which had 12 homophobic murders in 1995, had 1,177 overall in 1995. The data on aggregated assaults provide an even more startling picture. For example, all told, combining assaults with and without weapons and attempted assaults, there were 320 reported assaults against gays in New York City identifiable as anti-gay. The precise figure of assault with a weapon was 83. The total count of assaults in New York City, according to FBI data, was 52,322. Even allowing for discrepancies created by varying definitions and the size of the gay population, the gap in proportionality is huge. Living in urban areas is dangerous, regardless of sexual preference. Nor can these differences be explained away as gross underreporting by gays versus nongays. Such might be the case in minor crimes such as harassment or verbal abuse but not in murder or serious assault. Moreover, both gays and nongays probably underreport.

The Character of Alleged Homophobia: Campaigns Against Gay Teachers

The instruction of the young by homosexual teachers has emerged as an emotional hot-button issue. Polls have long revealed an aversion to gay teachers, especially for younger children. A 1993 CBS News/*New York Times* survey, for example, found that only 44.5 percent would not mind if their child's elementary school teacher were gay (50.5 percent said they would mind). By way of comparison, majorities would not demur if their doctor, accountant, or political representative were homosexual (CBS News/*New York Times,* 1995).[5] If public opinion polls dictated policy, thousands of gay and lesbian teachers would be dismissed tomorrow. Yet, alleged homophobia in education is not a simple matter of tolerating unconventional sexuality. The teacher's private sexual preferences are but one item on the agenda; an entire range of pedagogical choices, from textbook material about gays to allowable after-school gay-oriented clubs, inevitably bubbles up in these controversies. It is not surprising, then, that disputes between gays and nongays in education are often bitter and wide-ranging.

Is homophobia systematically driving gay teachers from their positions? The overall picture, though incomplete given the lack of systematic national studies, bears a familiar resemblance to the abusive hate-crimes tale: A gulf separates the provocative rhetoric and the less disturbing events beyond the limelight. Organizations and activists depict gay and lesbian teachers under siege. When describing the attacks on gays in education, a People for the American Way spokesperson talked of "whipping up hysteria" to "challenge issues at the federal level," while describing these local anti-gay activities as "a national witch hunt" (*Time,* April 29, 1996, 68). To gay organizations monitoring the situation, the absence of overt hostility plus greater openness of homosexuality among teachers only masks dangerous below-the-surface at-risk conditions.

Kevin Jennings, a leading gay-activist in education and the founder of the enterprising Gay, Lesbian and Straight Teachers Network, announces with consternation that only recently are we attending to the rise of homophobia in the schools (Jennings, 1994, 11). His collection of first-hand experiences of gay and lesbian teachers (*One Teacher in Ten*) also notes that this oppressive atmosphere is particularly powerful among lesbians, lesbians of color, and those living in the South (12). In fact, so mighty is this homophobia coupled with general societal racism that every lesbian of color teacher asked to contribute to *One Teacher in Ten* fearfully declined (13).

Many of the thirty-four participants in Jennings' symposium almost ritualistically pay homage to the inhospitable, fear-generating circumstances they confront. A dread of being "outed" is ubiquitous. Others, like Raymond Saint Pierre, a gay New York City teacher, hint at some larger conspiracy. As he forcefully put it, "I teach in the center of a maelstrom of homophobia expressed in the media, society, and consequently, in my classroom" (165). Ironically, his classroom displays posters on HIV, AIDS, the Gay Games, and other similar topics. Robert Parlin, a Newton, Massachusetts history instructor, is more typical in his unease, imagining a community up in arms should he come out of the closet. "I feared coming under attack from all sides, helpless to stop responses ranging from hurtful comments to malicious destruction of my property. I anticipated outraged calls from parents, who would remove their children from my classes. I imagined students running into my room, yelling 'Faggot,' through the open doorway. I expected to one day find my car in the faculty parking lot with its tires slashed" (220-221). Parlin did "come out" and none of this transpired. Evidence of homophobia is sometimes derived from off-hand remarks, jokes, and similar revelations rather than formal policy.[6]

Obtaining a clear and scientific picture of possible homophobic expulsions from teaching is presently a near impossibility. Nevertheless, I contacted various union representatives, legal defense organizations in New York and Chicago, and activist groups in education who monitor homophobia. Through either personal telephone interviews or questionnaires using a semi-structured format, respondents were asked about gay teacher problems—to their knowledge, had any been fired or otherwise driven out? were they at risk physically? what happened to those with troubles? and so on. Some inquiries drew a "we don't know of any" response or an unfulfilled promise to send accounts. Given the alertness of gay protection networks, I interpret inaction as evidence of no serious threat. Surely, if an illustrative story were to be told of inhuman treatment, it would be proclaimed loudly. The highly personal stories from *One Teacher in Ten* also furnish rich, complementary though unrepresentative, anecdotal evidence.

How many gay teachers have been fired, in their own or expert estimation, due principally to their sexual preferences? Or, if not dismissed outright, how many have otherwise substantially been harmed in their professional careers, for example, denied promotion or given unpleasant assignments? Before getting to numbers, some general statistical context is necessary. No official figures exist regarding "out" or "closeted" teachers, but the total must be substantial. Official government estimates of primary and secondary teachers (public and private) in 1994 was 2,890,000 (*U.S. Statistical Abstract, 1995,* 162). If claims of 1 in 10 are valid, this suggests about 289,000 gay teachers. One sympathetic study of gay teachers based on extensive interviewing (with referrals) estimated the proportion of gay teachers as exceeding their proportion in the population generally (Woog, 1995, 15). If gays make up merely 2 percent (not 10 percent), the predicted number of gay teachers would be approximately 60,000. Firing just 1 percent solely due to their sexuality could generate a sizable vocal group.

Our cursory inquest discovered not much vindictiveness. This does *not* mean that the schools are conflict-free, that all school boards and administrators sincerely want gay teachers, that harassment is only fantasized, or that parents are unbothered by homosexual instructors. No doubt, it is still easier to be a straight rather than a gay teacher, all things being equal. Still, searching for extensive, systematic expulsion efforts comes up largely empty-handed, especially given the alleged potential number of cases. Predictably, matters of dispute arise when gay teachers claim unfairness due to their gay identity. A New York Lambda Legal Defense and Education Foundation attorney noted that incidents are routinely reported to his organization, and many complainants receive professional legal representation (interview 10/31/96). These are quite real and perhaps traumatic. Nevertheless, cut-and-dried cases of rampant homophobia bringing about dismissal are rare; most accusations by gay teachers describe subtle irritation or other matters of intricate interpretation. And this assessment is made in an environment— New York City—that has witnessed some intense conflicts over gays in the classroom.[7] Make no mistake, gay teachers do unwillingly quit under homophobic circumstances; outright firing, however, is seldom the route. It is also worth noting, according to this attorney directly involved in many cases, that gay teachers forced out (justifiably or otherwise) typically receive financial settlements (a year or two of salary is typical). Many ex-teachers become independent entrepreneurs. We must emphasize, however, that the charge of "fired due to homophobia" is an accusation, not always an impartially verified fact.

A gay teacher in a small, conservative Pennsylvania town long active in the National Education Association, the largest of the teachers unions, volunteers a similar insight. As the elected president of his regional union branch (16,000 members) he has often worked with other gays in education at the national level (interview 11/12/96). Being an official union representative requires that he actively participate in teacher termination disputes, seeing a range of evidence, not just mere accusation. He recounts a familiar tale: Yes, stories pass along the grapevine of a few teachers having contracts vanish once their homosexuality surfaces and, yes, some teachers battle hostile administrators due to sexuality. Nevertheless, these sparse, sometimes vaguely remembered, accounts do not make up a documented account of abundant casualities. To emphasize, not a single clear-cut case of termination due to sexual preference was offered.

A corroborating account comes from another union representative, a lesbian teacher employed in Dade County, Florida, an area with a large, socially conservative Hispanic population (interview 10/29/96). In her conversations with gay and lesbian teachers still closeted, she reports serious anxiety over possible community reaction if they were discovered. This is quite typical and, undoubtedly, sincerely felt. Nevertheless, if past community reaction foretells the future, such nervousness is unjustified. To this union representative's knowledge, not a single gay teacher among the many thousands employed in the Dade County area was driven out for homosexuality. Her own personal experience, and that of fellow gay union members, was that coming out prompted heartfelt support among administrators, fellow teachers, and even parents and students. Indeed, her union position has awarded her news media notoriety as "the lesbian teacher" in Dade County with no adverse personal or professional impact.

What, then, are the incidents galvanizing gay groups to sound the distress-signal regarding dangerous homophobia ever-lurking in the schools? There are several events for which information exists and let us take a brief look. The most famous is "the Michigan story," which has gained national attention. Gerry Crane was a popular and successful music teacher at Byron Center High School, in the socially conservative suburb of Grand Rapids, Michigan. His problems began when his gay "marriage" became community knowledge. When a student used anti-gay language in class ("faggot"), Crane responded by speaking about tolerance for homosexuals and other unorthodoxies. The upshot of this classroom encounter was a formal reprimand from the school principal demanding that in-class expressions of tolerance for gays cease. The entire matter soon boiled over, with numerous parents demanding Crane's ouster despite his well-regarded teaching. A few students under pressure dropped his music class. Crane himself received hate mail, some with Biblical themes. Eventually, after protracted, accusation-filled negotiations and publicity, Crane resigned, receiving one year's salary plus continued health benefits as a settlement. According to the Byron Center, Michigan Board of Education, "Individuals who espouse homosexuality do not constitute proper role models as teachers for students in this district." Crane plans to continue in education, if possible (*The Grand Rapids Press,* March 19, 1996; America Online: DB LLDEF 8-13-1996).

A second incident involves a Chapel Hill, North Carolina English teacher who in 1992 began a well-publicized, officially sanctioned high school support group for gay and bisexual students. His class windows were soon shot out and stones, bottles, and even a dead possum were thrown in. "Bruton's a faggot" was spraypainted on the school, ten school buses, sidewalks and elsewhere in Chapel Hill for all to see. Some small structures and a truck were set on fire. The reply to this frightening outrage? The police responded fully, set a trap, and apprehended the three culprits, all of whom were Bruton's students. Fellow faculty and administrators were shocked and proffered their full support to the harassed teacher, with one proposing a faculty protest demonstration against the violence. This was agreed on, and when this "day of protest" occurred, discussions regarding homophobia were conducted in all classes. And to everyone's surprise, when the faculty as planned marched out, the students abandoned their classes to join in. Both the instructors and pupils locked hands to form a giant circle of support. Other students expressed their outrage over events more personally, a few offering to "take care" of any future troublemakers (Jennings, 1994, 180-181).

David Bruton's tale parallels other accounts in *One Teacher in 10* and similar accounts portrayed in Dan Woog's *School's Out* (1995). These histories frequently possess two recurring, pertinent themes. First, gay teachers *overwhelmingly* achieve full acceptance by administrators, fellow teachers, and their students when their homosexuality becomes public. This support can emerge from unexpected places, such as socially conservative administrators and rural, religious parents. This is true even when "the outing" is involuntary—for example, when students accidentally observe their teacher attending gay events. The anticipated nightmare of official and communal rejection *never* materializes. Woog, for example, recounts one tale of fearful gay teachers marching in a gay pride parade with paper bags over their heads. When TV coverage inadvertently outed them, the response from school administrators and colleagues was overwhelmingly favorable. When a lesbian industrial arts teacher in Goshen, Massachusetts took her partner to the senior prom, there was no backlash at all. At worst, the exposed teacher encounters a stray sexual innuendo or an expression of minor and inconsequential hostility from a parent.[8]

Furthermore, those maltreating the outed teacher are inevitably punished, never glorified. An offending student gets a swift trip to the principal's office for a reprimand. When serious problems surface with school boards or local political office-holders, the presence of sympathetic unions and political organizations offers effective legal protection. It cannot be overemphasized that the unionization of education plus legal redress impedes homophobia. Even in highly conservative rural areas such as Montana, efforts to "get" a gay teacher typically go nowhere (Woog, 1995, 187-196). In sum, to the extent that these accounts reflect overall conditions, being an openly gay teacher is seldom, if ever, a serious liability. There are costs to being gay but they are apparently modest.

The second theme is less obvious, more nebulous, and perhaps invisible to gay teachers. This concerns the basis of parental objections. Specifically, gay instructors often—what proportion, we cannot estimate—bring to the school an ideologically tinged agenda existing independently from private sexuality. Most commonly, this baggage is directly related to the contemporary activist notion of what it means to be gay. To be authentically gay, according to this concept, requires public pride, an affirmation of one's distinct sexuality, and sporadic outspokenness. This "gay pride" often translates into an open evangelical spirit in which even the disinterested must acknowledge the message of gay legitimacy. This can translate concretely into establishing a gay student club, promoting greater school awareness of homophobia, counseling students unsure of their sexuality, using instructional materials or entertainment explicitly depicting gays, and otherwise introducing homosexuality into contexts in which it was once unknown.

More understated than assigning gay-theme texts is interjecting "cultural liberalism" into the school environment. Given that so many frank, activist gay teachers reside in the cultural left part of the political spectrum, this is predictable.[9] The outspoken gay teacher may simultaneously advance both the legitimacy of openly facing homosexuality and, less plainly, other unsettled policies. In some instances, these controversial messages, judged as "obvious nondebatable reality" by the teacher, are conveyed to children as matter-of-fact instruction. For example, that sexuality is purely a matter of personal choice existing apart from moral imperatives. This leftist tilt is also revealed in who is chastised—conservative parents imposing their religion-based prudish views, parochial small town folk with narrow minds, and all those not in tune with the latest left cultural fashions. Significantly, many gay teachers express an almost compulsive need to come out to their students, even when their pupils are children. And, when they do come out, this experience seems to energize their "gayness" (Woog, 1995, 16). The message is thus conveyed that one's most private sexuality is critically self-defining in our society. Moreover, weighty matters incontestable to many families, such as the preeminence of parents in education, are matter-of-factly judged debatable in class despite these youngsters' naiveté. Some accounts in *One Teacher in 10* makes this perspective more concrete:

A lesbian teacher in a small rural Iowa town attended a school assembly in which U.S. flags were paraded and vigorous speeches offered on the importance of patriotism and the virtue of religion in protecting America from its enemies. When the audience stood for the pledge of allegiance, she conspicuously remained seated in protest. After the ceremony, she raised the issue of why patriotism was necessary among her students. Her classroom library was also designed to reflect *precisely* the U.S. ethnic population—11 percent of the books were about black people, 48 percent about men and so on. Though her actions caused a heated stir, she was rehired but opted not to return the following year (Jennings, 1994, 33-36).

A California English teacher assigned Larry Kramer's *The Normal Heart* to his students so as to explain that the killing of gays by AIDS is an example of the dominant culture's insensitivity to the plight of human beings. The existence of AIDS and HIV was portrayed as a form of injustice, almost a conspiracy. That this epidemic was self-inflicted and some of the proposed remedies—shutting gay bathhouses—were resisted by gays was, apparently never mentioned (Jennings, 1994, 235).

When a Cincinnati, Ohio lesbian teacher voluntarily announced her homosexuality in the local newspaper, she decided to share her views on being gay with her students who ranged in age from six to nine. She explained that lesbians were women who loved other women and how she and her lover planned to raise their teenager. When children asked about the gays in the military issue, she commented that it made her sad that some people discriminated in such fashion. (Jennings, 1994, 213)

The upshot of this ideological intrusion is that tolerating a gay teacher is far more encompassing than simply silencing gay teachers on private sexual preferences. For many nongays, particularly parents of schoolchildren, this is undoubtedly a highly consequential distinction and surfaces relentlessly in parental complaints. This is roughly reflected in survey data. A CBS News/*New York Times* poll, for example, found that 80 percent affirmed the right of gays to have equal employment opportunity, yet 60 percent would not permit their children to read a book portraying a homosexual couple. A similar number objected to children watching a TV comedy show with a gay character. (CBS News/*New York Times* poll, 1993). The distinction regarding accepting homosexuality as a personal choice versus openly flaunting one's gayness is murkier for many gay teachers, apparently. Thus, opposition to certain policies endorsed by gays, such as gay marriage, is (falsely) interpreted as opposition to private sexuality.

The Other Side of the Story

Gay organizations dogmatically see conspiracies among conservatives, especially Christian fundamentalists, to drive homosexuality from the planet.[10] This is a deceptively intricate accusation. Clearly, the public resists full legitimization of homosexuality. Polls, as Chapter 5 showed, routinely proclaim majority moral reservations about gay sex. Furthermore, a sizable number—38 percent in the 1993 CBS News/*New York Times* survey—would forbid this sexual practice altogether. Legal restrictions continue to apply, moreover. The Supreme Court in *Bowers v. Hardwick* (1986) upheld the constitutionality of a sodomy law involving the private behavior of homosexuals.[11] Sodomy laws also remain on the books in more than half the states (Posner & Silbaugh, 1996). Nevertheless, not every private hatred surfaces or funds calls to remake society. Chapter 2's explication of the many nuances of tolerance amply traced the huge gulf often separating desire and accomplishment. To conclude that the fact that most group members hate gay sex means that their membership fuels an extermination campaign goes too far.

Politics is the art of the possible, not constructing moral Utopias. Fathoming the inner, secret thoughts of those who loath homosexuality may be fascinating, but this task belongs to the psychologists. Our concern is political tolerance, and this demands attention to what public policies anti-gay organization seek.

What messages are sent forth by anti-gay groups in their brochures and press releases? Material from four prominent, seemingly typical, groups was collected: The Eagle Forum, Family Research Council, Concerned Women of America, and the Family Defense Council.[12] Regardless of group member private opinions, lashing out against private adult homosexual behavior is rare and, if voiced, quite mild. These organizations worry about the legitimization of homosexuality as "normal" and the conveyance of this vision to schoolchildren and its incorporation into law. The campaign, and it is not always a key element of a group's activities, is against same-sex marriages, gays in the military, sex education encouraging experimentation, adoptions by gays, and other aspects of traditional public morality. The fundamental distinction is between "culture" and "personal."

Didi Herman's "*The Antigay Agenda*" (1997), an avowedly pro-gay book that painstakingly scrutinizess the Christian Right's battle with homosexuality, *confirms* this portrait in far greater detail. She frankly admits that today's war is about legal issues and cultural acceptance, not re-criminalizing homosexuality (5). She further acknowledges that prominent Christian religious leaders exhibit a range of reactions toward gays, from charitable acceptance to admonishing them for their sins. But forced therapy or legal prohibitions are *not* on their agenda. Equally important, the catalogue of anti-gay actions committed by the Christian Right hardly constitutes burning suspected gays at the stake. Activities include warning parents about school materials, testifying at legislative hearings, publishing condemnations in the religious press, conducting research on gay behavior, and similar prosaic political endeavors. No evidence whatsoever is offered of abusive anti-gay behavior or organizing vigilante attacks, no trashing of gay bookstores or hurling eggs at those marching in gay parades. Private homosexuality is a nonissue, according to Herman. The very term *anti-gay* is largely a misnomer; the terminology should be *anti-gay political movement.* Anti-gay crusaders, at least those with a high profile in this field, want to return gays to the closet, not exterminate them, moral aversion aside. Perhaps John Locke's advice is being heeded: One must tolerate that which can never be banished.

Accepting private behavior is not pure fatalism. Society need not be so tolerant. A dramatically different scenario is quite possible. Given that many businesses illegally permit open homosexual sexual encounters, a frontal legal assault on certain gay practices via "simply enforcing the law" is perfectly feasible. Discrimination solely on sexual preferences is also still legally permissible in much of the country. Likewise, government possesses no statutory obligation to spend fortunes eradicating AIDS to the neglect of other equally worthy causes. Being gay could be viewed as no different from indulging in a risky weakness, a predilection akin to alcoholism and drug addiction. Forced therapy to cure those apprehended for succumbing to the temptation of risky homosexual eroticism is conceivable, just as drug addicts caught in criminal acts are occasionally forced into therapy.[13] Nothing of this, however, emanates from these organizations.

Rendering a Verdict

We initially likened our inquest to a trial. The charge was that contemporary American society and innumerable political organizations are indicted on charges of homophobic intolerance. Considerable evidence from two chapters has now been submitted on both sides. Here, then, is the jury's verdict:

Homosexuals live in a society generally inhospitable to gays and lesbians. Not guilty.

Government and "the establishment" systematically engender homophobia. Not guilty.

Citizen homophobic behavior, from criminal acts to hounding teachers from schools, is extensive and serious. Not guilty.

Homosexuality as a private, personal activity is seriously under attack by "Right Wing" conservatives. Not guilty.

Homosexuality, as a broad lifestyle heavily tinged with cultural/political principles that would transform existing society, has been resisted by many political groups. Guilty.

Justifying Intolerance

How are we to interpret the last verdict? Like justifiable homicide, is there something called "justifiable intolerance"? Does "democratic tolerance" require that Americans remove all barriers to the full acceptance of homosexuality, defined not as private behavior, but as a broad cultural vision? In concrete policy terms, is the "gay lifestyle" along with same-sex marriages, gay religious assembles, the teaching of homosexuality in school sex education, and all the rest—to be mainstreamed in the name of tolerance? Are homosexuals to be granted the total *cultural*—not merely full legal—equality they now insist on? Undoubtedly, volumes could be composed here without a resolution. Perhaps all scholarship is inadequate, judgments mirror heartfelt personal convictions, not skillfully analyzed statistical data. Nevertheless, drawing on Chapter 4's analysis of intolerance, let us offer an assessment. These are not necessarily personal beliefs; we explicate a position seldom articulated in a society in which tolerance of insurgent homosexuality dominates public discourse. Readers—the ultimate jury—are invited to render their own judgment.

A cautionary note, first. Untold gays live invisible, conventional lives save for their private bedroom behavior. Our discussion about gays advancing a distinctive cultural agenda purposely clashing with mainstream America *cannot* apply to them. Some gays might even dismiss the militant side of gay life as an unrepresentative extremist fringe. This possibility is readily acknowledged but irrelevant. Our concern is for that segment of the gay community, no matter how large or small, proselytizes for full communal legitimacy. And in some instances, the goal is cultural transformation. As one member of the militant ACT-UP! expressed it, "It's not merely tolerance we are looking for. It's something more profound than that, and something much more important too. Social institutions need to be redefined to encompass wider groups. And I think that is what the gay rights movement is doing; we're trying to change the culture" (quoted in Lockhead in Bawer, 1996, 56-57). Or, as one gay activist bluntly put it in a TV interview, "We don't want a place at the table—we want to turn the table over" (quoted in Bawer, 1996, 1). It is this often highly visible and quite strident request for full public admission, not merely being privately gay, that we review. Our answer, recall, is that it *could* be excluded.

Most apparently, that our society enjoys the right, some would say obligation, to govern public morality and decorum is beyond contention, especially to protect children.[14] Neither Locke nor Mill, the alleged patron saints of modern permissive tolerance would object. They might well join in this quest for restraint. Though some gays and lesbians define lewd public exhibitionism as integral to their gay self-identity, relish public billboards depicting naked teenage boys in provocative poses, and find collective pride in outraging heterosexual sensibilities with open homoerotic displays, this scarcely deserves tolerance-justified protection. Heterosexuals suffer nearly identical restraints. Provided uniformly enforced statutes conform to judicial guidelines, gays cannot unilaterally exempt themselves from state-imposed decorum by invoking a privileged lifestyle. It is not the case, as a federal court had to rule in a dispute involving Dow Chemical, that a gay male, dressing as a woman, had the legal right to use the company's ladies bathroom despite the vehement objections of female employees.

Furthermore, practical justifications abound. For example, tolerating establishments promoting perilous and anonymous unsafe sexual acts threatens the public health. Visiting gay bathhouses or X-rated cinemas for erotic encounters with dozens of unknown partners may be glorified for some, but it deserves as much protection as brothels for nongays or barbershop surgery. Ditto for police hassling gays "cruising" for sex in residential neighborhoods if this encourages boisterous rowdyism and violence. Controlling the spread of sexually transmitted diseases is likewise an established state function, and this enforcement can disturb those pursuing endless erotic encounters. Excluding HIV-positive immigrants is, in principle, no different from previous restrictions on tuberculosis sufferers. Overall, the pursuit of risky, and ultimately expensive to the taxpayer, pleasure in the name of living a valid lifestyle, whether homosexual or heterosexual, cannot be defended simply by cloaking it in "tolerance."

There are far deeper bedrock issues, as well. Though making cultural delineations is hardly precise, America *does not* interpret itself as a land in which unrestrained sexual freedom serves as the path to self-actualization. At least in principle, sexual fulfillment is not to be elevated above family stability, the welfare of children, work, religious devotion, public deportment, personal loyalty, and other values comprising what might be dubbed "bourgeois morality." Despite a notable recent and selective loosening, America remains essentially puritanical, at least publicly. The traditional orthodoxy is that one's self-definition does not arise from one's sexual preferences, and people surely should not seek self-actualization through sexual adventurism.[15]

Most important, not all sexual preferences are equal under the culture's accounting rules: Restrained heterosexuality is the *moral* norm, the preferred standard, regardless of the numerical incidence of homosexuality, crossdressing or any other unusual practice. Homosexuality may exist, even be accepted as inevitable, but it is inferior to heterosexuality as a habit. The chasm between accepting the inescapable and awarding respect is unbridgeable. The existence of a preferred sexual standard is no different from the dollar serving as the official unit of currency, though some establishments might also accept foreign currency. Not all gays, of course, situate promiscuous gay hedonism on the same plane as conventional heterosexuality. However, many do and, though seldom publicly broadcast, this is an explicit part of the gay culture. Properly understood, this insistency constitutes a *radical attack on the dominant culture.*

Recall Erikson's (1968) analysis of how all communities are obliged to delineate boundaries between the permissible and the forbidden. To say that an inclination is permissible simply because some prefer it or it presents itself elsewhere is to surrender the right to be a community. There is no authoritative dictum: If it can be done or exists somewhere on the planet, let it happily transpire here. Nor can the communally subversive automatically be shielded by claims of privacy or inconsequentiality. We do have laws on solitary use of narcotics. Some things must be beyond the pale or defining strictures themselves lack meaning. Nor is tolerance a call for unilateral moral disarmament. When gays insist that school-age children "must" know about wayward sexual predilections, even if none of them are so inclined, this does not pit truth against ignorance. The identical argument applies to slavery, human sacrifices, and other enduring but nonmainstream human customs. Ironically, many of those who insist that the subject of homosexuality be included in school curricula are horrified at the prospect of a similar welcome for religion. From the perspective of many nongays, no doubt, this insistence on "equality of conventions" is far closer to saying that honesty differs hardly at all from dishonesty. Backing up this assertion with proof that, in distant places or even among some Americans, almost everyone is happily dishonest by customary standards is fundamentally irrelevant.

It is perfectly appropriate to inquire what happens if moral absolutism slides into mere co-equal differences. This "defining deviancy down" (as coined by Daniel Moynihan) has already come to pass in illegitimacy, casual drug use, easy divorce, gratuitous sexual displays in the mass media, and various conspicuous urban ills, such as public urination, graffiti, annoyingly loud music, and aggressive panhandling. The argument that a small loosening of standards can lead to collapse must be taken seriously, not automatically dismissed as a scare tactic.[16] Repeated exposure to something previously "unthinkable" can eventually render it "normal." The insistence on tolerance without regard to consequences thus weakens our immunity system to matters far more perilous (see, for example, Himmelfarb, 1994 for a more complete discussion). It is now well understood that to be indifferent to so-called minor infractions of the peace, such as permitting begging or public intoxication, can inadvertently encourage more serious infractions. That is, potential evildoers witnessing these slight breaches of civility are signaled that more grievous harms might also be tolerated (Kelling & Coles, 1996).

Regarding homosexuality, some perceive a creeping acceptance of pedophilia—homosexual sex between adults and children (not teenagers, but *children*). Though still illegal, an organization—North American Man-Boy-Love Association (NAMBLA)—does venerate it. Though one might surmise that their immoral behavior would be universally condemned by the media, especially gays seeking respectability, this is not quite true. On May 8, 1995, *New Republic* (a reputable magazine) reviewed *Chickenhawk,* a movie depicting child molester Leyland Stevenson. The review paints a rather sympathetic "human" portrait. Stevenson and other NAMBLA members, according to the movie reviewer, have gotten a bad rap. (Rosin, 1995 cited in Eberstadt, 1996).[17] Similarly, *The Advocate,* few years back took a rather tender, nonjudgmental stand on NAMBLA. Their New York City convention was portrayed as an assembly of kind and gentle souls quietly milling about, seemingly no different from a "packaged tour chartered by the local Elks lodge" (Weir, 1994). Though some gay groups take exception to NAMBLA, this disapproval is largely rooted in the bad publicity it generates and less on the sexual pursuit of young boys. Mary Eberstadt (1996), in her aptly named "Pedophilia Chic," has argued that this once-taboo topic is slowly but assuredly creeping into respectability. Obviously, we cannot contend that tolerated pedophilia is just around the corner. Perhaps. Our point is that acceptance of odd practices can easily make the once truly brazen appear a little more normal.

A *One Teacher in Ten* story illustrates how acceding to the pull of gay sexuality, once almost unthinkable, becomes comfortably acceptable. Gretchen Coburn is a grade-school teacher in Andover, New Hampshire, a small rural town. She was married to the school board's president and has two young children. After falling in love with the local female school bus driver, critical choices presented themselves. Rather than live a lie, she left the closet, divorced her husband, and began a fresh life with her female partner and their combined four children. This was a costly option for everyone. She suffered threats, obscenities, ostracism, and even vandalism. It was also, admittedly, arduous for her ex-husband and children. When reflecting on this decision, she asserts, "I must live honestly, albeit dangerously, rather than in a cocoon or a web of deceptions. . . . I can hopefully do the most important things: Teach my schoolchildren and my own children by my example, to be caring, decent, honest individuals, no matter what the price" (quoted in Jennings, 1994, 227). In other words, given a choice between deceptive conventionality and open, disruptive homosexuality, the latter is compelling.

Let us be crystal-clear about what is being illustrated. Obviously, heterosexuals of both sexes routinely abandon families for enticing sexual encounters, with unfortunate consequences. The contrast is not between idealized dutiful straights and demonized immoral gays. It is the definition of the situation that matters. Ms. Coburn does not perceive her subversion of convention as wrong. She was not a powerless victim of an imposed, uncontrolled sexuality or moral weakness. This behavior represents free will and there is no remorse, no guilt, no expression of "I wish this had not happened, but, alas, it did." The opposite is contended—it was a *positive* experience, one promoting "diversity and change" (227), not a family tragedy. She acquiesced to her unconventional sexuality, despite the human wreckage, and this is, without any qualms, a noble choice. Resisting temptation, honoring convention via deception, even if satisfying erotic desires, are all unacceptable. It is the assessing of priorities, and then taking a step once judged unthinkable that makes this tale relevant.

Likewise, the need for tolerance cannot exclude display of private moral approbation. If J. S. Mill resided today in Andover, he might well join those townfolk aghast at Ms. Coburn's breach of convention because she has entangled others. A town council edict banning such misbehavior would be excessive, to be sure. Nevertheless, one could easily envision Mill defending her children's welfare, pitying the husband's social humiliation, and bemoaning the example she has set for others similarly tempted. "How could a community endure," he might admonish, "if every sinful passion were indulged?" Other utilitarian thinkers might step further, proclaiming that abandoning families for same-sex liaisons undermines society itself by weakening the definition of family. Kai Erikson would concur, interpreting the town's damnation of flaunting conventional morality as predictable— even essential—reaffirmation of communal mores. Without public outrage, how would innocents know impermissible behavior?

Finally, note that those "intolerant" of gay attempts for cultural equality use democratic political means to accomplish their goals. Recall our discussion of Didi Herman's (1997) gay-sympathetic *The Antigay Agenda.* Assassinations, bombings, arson are not on the agenda of anti-gay groups. Calls are to elected public officials for redress of grievances, not outcries for a harsh police state. Nor are those resisting gay demands the modern incarnation of the right-wing, conspiracy-seeing, anti-Communist 1950s "nut cases." To claim otherwise is deceit. Entering electoral politics to shape public morality is both legitimate and time-honored. Laws abound on gambling, alcohol use, prostitution, pornography, marriage, child abuse, drug use, sexual conduct, and abortion. To assert that citizens with an aversion to the gay political agenda should, in the name of tolerance, refrain from lobbying government on matters of private sexual morality, let alone school instruction, is absurd politically. One may surely point out the foolishness of anti-gay political efforts, labor to rout this enemy, and resist them at every turn, but one cannot assert that the First Amendment does not apply to those who yearn to banish homosexuality from the classroom.

Conclusion: An Epilogue
on The Study of Tolerance

American society, regardless of what some homophobes might privately crave, bestows ample tolerance on homosexuals. With regard to other unorthodoxies—Marxists or Nazis, for example—we cannot pronounce. Reaching this simple, circumscribed conclusion has required a laborious voyage. Obstacles for gays, even serious obstacles, surely continue, but the chilling rhetoric of homophobic crusade betrays reality. The patient reader surviving all the burdensome details, side-trips depicting obscure lesbian publishers, statistics of homophobic verbal abuses, and all the rest, now undoubtedly appreciates the "fast and dirty" lure of tolerance assessed via a few poll questions. Numerous pages have been consumed revealing what might be demonstrated in a single table. Hopefully, however, the virtue of our formula has proven itself in enhanced enlightenment.

To be sure, America may not be the 100 percent Garden of Eden version of affirmative tolerance demanded by purists, and our analysis admittedly has empirical gaps, but in the real world of human discord, our portrait is pretty encouraging for gays. If rampant repression lurks, whether by government or private citizen, it has miraculously escaped our inquest. To those who assert that we have employed evidence selectively, we can only rejoin that this alleged nationwide campaign of brutal homophobia has remained secret. Today's "out" homosexual easily enjoys opportunities and state protections unimaginable a few decades back. Flash points—same-sex marriages, access to spousal benefits, gays in the military, ordaining openly gay clergy, increased federal funding for AIDS research, and similar policy matters—are quite distant from whether homosexuality itself warrants condemnation. Not even the most ardent religious conservative calling for a return to strict morality endorses making homosexuality a capital offense, as it once was.

A peculiar irony lies here and screams out for attention. Our depiction will likely be judged *hostile* to the gay cause. This is certainly not derived from personal inclination. Affirming that conditions are pretty good and fears of imminent repression are groundless will, unfortunately, be taken as "bad news," not welcome tidings. That we use accounts by gays themselves in our evidentiary proceedings may undoubtedly compound our malfeasance. What gay-friendly organizations treat as dogma, we behold as contentions worthy of investigation. We repudiate the party line of ever-growing wretchedness and this, we guess, makes us heretical, perhaps even homophobic. What explains this infatuation with dismal tales? What has befallen the wise custom of once-downtrodden groups memorializing their accomplishments, not their misery?

The reward structure of modern politics contributes one answer. Claims of unmerciful victimization bestow a steady flow of government-mandated benefits, from easier victories in wrongful employment termination litigation to selective exemption from law enforcement. The conquest of the moral high ground—feelings of superiority—also may lie through loudly proclaimed tales of suffering. Material and psychological incentives also go to those exhorting the troops against weak enemies. Perhaps being immoderate serves well for getting a still useful half-loaf. As Oscar Wilde opined to Lady Hunstanton, "Moderation is a fatal thing. Nothing succeeds like excess."

A better clue to this puzzle emerges if we examine group self-definition. If endlessly repeated victimization becomes integral to collective personality— we are the "suppressed people" just as others are the "chosen people"—then challenging the vision of tribulation disputes the group's very essence. A question of empirical evidence is transformed into affirmation. To deny that people defining themselves as persecuted is a falsehood is conceivably akin to informing a hypochondriac that he is "a perfectly healthy person." This seemingly upbeat assessment offered the hypochondriac is hardly gladly received: It invalidates a cherished self-image.

A subtle but key message lies here for our mastery of tolerance. Once this self-definition of oppression takes residence, the quest for tolerance may be insatiable.[18] Affirming ceaseless intolerance authentically maintains identity as an oppressed portion of society. The permanently self-defined oppressed person craving unconditional acceptance lives beyond contentment. Even if justifiable, slights, hostilities, biases and exclusions—perhaps only visible to the self-defined victim—are irreducible conditions of existence. "I am oppressed, therefore I am." A final and lasting victory is both impossible and, deep down, unsought. Charges of intolerance easily take on a ceremonial character much like some associations display honored symbols in their yearly parades or shrines. Histories become narratives of martyrdom. Such are the unhelpful wages of a subjective understanding of tolerance, an understanding definitionally divorced from plain-to-see reality. Surely, if we have demonstrated anything at all, we have proven that judgments of tolerance or intolerance must lie beyond the psychological if they are to be meaningful.

NOTES

1. In the language of social science measurement, we are transforming "tolerance-intolerance" from a nominal to an ordinal or even interval level variable. Ironically, though this practice may be novel for social science, it nevertheless seems to reflect popular usage. We see no theoretical reason why nominal level measurement is to be preferred.

2. The police raid at a gay bar or bathhouse illustrates well the problems of disentangling homophobic behavior from conduct that tangentially involves such aversion. In New York City, where I have some personal knowledge of these practices, it was widely accepted that gay establishments were tempting targets for police extortion, given harsh state laws regarding lewd behavior or sexual solicitation. A lounge would forfeit its alcohol license or be forced to close temporarily if it "permitted" certain acts to occur on its premises. Thus, because a bar (or bathhouse) could be "busted" almost at any time, police bribery was essential for staying in business. Raids reminded owners of this police power or coerced those reluctant to pay bribes. Overall, police corruption is more the culprit than homophobia, though certainly a degree of repugnance to gays facilitated these shakedowns. In a sense, these harassed gays are "innocent victims," though some may have violated capriciously enforced law.

3. This complexity is made even worse because gay organizations do not publicly acknowledge unsavory and highly risky aspects of gay sexual behavior. These precarious amusements (often illegal when prostitution is involved) may put an entirely different spin on brutal murders. There is no formal documentation here, just a reliance on anecdotal information based on decades of witnessing the gay scene from a distance and talking with gay friends. For example, certain gay men have a predilection for "rough trade"—picking up lower-class tough-looking males for sexual conquest or prostitution. The very aroma of imminent violence can make these liaisons very sexually attractive. Combining this taste with high frequency is surely a recipe for violent risk. Other gay males pretend to be female prostitutes—"she-males" or "nobbers"—and hiding this from their clients. Violent retribution may well occur when this deception is accidentally revealed.

4. Also conveniently ignored when gay groups are outraged at anti-gay violence is the tradition of young male (usually heterosexual) hustlers bartering sex for money. Most of these youths are lower-class delinquents on their way to a life of crime. Because soliciting sex for money is illegal, the gay john is often almost defenseless against extortion or physical abuse. Matters are made even worse if the gay person is attracted to under-age hustlers (in gay parlance, those with a taste for youngsters are "chicken hawks"). Needless to say, reducing risks of bodily harm associated with pursuing male prostitute hustlers is not easily accomplished (See Comstock, 1993, Appendix D for a discussion of hustlers and the gay sex trade.)

5. The question only asked respondents to imagine having a child in elementary school; whether or not they had a child in that situation is unavailable. The real question, of course, concerns parents with children in those circumstances.

6. One case in particular deserves special mention. Here, two lesbians were "married" and went off for a Mexican honeymoon. This "marriage" was not announced to most of their fellow teachers (due to fear of coming out, undoubtedly). However, one of the lesbian teachers is deeply upset that she, unlike heterosexuals, is unable to receive engagement or wedding gifts. This incident of foregone recognition, at least in her estimation, makes her a "second class citizen." (Jennings, 1994, 152).

7. New York City witnessed one of the most well-publicized confrontations over the teaching of homosexuality: The conflict in Queens' Unit 24 when parents strenuously objected to young children being exposed to books with explicit gay themes. Despite all the highly charged rhetoric, threats, and the conflict spilling over into politics, not a single teacher lost his or her job. The only

casualty was the chancellor of the city schools, Joseph Fernandez, who eventually resigned in 1993, but his tenure was also troubled by many other issues.

8. The experience of gay teachers appears to be more general. One study of gays who have "come out" in corporations reports that nearly all found their supervisor's reaction to be positive. Only 5 percent were negative; 2 percent were "very negative." Of course, it might be argued that gays wanting to "come out" gravitate to more hospitable companies (Mickens, 1994).

9. The leftist character of organized gays is often obscured by purely sexual issues. Nevertheless, if one takes a close look at the platform of the 1993 March on Washington for Lesbian, Gay and Bi Equal Rights and Liberation, a well-attended "official" rally, one sees a far more expansive vision. Besides the predictable calls for pro-gay sexual policies, one finds demands for ending all poverty, the endorsement of affirmative action, stopping domestic and international economic oppression, abolishing censorship, greater effort to end racism, abolishing "English only" laws, support for abortion, and a truly massive increase in government spending in health-related fields. The latter would include, for example, the redefinition of sex-change operations as medical, not cosmetic, procedures (thus making it coverable by insurance). Save matters dealing with sexual practices and abortion, all these proposals entail the expansion of the federal government's power and higher taxes.

10. There is also the other side of this coin: How defenders of the gay agenda view religious fundamentalists. Harsh, unsupported accusations of bigotry and stereotyping are common. For example, one guide to alerting educators to lurking hate crimes singled out certain words as a likely tip-off to nefarious intent. These included *Church, Creator, Jesus, Christian,* and *Scripture* (Manatt & Dripps, 1994).

11. Though this case received extensive attention and may be construed as a lingering anachronism from the time when homosexuality was a capital offense, in reality this law is rarely enforced. When it is enforced, it is employed against public behavior or in situations on which the act is involuntary but the coercion is difficult to prove. In twenty-two states, there are no statutes against sodomy; in the others, sodomy convictions are roughly divided between misdemeanors and felonies (Posner & Silbaugh, 1996).

12. Groups were selected according to the following criteria: (1) their name was often mentioned by gays, (2) information in organizational directories indicated a degree of professionalism and sizable membership, and (3) signs of political activism, such as testifying before government, TV programs, and frequent mailings. There are, no doubt, many tiny groups escaping our attention, entities probably little more than small, localized self-publishing enterprises. A comprehensive canvass of all organizations would more than likely uncover a few that defied our assessment. But our findings resonate with the larger canvass conducted by Herman (1997) and she takes a decidedly pro-gay perspective.

13. Technically, according to the American Psychiatric Association, homosexuality was a treatable illness until December 15, 1973. On that date, largely due to intense pressure from gay activists, homosexuality was removed from the official list of sociopathic disorders. Some psychiatrists still treat being gay as an illness, however.

14. This chasm between protecting society and protecting children surfaces repeatedly in poll data. For example, a 1993 national survey found a clear majority of respondents adverse to permitting homosexuals to legally adopt children. In the same poll, equally well-defined majorities endorse anti-job discrimination laws to protect gays and expressed a willingness to work with gays, despite a potential AIDS threat (Rosenstone, Kinder, Miller, & the National Elections Studies, 1993).

15. Our analysis of sexual adventurism largely concerns men; lesbians have traditionally been more restrained in their sexual inclinations. An overview of the current lesbian scene, however, reveals that this may be changing: lesbians are also becoming more visible and celebratory in their erotic passion. This is particularly evident in parades in which at least some lesbians relish public sexual displays and partial nudity. Bars catering to lesbians enjoying openly lewd shows have also

become commonplace. Also recall the lesbian "'zines" described in the last chapter that rival gay male carnal appetites. One example of legitimizing this new orientation to female erotic exploration is *The Persistent Desire: A Femme-Butch Reader* (1992).

16. This argument emerges from both sides of the political spectrum. Some militant feminists, for example, make the identical case regarding pornography—even the innocuous *Playboy* begins the slide down the slippery slope toward the physical degradation of women.

17. Another example of this mainstreaming of pedophilia is the glowing critical reaction to the New York play *How I Learned to Drive*. The play offers a *sympathetic* depiction of a bisexual molester of an eleven-year-old girl. The *New York Times* gave the drama rave reviews, lauding the treatment accorded the molester. Similar sentiments were echoed by *New York Magazine*. Despite this favorable portrayal of child molestation, the play was judged "best new play 1996-1997" by the New York Drama Critics Circle.

18. The futility of this endless quest for tolerance is suggested by antagonisms surfacing within gay organizations. In particular, some gay organizations divide on who is an "authentic" community member worthy of full acceptance. For example, are men surgically transformed into "women" to be treated as women? Are transsexual hustlers praying on heterosexuals to be welcomed into the gay community? At least some gays, for a variety of practical and ideological reasons, express intolerance to such transgendered and transsexual people. In addition, some gay White men now complain of intolerance by radical lesbian feminists. In short, the quest for full tolerance is endless. This issue of intra-gay intolerance is further explored in Bawer (1996).

Achieving
Political Tolerance

Sustaining a reasonably heterogeneous and peaceful society is perplexing. Acrimonious divisions in North Ireland, Algeria, Russia, Lebanon,
Bosnia, Cyprus, Israel, Egypt and a myriad other countries well demonstrate
the obstacles to a peaceful "live and let live." Yet, tolerance of the disagreeable is a prerequisite for civil society. How, then, is this to be accomplished
while avoiding the twin dangers of intrusive government brainwashing and
abandoning community altogether in the name of "everything goes"? In the
United States, for example, how can we prevent animosities between, say,
Blacks and Whites from boiling over into strife?

Achieving an atmosphere of "live and let live" is hardly a novel task.
Proposals undoubtedly number in the hundreds; everyone has a scheme from
gentle admonitions to secession. Indeed, this problem is imbedded in the very
idea of governance. Prospective solutions surely go back to our civic beginning, the Constitution. It is a conceit to imagine that our current struggle at
managing diversity to ensure tranquillity is a fresh phenomenon. The United
States itself was created in the midst of a multitude of competing, often
hostile, interests. Even unity itself, let alone peaceful coexistence, was not
universally insisted on two hundred years back. The thirteen states were
divided along numerous lines—quarrels over religion, commerce, slavery,

and ideology all plagued the incipient government. A plethora of recommendations, from a strong monarchy to greater decentralization, abounded.

Today's nostrum of instilling a forgiving tolerance as the cure, however,
escaped the menu of therapies. Only recently has "hearts and minds tolerance" surfaced as the default option. We seem to be obsessed with collecting
people together into a heterogeneous society and then compelling them to
get along. Two hundred years ago, solutions were less ambitious. To hint, for
example, that New Englanders rewrite their history texts to better appreciate
Virginia slave-owners was unthinkable. The path to peaceful civil society lay
through judicious political accommodation and legal guarantees, not citizen
indoctrination. Constitutional architects assumed that human beings, by their
innate temper, were ill-suited to suffer noxious views. The narrowest of
tolerance windows was the ordinary human condition. Society was a bottled-
up collection of hatreds, animosities, and envies always on the verge of
turmoil. Impoverished farmers would not be deterred from seizing the
property of merchants by proselytizing respect for differences. The accommodation was to be imposed by the design of government, the distribution
of power, and the strict enforcement of difficult-to-alter laws. Tolerance was
to exist despite powerful urges to the contrary.

Relying on mechanisms far removed from the inner thoughts of ordinary
citizens has, alas, fallen into temporary neglect. Older devices facilitating
peacefulness amid strong differences—federalism, checks and balances,
separation of powers, geographical dispersion, constitution legal guarantees,
and super-majorities for alterations—have, unfortunately, become "mere"
history, despite their continued and successful presence. They are often
beheld as antique medical instruments suitable for a museum, not for contemporary applications. Today's infatuation with education, building better
citizens via masterful early state intervention, has crowded out these older
remedies as successful models. Here we dust off powerful mechanisms
outside today's repertoire when pursuing harmony in a society marred by
quarrelsome divisions. We draw deeply, though rather eclectically, from this
earlier, less fashionable spirit, namely, a reliance on political and social
arrangements rather than remolding citizens.

We avow no guaranteed universal cures for mayhem. Our nostrums might
prove beneficial, but only their future implementation can ultimately demonstrate worthiness. Nor are we arguing that our "old-fashioned" remedies
are inherently more effective than modern psychologically based contrivances. To repeat, we merely augment the agenda of solutions beyond hearts
and minds tolerance. Of the many hundreds of alternatives to inculcating
citizen respect for differences, we limit our canvass to three quite general

possibilities. All seem feasible, have proven themselves and, perhaps most important, neither impair a free society nor weaken communal identity.

The first is legal compulsion. People acquiesce to disagreeable tendencies because to do otherwise risks state-imposed punishment. Only outward compliance matters. The hated local Communist Party is ignored because courts routinely reverse prosecution or Communists successfully sue for harassment. Separation of antagonists, either voluntary or forced, is the second path toward political tolerance. This disengagement is no different, in principle, from dispatching brawling children off to their own rooms—in a phrase, imposed communalism. Finally, there are adaptive solutions. Those not tolerated learn to be invisible or otherwise adapt to a hostile climate. As in evolution, fragile creatures evolve to survive by altering their coloration, diets, or defensive strategies.

I. Compulsory Tolerance

The word *tolerance* invokes a voluntary spirit in the granting of acceptance. Embracing the disagreeable, gun to one's head, seemingly subverts the spirit of live and let live. "Police-state tolerance" is a bizarre concoction. Nevertheless, though seldom acknowledged as such, state-sanctioned compulsion is an oft-repeated technique of ensuring heterogeneity. After all, what is the criminal code other than imposed restraint? Hate-crime legislation or instituting campus speech codes prohibiting offensiveness similarly reflects recourse to coercive tolerance. More consequential are anti-discrimination laws, administrative edicts, and court orders forbidding citizens from making invidious distinctions. It is no exaggeration to characterize modern society as "tolerance or else." Refusing to "put up with" a person because of race or age, in employment or in housing, to cite but a couple of the criteria for forced acceptance, is now illegal.

Despite this popularity, however, forced toleration via legislation hardly proves to be a guaranteed cure-all. Ordinances demanding acceptance of differences abound, yet proponents of this stratagem ceaselessly call for fresh laws, more stringent enforcement, and greater citizen commitment. The germane question is when and how, not compulsion versus voluntarism. As in medicine, an excellent cure for one malady may exacerbate another. Enacting yet one more noble-sounding hate-crime bill may be more akin to a magical ceremony intended to invoke the spirit of tolerance than to assist. Here we observe but a single *successful* instance (out of innumerable attempts) of coercive tolerance proving effective, namely, the U.S. Army's far-reaching anti-racism campaign. It is to be hoped that we extract lessons on how potential antagonists can attain a reasonable *rapprochement* with judicious compulsion.

African Americans have continuously served in the U.S. Army from the Revolutionary War onward. Affinity between races and the treatment accorded Black soldiers have varied greatly, often depending on the military's needs and conflict intensity. Wartime necessity often brought improvement followed by peacetime deteriorations. The post-World War II era witnessed manifold shifts, as well. Prior to 1948, strict segregation ensured that racial conflicts were seldom personal. Segregation ended by the time of the Korean War, but African Americans remained concentrated in the lower ranks. Nevertheless, despite this inequality, the pre-Vietnam era army displayed far less racial strife than in civilian life. The military even optimistically portrayed itself as a harbinger of a forthcoming tranquil, multiracial society.

The Vietnam War, coupled with upheavals in society, more generally brought abrupt changes. Newly aroused racial discord fueled by the rise of militant Black Power, spreading racial nationalism, urban riots, the King assassination, and White resistance to integration, quickly crept into the armed services. That the anti-war movement successfully characterized the war as disproportionally lethal to economically disadvantaged black recruits added gasoline to the fire. Some civil rights leaders repeated these charges and further denounced military adventurism as hindering the resolution of pressing domestic issues. The upshot was agitated turmoil among recruits, innumerable fights, and self-imposition of racial segregation. Morale deteriorated sharply and combat effectiveness became a serious problem. The decline continued during the post-war 1970s, now compounded by spreading drug use (Moskos & Butler, 1996, Chapter 2).

By the early 1980s, racial antagonisms had sufficiently ebbed to attract intensive remediation. The underlying issue was hardly abstract: Fielding combat units in which soldiers viciously quarreled invited disaster. Weapons could just as easily be turned on each other, not the enemy. Several broad changes greatly facilitated the achievement of harmony. Most plainly, the shift to an all-volunteer, more technically adept force of reduced numbers increased the overall quality of recruits. The poorly educated, socially troublesome inductee of yesteryear soon vanished. The shift from cash up-front signing bonuses to post-military educational benefits likewise drew "better" enrollees while encouraging the completion of enlistments. The cooling down of highly charged rhetoric outside the services further helped.

Of critical importance were internal changes. Here, clues to sustaining tolerance emerge. Notably, unlike many universities and other civilian institutions occupied with vague, contentious "atmospheres," the army focused on discernible *behavioral consequences,* not lofty abstractions. Army rules forbid "provoking speech or gestures," but punishment for such offenses requires a precise demonstration of military impact. No attempt is made to protect troops, black or white, from "insensitivities" divorced from organization consequences. It is assumed that African American soldiers—and all others—can fend for themselves with the petty, day-to-day frictions endemic to close-quarter life. Only when comportment threatens military effectiveness is compulsion obligatory. Hate speech is not a stand-alone offense, it is punished only when engendering a more serious problem, such as rioting.[1] The upshot is credibility and respect when coercion is employed. This is a far cry from universities instigating encompassing campaigns against all offensiveness, no matter how innocuous (Moskos & Butler, 1996, Chapter 4). A similar restraint applies to soldiers affiliated with so-called hate groups. Membership itself is permitted though it is made plain that affiliation may hinder promotion. Only energetic hate-group behavior is prohibited.

To address the friction points of race (and now sex) relations—claims of bias, discrimination, favoritism, and additional factors impairing harmony— the Army has established special positions and training programs. Every command at the brigade level or higher is assigned a full-time noncommissioned officer who serves as an equal opportunity advisor (EOA). This is a temporary military, two-year rotated assignment and, significantly, it is not reserved for African Americans.[2] Indeed, in 1994 only about a third were Black, half were White. Thus, unlike universities and many corporations, there exists no enduring black or other minority mini-bureaucracy—for example, a campus Office of Minority Affairs—earning a livelihood uncovering grievances. This arrangement is consistent with the army's belief that intergroup harmony is an all-pervasive responsibility. It is the EOA's job to monitor alleged racial incidents, examine patterns of promotion, and generally attend to matters that could boil over into hostility. The EOA generally acts more like a facilitator and independent investigator than a police officer.

Training and research support for this monitoring is provided by the Defense Equal Opportunity Management Institute (DEOMI) at Patrick Air Force Base in Florida. In addition to focusing on racial discrimination or sexual harassment, the DEOMI in fifteen-week courses broadly covers leadership skills, writing and public speaking, social psychology, and military policy. Though this teaching superficially resemble the "awareness and sensitivity" training oft proscribed in universities, its overall orientation is pragmatic: to "enhance combat and/or operational readiness through improved leadership." (Code of Federal Regulations, 1996). Racism and sexual discrimination are not impediments to a better, more peaceful world; they undermine a unit's capacity to fight and kill people (Moskos & Butler, 1996, Chapter 4). In fact, soldiers are forever being told that divisiveness subverts unit cohesion and this togetherness, in turn, undergirds the military's ultimate violent mission.

Complaining soldiers possess copious opportunities to seek redress through formal and informal channels. Unit commanders are officially responsible for maintaining unpoisoned racial climates; professional advancement requires it, so charges receive prompt attention (and, on the other side, army rules punish those making false accusations). Most complaints involve relatively minor matters and are handled informally by the EOA. Punishments are finely calibrated by custom and rule, ranging from a friendly chat through an official reprimand to, rarely, expulsion. Serious gripes, such as regarding a denied promotions, are surprisingly rare, perhaps due to a combination of early intervention and the realization that serious accusations must be fully demonstrated.

Overall, the U.S. Army has adopted a "race savvy" policy in navigating racial tensions. A sizable effort keeps units from becoming racially homogeneous or having officers strictly of one race command those of another. Self-segregation, common on many university campuses, is generally unacceptable in military facilities. In the delicate area of promotions and assignments, the ratios of blacks to whites is carefully scrutinized, and the expectation is that minorities will share fairly in benefits. Nevertheless, no rigid formulae prevails nor are timetables and fixed goals imposed; discrepancies occur and are accepted, if reasonable. Moreover, unlike many private companies and educational institutions, the army will not promote the unqualified to "make the numbers." Yet, at the same time, an extensive effort takes place to train Blacks and others deficient in skills (such as writing proficiency) required for advancement. Careers may depend on preparing subordinates. The military, to its credit, often has far more success than civilian educational facilities (Moskos & Butler 1996, Chapter 5).

That the contemporary army has cooled divisive racial antagonisms often plaguing larger society is beyond doubt. Military installations may not be tolerance Gardens of Eden in which blacks and whites mingle as one big happy family but they compare favorably with many university settings, businesses, and urban environments. This is a formidable accomplishment, given the numbers and strife potential. What relevant lessons come forth? To be sure, some might rejoin none—the military's coercive and selective power are unique. Universities are not boot camps governed by fierce drill sergeants. Not quite true; drawing civilian-military parallels makes sense. Many civilian institutions, from universities to prisons, hold similar power. That many college administrators fail to use their power to punish or misdirect their efforts to vague behavior does not invalidate the comparability. Within the corporate world, troublemakers and bigots can always be isolated, punished, or expelled, just as they can within the army. In fact, in some ways these measures have greater applicability in the "outside world," especially given that many private sector "recruits" are more persuadable, with better education and stronger career incentives.

Three relevant and larger lessons are discernible. First, the army does not equate perfect acceptance of differences with acceptable levels of de facto overall tolerance. Perfection—ridding the military of all illegitimate hatreds and offensiveness—is not the operational gold standard. The tolerance window is wider than it might be in a perfect world. Many black soldiers still believe that equality remains an uphill battle against deeply rooted bias (Moskos & Butler, 1996, Chapter 4). Nevertheless, these reservations aside, in their outward behavior African Americans do not visualize the army as an inhospitable battleground between "us" and "them." People can still get along amicably amid lingering perceptions of inequality, intolerance, and discrimination. That the military also provides blacks with a decent standard of living and many other material benefits also helps.

Second, keying on conduct, as distinct from an unbounded concern for hearts and minds inner-tolerance, more effectively cools a once quarrelsome situation. The army now concedes—especially after past failures with the opposite strategy—that remolding a soldier's innermost thoughts, values, beliefs, and perceptions is unworkable. Instead, wisely, it admonishes recruits against being disruptive regardless of what might pass through their minds. There are no *thoughtcrimes* among recruits. Only if intolerance subverts the army's basic mission are sanctions forthcoming. This pragmatic attention to behavior is a far cry from universities imploring their students to change their private thinking.

Finally, the forceful imposition of live and let live is possible under arduous conditions. This is an intricate and demanding task; merely promulgating edicts and sanctions is insufficient. Re-working training manual language or photographs to be "sensitive" is not on the menu here. Details are critical and these are seldom initially self-evident. The army's journey to a live-and-let-live environment experienced several setbacks; today's formula was not the initial proposal.[3] Not every good idea is guaranteed to succeed. It would probably be disastrous, for example, if the army created a distinct career corps of all-black civilian "tolerance police" to impose harmony. Equally calamitous would be attempts to punish each and every breach of the peace. Accepting limited intolerance—largely personal expressions of slight organizational consequence—results in a larger amity. Slack is essential—purging all bigots, hatemongers, racists, or Black power extremists from the ranks would probably only inflame divisions. In sum, though these lessons may be of debatable application (though we think not), they do suggest a role for coercion in bringing peace to disputatious situations in society more generally.

II. Communal Separatism

Contemporary discussions of tolerance occur within a context of universalistic national citizenship: All citizens are equal before the law. The 14th Amendment's equal protection under the law" provision clearly articulates this principle. Though laws may treat people differently—for example, children or incompetent adults—such distinctions are permissible only under limited, specified conditions. Older, once-common particularistic group-centered practices, such as prohibiting Asians from testifying in criminal cases, are now both illegal and unthinkable.

Against this universalistic ideological backdrop, splitting people into separate administrative racial or religious entities, each governed by distinct rules, appears retrograde. If done, as in the case of, say, affirmative action for African Americans, it must be understood as a temporary, ameliorative remedy for past inequities. Legal communalism here would be but a detour on the road to full equality. An arrangement of distinct "nations within nations" evokes a pre-modern feudal image, a society populated with tribes or clans, and one hardly conducive to modern appreciations of tolerance. Indeed, our core notion of tolerance—different peoples living together and accepting their differences—closely corresponds to the modern emergence of universalistic conceptions of citizenship. Applying tolerance to particularistic feudal arrangements seems eccentric.

Tolerance and distinctive communalism are not, however, inherently incompatible. Much depends on how *tolerance* and *rights* are conceptualized and on circumstantial detail. The flourishing of multiple views need not be interpreted exclusively in the context of universalistic *individual* rights. Traditions exist in which the primary societal unit is the group, and it is the ethnic, religious, economic, or family entity claiming the right of toleration (see, for example Kymlicka, 1996). That separate individuals are not permitted deviancy is irrelevant *if* group interests are protected and expressed. Group identity—not personal liberty—is sheltered by tolerance. Hence, a society in which ethnic identity is the elementary defining trait might be judged tolerant, though innumerable political heresies were vigorously persecuted. Such prosecution does not count if it lies outside society's organizing principle.

Equally material are circumstances regarding the level of tolerance achievable. As depicted when calibrating intolerance, affirmative tolerance is hardly the sole standard. Imagine a Hobbesian world war, savage repression, misery, or endless slaughter, not uncommon features of the human condition. Separating warring factions substantially moves *toward* an environment of political tolerance—perhaps a .75 on our 0 to 1.00 scale depicted in the previous chapter. Separation advances, even engenders, tolerance though this act itself is not tolerance. The 1947 partition of British India into separate Muslim and Hindu nations may not delight those envisioning a "one big, happy, diverse family," but the alternative was mass extermination until the happy family was a uniform faith. Everyone gets along but not necessarily in the same place and not necessarily governed by identical rules.

As in our *tour d'horizon* of Marxist and gay groups (Chapter 5), bountiful though selective detail is necessary. It is insufficient to insist "survival of differences sometimes requires disengagement" and retire. To be demonstrated is that separatism to secure mutual accommodation has worked and remains applicable. Our eclectic canvass begins in an unlikely place—the pre-World War I Ottoman Empire—and then proceeds toward unorthodox religious groups and concludes with urban neighborhood sanctuaries. Our underlying theme is familiar: Strong differences can coexist, even flower, without tolerant people.

State-Coerced Separation: The Millet System

The *millet* (governing unit) system arose in the Ottoman Empire in 1454 and continued with modifications until the end of World War I, the Empire's collapse. Though the *Quaran* provides its theological justification through its expressed acceptance of separate tribes and people, its initial implementation was politically motivated (Karpat, 1982). Its purpose was to ameliorate widespread religious, ethnic, and linguistic strife within a polity of extreme heterogeneity. As the Empire expanded into the Middle East, North Africa, and especially into the Balkans, it acquired territory plagued by savage civil discord. How, then, was peace to be kept? Recent turmoil in Serbia, once part of the Ottoman Empire, demonstrates this quest to be hardly a passing problem. Rather than impose uniformity or brutally bottle up antagonisms, practical accommodation via *millets* was devised. This system also recognized the political reality of ruling Muslims being minorities in many areas or non-Muslims possessing critical skills (Braude & Lewis, 1982, 5).

Though administrative details were often ad hoc and shifting, at the *millet's* core was the division of citizenship into distinct religious and civil components. Civil subject status applied within the Ottoman Empire regardless of ethnic or religious membership; the Sultan governed all under Islamic law. Coterminous with this civil rank was inclusion in a religious *millet,* or congregation-writ-large.[4] What is today called "Greek Orthodox" was the initial *millets,* soon followed by the Armenian and Jewish. Together with the Muslim *millet,* this arrangement granted dual legal identities—religious and civil (though civil here accorded with Islamic law). Within one's religious community, heresy was forbidden—religious toleration meant *only* the right to profess one's designated, officially recognized faith though each persuasion might afford doctrinal latitude. As Kymlicka (1996, 82) put it, the *millet* system was "a federation of theocracies."[5]

The sharp contrast with present-day liberal, individual-centered political theory is noteworthy. When modern western conceptions of tolerance initially emerged, Locke and others saw the disengagement of the State from private religious affairs as a necessary precondition of tolerance. Kings (unfortunately) imposed official dogma on reluctant subjects, and government slaughtered millions who advanced "false" religion. Within the Ottoman Empire, the reverse held sway: State intervention guaranteed the survival of religious privilege, albeit only certain religious bodies (Kymlicka 1996). Communal subsistence, not individual liberty of conscience, was paramount. Religious tolerance simply meant the acceptance of specified, officially designated orthodoxies. Denominational self-government, moreover, was not an unalienable contractual right but a gift of the Sultan. Ottoman Sultans seconded Locke without accepting the principle of freedom of conscience—since doctrinal differences were inevitable and beyond eradication, one might as well accept the inevitable to preserve civil peace. Ironically, when liberal western ideas of individual rights and democratic universalism filtered into the Ottoman Empire in the 19th century, they were advanced by civil authorities and, predictably, strongly resisted by established religion (Kymlicka, 1996).

Religious inclusion existed independently of physical proximity—all the Empire's Jews, for example, were communally bound together. Thus, a Jew and a Christian in Istanbul were ruled by different officials—both by the Sultan, and each by their respective religious leader. To be outside the *millet* system, whether by choice or given one's unrecognized religious preference, was the modern equivalent of statelessness. Officially accepted religions enjoyed substantial autonomy within these well-defined boundaries. Each enjoyed separate courts, legal codes, schools, and monasteries. Spiritual leaders, the Chief Prelate, Patriarch, or Chief Rabbi, were nominally appointed by the Sultan and shared the prestige awarded to the Ottoman bureaucracy. Spiritual leaders could own or administer property, thus permitting financial independence. Local religious and secular officials (often sharing the same faith) cooperated in the administration of collecting taxes, allocating tillable land, and other governmental functions. Non-Muslim denominational officials could not challenge Islam nor seek to undermine the Sultan's rule. Moreover, churches or synagogues could be constructed only under license, non-Muslims could not proselytize, Jews and Christians were required to wear distinctive attire or emblems so as to be recognizable, inter-marriage was limited, and interdenominational dealings were carefully regulated.[6]

Nevertheless, the preservation of separate beliefs, customs, languages, and other distinctive communal elements was guaranteed not only by the force of law but by the Sultan's enduring political self-interest. Diverse peoples accommodated each other amicably. As Braude and Lewis (1982) expressed it:

> For nearly half a millennium the Ottomans ruled an empire as diverse as any in history. Remarkably, this polyethnic and multireligious society worked. Muslims, Christians and Jews worshipped and studied side by side, enriching their distinctive cultures. The legal traditions and practices of each community, particularly in matters of personal status—that is, death, marriage and inheritance—were respected and enforced throughout the empire. Scores of languages employing a variety of scripts flourished. Opportunities for advancement and prosperity were open in varying degrees to all the empire's subjects. (1)

Non-Muslims were not systematically singled out for permanent harsh subordination as were Jim Crow-era African Americans. Denominational distinctions hardly constituted repression. For example, non-Moslims were forbidden to use Muslim names or, in the case of common names such as David and Joseph, different spellings were required. Civil peace, with the open acknowledgment of Islamic superiority, not forced subjugation, was the object. To be sure, taxes on non-Muslims and other disadvantages were instituted, though some historians have suggested that the medieval state's administrative weakness often rendered these unenforceable (Braude & Lewis, 1982, 6) In some instances, these unequal taxes were for cause, such as payment for a military service exemption. On the other hand, some non-Muslims, such as the elderly and the ill, escaped taxation. Also, as tax burdens were calculated according to civic service, Christian towns supply-

ing useful services—for example, maintaining bridges or metal-working—
often secured a privileged tax-exempt status.

What is germane here is not the oft-murky, fluid details of the pre-WW I
Ottoman Empire. Nobody today, save a few racial separatists, suggests
reinventing *millets*. What is relevant is a radically different conceptualization
of tolerance and its implementation. Namely, that the state can partition
society into distinct bodies, grant limited though substantial autonomy to
these entities, and then safeguard their survival. The model for ensuring
harmony amid divergence broadly understood is critical, not the administrative peculiarities. Reconciliation of differences is embodied in legally
defined collectivities, not autonomous individuals.

Negotiated Disengagement:
The Amish, the Doukhobors and Mormons

The separatism of the *millet* system largely is state imposed. An alternative is group-instigated separatism via political compromise and negotiation.
Here, as in marital separation without divorce, both parties "decide" that
balancing tranquillity with irrepressible distinctiveness requires some physical disengagement. Accommodating antagonisms behooves innumerable
compromises—the unconventional can flourish but not in the midst of the
conventional. Community and unorthodoxy thus coexist at a distance though,
as we shall see in our example from Brooklyn, New York, this distance can
be physically small.

Though barely on today's menu of prescriptions for harmony, this solution
has enjoyed striking success. Partition has repeatedly mollified our disputatious religious divisions. The holy wars that ravaged Europe for centuries
and still persevere today in the Middle East are, most fortunately, barely
known in the United States. This accomplishment is presupposed and un-
derappreciated, though most societies have failed in their efforts. Our analysis here singles out only three of innumerable reconciliations via physical
separation and negotiation, namely, the Amish, Doukhobors, and Mormons.
These religious sects uniquely pushed the tension between acceptance and
community to the limits, yet all now enjoy reasonable accommodation.

The Amish

The Old Order Amish remain theologically rooted in the 16th century
Central European Reformation. This broad movement of pietistic sects, of
which the Amish are a splinter, swelled as a reaction against the hierarchical
Catholic Church with its ornate cathedrals and embellished liturgy. Inspira-

tion flowed from a "primitive" early first century Christianity: personal spirituality, communal equality, a withdrawal from worldly endeavors, and rejection of a professional, authoritarian clergy espousing formalized dogma (Ahlstrom, 1972). The state's authority over faith and behavior was discarded as contrary to God's laws. Predictably, these dogmas were condemned as revolutionary, subversive, and affronting both civil authorities and established churches. Amish unwillingness to swear oaths or allegiances was judged tantamount to treason (Yoder, 1993). Outside of a few localities, such as Holland, these nonconformists endured relentless persecution. During the mid-16th century, thousands were burned at the stake, drowned, died in prison, or were executed. The original dissenting sect, the Anabaptists (so named for their requirement of a second, adult baptism signifying church membership), nearly disappeared (Kraybill, 1993).

Like related persecuted religious groups trekking through central Europe, the Amish eventually sought refuge in America. Beginning in 1727, they settled in Berks and Lancaster counties of Pennsylvania. As immigration increased, colonies moved westward. Today, it is estimated that some 130,000 Amish reside in the United States and Canada. Though they reside in twenty-two states, Pennsylvania, Ohio, and Indiana have the largest settlements (Kraybill, 1993). Significantly, Amish towns are modestly populated, fairly isolated rural areas dependent on agriculture and small craft-type businesses. Unlike their close theological cousins, the Mennonites, the Old Order Amish maintain a visibly unique existence. Their attire—for example, all black suits and distinctive hats— and beards for the men, horse and buggy transportation, a German dialect instead of English, and intense clannishness clearly set them apart. All personal adornments, even wedding rings, are taboo.

Nevertheless, it is not this outward uniqueness that instigates the potential conflicts and possible repression. After all, many religious denominations comfortably persist with equally "odd" theological tenets and physical distinctiveness, such as the similarly attired Hassidic Jews. Critical is the Amish's insistence on their religious ways even if this collides sharply with civil law. Such discord, moreover, is not just over superficial, easily ignored details, such as a fondness for horses over cars, but occurs over the central statutory dictates of modern government. For example, the Amish adamantly refuse military service, and for over a century this has clashed with the draft. Similarly, the modern state requires school attendance well into high school; the Amish not only reject schooling past the 8th grade but will only accept education in their own Spartan 19th century vintage schools. At least since the 1920s, conflict has been frequent, especially during wartime when clannish German-speaking people were viewed suspiciously (Meyers, 1993).

Workplace regulations—compulsory Social Security enrollment, mandatory unemployment compensation contributions, and conforming to incessant safety requirements, such as hard hats—similarly confront deep-seated Amish religious beliefs. Certain Amish medical practices—for example, noncertified midwives and objection to vaccination—likewise engender friction. Their religion also forbids oath taking, a common legal requirement. Local battles erupt over zoning regulations, sanitation requirements, the in-town quartering of horses, pollution abatement, and horse-inflicted highway damage. As one analyst put it, "Many of the feuds between the Amish and the state involve fundamental clashes between diverse social orders. Anchored in opposing values and differing social structures, these duels are essentially face-offs between the Goliath of modernity and shepherds from traditional pastures" (Kraybill, 1993, 17).

Not only does Amish unorthodoxy invite heavy-handed state intrusion but their faith strictly forbids resistance. *Gelassenheit*—a German term signifying complete submission to divine will—governs Amish life. It entails self-denial, the stoic acceptance of suffering, and a quiet spirit of contentment and resignation. During 16th century persecution, resistance was impermissible—a death sentence for one's faith was uncontestable. To seek recognition, promote oneself to leadership, or claim credit violates spiritual doctrine. *Gelassenheit,* in turn, reinforces a religion-sanctioned rejection of the "worldly," that is, life outside family and community of the faithful. Mixing with outsiders is highly bounded; non-Amish newspapers, television, movies, gambling, sports, airplane travel, and similar outside ventures are strictly forbidden. Violators are socially ostracized or expelled.

Politically, at least according to modern speculations regarding civic influence, the Amish are essentially defenseless. Except in rare local situations when issues directly affecting the Amish are on the ballot (e.g., school policy) voting is verboten by custom though not by specific dogma. Doctrine similarly forbids campaign contributions, political parties enrollment, or similar "worldly" politicking. Even the innocuous local Chamber of Commerce is usually off-limits. The Amish disdain public relations—they almost never grant newspaper interviews, and they seldom articulated their cause well. No media-savvy Amish chieftains catch the public eye, nor are there attention-getting marches, demonstrations, and boycotts.[7] The most common Amish response is a mild-sounding petition to authorities or a humble delegation of church officials politely seeking relief from a burdensome regulation. Political sophistication is generally minuscule; civic knowledge is disdained. Equally relevant, utilizing courts for redress of grievances is unacceptable. Lawsuits against government or private citizens, court orders, injunctions, and volunteered testimony are, by creed, unthinkable. Jury service is impermissible. At most, a few Amish settlements enjoy local influence by their ability to attract free-spending tourists (Kraybill, 1993).

How, then, can this stridently contrarian, politically weak people resist aversion? Why should non-Amish "put up with" an "odd," passive people who refuse military service, reject welfare state enrollment, violate untold economic regulations, feel unbound by commonplace statutes, and otherwise rebuff the authority of the larger civil community? What facilitates tolerance with the larger society when severe culture clashes are endemic?

Amish survival against a contrary larger community rests on several factors. Each smoothes out potential frictions, thus facilitating a complex accommodation. Important lessons regarding political tolerance are imbedded here. Most plainly, the relatively isolated, rural, and smallish size of Amish communities affords accommodation. The Amish, unlike some others believing themselves aggrieved, shun confrontation with outsiders, especially government. Amish *never, never* proselytize or hint that their dogmas deserve an equal footing. This contrasts sharply with many gays, for example, who insist nongroup members heed pleas for equality.

Contacts are initiated only most reluctantly, as a protective reaction when governments compel Amish to violate religious convictions. Even then, the Amish often accept imprisonment or pay heavy fines rather than resist. Government benefits, programs, or entitlements are never demanded in the name of tolerance. "Affirmative tolerance" is grossly inappropriate here. Modest population size also minimizes overall risk—the insistence on restricted schooling for a few thousand future agricultural and craftworkers hardly endangers public policy (indeed, judges sometimes note that simple Amish instruction may be more effective than public high school education). A peculiar parallel holds with the hippie communes of the 1960s and 70s—out of sight, out of mind: Small numbers encouraged a tolerance of obviousness.

A widespread admiration for the traditional Amish values also fosters acceptance. Legal disobedience is not an insurmountable obstacle to being viewed fondly. Traditional values—strong families, self-sufficiency, strict personal morality, self-discipline, thrift, hard work, absence of crime, a mannered politeness, and shouldering tax burden despite nonuse of services—impresses would-be enemies. One analyst suggests that many non-Amish deeply admire the Amish for performing what they themselves fail to accomplish (Kidder & Hostetler, 1990, cited in Olshan, 1993). Few question Amish sincerity and religious devotion; no hint of self-aggrandizing opportunism exists.

This respect often surfaces in legal disputes upholding Amish distinctiveness. Courts in religious cases generally follow "the secular regulation rule."

That is, only religious beliefs, not religiously motivated behavior, is protected by the First Amendment, though judges can, usually reluctantly, make exceptions. For example, polygamy was struck down under this principle despite its requirement by the Mormon faith (*Reynolds v. United States,* 1878). In fact, state court decisions in the first half of the 20th century often assailed Amish uniqueness. Nevertheless, especially in recent decades, both state and federal judges have been more generous (Place, 1993). *State v. Yoder* (1971) upheld the right of Amish parents in Wisconsin to withhold their children from education beyond the 8th grade. The primacy of religious faith in this matter was explicitly acknowledged. The U.S. Supreme Court in *Wisconsin v. Yoder* (1972) confirmed that Amish creed required their children be isolated from the larger world. The state's strong interest in promoting education could not supersede preserving a religious community. In *Commonwealth v. Sykes* (1989) a Pennsylvania court rejected the State Board of Medicine's effort to prevent unlicensed Amish midwives from practicing their profession. Similarly, several state cases have exempted Amish buggies from displaying slow-moving vehicle signs. Only when Amish claims are not rooted in dogma—for example, an Amish man's refusal to pay employer's Social Security taxes—have the courts resisted (*United States v. Lee,* 1982).

Less observable is the Amish's peculiar skill in negotiating with government. A paradox exists. Clearly, the Amish avoidance of worldly contact, speaking a German dialect and otherwise shunning modern travel and communication are political liabilities. Nevertheless, their successes at keeping Caesar at bay are extraordinary. The secret lies in a combination of great patience, a sense of priorities, and a gracious nonconfrontational style. And, when necessary, a willingness to suffer stoically the consequences of their beliefs, even if this means jail.

Much of this accomplishment is attributable to the National Amish Steering Committee, the one national Amish organization that loosely speaks for all Amish.[8] The committee has little money, no up-to-date professional staff, and lacks formal authority over individual communities. Yet, despite all practical and doctrinal limitations, it still serves as an expert assembly of lay lawyers lobbying, negotiating settlements, discovering unique legal loopholes and otherwise advancing Amish civic interests (Kidder & Hostetler, 1990, in Olshan, 1993, 78). The Amish abiding limited agenda also helps. For example, Amish leaders developed close personal ties with General Lewis B. Hershey, the long-time Selective Service system head. This enduring relationship permitted the Amish to resolve innumerable intricate conflicts between government military needs and their religious nonparticipation in anything warlike. The precise jobs assigned young Amish men as alternative service—home-front fence repair but not distant hospital work—

resulted from protracted bargaining. And when the government would eventually acquiesce to their requests, the Steering Committee would humbly express its profound gratitude, declaring its highest appreciation for being given the privilege of working with such honorable people (Olshan, 1993).

This Amish bargaining style is unconditionally nonconfrontational. It emphasizes amicably sitting down with the right person and patiently reaching mutual understandings, however tediously. There can be no threats of litigation, unfavorable publicity, voter retaliation or any of the other commonplace contemporary tactics. A genuine give-and-take governs, though some principles must be off the agenda. For example, during World War II, the Amish refused service in any combat-related situation, but being drafted for nonmilitary work "of national importance" was acceptable. Compulsory education laws were sometimes finessed when Amish youth attended vocational training schools located within Amish settlements (Kraybill, 1993). When some states required that milk sold for public consumption be refrigerated prior to shipment, the Amish agreed to diesel-powered cooling systems but refused commercial electricity.

The Doukhobors[9]

Like the Amish, the Doukhobors are a small, Christian sect profoundly challenging conventional Christianity. And, also like the Amish, they steadfastly persisted in their faith and thus long suffered persecution before achieving a rapprochement with modern society. Two features of their tribulation are especially relevant here. First, their modern travail occurred in Canada, which permits us to view accommodation under distinctive political-institutional conditions. Second, Doukhobor unconventionality has periodically pushed the limits of societal accommodation even further than do the Amish. It is only a slight exaggeration to contend that if the Doukhobors and the rest of society can cohabit the same nation, almost anything is possible.

The Doukhabors originated in Russia sometime during the mid-17th century, probably associated with the upheaval within the Russian Orthodox Church. Like the Amish withdrawal from elaborate, formalized Christianity, the Doukhobors rejected all institutional features of organized religion and carried it a few steps further. Not only was a priesthood rejected, but so, too, were basic tenets such as baptism, the Eucharist, and all ceremony, icons, and saints. The Bible, as well, was only of slight significance. For the Doukhobors, each person, as God's child, was to be guided by the "Christ within." Indeed, Jesus Christ himself was but a mortal person possessed with "the Spirit," and this Spirit can periodically reappear in chosen men. Moreover, Spirit followers are incapable of sin (Whalen, 1979).

This doctrine removed not only the need for civil government but virtually its entire authority as well. Government endured only for the wicked, and thus to bear arms or swear oaths was absolutely forbidden. Even minor civil matters—marriage licenses, death certificates, mandatory education, property deeds, dealing with courts and police—are condemned. Marriage, for example, occurs merely when people (nonlegally) acknowledge mutual love (Stamouli, 1912). This was a spiritual philosophy of all-encompassing egalitarianism and civic non-cooperation, not unlike anarchism. Like the Amish, life was always rural and isolated, a Spartan existence of agriculture and a few handicrafts. Significantly, though this feature varied over time and by settlement, Doukhobors practiced a primitive communism with collective property ownership. This practice, apart from its ideological overtones, would repeatedly bring the Doukhobors and modern state legal requirements into battle.

Their Russia experience alternated between long periods of severe repression and fleeting acceptance. The Russian Orthodox Church relentlessly sought eradication. Periodic waves of Russian xenophobic nationalism immovably collided with their insistence on maintaining a distinct, and seemingly non-Russian, communal identity. Persecution became so intense that by the end of the 19th century, an exodus of nearly 7,500 Doukhobors trekked to Canada, lured by an expansive territory needing settlement by industrious farmers.

Unlike earlier Amish migration to the United States, the Doukhobors settlement in Canada involved prior negotiations between communal spokesmen and administrative agents. In some matters—for example, the number of Doukhobor settlements, their location (present-day Saskatchewan), and exemptions from military service—final accords were well understood. In other instances—schooling, state vital statistics records, and requiring oaths—matters remained ambiguous and ultimately caused continuing friction. Nevertheless, despite unsettled points, Canada and various U.S. Quaker organizations warmly welcomed these refugees. All seemed content, at least momentarily.

Tranquillity was but short-lived; discord soon arose between the Doukhobors and settlers already residing in supposedly reserved land. Though this initial bickering was eventually resolved, further land ownership conflicts soon followed, and Doukhobors strained their once-warm welcome. Open confrontation with the central government now occurred over registering property titles. Canadian law required that land be registered in individual names regardless of communal usage. Many devout Doukhobors, encouraged by outsiders (including Leo Tolstoy), resolutely refused to yield to this seemingly minor technical demand. Gentle admonishments from Quakers to accede to harmless government requests fell on deaf ears. The government stood firm. Soon, talk of retaking Doukhobor land and distributing it to new settlers surfaced. A convoluted legal compromise was, fortunately, concocted to halt a crisis.

Fresh troubles again forced Canadians to re-think their generosity. Simultaneously with this legal turbulence, a band of 1,700 indigent Doukhobors heard God's call, rejected worldly behaviors such as using money, work, and physical labor, and marched across the prairie on a religious pilgrimage. Fortunately, intense last-minute negotiations averted skirmishes and, at least for awhile, peace and prosperity reigned. Divisions among the Doukhobors now provided new irritations. In May of 1903, internal conflicts broke out among the Doukhobors over communalism, and protests included a nude pilgrimage by sect members alarmed at growing materialism. Some protesters were jailed for three years (Janzen, 1990, Chapter 3). Non-Doukhobors began grumbling that land assigned to the Doukhobors—nearly 450,000 acres—was not being cultivated as legally required and deserved redistribution. In some cases, this was done, further exacerbating tensions. Public clamor against the Doukhobors mounted as recent immigrants saw huge tracts of uncultivated land denied to them. Public officials grew louder in their attacks on their communistic arrangements as wasteful economically and on Doukhobor reluctance to become assimilated Canadian citizens.

Under pressure from fresh land-hungry immigrants, the Canadian government reclaimed tracts of uncultivated land once ceded to the Doukhobors. Provisions were made for Doukhobors to regain land as individuals but, given a choice of retaining land individually or abandoning it, many Doukhobors elected faith over farmland. Some, however, chose otherwise and joined a growing number of "independent" Doukhobors rejecting communal property. Delegations and petitions from the faithful invoking past agreements and religious creed were, at least for the moment, ignored. As non-Doukhobor settlers moved into their midst, blurring communal boundaries, thousands moved westward to British Columbia, reestablishing tighter Doukhobor communes (Janzen, 1990, Chapter 3). In 1918, swelling immigration and the availability of millions of untilled acres again compelled the Canadian government to confront the Doukhobors. This time, perhaps fearing being crowded out altogether, many Doukhobors bowed to legal reality and bought land individually.

Military service contributed the next friction point. The original agreement granted "the fullest assurance of absolute immunity from military service" (Janzen, 1990, 166). This assurance, moreover, conformed to long-standing Canadian policy of granting military exemptions to similar "peace" groups, including Quakers and Mennonites. Generally, this promise was honored, though contentious incidents occurred. For example, in 1918 several draft-age Doukhobors were arrested in Saskatchewan, fined, and turned over to the military. Protests and work stoppages followed. When police demanded that draft exemption certificates be signed by ministers (a legal requirement of the exemption law), Doukhobors rightfully argued that their religion did not have ministers. Eventually, however, the commotion abated.

World War II similarly tested Canadian patience. Initially, the government proposed that Doukhobors would register, though, of course, there would be no military service call. Some Doukhobors rejected the very idea of government-administered registration, insisting on performing this task themselves. This was accepted after much negotiation but, alas, not all Doukhobors recognized even this mild state intrusion. Protests and violent demonstrations broke out and several militant Doukhobors were arrested. Alternative service also proved contentious. Originally, some Doukhobor leaders—though not followers—accepted it to reduce public hostility, but their position soon shifted. When Ottawa called up Doukhobors for alternative service, such as road building, most refused. Demonstrations and legal prosecution predictably followed. Efforts to give Doukhobors medical exams as part of the national registration also failed. When government toughened its stance, militant Doukhobors responded with everything from arson to nude public demonstrations. Eventually, sensing the futility of further calls, the government, despite fears of awarding unique privileges, adopted generous compromises or simply surrendered (Janzen, 1990, Chapter 9).

This strife typifies other encounters. Doukhobors often shield their children from the outside world by resisting mandatory public education. This has, predictably, spawned resentment and fears of cultural balkanization. Conflicts over obtaining death certificates, registering vital statistics, and social welfare policy continue. Assimilation still remains partial. All told, the "marriage" between Canada and the Doukhobors remains strained, occasionally marred by mayhem. Nevertheless, today's conditions are light-years away from, say Northern Ireland or Bosnia.

Explanations for this accommodation are not obscure. Clearly, Canada needed industrious, agricultural-oriented settlers to populate its immense territory and thus easily offered sturdy legal promises of live and let live to unorthodox sects. Even as continued immigration rendered this population urgency less pressing, the original guarantees were generally mutually honored, though maneuvering continued (Janzen, 1990, Chapter 12). Respect for legal obligations, notwithstanding contrary public pressure or wartime necessity, sets Canada well apart from Czarist Russia, which shared similar settlement and military requirements. Given their small numbers, plus principled passivity to state coercion, expelling Doukhobors as unwelcome pests to "preserve the Canadian way of life" would not seem especially outrageous. Though common in other nations, this expulsion alternative was not an option. Legality counts.

That both sides negotiated patiently in good faith also helped greatly. The pattern of nonconfrontational flexibility resembled that of the Amish, though the Amish never resorted to nude romps. Ceaselessly, Doukhobor leaders visited Ottawa or local administrators and graciously pleaded their case as a gentle, naive, religious people seeking a quiet, isolated life. Officials were likewise usually noncombative. Doukhobor demands were, essentially, to be left alone; no petitions were advanced to repair past injustices. No non-Doukhobor was harmed by their strict doctrinal adherence. Compacts imposed minimal tax or regulatory burdens and all but the most militant Doukhobors did not feel their creed dishonored. Politics was to escape harmful collisions, not gain fresh advantages.

Finally, despite their oddities, Doukhobor industriousness and sobriety draw respect. As was true for the Amish, why dispossess economically useful citizens? This grudging acceptance is hardly preordained. Remember, arcane divergences in religious dogma, even among similar people, routinely instigate mass slaughter. An occasional outburst by naked fanatics running through town may enrage some Canadians, to be sure, but this is hardly a fundamental assault on society. The issue is one of group eccentricities in largely out-of-the-way localities. Even their reluctance to avail themselves of public education has gained a degree of tolerance as it has not brought mass juvenile delinquency. In short, strong differences aside, an accommodation based on usefulness and largely decent behavior has been successfully brokered.

The Mormons[10]

The rise of the Mormon church offers yet another possibility of nonconformism surviving intense animosity. Outwardly, unlike the Amish and Doukhobors, Mormons appear conventional. Nor do Mormons seek a premodern refuge in rural agriculture. Historic, doctrinal-based disputes between the state and Mormon religion are relatively few, polygamy being most conspicuous. Mormons fully accept the modern state, military service, and gladly mix with non-Mormons. Nevertheless, the travails of the Mormon church to gain acceptance often rivaled the difficulties faced by European Amish and Doukhobors—banishment and harsh persecution. The achievement of tolerance has been laborious, but it has been accomplished.

The Mormon faith was founded by Joseph Smith, Jr., born in Vermont in 1805. He grew up in western upstate New York, a region of intense religious revivalism during the first half of the 19th century. As a young man, he hunted buried treasure, occasionally running afoul of the law for false claims. He was strongly shaped by the religious movements, cults and fads then sweeping through western New York. In 1827, Smith allegedly discovered a long-lost Indian treasure revealing past secrets. The angel Moroni, Smith announced, revealed in a vision the location of golden plates inscribed with "reformed Egyptian" hieroglyphics and a set of seer stones. With the assistance of his wife, Emma, and other helpers, Smith translated these plates. This rendering was published in 1830 as the five-hundred-page *Book of Mormon*. An angel then swept away the original plates (Ahlstrom, 1972).

Like the Old Testament in language and structure, the *Book of Mormon* offers elaborate tales—wanderings, intrigues, exhortations, mystical doctrines, colorful personalities, unusual events, and divine interventions. It hints at doctrines—polytheism and reincarnation—diverging substantially from traditional Christianity. According to Smith, the original plates were buried in 384 AD by Mormon and his son, Moroni, as their saga's chronicle to be bequeathed to their descendants who could, before the Last Day, establish the state of Zion. Smith, now officially titled "Seer, a Translator, a Prophet, an Apostle of Jesus Christ, and Elder of the Church through the will of God the Father, and grace of your Lord Jesus Christ," quickly attracted followers. Revelations, faith healing, and warning regarding the impending Millennium followed. That a "new Jerusalem" would be found "on the borders by the Lamanites" was proclaimed, and Smith dispatched a three-person party seeking land. In 1831, as the new Mormon church added fresh converts, the congregation moved westward to Kirtland, Ohio, believed to be the eastern boundary of the Stake in Zion.

Smith's preaching and claims of divine revelations antagonized neighbors. He was once abducted from his home, tarred, and feathered. Nevertheless, the sect gained numerous enthusiastic adherents and constructed a stately temple in Kirtland with borrowed funds. When the financial crisis of 1837 struck, the Mormons defaulted on their financial obligations and chaos—fires, riots, and theological schisms—ensued. Again, the Mormons sought safety by fleeing westward to Missouri, joining a band of believers in an already established colony. The situation became even worse than matters in Ohio. Near Independence, Missouri, Mormon followers were mobbed and forcibly expelled when the local townfolk discovered that the Mormons disagreed with them over slavery (Braden, 1950, Chapter 13). The flock moved northward in Missouri. Smith's penchant for highly charged oratory and threats of divine vengeance against enemies once more drew animosity. Smith was even sentenced to death, though the sentence was never carried out. All Mormons were expelled from Missouri and the faithful fled, now eastward across the Mississippi to Nauvoo, Illinois.

Temporarily, all went well. The Nauvoo Mormons numbered fifteen thousand and their political clout gained them a charter transforming the town into a virtual independent theocratic principality. Evangelistic success transformed Nauvoo into the largest, most prosperous, and fastest growing Illinois city. Success attracted converts and the local militia, commanded by Smith—newly titled "King of the Kingdom of God"—became a disciplined military force decked out in impression uniforms (West, 1957, Chapter 5). Revelations and new teachings, such as baptizing the dead and plural marriage (polygamy), continued from an increasingly despotic Smith, and Mormonism became less and less Christian in character. An entirely new religion was forming, at least in the eyes of non-Mormons.

In 1844, an ever more ambitious Joseph Smith declared his quest for the U.S. presidency. Tales from ex-Mormons filtered out of widespread lawlessness, corruption, and polygamy. Local Nauvoo newspapers criticizing Smith were abruptly suppressed. Responding to a highly tense situation, Smith, officially charged with inciting to riot and treason (for calling for the creation of a separate kingdom), sought safety by surrendering to Carthage, Illinois authorities. On June 27, 1844, the Illinois militia turned into an angry mob, removed Smith and his brother from jail, and murdered them. Now under the leadership of Smith's disciple, Brigham Young, the Mormons once again migrated westward to seek a new empire. The first wagonload of Mormons entered the Utah Great Salt Basin in 1847. An 1849 constitutional convention created the theocratic Mormon state of Desert. Within a decade, ninety Salt Lake communities were established, plus a few as far distant as California.

Tranquillity was but momentary. In 1852, Brigham Young published Joseph Smith's revelation on "the order of Jacob," openly reaffirming plural marriage as a fundamental religious tenet. A clash with the national cultural and legal norm of monogamy was now inevitable. Moreover, not only did the Mormons embrace polygamy contrary to territorial law but they continued their vigorous and successful attraction of converts (West, 1957, Chapter 15). Mormons also acknowledged their controversial doctrine of "blood atonement," which, especially to outsiders, seemingly sanctioned ritualistic murder. Sensationalist books spoke of alleged barbaric Mormon rites, human sacrifices, and sexual lewdness (West, 1957, Chapter 10). These well-publicized stories of atrocities, lechery, and lawlessness had become commonplace in the outside world.

When President Buchanan in 1857 replaced Young as Utah's territorial governor, a bitter "Mormon war" ensued. Before Congress, Buchanan forcibly denounced the Mormons as religious fanatics bent on establishing an independent theocracy with Brigham Young as king. Twenty-five hundred federal troops were dispatched to Utah to seize control. With memories still fresh of past persecutions, Young ordered Mormon resistance, and armed skirmishes broke out between Mormon and federal troops (West, 1957, Chapter 12). At one point, all the Mormons in Salt Lake City fled. The most serious incident was a massacre of noncombatant California-bound settlers by Mormons and Indians. Only after arduous negotiations was full-fledged bloody military conflict avoided. The Civil War's eruption, and both Lincoln and Brigham Young's desire to dodge the slavery issue, muted further conflict. Nevertheless, the strife between outside society and the ever-growing Mormon population smoldered for decades.

Congress in 1862 formally declared bigamy illegal but hardly settled the matter despite the Supreme Court upholding the law as constitutional. In 1882, Congress again tried to compel Mormons to forego plural marriages, this time by withdrawing their franchise and right to serve on juries when charges of polygamy were involved.[11] Some sixty-five thousand Mormon men and women beseeched Congress to reject this legislation. Eastern anti-Mormon clergy organized mass rallies protesting Mormonism, a faith likened to a "political cancer." (West, 1957, Chapter 15). Additional federal legislation was aimed at destroying the Mormon church ordering, among other things, the confiscation of church funds and rescinding Utah women's suffrage provisions (West, 1957, Chapter 15). Anti-polygamy enforcement was stepped up, often with midnight raids into bedrooms and lengthy prison terms meted out to violators. The persecution brought the church to near bankruptcy and saddled it with a huge debt. The faithful, including top leaders, often went underground or resorted to deception, including secret bedrooms.

In *Davis v. Beasom* (1890), the Supreme Court concluded that bigamy was not a religious tenet; rather, it violated Christian faith, regardless of contrary claims. *Church of Jesus Christ of Latter Day Saints v. United States* (1890) denied the Mormon church status as a religious corporation because the doctrine of polygamy was religious fantasy. The justices even invidiously compared Mormons to the Thugs of India, a sect exhorting ritual murder (Pritchett, 1977, 398). For Mormons, long convinced that their practices were protected religious doctrines, these decisions were shocking. The "culture war" seemed almost eternal.

Today, "Mormon Wars" and the once bitter antagonisms survive as dim historical memories. The expression "intolerance against Mormons" sounds inappropriately odd. Mormonism, despite its controversial origins, unconventional religious doctrines, and tumultuous past is, undoubtedly, "just another Protestant creed" to most Americans. The problem of intolerance toward Mormonism is fundamentally resolved. When non-U.S. religious conflicts are reflected on, this transformation of doctrinal antagonism into benign acceptance in "only" 150 years is remarkable. After all, Christian-Moslem strife has survived centuries in the Balkans whereas the aftershocks of the 16th century European Reformation still linger in Holland, Switzerland, Northern Ireland, and Germany despite secularism's decisive triumph.

What explains this peaceful transformation, this live and let live attitude against the backdrop of turmoil? Clearly, as with the Amish and Doukhobors, physical disengagement facilitated accommodation. Had the Mormons dug in their heels in Kirtland or Nauvoo, insisting "take us like we are or not at all," mayhem would have predictably ensued, particularly given their evangelical, aggressively expansionistic character. Isolated, thinly settled areas, scattered across the West offered a safety valve. And, as mentioned, those who absolutely refused compromise further retreated into isolation. Here, the United States differs substantially from most other nations, where land shortages and deeply rooted territorial attachments make this less feasible.

Equally contributive was a social and economic transformation. The Mormons rapidly evolved from a tiny militant sect, led by fiery leaders bent on fierce confrontations, to modern dull, conservative respectability. The controversial establishment of an unforgiving theocratic desert kingdom faded away. Twentieth century Mormon leaders were not young, charismatic, fanatical orators but elderly, cautious administrators tending to financial stability and pedestrian good deeds. Doctrine became more private and church deportment more secularized though the church's missionary commitment expanded. Mormonism, at least superficially, closely resembles mainstream Christianity. If church members are physically distinctive, it is their conservative grooming and attire.

The Church's mainstream image has been carefully polished: the traveling world-renowned Mormon Tabernacle Choir, friendly guided tours of impressive temples, and world-class universities such as Brigham Young University now define contemporary Mormonism. Spiritual bellicosity has given way to energetic capitalism coupled with a strict personal morality, including abstinence from alcohol, tobacco, coffee, and tea. Mormon commitment to self-help social welfare, administered through the church and financed via tithing, is similarly admired. Today's Mormons, without surrendering their evangelistic fervor or beliefs in the Book of Mormon, unambiguously project the image of a law-abiding, thrifty, education-minded people. Literacy, low crime rates, work ethic, and similar freedom from "social pathologies" have made Mormons attractive employees and Mormon areas in states such as Utah, Idaho, and Nevada growing commercial centers.

The Mormon leadership's willingness to compromise, and followers' acquiescence, has proven essential. When the Edmunds-Tucker Act of 1887, a direct assault on the church, was declared constitutional in 1890, a Mormon delegation to Washington sought an armistice. No instructions were given to surrender on the principle of polygamy; rather, the delegation was to sound out Congress on reactions if the church altered its stance. Washington's mood was conciliatory. On September 25, 1890, the church's president openly bid for Mormon submission to civil law. This reversal was not a doctrinal revelation nor a rejection of polygamy's divine character; it merely solicited legal obedience to the secular state (West, 1957, Chapter 15). Though Mormon officials never formally renounced polygamy's exalted status, this artful concession satisfied Congress. Compromise opponents withdrew to more isolated areas or immigrated. Utah gained statehood and thus acceptance in 1896, though an early Senator-elect (Brigham H. Smith) was denied his seat for he was believed to be a bigamist.

Finally, though Joseph Smith initially imaged an autonomous theocratic Kingdom of Zion, Mormon citizens have become thoroughly integrated politically in existing society. No lingering traces of separatism are discernible, no call for a distinctive communalism as might occasionally be detected among African Americans or Latino/a political groups. Utah is hardly Quebec. Mormons customarily vote and church officials often hold high elected positions (a fact that initially exacerbated tensions between Mormon settlements and their neighbors). However, once Utah achieved statehood and enmities cooled, more conventional political demarcations followed. Mormons, like the rest of the nation, divide between Republicans and Democrats and share the familiar intra-party disputes. No "Mormon Party" akin to Middle East or Indian religious factions competes, and partisan politics does not mimic religious cleavages (O'Dea, 1957, 172-173). Potentially troublesome citizen-state contact points—taxes, education, military service, patriotism, accepting legal authority—have long been smoothed over.

This saga illustrates a viable, contemporary-relevant model for building political tolerance. The recipe's principal ingredients included healthy measures of mutual compromise, intermittent physical isolation, and an outward acceptance of the dominant morality. Selective accommodation is indispensable. Political tolerance would have been impossible had Kirtland Mormons forcefully demanded an autonomous theocratic duchy built on open plural marriages.

Urban Enclaves

Our exploration of communalism has till now focused on a specific institutional arrangement (the Ottoman *millet* system) or distinct, well-defined religious groups. The pivotal role of physical separation, in some instances hundreds of miles, to facilitate accommodation was emphasized. We now shift gears, concentrating on the modern city in which insulating distances may be a street. In sociological language, an "elective affinity" connects big cities and political tolerance. Though not their primary purpose, large, heterogeneous urban environments afford distinctive opportunities for even bitter historical enemies and deviant sentiments to live and let live.[12]

This accomplishment has been long-grasped but seldom placed in the context of political tolerance.[13] Cities balance intimate proximity and unruly distinctiveness. In the words of Robert Park, an early student of city life, cities are "a mosaic of little worlds that touch but do not interpenetrate" (cited in Abrahamson, 1996). Precisely defined discernible areas constructed around distinct ethnic identities—Chinatowns, Little Italys, African American ghettos, the Little Havana area of Miami, Florida—dotting tourist maps are well known. Most enclaves, however, are less conspicuous to outsiders, though usually familiar to locals—for example, the Greek section of Astoria, Queens, New York. Some urban "villages" are nearly physically imperceptible— for example, certain streets of the Hyde Park area surrounding the University of Chicago. No doubt, American cities possess innumerable enclaves, gradually shifting over time, and those attracting immigrants—New York and Los Angeles, for example—may possess hundreds.

Such unique communities within communities comfortably invigorate group stability. Orthodox Jews residing in the Williamsburg section of Brooklyn, for example, can easily buy kosher food, walk to synagogues, conveniently arrange weddings and funerals, find religious articles, and otherwise follow their exacting creed. African American culture persists more readily in Harlem (New York City) where black music stores abound, black political organizations flourish, retailers carry books on Africa, and locally owned businesses meet black grooming needs. Physical concentration, whether voluntary or coerced (as was once the case for many groups), also powerfully reinforces group identity via informal social pressure on deviants. To scatter Hasidic Jews or Harlem Blacks across the entire city involuntarily would be no different from dispersing the Amish into suburban sprawl—the end of community.

Preserving communal distinctiveness is often more subtle than the existence of ethnic stores or specialized churches. Government agents—the police, educators, planners, garbage collectors, fire inspectors, and other minor bureaucrats—typically make various "non-legal" adjustments, accommodation, and tailoring of local ordinances to the peculiarities of place. Political universalism bends to communal compromise. For example, New York City police might well tolerate boisterous young men loitering in public parks, with loud radios, drinking alcohol, perhaps gambling, all actions nominally illegal, provided this occurs in certain well-defined areas. This "culture" is locally accepted so a police crackdown would be perceived as an outrage. Identical behavior in Bensonhurst, a subdued Italian section of Brooklyn, might draw immediate police attention. Community schools routinely acknowledge insular identities, perhaps adopting a revered name ("Booker T. Washington JHS" in an African American neighborhood) or highlighting group holidays (St. Patrick's Day school murals where the Irish predominate). The enforcement of ordinances regarding public noise, street peddlers, illegally parked cars, food handling, public intoxication, graffiti, zoning, and littering are all to some extent neighborhood-sensitive.

These well-defined urban enclaves are not the only mechanism supplying sanctuary to the unorthodox. Urban scholars have long noted that some urban terrains constitute a no-man's land, permitting socially marginal, even vaguely illegal, activities to flourish (Gans, 1995). These domains belong to no group and are economically fragmented, sufficing as "free zones" in varying degrees beyond the pale of urban civility. Skid-row and red-light districts populated with panhandlers, homeless vagrants sleeping in doorways, people openly urinating, and prostitutes soliciting passing motorists are the most extreme examples. The police typically keep a modicum of restraint, confining activities to a generally understood locality, not eliminating offenses altogether. Only if prostitutes grew too numerous, became too aggressive, and spilled out into a nearby "nice" locality might the police crack down.

Less obvious, but more commonplace and pertinent for our purposes, are larger urban tracts characterized by mixtures of low-density nondescript housing, modest-income transient residents, and commercial enterprises unaffected by their proximate environment—gas stations, small wholesale and manufacturing businesses, auto repair facilities, or specialized off-beat retail stores. Populations tend to be heterogeneous with a fair sprinkling of the elderly, unattached adults, the economically marginal, or "Bohemian" artistic types. Few intact families and children reside there and, therefore, schools and playgrounds are absent. Outwardly, they stand in sharp contrast to vibrant densely packed communities such as Chinatowns or Little Saigons.

Residents here are nearly oblivious to neighbors, save disruptive criminals. Landlords rent apartments and storefronts to those paying, regardless of race, ethnicity, sexual preferences, or political ideology. Few complain of their milieu "going downhill." Because daily neighborhood visitors are largely passing strangers or daytime workers, an easy tolerance prevails. For the outrageous, these rundown, jumbled environments offer wondrous sanctuaries. Provided unassuming requirements are satisfied, largely paying the rent or not being outwardly criminal, nearly everyone is welcome.

Many of today's vibrant gay areas—West Hollywood, California; the Castro area of San Francisco—have sprung from such slightly "seedy" districts.[14] They are also hospitable to political radicalism. Scanning Marxist group addresses depicts a physical clustering of controversial organizations in these zones. Cheap rent, low residential population densities and nonchalant nearby residents serve as powerful lures. In New York City, for example, the area generally surrounding Union Square Park (14th Street between Park Avenue South and Broadway) typifies this marginal hodgepodge neighborhood with a reputation for accepting even the most radical. In 1989, for example, one could find within walking distance divergent groups such as the Socialist Party USA, Union of Radical Political Economists, Workers Defense League, the Nationalist Anti-Imperialist Movement, Revolution Book Store, National Coalition for Economic Justice, the Workers World Party, the Marxist Research Center, and myriad other radical leftist organizations (Wilcox, 1989). It is quite unlikely that neighborhood locals share these unconventional sentiments or, for that matter, even notice outcroppings of revolutionary activity. Such invisibility would evaporate if these organizations had migrated *en masse* to Madison Avenue in the 1970s, when it was home to conservative, wealthy residents more attuned to exorbitant designer boutiques than proletarian bookstores.

To make this point concrete, consider the Revolutionary Bookstore, located just off 5th Avenue on West 19th Street in a Manhattan neighborhood housing everything from tiny factories to avant-garde boutiques. Run by the Revolutionary Community Party, a Maoist sect that denounces nearly all present-day Communist countries as "capitalist" (including Cuba and China), it hardly disguises its intense revolutionary ardor. A casual visitor immediately sees outcries for demonstrations against capitalist oppression, stacks of revolutionary tracts, and all the other trappings of a genuine rabble-rouser party. Nor are sales clerks shy about voicing the objectives— inquiries will unleash an anti-American torrent and the urgency for a proletarian revolution. Nevertheless, this outpost of the fundamentalist Marxist revolution has only once in recent memory experienced any local hostility— when a window display during the 1991 Gulf War invited solidarity with Arab people. Even then, the bother was inconsequential and, more significantly, local government has totally ignored this vanguard of radical revolution (personal interview, March 28, 1997).

Many modern urban settings can abet even those testing the limits of communal acceptance. Beyond the thriving enclaves, past the mixed "neighborhoods without community" are fringe localities where behavior judged unacceptable, even blatantly illegal, elsewhere is tolerated. Recall our contention that the Amish, Doukhobors, and Mormons gained much of their acceptance by upholding strict moral values—hard work, thrift, strong families, and so on. This does not mean, however, that conformity to strict morality is the only ticket to tolerance. Toleration of the intolerable *is* possible. Many large cosmopolitan cities unofficially permit severe violations of societal standards to flourish *provided* they are limited to specified hidden locations.

The far west side of Manhattan's Greenwich Village is a decaying, isolated waterfront/warehouse borderline commercial area that is largely deserted at night and has few conventional residents.[15] It is a physically unattractive place, almost inviting crime and decadence. Below this public facade, during the 1980s, were businesses catering to flamboyant, sexually liberated gays— leather S&M bars, transvestite cabarets, stores hawking erotic paraphernalia, clubs facilitating open sexuality, and similar entities tolerable no place else in New York. Similarly, on the West Village's long-abandoned, out-of-the-way piers, today's gays can freely sunbathe virtually nude, a behavior hardly acceptable to the Russian immigrants of Brighton Beach, Brooklyn a few miles away. Again, "out of sight, out of mind" can foster tolerance.

More is involved, however, than enclaves of like-minded citizens or all-forgiving mixed-usage urban tracts. Urban balkanization, contentious feuds between neighborhoods, and raids into unclaimed territory are equally imaginable. Indeed, turf battles among ethnic-based gangs have long plagued cities. A psychological element must also be present to guarantee political tolerance. Needless to say, this necessary psychological ingredient is exceedingly complicated, but an abstract fondness for tolerance does not seem part of the concoction. It is unlikely that the Italians north of Canal Street in New York City "put up with" the recent Chinese immigrants across the street largely out of a deeply felt appreciation of cultural differences. Nor do these Italians extend a warm multicultural hospitality to the many gays residing a mere block from their Bleeker Street territory. Ditto for the Italians of "Spanish Harlem" living in intimate proximity to African Americans and Puerto Ricans. Tolerance exists despite hostility.

Far more germane are feelings like obliviousness and emotional detachment (Gans, 1991). For these New Yorkers of Italian decent, the nearby Chinese, gays, African Americans, and Puerto Ricans barely enter daily consciousness. They may be there in the sense of being encountered, but these strangers—unless they are posing a threat—could just as well be on Mars.[16] In fact, such mental callousness is endemic to urban life and is not limited to urban Italian culture. Furthermore, modern city life permits—

perhaps even requires—emotional and physical detachment. Wealthy residents are insulated from loathsomeness by doormen, delivery services, taxis, exclusive stores and restaurants, vacation retreats, private schools, and a selective social life. Even the less wealthy acquire a city-wise prudence— shunning subways during certain times, averting eye contact, pursuing solitary hobbies, or otherwise hardening themselves against unpleasantness. Tolerating the invisible is easy.

An exquisite illustration is the peaceful coexistence of Orthodox Jews and devout Muslims in Borough Park, Brooklyn, New York (*New York Times,* August 17, 1995). Both are substantial and growing communities in close proximity to each other. Given that incessant strife between devout Jews and Muslims is notorious, the question becomes: Why peace in Brooklyn despite endless potential friction points? Most evidently, both communities share innumerable cultural attachments—strong patriarchal family life, puritanical moral code, severe public modesty in attire, respect for religion, common dietary restrictions, avoidance of alcohol, strict discipline for children, and an abhorrence for Hollywood-style movies and other contemporary libertine "distractions." Occasional economic incentives further promote cordiality— for example, Muslim-owned food shops now stock kosher milk alongside items imported for their Muslim customers. Some Muslims buy their Arabic newspapers at newsstands owned by Orthodox Jews.

More fundamental is psychological distance despite physical proximity. As Dr. Faizul Kabir, a dentist and Muslim community leader put it, "We see each other during the day's business, we make our transactions and then we go our own ways. We are both people that keep to themselves, and we complement each other in this way" (*New York Times,* August 17, 1995). An informal norm exists that neighborhood Muslims and Jews avoid political discussions or other potentially conflictual matters. Jewish storekeepers learn Arabic phrases out of politeness and good business sense, but this mingling does not go any deeper. Transactions occur with a polite distance. This "oil and water" urban coexistence pattern is hardly unique. It is a ubiquitous feature of many great cities, especially in so-called transitional neighborhoods. In the 1950s and 60s, for example, San Francisco's North Beach neighborhood found socially conservative Italians in close proximity to "Beatniks" preaching cultural revolution. A stroll through Miami Beach, Florida's South Beach section, reveals elderly religious Jews, gays and lesbians, boisterous teenagers, yuppies, and conventional tourists all sharing physical space though hardly interacting. Urban environments offer wondrous opportunities for highly divergent people to live peacefully if psychological distances are kept. To attempt to break down these walls of obliviousness in the name of "appreciation" would probably prove disastrous.

III. Resisting Intolerance

Depictions of intolerance typically envision powerful forces wielded against defenseless victims. We hear of government repressing Marxist groups or angry homophobes harassing gays. Lacking in these accounts is resistance from the targeted victim. It is assumed that third parties—the courts, community leaders, First Amendment-attuned citizens—are charged with offering protection. However, as in criminal assaults, the prey can resist successfully. And if sufficient numbers of intended victims defy, both criminality and intolerance will diminish. Conversely, potential marks can multiply the likelihood of attack. Wandering around intoxicated and flashing expensive jewelry, for example, invites robbery. Of all the potential items on the promoting tolerance menu, it would seem industrious resistance is particular useful.

A particularly adaptive counteractive strategy is physical invisibility. Of course, as in the case of racial or ethnic identity, this is unfeasible. Ditto for required religious garb—for example, Hasidic Jews. Nevertheless, America is not a medieval society of prescribed attire, and mavericks need not exhibit their deviancy in public. This camouflaging of unorthodoxy is deceptively complicated. It extends from clothing to details such as hairstyle, jewelry, beards and mustaches, wearing propagandistic items (e.g., political buttons or emblems), carrying conspicuously provocative books, and otherwise openly announcing one's identity. Even one's vocabulary is a source of revelation—terminology often reflects ideology—for example, using "queer" instead of "homosexual." This signaling of views via outward appearances is frequently conscious—in the 1960s, for example, counterculture hippies sought to achieve the right look with colorful headbands, love beads, and psychedelic tee-shirts despite their claims that appearances were superficially irrelevant.

The outward appearance of controversial groups reflects diverse strategies. The Communist Party USA has consciously implored followers to appear "normal." During the 1930s, for example, party officials directed that members resemble typical American workers, not "radicals," and thus should regularly get haircuts (Klehr, 1984, 308). This "passing" was especially apt when Communists ventured into hostile territory, as in 1932 when a band of youthful Marxists traveled off to organize Kentucky coal miners. Leaders admonished them to avoid black leather jackets, the then-fashionable "proletarian look," and instead opt for respectable suits and skirts (Cohen, 1993, 47). Photographs of party leaders from the 1940s and 50s exhibit a predilection for nondescript suits, white shirts, dull ties and other conventionalities, rendering them indistinguishable in a crowd. A similar inclination toward visible respectability characterized 1950s southern civil rights leaders. Demonstration organizers sought approving publicity and thus insisted protesters dress neatly, be well-groomed, and eschew anything proclaiming radicalism. Picket lines typically resembled an assembly of conservative churchgoers.

Insistence on hyperconventional attire goes beyond making a fashion statement. Distinctive demeanors, especially in the case of the CPUSA and similar despised radical groups, offered easy targets for unfriendly police or hostile citizens. Arresting revolutionary students is far simpler when they appear in unique proletarian costumes. Outward conventionality also reaffirms—perhaps deceptively—a deeper cultural commitment. A wholesale rejection of society invites intolerance, and this affront is customarily proclaimed by ostentatious weirdness, such as purple hair, going barefoot, outrageous body piercing, or frequent vulgarity. Flaunting outward conventionality needlessly hinders proselytizing among the unconverted. Imagine the self-imposed obstacles faced by Communists appealing to laborers if they were outlandishly dressed and peppered casual conversation with "fellow revolutionary toiler." Resentment, if not outright hostility, would replace tolerance.

The reverse tactic—manipulating outward appearances to antagonize—is equally familiar. During the mid-1960s, for example, anti-Vietnam War resisters routinely enjoyed taunting middle-class sensibilities. Indeed, the male protester style—long, unkempt hair, scraggy beards, rumpled clothing, defilement of patriotic symbols such as flags, open marijuana use, ceaseless talk of subverting authority, permissive sexuality, and mocking regular employment—became clichés. Similar derision of conventionality characterized the militant Black power movement—extreme hairstyles, paramilitary garb (often with bullets as a fashion accessory), a violence-laced vocabulary, and conspicuous rejection of bourgeois values. Today, militant gays continue this "tradition" of outwardly broadcasting unconventionality in their flamboyant attire, patent sexuality, and provocative language. Gays also occasionally accent their sexual identities—and thus make themselves easier targets for harassment—by affixing distinctive rainbow flag decals to car bumpers or hanging their identifying multicolor flags from gay-owned businesses.[17]

A parallel choice of tactics prevails among organizations. Groups can avail themselves of multiple alternatives. The Amish and the Doukhobors, for example, emphasize mild-mannered delegations gently appealing to public officials, invoking cherished principles of religious freedom. The Mormons likewise favored amicability despite periodic violence. These are nonconfrontational, nearly invisible, often tedious styles of redressing grievances. They commonly brought success—nearly everyone easily tolerates exemptions when pursued in this "don't make waves" fashion. Even Marxists, such as the early Socialist parties located within ethnic enclaves, once adopted this image of wholesome respectability by sponsoring educational public lectures, self-help and hobby groups, family social gatherings, and similar ultrarespectable "bourgeois" activities. Socialist mayors, notably Milwaukee's Victor Berger, prided themselves on well-run, efficient civic administrations. No doubt, even staunch capitalists had to tolerate, even admire, this no-nonsense brand of dour Marxism.

At the opposite pole are contemporary "in your face" groups that, apparently, thrive on shocking. This style originated in the mid-1960s when anti-war groups ransacked draft induction centers, vandalized government-sponsored research facilities, and otherwise redefined "political protest." A notable example today is AIDS Coalition to Unleash Power, better known as ACT-UP!. Among their demands are free medical care for all HIV/AIDS-infected people, free needles and other drug paraphernalia, and similar cost-reduction measures. ACT-UP! has covered buildings with red tape to expose government inaction, chained members to the balcony of the New York Stock Exchange, stopped traffic for "die-ins," conducted disruptive stand-up protests during church services, spray-painted body outlines on streets to symbolize the mounting death toll, and conducted innumerable other high-profile, flamboyant public protests. An especially controversial ACT-UP! tactic is disrupting government hearings, medical society meetings, and scholarly conventions (Button, 1995, 353).[18]

Unpopular groups possess multiple options to escape unwelcome attention. One's name is unmistakably a critical choice. Contrast, for example, innocuous-sounding designations such as Human Rights Campaign Fund, Lambda Legal Defense and Education Fund, and the Hetrick-Martin Institute with, say, Queer Nation, Lesbian Avengers, or Queer Women/Men Support for Prisoners, all gay organizations. On the Marxist side, compare the Maoist International Movement with The Center for Popular Economics in terms of the image evoked. This choice of formal identity is compounded by other outward, seeable displays—publication titles, identifying symbols, rhetorical flourishes, and those spokespeople put forward to publicly represent the organization. Points of contentious conflict can be softened by clever language or avoiding provocations altogether—for example, using "Public Relations Coordinator" in lieu of the dictatorship-sounding "Minister of Information." As alluded to earlier, to promote its American image, the Communist Party USA sought "authentic" American leaders with Anglo-Saxon sounding names (for example, Gus Hall).

An equally time-honored hiding technique is joining established, more acceptable causes. The CPUSA's anti-fascist Democratic Front commencing in 1938 is a classic example. Under Moscow directives, Communists embraced the Democratic Party "to preserve and extend democracy, all those things that have been the heart of the American tradition in the past, ever since the revolutionary foundation of the United States" (quoted in Klehr, 1984, 208). Alliances were also formed with several leading state-based political parties—the Farmer-Labor Party of Minnesota and New York's American Labor Party, for example. Once strident anti-capitalism was toned down in the name of lesser evils, and President Roosevelt's New Deal now became middle-of-the-road-progressivism. "Revolution" evaporated from public vocabularies, replaced by eulogies to Thomas Jefferson (now conveniently placed in the tradition of Lenin). The CPUSA gladly endorsed the highly popular Roosevelt and his liberal programs while keeping silent on obvious disagreements. The CPUSA even criticized opposition to Roosevelt as "treason" and sought to mend relationships with the Catholic Church (Klehr, 1984, Chapter 12). Predictably, the Communist Party now enjoyed relatively high levels of public support, attracting thousands of fresh recruits.

The Cyberspace revolution affords even greater opportunities for unorthodox views to hide while still soliciting adherents.[19] Indeed, the proliferation of oddball groups, including openly racist, White-supremacist organizations, such as the KKK and the American Nazis, in addition to those noted in chapter 5, is such that an intolerant person might be overwhelmed by tracking them, let alone obliterating them. Compared to "real" organizations that inherently require a physical presence, website entities need not worry about rent, printing stationery, newspapers, and other burdensome operating costs. The entry fee for political visibility and interchanges is but a pittance. For $20 a month, they can subscribe to a service like America OnLine, and with a server plus modest technical assistance, access is gained to an estimated 30 million web browsers. This has proven a bonanza for the once marginalized. The *Knights of the Ku Klux Klan* in the first of its eight websites received some 10,000 visitors (e-mail communication, April 9, 1997). The Southern League website, with its call for southern political independence, averages about 100,000 visitors a year. Obviously, not all these "hits" were messages from fellow-believers, and many are duplicates and the merely curious, but this represents notable exposure for those residing on the fringe of acceptability (e-mail communication, April 9, 1997). This form of interchange has often proven invaluable for gaining fresh recruits and keeping sympathizers up-to-date.

More relevant for our purposes, however, is the invulnerability provided by this electronic medium. Like noxious weeds, these contentious sites thus far have resisted all efforts at eradication; calls for government intervention from hate groups have thus gone nowhere. When Congress enacted the Communications Decency Act in 1996 to protect citizens against an unregulated Net, it was almost immediately declared unconstitutional by a federal court of appeals. When nervous access providers fearing retribution expel controversial groups, groups inevitably resurface elsewhere. The KKK, for example, has migrated several times; other controversial groups hold their ground by threatening legal action. Nor has a flood of hostile e-mail and electronic sabotage silenced these odd voices. *Crosstar,* a vehement White racist organization, has endured multiple attacks by hackers by upgrading its electronic defenses and constructing elaborate backups. It still manages to receive some 2,000 hits a month (e-mail interview, April 9, 1997).

The information available at websites may also assist those living beyond Cyberspace in fending off adversaries. The *Witches Voice* homepage, for example, offers free, expert legal advice to harassed witches. Especially noteworthy is the insulation from inevitable verbal denunciations, economic intimidation, and threats of violence. The web's removal from a physical place constitutes a shield against direct confrontation: You cannot destroy the physically invisible. Intolerance remains unconsummated. This anonymity likewise affords nearly complete privacy to those who might fear public exposure. KKK sympathizers and others beyond the mainstream can privately keep up and e-mail their encouragement without arousing suspicion from neighbors, anti-hate groups, and government watchdog agencies. To borrow a health-care phrase, net politics may be the ultimate "safe politics" for those fearing retribution. No doubt, as access to the web grows both domestically and internationally, proliferation of difficult-to-harass unpopular groups will increase geometrically. And, should they be attacked, like viruses they can quickly mutate, adopt protective coloration, and otherwise continue largely unchecked.

Conclusions

Our tour of achieving political tolerance without hearts and minds indoctrination has only sampled multitudinous possibilities. We do not submit *the* definitive alternative or a particularly worthy hierarchy; we simply reveal a range of historically viable options. None, not even the U.S. Army's coercive stratagem, demand citizens alter their private, innermost thoughts. It is inexcusable to contend that hearts and minds tolerance is the exclusive or historically most popular path. Of course, some will insist that this journey is without real relevance to our contemporary dilemmas: Today's problems are too unique, too tenacious, and thus amenable only to wholly innovative solutions. Not true. *Everything* we have explored remains relevant though not necessarily perfect.

What enduring lessons are revealed here? Surely one message is that *political* tolerance can coexist with overwhelming *personal* intolerance. No doubt, many Army recruits continue to harbor private racist sentiments but unit cohesion coupled with career incentives demands their suppression. Only outward behavior counts. The three religious groups described—the Amish, Doukhobors, and Mormons—long confronted far-reaching animosity. It is all too easy to forget that, given these bitter disputes, present-day peace and ultimate resolution were far from inevitable. All those involved robustly survived hatreds without government waging psychological campaigns of mutual *rapprochement.* Even today's outcast groups—gays and Marxists, for example—persevere without serious annoyance nearly everywhere. Live and let live transpires *despite* innumerable desires to the contrary.

It might be contended, predictably, that these lessons are irrelevant to contemporary sentiments facing aversion. What, for example, might urban gays learn from rural Doukhobors? Our answer is "something," though the parallel is evidently limited. Physical separation, recall, engenders a serviceable tolerance. This principle is hardly irrelevant for gays uncomfortable in mainstream society; there are entire towns off the beaten path in which gays enjoy unbridled freedom—Provincetown, Massachusetts and Fire Island, New York, among others. Urban enclaves serve a similar purpose. The benefits of a Doukhobor-style nonconfrontational, willing-to-negotiate approach is equally relevant to gays insisting on raucous confrontation. Perhaps most important, tolerance is more forthcoming when one seeks detachment, not an uninvited intrusive campaign to alter society. A radical call for sweeping social transformation is not the best prescription for accommodation; it will draw a rebuke.

More theoretically, our excursion suggests that today's dominating conception of tolerance is overly constrained by a universalistic and individualistic conception of citizenship. This is not preordained, choices exist. Our tour of the Ottoman Empire's *millet* system prompts one pertinent alternative—government guardianship of distinctive group rights, even when these rights collide with the larger community. The partitioning of society together with group-specific rules may affront those envisioning one big, happy family adhering to like rules, but this may cheaply avoid bloodshed. To wit, gays can have their life, heterosexuals theirs. Surely the 18th century Ottoman Empire was spared the immense carnage transpiring in Europe during the same era, despite all the learned calls for greater tolerance. Indeed, this may be the *de facto* convention in urban areas where distinct codes apply to particular groups and localities.

Finally, the irresistibility of intolerance must not be exaggerated. The constitutional order, with its decentralized, fragmented distribution of power, facilitates the survival of unpopular causes. Stamping out heresies—at least in contemporary America—is undoubtedly hopeless. If our tour has demonstrated anything, it is that our landscape thrives with a variety of political flora that rivals a tropical rainforest in novelty. Unpopular groups often, though not inevitably, resist successfully—much depends on tactics. Marxism still carries on despite innumerable eradication efforts. Conversely, unpopular groups may almost masochistically *invite* intolerance. The appeal of needless provocation is beyond our analysis but, apparently, self-generated intolerance is not unthinkable. We cannot condemn people for loathing groups who insist on inflaming. Without doubt, almost any tendency or inclination—and many unconventional behaviors, to boot—can be tolerated if reasonable accommodations are made. Tolerance is a two-way street.

NOTES

1. The military's treatment of hate speech is thus consistent with much older conceptions that focus on impact apart from intent. Moreover, the military code expressly exempts harsh epithets used in training given the army's long tradition of cuss words to mold fresh recruits.

2. It is also worth noting that this assignment does not carry any stigma that could hinder one's military career, though repeated assignment as the EOA is very much unwelcome. For the upwardly mobile soldier, doing the job well is part of the normal advancement process. Being excessive, alleging harms where none exists, to establish a reputation for fanatical diligence thus has no pay-off in the army. Conversely, a white who ignored the grievances of Blacks would ultimately be judged a poor EOA and this would hurt his or her career. In sum, the stress is on competence, not some larger political agenda.

3. Interestingly, early—and largely unsuccessful—army efforts resemble some of today's tactics employed by college campuses, namely a stress on altering attitudes via confrontation. This approach was ultimately abandoned as counterproductive (Moskos & Butler, 1996, 57).

4. This raising up of religion as the preeminent citizen characteristic in a system of governance does not mean that religious differences were the sole differences tolerated. Religion was typically a proxy indicator of other salient characteristics—language, economic status, and cultural values. Thus, protecting a faith also extended protection to these traits. Ironically, in its structure, the *millet* system mimics those contemporary thinkers who interpret individuals exclusively in terms of race, sex, and class.

5. The *millet* system was capable of absorbing a variety of religious creeds, but under Islamic law there were clear limits as to the types of religions admissible. Specifically, a distinction was drawn between monotheistic faiths based on revelation—Judaism and Christianity—and

polytheism and idolatry. The former are tolerable under certain restrictions whereas followers of the latter may be put to death or offered slavery as an alternative if they refuse to convert (Braude & Lewis, 1982, 4-5).

6. The yellow badge worn by Jews during the Nazi era was first used in the 9th century by Muslims in Baghdad and eventually became part of the *millet* system.

7. There are, however, national organizations that occasionally convey the Amish view to government. But these are hardly traditional interest groups. For example, the National Amish Steering Committee recently discouraged its members from voting and signing up for jury duty. Perhaps the closest step the Amish would take in attempting to influence government would be to advise praying that those in authority follow God's will (Yoder, 1993).

8. It should be noted, however, that this Amish committee is assisted by an organization called the National Committee for Amish Religious Freedom, which is composed of non-Amish who legally assist the Amish in things such as providing counsel, raising necessary funds, and providing a public voice for their concerns (Lindholm, 1993).

9. Doukhobor comes from the Russian meaning "spirit-wrestlers." The formal name of this sect is Christians of the Universal Brotherhood but our analysis follows convention and employs "Doukhobor."

10. The proper name of the Mormons is The Church of Jesus Christ of Latter-day Saints. Our use of "the Mormons" follows the convention of other scholars and is merely a shorthand term. We also do not use official Mormon terminology for leadership positions—for example, First President—insofar as they are generally unknown to non-Mormons.

11. This 1882 Act, the so-called Edmunds Act, had as its official purpose "the purification of the American home." Thus, it pre-dates by over a hundred years current discussions of preserving family life against attacks by those who define "family" differently. The success of this Act and subsequent Mormon acquiescence to civil law has been much debated. Even Mormons themselves acknowledge that a few of the faith continued in secret to maintain polygamy; outsiders estimate a higher proportion. This compliance issue was at one time a highly charged issue but has currently vanished from the agenda (O'Dea, 1957, 246-247).

12. To single out large urban areas as bastions of tolerance is not to suggest that small towns do not permit political tolerance. In fact, as John Roche forcefully argues, small-town America during the 19th century greatly facilitated such tolerance but *only* by allowing each civic entity to impose homogeneity within its borders. America was a mosaic of tiny tyrannies in which people could pick and choose agreeable settings. It was the *array of choices,* not freedom within each town that was critical (Roche, 1958).

13. Ironically, the customary connection between tolerance and urbanness *reverses* the logic of our argument. Tolerance scholars (going back to Stouffer) and others celebrating city life argue that routine contact with heterogeneity breeds tolerance. That is, people learn to appreciate differences by coming into contact with them. Our argument is different though not inconsistent: Separation preserves differences and, thus, heterogeneity.

14. It is sometimes argued, of course, that this "ghettoization" is a sign of larger societal intolerance. This would be correct if such proximity were forcefully imposed and, in the past, it often was. Nevertheless, it is also true that such concentration of like-minded residents is a precondition for a critical mass to support a group culture. For example, the existence of hundreds of gays living in proximity with each other easily allows the flourishing of businesses specifically catering to gay needs. The principle is no different from that facilitating religious communities, such as the Orthodox Jews.

15. These off-the-beaten-path neighborhoods are nearly invisible to the general public. Moreover, the combination of low rent and "exotica" may make them attractive to commercial developers. San Francisco, until the economic boom of the 1980s, had a similar decrepit waterfront area (the Embarcadero). No doubt, many major cities have such areas, though it is difficult to identify them precisely at the moment.

16. The interaction of many Italian Americans in New York City with their neighbors is far more complex than we have depicted here. It can be simultaneously quite violent and highly peaceful depending on specific circumstances. Indeed, the public face of tranquillity may be a direct consequence of a heightened willingness to employ force against disruptive outsiders. This matter is consider at length in Rieder (1985, especially Ch. 2).

17. The outward proclamation of one's gay sexuality has merged with capitalism and organization fund-raising. For example, the January 1997 *National Now Times* offers several pages of NOW-distributed tee-shirts, bumper stickers, coffee mugs, books, and similar items making a feminist ideological statement. Several of these are openly lesbian in character. A company also advertises bank checks with an ideological imprint.

18. That this public rambunctiousness has proven a windfall for anti-gay groups has often been noted by other gays. See, for example, Bruce Bawer, "Truth in Advertising," in Bawer (1996b).

19. Analysis here draws heavily on the research of Laura Huntington's "The Floodgates are Open: How the Internet Unleashes Purveyors of Strange Politics," independent study project, University of Illinois, 1997.

8

Propagating Tolerance

Chapter 1 depicted a growing, seemingly unreflective, celebration of hearts and minds tolerance. This nostrum was popularly judged the consummate cure-all for the myriad problems plaguing modern society. Nevertheless, this rendition of tolerance is but one of several and suffers, both conceptually and in measurement, from copious flaws, particularly its vagueness regarding limits of acceptability. We now zero in on this pernicious, seductive, blank-check vision of "live and let live." Installing this alleged virtue, we contend, undermines ordered liberty. To tutor citizens in an unreflected "accept everything" as a means of escaping acrimony is, in our estimation, a critical step in the march toward totalitarianism. This is surely not the intent of advocates, but it may well authorize a friendly and benevolent *1984* or *Brave New World*.

Not everyone will share this disheartening vision, this perceiving nefarious intent behind a pedagogy ever-so gently venerating "respect differences." Ours is most surely an assessment contrary to ruling opinion and will be undoubtedly deemed ideologically strident. Others will take issue with the empirical side of our analysis. For these defenders of the faith, our unease regarding hearts and minds tolerance subverts social harmony, the full development of people liberated from hated and bigotry. After all, the opposite of tolerance is intolerance, and who could possibly wish for wicked intolerance? To escape such facile—and mistaken—charges, let us dwell further on what we propose.

225

All societies, as Chapter 4 argued, are obliged to defend against seditious ideas, principles, and behaviors lest they crumble. This protective prescription is imbedded within the very notion of community independent of ideological inclination. Defense need not entail harsh pogroms against dissenters; proclamations of right and wrong may be sufficient without inflicting physical harm. A peaceful partitioning of "us" and "them" is also often adequate, as we just depicted. Surely no people are obliged to embrace radical assaults. Yet, having accepted the necessity of safekeeping against subversion, it is equally true that the imposition of total uniformity is both impossible and undesirable. Difficult balances between homogeneity and heterogeneity deserve careful attention. Though this equilibrium is typically uncertain, this inherent grayness is not an open invitation to abandon all standards. Nor does uncertainty over adjudicating rules mean that resolution is hopeless. Tolerance is not anarchy; it exists within a community, and communities require delineation.

In a free society, plainly, the preservation of heterogeneity is particularly difficult and querulous. Surely state coercion is part of the mix—citizens (though perhaps not the state itself) cannot execute deviants violating community norms. Laws legitimately forestall breaches of the peace by those who would subvert civil society. It is also true that government in an open society has a justifiable right to intrude into citizen thinking (see, for example, Tussman, 1977). Just as the criminal code announces the legitimacy of force, imposing educational commitments proclaims the necessity of molding young louts into "good citizens." Moral education has always been integral to schooling. The teaching of blank-check, hearts and minds tolerance is not to be condemned simply because it intrudes coercively into citizen thinking. How then do we navigate this uncertain terrain? What are the relevant standards? After all, who is to say authoritatively that one technique of deciding tolerance is superior to another? Without belaboring each intricacy of this immense issue, we propose the following principles regarding squaring tolerance with the preservation of community. We confess at the onset that this listing is somewhat subjective, but it is inconceivable that any such listing could qualify as impartially objective given its subject matter.

1. Mechanisms of preserving acceptable heterogeneity without requiring citizen psychological transformation are preferable to those that do, *ceteris paribus*. Laws demanding outward acceptance of the heretic are superior to insisting that citizens genuinely appreciate the nonconforming. Physical separation of antagonists is favored over forcing affinity among adversaries. This aversion to state intervention sustains the principle of limited government.

2. If tolerance is to be taught, teachings should reflect communal values and beliefs, from parents to the nation. Parents do not send their children to

school to be surreptitiously reshaped into young pioneers settling a school administration-defined novel Utopia. Parents need not insist on strict replication of their culture via schools. Indeed, immigrant parents may be quite content for schools to "Americanize" their children into something unlike themselves. Schooling should reflect parental desires; it is not revolutionary cultural kidnapping.

3. Education must involve parsing right from wrong, good from bad, in a graspable manner. Tolerance itself implies that something is better than something else. This promotes communal identity, a precondition of tolerance. This instructional responsibility is not painlessly discharged by raising moralistic questions or dwelling on empty abstractions sans strong conclusions. Claims of "value-neutral" indoctrination are bogus: Insisting that nothing is better than anything else is not value free. Lessons, moreover, must be appropriately clear—youngsters can hardly tease out subtle lessons resting on arcane principles.

4. Compulsion—if necessary—should center on outward behavior, not private thoughts. It is not that thoughts are inconsequential, and molding outward behavior may certainly shape innermost beliefs. Rather, schools in an open society are limited in coercive power. Parents, of course, are not bound by this restriction: For them, psychological identities are critical.

5. Inescapable techniques of state-sponsored indoctrination involving degradation, humiliation, physical abuse, harassment, and other techniques involving trauma are generally impermissible as public—though not private—policy (an exception might be the military). Nongovernment bodies are not, however, so constrained. A religious group may degrade a sinner before all, but this sinner need not worry that his or her church may confiscate property or take a life. Government's immense power, on the other hand, requires greater constraints. The policeman is not to be raised up to the ever-intrusive bully unless absolutely necessary.

This, then, constitutes our rough and ready framework for evaluating the contemporary inculcation of tolerance. We balance some overall need to teach tolerance, impart communal standards, and constrain state power while not elevating "anything goes" into official dogma. Of course, this list hardly resolves the innumerable honest differences over what is to be tolerated and what transgressions punished. There can be no official, rigid resolution to the untold complexities. Universal assent for these five propositions is not to be expected. They certainly do challenge today's fashionable and facile infatuation for differences. Our purpose is, however, not to persuade unbelievers; we merely make clear how we judge.

We begin with pronouncements by professional educators regarding the teaching of tolerance. Ideally, this should be complemented by accounts of classroom activity, for discrepancies often occur between pedagogical prescription and daily instruction. Nevertheless, for our purposes *intent* is as consequential as practice for it displays the goals of this "tolerance industry." Of particular relevance will be underlying guiding theoretical frameworks, such as the rules governing inclusions and exclusions on the to-be-tolerated list. Who is authorized to decide what is to be accepted and what is to be expelled from the community? We shall find an approach that differs substantially from the behaviorally driven U.S. Army strategy. Finally, these tolerance efforts will be examined in the context of promoting a free and open society in which reasonable differences can survive. This will not be a heartening conclusion.

The Call for Tolerance Instruction

Searching electronic data bases such as ERIC plus tracking down citations yields a plethora of books and essays devoted to inculcating tolerance. Some are grade school textbooks, others are more scholarly contributions. A few exist as resource kits or pedagogical blueprints. These are but a modest outcropping in an exploding enterprise. Again, as when portraying the Marxist and gay presence, this is a *tour d'horizon,* not a systematic inventory. Furthermore, whether these missives are but barely audible voices in a sea of divergent proposals or a mighty chorus in a soon-to-be-dominant pedagogy, we cannot surmise. Nor can we claim that our cullings are especially influential, though we have made a reasonable effort to concentrate on schemes eliciting widespread attention. All we can say is that these pedagogical formulations constitute the "educate for tolerance" impulse; those who demur remain silent, according to our survey.

What, then, do we encounter marching through this varied collection? Most plainly, whether it is a lone educator voicing singular convictions or an elaborate report from a generously funded ongoing project, the call for toleration is generous. Though each writer promotes his or her own special vision, in the aggregate, little is deemed beyond the mantel of acceptance. Thus, given the scope of ideas and behaviors that "must" be accepted, almost everyone is probably guilty of intolerance. Even obesity, a condition doctors deplore as unhealthy, draws a plea for tolerance. As one *NEA Today* tract pleaded, students of variegated sizes should feel equally welcome in the classroom and educational material should be screened for unflattering references to being overweight. It is wrong, according to this tolerance advocate, to exclude fat children from cheerleading squads or otherwise to ridicule them. And, to rally others against prejudice, names and addresses for obese support groups are provided (*NEA Today,* December 1994).

Predictably, especially in light of our discussion of gay teachers in Chapter 6, calls for teaching tolerance toward homosexuality are commonplace. A particularly illuminating example is offered by Laura Ellis-Stoess who shrewdly advises those committed to inserting homosexuality into the classroom on how to parry parental and school board objections. She prudently warns against spontaneously discussing homosexuality. Yet, in the same sentence of this advisory, she adds, "educators should be free to address these controversial sex issues that have been *forced on them by society*" (188) (italics added). Though official consent at every step must be secured, the lesson plan demands the teaching of respect and compassion for gays (Ellis-Stoess, 1996). The reasonable prospect that parents and school boards might wish homosexuality to be taught in a *negative* light is not addressed. Even mentioning the teaching of heterosexuality as the preferred form of sexuality escapes attention.

Perhaps the most ambitious assault on intolerance is the one sponsored by the Southern Poverty Law Center. Of the entire "tolerance industry," this best approximates a vital nerve center.[1] Their handsomely produced magazine, *Teaching Tolerance,* is dedicated to promoting this virtue and is mailed free twice a year to every public and private school in the country. Some 40,000 video kits have also been shipped out. Even this huge undertaking involves but a small part of the Center's larger Teaching Tolerance Project. The Center weekly receives hundreds of telephones calls and suggestions from people all over the country to expulse intolerance (Heller & Hawkins, 1994). According to *Teaching Tolerance, tolerance* means "recognition and respect for diverse practices or beliefs." Acceptance of differing lifestyles is also included under *tolerance* (Heller & Hawkins, 1994). Generally, children should appreciate those traits characteristic of divergent religious, ethnic, sexual, or racial groups (*Teaching Tolerance,* Spring, 1994). The popular magazine typically offers stories teaching children to appreciate cultural diversity, reviews worthy films and books, and provides a forum for the exchange of instructional inspirations and tales of students conquering bigotry. The theme of multiculturalism as applied to race and ethnicity dominates. Though the Center explicitly asserts its nonpolitical, nonideological character, there is a heavy emphasis on the civil rights struggle as the paradigm of achieving reverence for differences.

Especially common is casting tolerance as a defensive weapon against the familiar evil trinity of sexism, racism, and homophobia. Typical in this regard is Judith A. Swearingen's effort to expose and root out these biases among novice teachers in training before they can infect their own students (Swearingen, 1996). This is a grim problem, claims Swearingen, for "Our society is fractured by violence, racial prejudice and intolerance, and religious and gender bias" (152) and these troublesome notions have even permeated her students. Class discussions highlighted women in the military, dates among gays, and bias against Islam. Significantly, as the class progressed these teachers-to-be realized that they were not nearly as liberal and open-minded as they once believed, and now discerned the need for personal change. Swearingen's grim assessment of contemporary society racked by hatred is hardly unique; it appears as an unchallenged *leitmotiv* in much of this literature. As Barta and Winn (1996) express it: "In a society where racism, bias, prejudice, and discrimination continue to exist, it should be no surprise that children reach our classroom carrying these harmful attitudes and behavior." Predictably, these authors endorse vigorous medications for this disorder, just as a public health official might wage war on AIDS.

A different instructional approach is the "Tolerance for Diversity of Belief" project being conducted through the University of Minnesota (Avery, Bird, Johnstone, Sullivan, & Thalhammer, 1992; Bird, Sullivan, Avery, Thalhammer, & Wood, 1994). Here the *a priori* assumptions regarding what is to be tolerated are not as explicitly imposed. Tolerance is initially conceived as the willingness to acknowledge the civil liberties of personally disliked groups. Operational measurement is via the content-controlled method previously described in Chapter 3 (John Sullivan, the technique's developer, is a project investigator). Specifically, students are presented with a brief researcher-supplied, ideologically balanced list of controversial groups, from the American Nazi Party to the Communist Party. Young respondents then decide whether selected disliked group members could engage in specified legitimate activities, such as running a candidate for the presidency or holding rallies. To deny a civil liberty to a self-selected group constitutes intolerance. Significantly, and this cannot be over-emphasized, there are no groups on this researcher-supplied list that do *not* warrant tolerance: Students can *only* be unjustifiably intolerant when imposing limits.

As one scans these tolerance education programs, sincerity and devotion are indisputable. Everyone seeks harmony, a world free of violence and persecution. The message of peaceful coexistence, sporadically buttressed by illustrations of intolerance drawn from horrible historical events, is forcefully preached. Superficially, everything looks commendable and beyond contention or, at worst, harmlessly inefficacious. Nevertheless, further reflection on these and similar efforts to enhance the peaceful acceptance of differences raises several troublesome issues, issues obscured by this enthusiastic pursuit of virtue. There are serious flaws here, not merely technical pedagogical impediments.

Evidently, if one imagines oneself as the recipient of these admonishments, the single permissible conclusion would be that only the acceptance of all—save one—differences is permissible. The single exception would be intolerance itself: Feelings of loathsomeness are to be exiled from society and within one's inner thoughts. Leaving aside obvious specific evils such as the Klan and White militias, it is a promiscuous tolerance that is being advanced. When a rare concrete example of something "not to be tolerated" does surface, it is very extreme and far distant from contemporary life—for example, Nazis who killed Jews. Many analyses lack a single example of something forbidden, though one can well imagine the distant content if one were to insist on an example. Beyond these few unequivocal historical examples, immense vagueness surrounds what else is evil. It would be as if legislators drafted laws banning "bad things." To express an aversion to a proclivity, to an unorthodox sexual preference, to somebody who was physically or culturally "different" is a crime against the spirit of tolerance. In a nutshell, students are being instructed to raise up acceptance of expansive differences to the highest personal and civic virtue. Unfortunately for all these captive students, such unreflected generosity is not what tolerance is all about.

To appreciate the flawed nature of this understanding, let us return briefly to our earlier characterization of tolerance as a window dividing the commendable from the legitimately unacceptable. This principle of a range, not a measureless territory lacking boundaries, is inescapable, not a matter imposed by choice. Disregarding this window negates the promise of civil society. Recall that both Locke and Mill, two central founders of the modern tradition, frankly acknowledged boundaries for putting up with the objectionable. Locke might tolerate dissenting Protestant sects, but Catholics were unwelcome (as Locke believed them to be foreign agents). Nor would Locke "put up with" sexual immorality. Mill similarly granted acceptance to personal eccentricities and private beliefs; conduct undermining the public good lay beyond the frontier. Chapter 4 demonstrated that a firm, though not always easily located, line separated honest dissent from subversion. Both Locke and Mill (and much else in the tolerance tradition) permit citizens to exhort, counsel, or entreat the untolerated to reform their ways. Tolerance does not demand silence or passivity, let alone coerced acceptance. A sharp distinction separates state coercion, to be employed only reluctantly, and the continuing moral obligations of citizens to promote virtue.

Consider a simple example—tolerance for obesity. Recollect how a teacher—Russell Williams—campaigned to protect fat students from being ridiculed and ostracized (Faber, 1994). Surely one could argue that childhood obesity is worthy of personal chastisement given its injurious health conse- quences. Tolerance would preclude, for example, a state-imposed diet but surely entreating fat students to lose weight seems an act of kind concern, not harassment. In principle, how are we to distinguish warnings against bad eating habits from, say, school-sanctioned campaigns against smoking or drunkenness? Might not a compassionate "tough-love" teacher occasionally chide the roly-poly student to reform him or her? Indeed, *not* to make such intervention, perhaps erroneously justified by "respecting different body shapes" might be an act of sinfulness, given the detrimental consequences of stoutness.

Dwelling on fatness to highlight misdirected tolerance is not an attempt to amplify a weak argument with a bizarre example. If the approval of being overweight were the only illustration of the anti-bias, combat-the-evils-of- prejudice curriculum we could muster, matters would be less alarming. The campaign is far more expansive. Venerating differences in school textbooks at all levels has become the ticket to financial success for ambitious pub- lishers in a multitude of subjects. It is almost as if commercial competition encourages enlarging the perimeters of inclusiveness. Inclinations once deemed reprehensible now are being invited into the ever-inclusive tent of respectability. Unstudious first-graders can take solace in *Leo, The Later Bloomer.* Children who are grammatically challenged and lacking employed fathers can validate their lives with *Daddy Don't Go To Work.* Those young- sters who shun advancement will find comfort from a textbook insisting that upward mobility depends on power and force, not education or hard work (Brown, 1992). Children too lazy to master conventional spoken English, a prerequisite for economic betterment today, may find a sympathetic teacher appreciating this "difference." Indeed, one professor charged with instruct- ing future teachers pleaded that children have a *right* to have their non-stan- dard English validated by the school in the name of "linguistic tolerance" (Terry, 1994). An insistence on standard English was likewise portrayed as "language imperialism" (Byrd, 1995). If school-age children are homeless, it is up to schools to improve their self-perception and social standing, not restore them to adult supervision (Heller & Hawkins, 1994).

Of all the inclusionary efforts, however, the most far-reaching is the infatuation with unconditionally accepting "group-based differences" almost regardless of what makes up the difference. This welcome seems to be the emerging definition of authentic tolerance. Youngsters are enlightened to grasp that each discernible classification—African Americans, Hispanics, Chinese Americans, and so on—has its own special culture, all cultures contribute, each is worthy of unconditional respect, and no one culture is superior. Indeed, according to one professor of education (Terry, 1994), children have a right to have their nonstandard English validated: "The goal of a cultural diversity course should be to foster tolerance for and (sic) unconditional acceptance of all human beings regardless of differences of self. Tolerance for human diversity implies the recognition of the inherent worth of another human and that person's right to exist." (5) This sentiment is not a lonely voice in the wilderness. Portland, Oregon's famous Multicultural/Multiethnic Education program constantly reiterates this strict cultural equality theme and has found widespread popularity both in the U.S. and abroad (Billingsley, 1997). And what might constitute intolerance according to this vision? Judging from a suggested questionnaire designed to assess "inappropriateness," feelings of unease in dealing with differences are the problem. Actual behavior lies beyond inquiry. (Byrd, 1995).

This multiculturally laden tolerance involves far more than the old-fashioned "group appreciation programs," ethnic holidays, or other forms of prizing foreign cultures via special food or recounting a people's history. In fact, such episodic special attention may itself be reprehensible, as it only highlights a group's minority status. The message, at least for those at the cutting edge of pedagogical theory, is supposed to permeate the entire curriculum whether it be mathematics or English. Tolerance tinged with multiculturalism colors the entire education experience, not just an instructional module, and goes well beyond the classroom.

If this broad message were judged by factual standards much like one would assess the accuracy of a history book, it would be found to be deeply flawed. It requires an enormous stretch of the imagination and bending of reality to make it credible. No doubt perceptive students will readily notice that not all cultures are equal, save in their very existence as cultures.[2] The concept of tolerance is clearly being employed in the service of mendacity, albeit for an allegedly noble purpose; one might even conclude that the very idea of tolerance is being corrupted. In a few extreme instances, the teaching of tolerance employs gross misrepresentation of history. Portland, Oregon's promotion of multicultural acceptance entails teaching students that ancient Egypt was a Black African society that gave the modern world its science, mathematics, and religion (Billingsley, 1997). Needless to say, this is hardly an uncontested scholarly vision (see, for example, Lefkowitz, 1996, especially Chapter 2).

Surely government policy itself suggests that not all racial or ethnic group attributes are to be embraced as is. Embarrassing, controversial issues here lie just below the surface, and it is understandable why public schools might shun them, but awkwardness is certainly no excuse for mis-education. If this argument were convincing, sex education would be banished from the curriculum because teenage illegitimacy might be "valid" within certain cultures. It is well-known, for example, that many African American children perform poorly academically. Governments acknowledge this problem by pouring billions into targeted remedial programs, from Head Start to school lunches, and courts have likewise intervened to correct deficiencies. It is equally clear, though honest differences arise over proportions, that this problem partially derives from African American students themselves—a disinterest in education, poor discipline, and noneducational distraction such as sports. Sharply put, how are we to treat African American children who announce that "grade school is worthless"? Is this to be tolerated as a valid expression of a beyond-reproach cultural perspective, no different from an Asian student infatuated with the opposite view? Pushed further, how can we square the easy acceptance of equal validity with other "bad" behaviors such as teenage pregnancy, gang violence, or drug use? Are grade-school children to be told that the "gangsta culture" is precisely equivalent to any other lifestyle?

More important than promoting distortions justified as tolerance, this quest abandons a central function of education. Though hardly an easy, noncontroversial task, distinctions regarding good and bad can—*and ought*—to be made regarding what is desirable and what is loathsome behavior. Schools are a critical agency in cultural transmission, and a posture of neutrality—save an aversion to hatred—does not convey culture. Cultures cannot be cultures of everything; insisting on absolute permeability is not an act of kindness. Governments, often at the behest of African American or Latino/a group leaders themselves, make such separations when demanding intervention. Not even the most ardent civil rights leader would hold that many African American children are fine as is and nothing needs to be altered. If all differences were equally valid, if literacy and illiteracy were merely distinct lifestyles, why spend massively to transform (deficient) attitudes and behaviors? Again, for a teacher to tell students that all traits, so long as they are characteristic of a group and no matter how personally objectionable or economically debilitating, are worthy of full acceptance, is surely extraordinary.

Any why this rush to advance cultural relativism? Why must children of European ancestry hurry up and come to appreciate schoolmates from Asia? At least three reasons come to the fore. First, no doubt, tolerance preaching is partially crassly selfish. For some it is economically driven—"tolerance for diversity" is a hot fashion within education and money is to be made by authors, publishers, and experts counseling eager teachers (Brown, 1992). Others may not enrich themselves financially, but they still nevertheless profit by insulating themselves from strict, conventional, pedagogical standards. Both students and teachers are not challenged by planning this new inclusive Utopia. Avoiding "hard" subjects such as Shakespeare's plays or the poetry of Milton may be a welcome relief for some teachers.

Leaving avarice and slackness aside, however, and assuming complete sincerity, its seems indisputable that these tolerance devotees see American society seriously at risk lest we mend our evil, bigoted ways. Appreciation of differences beginning with young children is but essential preventive medicine. Teachers under the guidance of education professors and administrators are to be the new physicians of societal disorder. The burgeoning menace of sexism, racism and homophobia is especially singled out when starting to call for medicinal tolerance. Dread of imminent strife is the theoretical launching pad. Typical is David Aronson, a writer for *Teaching Tolerance,* who easily gathers together Beirut, Belfast, Sarajevo, and Soweto with Los Angeles and New York. Racial epithets among students, for Aronson, resemble the forced inculcation of a depilatory communal virus (Aronson, 1994). Securing parental acceptance for (favorable) classroom treatment of homosexuality similarly invokes a societal medication image. One advocate, for example, suggests that parents be informed that such instruction is an attempt "to diffuse a classroom and societal problem" rather than merely advocate a personal view. Wise counsel here easily assumes that aversion to homosexuality, not homosexuality itself, constitutes the obstacle confronting the community (Ellis-Stoess, 1996). Needless to say, as we have demonstrated earlier, the United States is scarcely awash with the brutal repression of minorities. If anything, diversity in nearly every form is exploding.

Finally, the inculcation of tolerance becomes an essential precondition for future citizens surviving an ever more diverse America. In a word, multicultural appreciation is "practical." This verdict is ubiquitous throughout (see, for example, Banks, 1994, Chapter 3). Typically, authors cite census-like future population projections—by the early 21st century, it is alleged, residents of European ancestry will be a minority. And because, it is safely assumed, nonmainstream cultures will not assimilate to the now dominant European environment, Whites "better get ready" for the big transition. Acquiring tolerance (defined as valuing differences) in a sense resembles learning foreign languages—a survival tool. Leaving aside all the arguable demographic assumptions, it is never explained why coexisting in the same nation requires *all* Whites to accept unconventional cultures.[3] Recall our example of Orthodox Jews and religious Moslims surviving in physical proximity without much regard—or appreciation—for each other's faith. Must rural folk in Montana learn about the African American contribution to urban society? The argument's unfounded, almost *non sequitur* character is amusingly revealed by David Aronson's rejoinder to Saul Bellow's anti-multicultural comment. "I will read the Zulus when they have produced a

Tolstoy," said Bellow. Aronson's answer: "Next time you get on a bus, look around: No matter who you are—Black or White, Protestant or Hindu—you will discover that not only are they among us, they are us. We as a community, could do worse than start to recognize ourselves" (Aronson, 1994, 30).

Refusing to draw distinctions regarding good and bad in the name of easy tolerance involves more than just escaping awkward realities or enjoying a harmless feel-good fantasy. Over and above offering students lists of "good" and "bad," instruction can convey *the very idea* of drawing distinctions. Teaching discernment as a cognitive habit parallels instruction in other subjects: The need to separate fine art from trash or safe sex from unsafe sex, independent of precise content, is part of the lesson. It would not seem especially difficult for educators to devise lessons in which students discover how to detect good from bad traits, learn, for example, that hard work is virtuous and sloth is wicked. Teachers must be *judgmental* though this term is anathema in the tolerance literature. In other words, lessons on discrimination should elucidate formulating distinctions regarding worthy and unworthy cultural/personal traits.

Unfortunately, the modern incarnation of tolerance makes *discrimination* a wholly negative term: *To discriminate* exclusively means to perform something unjustifiably "bad" as in "discriminating against gays." Only "bad citizens" discriminate. As one study put it, "Anti-bias curriculum in classrooms educates children to diffuse the bias which precedes prejudice and discrimination" (Barta & Winn, 1996).[4] This ever more common one-sided understanding of discrimination represents a notable and consequential shift; more than mere words are involved. Etymologically speaking, *to discriminate* need not imply exclusively negative behavior. The Oxford English Dictionary II defines the verb *discriminate* as:

discriminate *v.*
[f. L. discr mina t- ppl. stem of *discr mina re* to divide, separate, distinguish,
f. *discr men,-cr min*-division, distinction, f. stem of *discerne re* to distinguish.

Discrimination is defined:

discrimination.
[ad. L. *discr mina tio n-em,* n. of action from *discr mina re* to discriminate.]

1. a. The action of discriminating; the perceiving, noting, or making a distinction or difference between things; a distinction (made with the mind, or in action). Also with *against.*

To emphasize, this displacement comprises more than unguided, evolving linguistic convention. Substituting an ill-defined "acceptance of differences" while neglecting specific, balanced lessons in discrimination undoubtedly ill prepares students to navigate the inevitable choices they will face. Instruction against abstract bias or discrimination is hardly useful. After all, when legislatures enact nebulous statutes against "bad behavior," the courts strike them down as unconstitutional. How are citizens and officials to be guided by vague strictures? If being overweight resides within the boundaries of acceptability, how are ten-year-olds to judge similar unhealthy inclinations such as smoking? How about heroin addiction? A remarkable feature of this literature is that the appropriate role of teacher-supplied guidance draws scant attention. The possibility that teachers are responsible for inculcating communal values apparently escapes attention in tolerance discussions. There are two important underlying issues here. The first pertains to actual classroom instruction—what is being taught and how. The second concerns the ultimate source of educational inculcation—whose views are to be reflected when telling youngsters what is to be admitted or rejected. Let us address each.

Classroom Instruction

Residing at the very heart of this multicultural colored tolerance instruction are assumptions about culture and personal morality. "Tolerance industry" educators erroneously assume that the expression of moral disapproval is inappropriate if not reprehensible, and that to condemn is tantamount to insisting on unwelcome, forcible intervention. Legitimately disliking something, let alone attempting to repress it, seems inconceivable in a "real" democracy. Only hatred, prejudice, and discrimination are officially reprehensible.

A generous cultural relativism and tolerance are wrongly conflated. The former is being passed off as the latter though the two concepts share only the most superficial commonality. Remember that tolerance is almost always—correctly—defined as somehow putting up with what is *objectionable*. Our disagreement with convention is over the substitution of individual attitudes for collective behavior, not the definition itself. To impose appreciation on the once despicable via tutoring is *not* the inculcation of tolerance. This transformation is better categorized as advancing value neutrality or nonjudgmentalism, but is hardly training for tolerance. To repeat yet once more, tolerance, properly understood according to the OED II, is "The action or practice of enduring or sustaining pain or hardship; the power or capacity of enduring; endurance." To tolerate fat people or those unable to speak English correctly denies a warm embrace—we *suffer* these weaknesses and incapacities, not hallow them. Recall our much earlier discussion (Chapters 2 and 3) in which we argued that for, say, a Communist to say that he "tolerates" Communism was hardly tolerance.

Imbedded in tolerance is the idea that something is better than something else. As John Gray aptly put it, "When we tolerate a practice, a belief or a character trait, we let something be that we judge to be undesirable, false or at least inferior; our toleration expresses the conviction that, *despite* its badness, the object of toleration should be left alone (Gray, 1993). The political philosopher J. Budziszewski (1993) likens this divorce of tolerance from moral valuation as equivalent to postulating a "square circle." If tolerance were being properly taught, a teacher might say, "We must disapprove of laziness, but, alas, we nevertheless must accept this unfortunate disposition for we cannot alter it." Properly grasped, a tolerant person would *not* accept a serious, correctable flaw, such as incomprehensible speech. Such an understanding of tolerance, alas, might be construed as insensitive to those who choose a deplorable yet "valid lifestyle," talking without being understood.

Whether nuanced delineations between moral relativism and tolerance are either grasped or judged worthy of discussion in this proselytizing literature is debatable. The two ideas merge by expedient, even careless, fiat. A brief exchange reported in the Teaching Tolerance Project illustrates this reluctance to think through properly the connection between having standards and accepting differences. If this case typifies reasoning among those promoting all-inclusive tolerance, this disentangling may be too challenging. An Iowa school board member troubled about the implication of multicultural tolerance wrote to *Teaching Tolerance,* inquiring, "Must our children be tolerant of the lifestyles of child molesters, drug dealers and rapists?" The writer patently used extreme examples to contend that, without clear, explicit guidance, children might be unable to disassociate good from bad in general. The rejoinder was that the Teaching Tolerance Project reviews thousands of children's books and other classroom material, and "To date, we have yet to come across any materials praising the lifestyles of child molesters, drug dealers or rapists. Any reasonable, thorough review of the *empirical* research literature on teaching tolerance or multiculturalism will result in the same conclusion. Such material, such teaching, simply do not exist" (344) (Heller & Hawkins, 1994). Evidently, the abstract implications of "cultural relativism" were not comprehended. The Iowa school board member's argument was literalized—as no explicit call for tolerating child molesters was uncovered, then children will not tolerate child molesters. The deeper issue of *any* standards was sidestepped.

This neglect of perceptible guidance in the name of nonjudgmental inclusiveness is further accentuated by nondirective instructional styles. This pedagogical student-centered fashion apparently pervades tolerance inculcation—teachers scarcely lecture or otherwise impose doctrines; they stand distantly apart to help facilitate a student-developed consensus. In the education profession's latest jargon, this shift toward students as sources of insight is christened "student empowerment." Lessons in tolerance are thus (superficially) free-ranging, student-instigated discussions in which youngsters "share" their ideas, occasionally assisted by the distribution of resource materials while teachers unobtrusively keep order. If, perchance, a student offers the "wrong" judgment—for example, homosexuality is a sin—the appropriate pedagogical response is not to condemn harshly but to elicit other opinions as to why this notion may be mistaken. Students develop and achieve "personal growth" from formulating their own views via peer interaction.

To appreciate this style, let us review two exemplars of tolerance instruction in greater detail. Marilyn R. Cover, an adjunct professor of law at Lewis and Clark College, Portland Oregon, directs the Classroom Law Project. Her lesson plan for high school students begins with the contention that tolerance is a fundamental part of democracy, and this tolerance means respect for diverse ideas. One of these to-be-respected ideas is homosexuality, so the task at hand is teaching acceptance of homosexuality. Students first develop their own tolerance definition, then identify tolerance-related issues in their daily lives, followed by reviewing Oregon's proposed amendment forbidding sexual preference-based legal classifications or spending public funds to advance homosexuality. Finally, these high school students formulate a response to potential conflict within the school. Miscellaneous resource people are provided—state legislators, fellow students, and attorneys. Students work in small groups using historical documents that stress equality of rights, such as the Declaration of Independence. Cover expressly notes that the discussion is to focus on tolerance, as expressed in the proposed amendment, not the morality of homosexuality. Though pro-amendment arguments are presented, it is abundantly clear that this position is officially conceptualized as intolerance. However, rather than express this far-from-axiomatic view plainly—a potentially risky act given the serious disagreement surrounding the amendment's interpretation—it is more subtly conveyed via "spontaneous" student-run discussion using teacher-provided materials (Cover, 1995). "On their own," students thus come to realize that prohibiting homosexuality as a statutory classification constitutes intolerance. That one might be tolerant of homosexuality *and* still oppose the Amendment on legal or other nonpersonal grounds is not considered a legitimate option.

Perhaps the most ambitious and systematic exemplar of relying on students themselves to ferret out intolerance appears in the Tolerance for Diversity of Beliefs Project. This curriculum consists of seven lessons lasting three to four weeks. Again, teachers appear most like referees or suppliers of resource material than like active instructors. It is assumed that with the proper staging and encouragement, high school students more or less autonomously will acquire tolerance for the once condemned. Students begin in groups, defining tolerance and deciding what deserves acceptance. Journals are kept, and each group reads a case study on one of three tolerance-related situations—the Holocaust, the Chinese Cultural Revolution, and the World War II U.S. internment of people of Japanese ancestry. This self-education continues as these teenagers record their own tolerance feelings in journals. They read a fictional story about a class bully to personalize their appreciation of intolerance. The topic of human rights is introduced by having the youngsters themselves list and rank human rights while also considering the limitations of those rights. This newly acquired knowledge is applied to a video "I-Team Hate Mail," which examines hate mail sent to couples in racial or religious mixed marriages. Additional case studies appear—wearing black arm bands to protest the Vietnam War, a Nazi march in a largely Jewish community—and participants simulate cases with role playing. Students repeatedly pursue the quest for understanding—analyzing U.N. documents, collecting library materials or developing programs to enhance the right of free expression.

From the perspective of those designing this involved pedagogical exercise, the project was successful—overall, the appreciation for tolerance modestly increased. More students were now sensitive to the rights of minorities though a few also aired a heightened fear of violence if controversial ideas are permitted to flourish. This increase even occurred across schools with enrollments differing substantially by class and race. For the authors, this didactic experiment represents a glimmer of hope for democratic society.

Though the motives for this approach may be noble and it may conform to fashionable educational doctrine, a degree of disingenuousness is present. From a more sophisticated perspective, this inculcating of an appreciation for differences is less spontaneous than outwardly claimed. These education rituals, despite the absence of direct teacher lecturing, are hardly impromptu encounters whereby the incontestable truth miraculously drops from the sky. The teacher's hidden hand and the positions of others formulating the lessons is inescapable, from the selection of the allegedly unbiased resources and exemplars to defining the endeavor's ultimate thrust. The mission is to promote a permissive acceptance, not one to let the chips fall where they may. No doubt, had students spontaneously concluded that America needs a dictatorship or gays forcefully need to be converted to heterosexuality, the entire exercise would have been reformulated. Furthermore, regardless of their academic weaknesses, most students fully know that "right" and "wrong" answers exist, to be revealed in grades. The freewheeling, unrestrained nature of this quest is largely—if not entirely—illusionary.

What is pernicious about such hidden-hand instruction is its (false) presentation as the voluntarily determined end-product of the students' personal thinking. These teenagers are told that they autonomously "discover" the vague principle of virtually unlimited acceptance of differences in ways seemingly indistinguishable from "uncovering" Boyle's Law in chemistry class. Thus, what is merely one of several arguable stands on managing differences becomes revealed as a universal, transcendent truth.

This pedagogical stratagem, this facile escape from accusations of judgmentalism, is hardly the sole alternative. Conventional morality has long been unashamedly taught not by having students fabricate their own definitions of right and wrong, but by teachers minutely conveying clear "do's" and "don'ts." Students learn what is culturally required they do not concoct their unique moralities by talking among themselves. Wisdom regarding acceptability—the window of tolerance—is imparted, not singly "discovered." This is what schooling is all about; the classroom is not a deftly manipulated marketplace of ideas in which teenage "scholars" debate civic rules and reach authoritative conclusions. Lessons in civics should teach conventional virtues—in our case, patriotism, reasonable obedience to authority, the obligation to participate, respect for majority rule balanced by minority rights, the rule of law, and so on, not some ill-defined vision that there are many unspecified ways of conducting politics, and who is to say what is best for all people. Added to this might be rules for public decorum— one does not, for example, impose one's obnoxiousness on an unwilling public even if this behavior is a "valid" subcultural artifact. To argue otherwise denies the inherent possibility of community and its right of survival. Along with multiplication tables, pupils absorb that it is okay to read about communism, not so good to actually subvert the existing government. The Constitution is our fundamental law that has proven immensely valuable; it is not reducible to a malleable resource that assists teenagers to decide freely whether passing laws making homosexuality a protected category constitute an act of tolerance. This is an adult responsibility and, when decided, it should be stated plainly. Role playing with the Fourteenth Amendment is certainly fine, but to argue that teenagers can actually decide on interpretations for themselves is ludicrous.

Beyond qualms regarding vagueness and disingenuity, the question arises whether more can be acquired than hollow slogans. "Respect differences" is an abstract, imprecise dictum that will prove practically worthless beyond the sheltered classroom unless details can be drilled in. Imagine if the Ten Commandments simply advised one to "be good." And how are particulars to be forged in novel situations without teachers and resource people always standing by? Few situations permit the luxury of discussions and self-reflection. Such incapacity, moreover, is probably most acute among those with modest cognitive abilities, the same students needing clear guidance. What is the appropriate response if one's future college roommate insists on playing music loudly, wallow in filth, display graphic homoerotic art, or otherwise pursue a culturally different lifestyle? Is such behavior merely different? As a citizen, how is he or she to assess a nation that tolerates physical mutilation of children? Perhaps, to hazard a speculative guess, future citizens will simply surrender the right to personal judgments. This responsibility might be relinquished to a state-run agency of certified experts charged with resolving such dilemmas. Responses to complex situations may be uncertainty and bewilderment.

A final point here is that limited, and admittedly anecdotal, evidence suggests that pressures to accept differences can be harshly intrusive. At least occasionally, youngsters rejecting the officially sanctioned permissive tolerance viewpoint are made to feel uncomfortable, and are ridiculed, humiliated and otherwise chastened by teachers. All, save traditional morality, is to be accepted without resistance. One analysis of this phenomenon invoked the image of "Chinese Communist brainwashing" to describe how children are involuntarily refashioned into more forgiving moral creatures. In one particular case in which a teacher preached premarital sexual relations and homosexuality, a child possessing a strict moral code was constantly called on by the teacher (up to 23 times per class period) to defend his views before a hostile audience. In another instance, a junior high school student was compelled to justify her religion against extreme derision from the group leader and fellow students. Shock tactics—graphic accounts of death, explicit sexual depictions, emotion-laden language—are also employed to jar loose pre-existing, traditional views from children. Student journals are common devices to elicit "confessions" of bad thoughts. If the opinions expressed did not conform to teacher-defined acceptability, they often had to be justified in public (for additional examples, see Sowell, 1993, Chapter 3).

We cannot claim that such abuses are rampant—the evidence on either side remains inconclusive. We merely acknowledge a revealing phenomenon: Intolerance can be disguised as tolerance. In a sense, this is no different from the familiar selective invocation of free speech in which doctrinal positions are quickly changed to reflect specific content. Here, those repudiating moral or cultural neutrality, those who insist that some things are sinful, are to be excluded from the tent of acceptance until they mend their dangerous ways. Religious fundamentalism is hazardous to civic life whereas moral relativism promotes personal growth. We are not demanding strict classroom monitoring to ensure equal respect for those who profess traditional views. And it is certainly permissible for parents to have their children instructed in moral relativism. The more important point is that "something else" is often imbedded in the fine-sounding neutral calls for generosity. And this something else may not be all that welcome by many outside this tolerance advocacy.

Sources of Values

Deciding educational content—for example, creationism versus evolution—is a familiar educational clash. Chapter 6 briefly touched on one especially bitter battle—classroom coverage of homosexuality. Given that instruction on unsettled topics inherently reflects somebody's values—regardless of "value neutrality" claims—the key question, then, is "Whose values *ought* to be conveyed?" This is a deceptively complex issue. Even if we answer "Community values," one still must ask, "What community?" The town? The state? The entire nation? What if communities are fragmented over values, as is often true? Do we take a majority vote? Must parental opinion, no matter how misinformed or wrongheaded, ultimately govern? Do taxpayers possess the final say? Do we obey professionals—school administrators, professors of education, textbook publishers, and all the auxiliary experts surrounding today's schools? Surely some amalgam is inevitable, so choices reside in the proportion.

Though we cannot resolve this quandary in detail, let us again assert the principles suggested at the chapter's beginning: All else being equal, community values (however imprecise or inarticulate) should prevail, and this means attending to parental preferences. At a minimum, parental predilections should not be subverted, attacked, and made reprehensible. Parents, of course, seldom profess an opinion on many technical aspects of education—for example, the worthiness of instructional techniques. In other instances, such as keeping order, parents may hold clear preferences though conceding to professionals wide discretion on means. However, educators, whether kindergarten teachers or distinguished professors of pedagogical philosophy, never have *carte blanche* to transform the culture. Public schools are not covert revolutionary academies. If an uprising is to commence, it is not to flow from educators through children, contrary to community intent.

It would be preposterous to submit that our schools are now battlegrounds where "revolutionary" teachers kidnap students to advance radical agendas draped in tolerance. To be sure, some portion of the education elite—professors and government bureaucrats far removed from the classroom—are intent on capturing the culture. Nevertheless, no doubt most schools overwhelmingly continue down the traditional path, and innovation almost always falls within the range of parental acceptability. Schooling is always part of the status quo baggage, and continues to evolve with it, despite occasional strife. Yet, having acknowledged this prevailing conventionality, it is also true that certain educators—their precise number we cannot say—*actively* pursue a notably different course. For them, classroom instruction is less the teaching of skills and transmitting communal culture, more an opportunity to re-engineer society furtively. Accounts in Chapter 6 of how a few gay teachers gratuitously drag the "normality" of their sexual preference into the classroom exemplifies this tactic. Others, perhaps, use the classroom as a bully-pulpit to sneak in attacks on gays.

Without attempting to quantify this radical urge, let us at least highlight its presence. This inclination is especially marked among professional educators stressing pedagogical innovation to remedy the problems of society. Thomas Sowell (1993), in his wide-ranging analysis of American primary and secondary education, makes the strongest case for its pervasiveness. He argues that radicalization efforts are commonplace, though often deviously hidden from nonprofessionals. What is officially labeled as "health" may be little more than propagating the acceptability of lifestyles widely judged socially undesirable or even dangerous. Pushing beyond the edges of acceptability, even when dangerous, is innocuously depicted as "an adventure." Foolish behavior becomes "an experiment" akin to chemistry class exercises. Meanwhile, "value clarification" in World History may amount to unrelenting, one-sided, critical, communal self-appraisals. Blatant seditious dogma is passed off as innovative scholarship from prestigious universities. Recall that publishers have plunged into the multicultural "accept-all-differences" textbook market with enthusiasm. Some of this intoning has little good to say about our own culture.

The most evident, and no doubt radical, element in this agenda is the disregard for parental values. That the educational process owes its allegiance to parents seldom appears when professional educators clamor for uplifting society. The anti-parent message is not explicit; rather, that values must flow from sources outside the home is the abiding assumption. Textbook chapters titled "How do we satisfy parents and community?" are conspicuous by their absence when preaching the gospel of improving humanity. Thus, if a child confronts the issue of homosexuality, he or she will be directed toward self-reflection, peer discussion (under teacher guidance, of course) or school-supplied materials, exercises, and outside technical experts. Not on this "list to consult" are parents, relatives, or the family's religion. Even the roster of tolerated outsiders is constrained. Inviting a minister into the classroom to present an unfriendly, morality-driven view of being gay is beyond the pale. This invitation might well constitute bias and intolerance (unless, perhaps, this was a pro-gay minister bidding acceptance). Occasionally, avoidance of parental contribution is tacitly acknowledged when schools warn teachers about letting parents view provocative materials or misrepresenting debatable instruction (Sowell, 1993, Chapter 3).

To appreciate this underlying anti-parent mentality, consider a journal article deceptively entitled "Involving Parents in Creating an Anti-Bias Classroom" (Barta & Winn, 1996). The authors embark by affirming the doctrine of permissive acceptance of group differences: "The problem is not the differences between people; rather, it is how people value and respond to these differences" (28). In other words, antagonisms, not being "real," are resolvable via mutual appreciation. Predictably, an "anti-bias classroom environment" requires parental support. And what about biased parents? The good news is that "some parents are aware of the necessity of cultural validation and raise their children congruent with this belief." Unfortunately, exceptions exist: "In other homes, however, opposing perspectives expressed by parents model long held biases and prejudices which are passed on to the next generation" (29). How, then, do we remedy the predicament? The answer is simple: Parents are to be invited into the classroom and together with teachers,"chart the direction of their efforts congruent with cultural influences of the particular school" (29). Advice on programs is then offered—multicultural days, grandma appreciation days—to help assist parents and "empower children," to advance this anti-bias diversity curriculum.

What these experts insist on is that teachers arbitrate the teaching of differences. Multiculturalism, newly defined as tolerance, is the official doctrine. Parents may help teachers *only* if they have the correct permissive stance; if they do not, then it is up to the teacher to reform parents. The possibility that mothers and fathers might have something legitimate to impose is, apparently, inconceivable. In a clash of values, teachers are to side with professors of education, not parents. Imagine if family members rejected cultural relativism—if they sincerely believed, for example, in prescribing standard, unaccented English, patriotism and similar "bourgeois values." For them, glorifying "foreign habits" is inappropriate for American children, a waste of time that would be better spent mastering skills such as writing clearly. Surely these are not disreputable notions, evidence of a pathological bias; indeed, they have always been commonplace. In the guise of "building a better world" there is an arrogant contempt for the status quo.

This radical proselytizing is hardly exceptional in this "tolerance literature" though, again, we cannot assess its overall popularity within the education profession. If there is a contrary viewpoint, it has escaped out attention despite multiple computer-assisted literature searches. Let us be unequivocal; celebration of differences goes far beyond acknowledging the contribution of non-U.S. cultures. Tolerance and multiculturalism are seamlessly joined to yield an easygoing clamor for permissive acceptance. To demur invites the charge of intolerance. More than curricular "enrichment" is insisted on; society itself is in need of transformation. Without this metamorphosis, inclusionary efforts can only fail. Various textbooks on instructional methods often proudly—and matter-of-factly—proclaim teachers as foot soldiers in the war of liberation against oppressive conventionality. Appreciation of differences masquerading as tolerance is the battle plan. Typical in this regard is James A. Banks's *An Introduction to Multicultural Education* (1994), which proclaims:

> Education within a pluralistic society should affirm and help students understand their home and community culture. *However, it should also free them from their cultural boundaries.* To create and maintain a civic community that works for the common good, education in a democratic society should help students acquire the knowledge, attitudes, and skills they will need to *participate in civic action to make society more equitable and just.* (italics added).

Banks is no little-known teacher voicing an obscure opinion; he is a highly visible, well-published professional educator.[5] Devising culturally sensitive techniques for imparting traditional skills is *not* what concerns him. The schools are now to cure "racism, sexism, poverty and inequality [that are] widespread within U.S. society and permeate many of the nation's institutions, such as the workforce, the courts, and the schools. To educate future citizens merely to fit into and not to change society will result in the perpetuation and escalations of these problems, including the widening gap between rich and poor, racial conflict and tension, and the growing number of people who are victims of poverty and homelessness" (39). Within the school itself, Banks calls for teaching black students Ebonics ("Black English') and assigning those in gifted and talent programs strictly according to race and ethnicity. Indeed, as ethnically sensitive learning is a prerequisite for future adult decision making, the entire school curriculum must be taught from a "culturally sensitive" perspective. Moreover, all school staff, from teachers to administrators, must heed school demographics; even disciplinary measures must mirror demographic proportionality (Ch. 7). These prescriptions, no doubt, are hardly conventional, and if proposed to parents, would draw considerable opposition. "Tolerance" differs substantially from its traditional meaning, and this multiculturalism is hardly Black History Month.

Whether Banks's vision is burgeoning orthodoxy we cannot say; we can say, however, that this radicalism is not unique. Sonia Nieto (1994) is another prominent, well-published authority in this multicultural movement and, like Banks, endorses far more than acknowledging diverse contributions to our collective identity. In her aptly titled "Moving Beyond Tolerance in Multicultural Education," she confronts the traditional definition of tolerance and finds it woefully lacking. Just putting up with differences is grossly insufficient: Differences must be highly esteemed and afforded unqualified acceptance. Even inserting material about previous neglected group contributions is worthless, a mere cosmetic sop, as is being "color blind." The traditional school, with its emphasis on maintaining order, imparting skills and training future citizens for the status quo, is the enemy. Two other much published professors of education enthusiastically concur in the need for social transformation. According to Grant and Sleeter (1993) "The societal goals of this approach [multicultural education] are to reduce prejudice and discrimination against oppressed groups, to work toward equal opportunity and social justice for all groups, and to *effect an equitable distribution of power and members of the different cultural groups*" (italics added).

Stripping away the educational jargon reveals an underlying philosophy best understood as "radical collectivist egalitarianism."[6] This is a sweeping radical agenda though it may not be fully understood as such by its advocates. Commitment to individualism and universalism is to be replaced by collectivist, group-based identities, a modernized tribalism. Merit is suspect, if not outright dangerous elitism. Beliefs about good and bad, at least for Banks, Nieto, and numerous others, are to be supplanted by some (ill-defined) theory of moral equivalence. In English classes, for example, literature readings are foremost interpreted by their ethnic origins. The idea that writings can transcend race, class and sex appears inconceivable—Joseph Conrad, for instance, can only reveal Polish perspectives. And science? "Science classes" in the ideal middle school, according to Professor Nieto, "do not focus on contributions made by members of specific ethnic groups, but have been transformed to consider how science itself is conceptualized, valued and practiced by those who have traditionally been outside the scientific mainstream" (38). Science topics include AIDS and racism but not traditional science like physics. Predictably, ability classifications are forbidden (as all children are judged to be "talented," though in different areas) and schools impose no official language, including standard English. Staff hiring, she continues, is strictly proportional to enrollment. Middle school youngsters are instructed to be critical of *everything,* that *everything* is bias, that *nothing* is taboo and that *all* is relative to one's position and ethnic/racial/gender identity (37). Finally, not surprisingly, if there is anything that is bedrock knowledge, it is that the status quo is plagued by about-to-explode inequality, oppression, and similar vices.

Further examples, all drawn from certified-expert writings and published in reputable scholarly outlets, can be gathered, but we shall refrain from beating a dead horse. The pattern is evident: Promoting greater tolerance is taken as the starting point, reworked into gladly embracing differences, and the acceptance of differences metamorphoses into radical egalitarianism. Outsiders, especially naive parents, are probably oblivious to this important philosophical shift shielded by high-sounding rhetoric. For them, perhaps, this multiculturalism is inseparable from the admirable, and hardly arguable, heightened attention to previously ignored historical and literary contributions. If this more radical nature were exposed, if parents now discovered how their children were to be conscripted to this radical campaign, justifiable outrage might ensue. Though parental indifference is often bemoaned by these experts, such distance undoubtedly permits this agenda to proceed. Without question, this refashioned tolerance, at least for those educators writing about tolerance in the education literature, has become a political weapon inconsistent with communal values.

Results?

The classroom promotion of tolerance depicted here is generally understood as a prescription to cure societal defects. Though one could dispute the diagnosis, if a medical metaphor is to be invoked, if millions are to be spent for reform, these would-be doctors must supply proof. This requirement that betterment be demonstrated is, after all, customary among educators. After all, partisans of a new math approach must confirm that a new technique boosts proficiency. Progress cannot be built on hope and worthy intention. What, then, is the evidence regarding the reward of heightened tolerance, especially tolerance defined as enthusiastic acceptance of differences?

Other than the University of Minnesota-based Teaching Tolerance for Diversity of Belief Project described above—in which some attitudes did shift[7]—attentiveness to strict standards of accountability seem rather casual.

What drives the commitment to tolerance/multiculturalism has far more to do with dogmatic passion than emerging results. Even advocates of the massive Teaching Tolerance Project frankly acknowledge that the empirical evidence buttressing their efforts is skimpy (Heller & Hawkins, 1994, 363).[8] Perhaps for outsiders to even insist on hard proof for these now-fashionable schemes hints at covert resistance to "improving" society. Considering the immense cost of reforming the curriculum and anticipated opposition, the entire enterprise must be judged a gigantic leap of faith, a pedagogical crusade. What is more germane for our purposes, however, is the neglect of injurious consequences in this promotion of "multicultural tolerance."

At the outset, we must confess difficulty evaluating this effort as its goals are often nebulous. One sympathetic overview of this passion frankly conceded that a wide range of ends—several at cross-purposes to each other—are commonly associated with this embrace of multicultural tolerance (Bullard, 1991). Given that *educational* reforms are advanced, one might guess that instructional benefits are to be anticipated as a dividend. Students, thanks to a greater sensitivity to their personal attributes, will become "better" pupils, measured by the customary professional standards. Unfortunately, talk of improved mastery of skills—reading, science, or mathematics—scarcely arises in these sermons. Indeed, skill testing is assessed condescendingly, almost as if objective measurement, grading, and diagnosis of academic deficiency smack of a mischievous, judgmental "European" culture. The operative doctrine seems to be that "everything is good, no matter how different, and democracy requires equally of acceptance." We can only conclude that whatever the alleged benefits of this new and improved tolerance, it does not yield scholastic improvement.

This remediation effort is also financially burdensome, no small consideration given the growing demands on public education. The resource kits, training manuals, and thousands of hours spent in workshops to train teachers in tolerance are not free. However, far more serious than misallocated funds is potential harm. Unfortunately for those who might appreciate balanced assessments, the possible nonfinancial downside of this tolerance/multicultural adventure receives the briefest of mentions. Critics are typically dismissed in a few sentences, if at all. That imposing cultural relativism shrouded in calls for tolerance might *exacerbate* group conflict and engender divisive balkanization, not harmony, is not on the discussion menu. Also not examined is the possibility that bombarding students and parents with relentless diversity proclamations in the name of energetic tolerance might elicit resentment. These antagonisms, in turn, might mean diminished support for public education, even public school abandonment by affluent parents.

Surely the philosophy of radical egalitarianism hardly sounds like a prescription for tranquillity despite admonitions against oppression, inequality, and all the other alleged disruptive evils.

Moreover, the neglect of primary skills, the acceptance of academic weaknesses in the name of cultural uniqueness, and the managing of schools according to the tenets of demographic determinism may facilitate the very malady this prescription is intended to cure: the permanent consignment of the less-privileged to economic and social inferiority. Of course, promoting inclusiveness does not inherently conflict with imparting traditional skills, but this circle cannot be squared unless classroom hours are extended, and nobody suggests this prescription. For better or worse, the ticket out of impoverishment is mastery of the traditional academic curriculum, especially language and reading skills. To shield deficient youngsters with "tolerance for diversity" doctrines ultimately gravely harms them. If teachers and administrators are hired and retained because of skin color, not demonstrated competence, this compounds the crime. This novel and wide-ranging understanding of tolerance is a far cry from merely suffering the disagreeable.[9]

Does the Inculcation of Tolerance Pass Our Tests?

Our excursion initially posed five criteria for content and approach to be employed in assessing the contemporary inculcation of hearts and minds tolerance. Though limited, our review has uncovered a sufficient number of disturbing outcroppings—the requirements are often violated. Tolerance—at least in the corner of the universe that we can search—has been refashioned into unqualified acceptance of differences merged with multiculturalism. This is hardly a disaster demanding a mobilization, but—especially if our findings foretell the trend—it is far from a cheerful situation. More than a few educators are infatuated with psychologically remolding future citizens in ways contrary to standing convention. Though these experts might not define themselves as revolutionaries, this is their intent. How deeply, and with what ultimate consequence we dare not say, but it does occur. The alleged problems of American society are to be cured with untested schemes and novel philosophies, not a reaffirmation of nostrums already proven successful. Dutiful teachers are no longer to assist in acquiring the civic culture; they are to be midwives in remaking the culture.

Repeatedly, parents are construed as the ideological adversary if they fail to embrace those professionally certified relativistic doctrines. Prestigious authorities are hardly shy about making their radical political agendas plain to teachers. And teachers are scarcely embarrassed about imposing these contrivances on students. Just how far and how deeply this radical vision has penetrated into the education system, we cannot say. What we can pronounce is that it is rampant in the education literature wrestling with group antagonisms. The upshot of this push for inclusiveness, we maintain, will not be heightened harmony or capacity to suffer the disagreeable; it will be vacuous confusion as young "scholars" in due time struggle to navigate murky moral and political distinctions. One can only imagine a twelve year old trying to determine why homosexuality is "blameless" while smoking is "regretful." Will they venture to the library to gather historical documents? Consult with fellow pre-teens or study old journal entries?

A notable disingenuousness prevails regarding pedagogy. To be sure, a degree of intrusive coercion suggesting brainwashing might be detected by some, but we find this possibility less troublesome than guidance deceptively passed off as autonomous learning. Convention is not plainly presented as "our way"; rather, students are gently encouraged to conclude that they themselves have "discovered" immutable democratic principles that are actually doctrines residing on the far edge of conventional political values.[10] Leaving aside the inculcative merits of this instructive technique, it surely constitutes an easy escape from the school's civic responsibility. If accused of promoting a radically inclined political permissiveness, educators can glibly defend themselves with "The students decided by themselves." The supposition that external communal standards exist and are worthy of absorption is now replaced by a citizenship model whereby children—often lacking rudimentary cognitive skills—resolve weighty dilemmas. It is, indubitably, a trouble-inviting progression from philosopher kings to philosopher citizens to philosopher children.

The Wages of Tolerance Inculcation

The foregoing analysis has depicted the adulteration of tolerance verging on a complete refurbishing. Though tolerance surely lacks a pure, crystal-clear definition (see, for example, the excursion into this murkiness in Chapter 2), to assert that it now encompasses a heightened—even coerced—appreciation of once disliked differences corrupts the term's core meaning. The stretch has produced a rupture. Convincing heterosexuals averse to gays that tolerance requires them to esteem gays is *not* tolerance. Tolerance would be telling heterosexuals that they should accept gays *despite* antipathy. And, if this were not feasible and it was somehow decided that gays still deserved refuge, other arrangements must substitute for the shortcomings of harmful personal predilections. As Chapter 1 emphasized, a free and open society is incompatible with *thoughtcrimes*. We applaud efforts to constrain intolerant *behavior* (provided that the object of intolerance deserves protection), but consigning detestable thinking to the list of offenses undermines liberty.

This imposition of corrupted tolerance, this rush toward an imagined amicable Utopia of endless differences, involves far more than misdirected, wasteful education. Because this pursuit confounds reality—humans can never sincerely cherish everything save hatred itself—the endeavor stands as a permanent invitation to swelling resource commitment and, more serious, enlarging state coercion. A monster of rapacious appetites is being assembled. To wit, if children fall short in appreciating all those people who "differ," no matter how obnoxious or dangerous this uniqueness, the only sensible remedy is to push even harder, develop fresh programs, and tinker even more with the deficient curriculum. Permanent failure authorizes permanent effort. And, as this shortcoming is psychological in nature, the remedy must be psychological—the state must direct itself to altering thinking by whatever means necessary. If hiring teachers on the basis of demographic proportionality does not bring academic improvement, perhaps one might consider assigning grades by statistically norming them within ethnic/ sexual categories. No doubt, some innovators will demand that all textbooks be written in the prevailing street talk so as not to marginalize functional illiterates. Conceivably, one could make repugnance a criminal pathology or a medical malady requiring therapy. Machinations to implement universal cultural valuation are, no doubt, boundless.

And will this quest bring us any closer to tolerance? Probably not. At best, intensive pedagogical intervention to alter thought might yield some attitude shift of uncertain consequence. Quiet cynicism is a more likely outcome. A review of these ventures generally also shows that there is seldom much concern for demonstrated behavioral success. Discussions of programmatic efforts merely implore readers to sympathize with a greater commitment; evidence regarding exterior accomplishment—improved skills, harmonious groups relations—seems almost irrelevant. More important than wasted effort, however, are opportunity costs. Building citizens attuned to the virtues of a falsely maligned group is only a single tool in the tolerance repertory. If there are serious problems about—and this remains debatable—better panaceas are available. Chapter 7 proclaimed this message in detail—a multitude of effective, hardly challenging solutions beyond hearts and minds wait in the storehouse of historical knowledge. Many modern educators, sadly, thus resemble workers determined to build a house with only a hammer, a project both hopeless and pointless. When progress does not come, they call splendid conferences to invent new hammers or insist that their hammers are not being used with sincerity.

Nor must those hating one another be made to appreciate displeasing traits. Violent urges are controllable via the criminal code or material incentives. Tolerance, as we reiterate, can prevail between communities; it need not necessarily exist universally as a precondition of peaceful heterogeneity. Cities have long been accumulations of historical hatreds without boiling over into perpetual turmoil. Outcast groups readily learn to survive, fight back, and reach amicable settlements. A New York City or San Francisco tour will easily convince on this point. The quest for accommodation is not dedication to reshaping of human nature.

What, then, can we surmise regarding all this hurried activity to rescue America from the calamity nearly on us? It is a dangerous prescription for failure. Tolerance, properly understood, is a wondrous virtue helping people to achieve the good while accepting the shortcomings around them. It confirms the judgment that some things are bad, though sufferable, whereas others are beyond the pale. In the words of A. T. Nuyan (1997), "In true tolerance, the source of irritation remains in sight. That which is different remains different and so continues or grate and irk" (9). With tolerance, communities may survive *qua* community while nevertheless still entertaining a wide range of disputable notions. To somehow insist that democracy requires a tolerance built on some poorly articulated, all-inclusive admiration of differences subverts what tolerance can accomplish. As the English poet Blake put it, "You don't know how much is enough until you have too much."

NOTES

1. Despite the word *poverty* in its title, The Southern Poverty Law Center is hardly indigent. In 1995, for example, it spent some 10 million dollars on programs and litigation. Recall that this was the organization that reaped considerable financial benefits from the panic over Southern Black church burnings. Its endowment is about 60 million dollars with top executives drawing handsome salaries (Wilcox, 1996, 355)

2. The inherent difficulties of this relativism are revealed when "stereotypes" are addressed. In this tolerance cosmology, a stereotype seems to be a common belief that reflects poorly on a group or, if positive, its expression hints that other groups are deficient in this attribute. That this belief may be factually valid is totally ignored. Hence, to say that "African Americans are more likely to commit crimes" is a stereotypical phrase worthy of banishment, though statistical data would confirm it to be true. This tension may, however, be solved by addressing inconsequential matters. For example, in one uplifting tale from *Teaching Tolerance,* a high school instructor artfully convinced his students that "Jews always drive big cars." This was a stereotype (no data on vehicle ownership was presented, however). Having demolished this reprehensible stereotype, the essay concluded on the upbeat note that progress in intergroup relations was possible (Lefton, 1992).

3. This "get ready for demographic change" argument often collapses from internal contradictions though, predictably, this is left unsaid by its advocates. Specifically, the future economy will require an ever-more skilled workforce but, alas, many of those whose existent culture should be cherished "as is" cannot compete. How, then, are we to make them economically competitive without altering their culture? Save the U.S. becoming—at least partially—an underdeveloped nation, this conundrum is unsolvable. For a tortured example of a solution, see Banks (1994, Ch. 3).

4. The politically inspired etymological transformation of "discrimination" and "prejudice" into wholly negative terms among those preaching tolerance is a fascinating topic beyond our scope. The OED II defines prejudice as a harm inflicted on others or as a judgment rendered without prior knowledge. In more contemporary parlance, however, it is assumed that an act of prejudice is wholly capricious, without basis or evidence. Thus, to say a person is "prejudiced" is to strongly imply that he or she has no basis in fact for inflicting harm. This basis is, of course, a purely empirical matter though it is never treated as such by those who rail against prejudice.

5. Banks's professional biography in *Who's Who in American Education* runs some 3.5 inches, which is comparatively long. The listing of publications, awards, and accomplishments is extensive.

6. It is also perhaps worth noting that not only is this curriculum at odds with traditional notions of education, as described here it also draws teachers away from classroom duties. The accomplishment of a multicultural school demands teachers attend numerous outside conferences, hold multiple meetings with faculty and facilitators to coordinate the curriculum, and otherwise spend prodigious non-classroom time unconnected to enhancing traditional student skills. Given the ever-growing "innovation" in this field, and the need for more and more experts specializing in newly arrived groups in need of special attention, it is no wonder that educational costs soar while basic skill levels decline.

7. It remains to be seen whether this shift survives maturation and changed attitudes shape future behavior. Recall our previous analysis of the uncertain connection between attitudes and behavior, especially in areas far removed from daily experience.

8. The one item of supporting evidence claimed concerns shifts in racial attitudes among young children. No evidence regarding behavior, individually or collectively, is offered. Moreover, judging from the space allocated to this critical issue—a brief mention—it hardly appears to be a pressing concern.

9. The original plan of this chapter included a discussion of similar tolerance-enhancing projects at the college level. These are often conducted not by the regular faculty but by instructors employed by the housing divisions or offices of student affairs. Unfortunately for our purposes, the published literature is sparse, though what exists conforms with what is found at the primary and secondary levels—fervent calls for accepting all differences in the name of multicultural tolerance (see, for example, Schreier, 1995; Scott, 1995). What is noteworthy is that several major educational efforts were identified, and instructional materials were solicited. In all but one case, however, either our inquiries were totally ignored or, more commonly, unfulfilled promises were made to forward materials. One can only suspect that college-level diversity training experts were reluctant to have their materials made public to audiences outside their industry. That these efforts do not pass faculty scrutiny, are imposed on unwilling students, and have occasionally attracted highly negative publicity (e.g., Shalit, 1995) is all the more reason for practitioners to be less than perfectly forthcoming.

10. We have refrained from joining the debate over how democracy relates to accepting differences. Nevertheless, this matter cannot be ignored entirely. No serious student of democracy would argue that it requires the unquestioned embrace of cultural differences. This would be a radical transformation of a venerable concept. At democracy's core is *political* equality, not even-handed judgment of language or lifestyle. Like tolerance, democracy has also been expropriated to serve the multicultural agenda.

A Personal Postscript
on Political Tolerance

This has been an extended, and we hope absorbing, journey with innumerable stopovers. The persevering reader has gained a passing acquaintance with a plethora, almost Hieronymus Bosch-like, collection of unusual creatures habituating our landscape: Marxist political parties, gay and lesbian campaign organizations, the U.S. Army, the Ottoman Empire, various uncommon religious denominations, and minuscule sects advancing the oddest of odd views in zines and Cyberspace. And, as we regularly note, these are barely highlights. *Political Tolerance* may be likened to one of those wondrous zoological collections housed in scientific depositories.

A deeper purpose informs our endeavor beyond this fleeting cataloguing. *Political Tolerance* has set out to demonstrate a point seldom articulated in a world in which scholarship is inclined to stress repression: We are an *incredibly* tolerant nation. This abundance endures regardless of what most citizens desire; it is political tolerance, not necessarily psychological tolerance. The alarm monotonously sounded (typically by comfortable academics) over the immanent onslaught of subjugation—usually of the homophobic, sexual, or racial pattern—is a flagrantly specious alert. It assumes far too much about the connection between what citizens crave and what transpires. This scare tactic might well be compared to those 1970s environmentalist distress signals—Earth is about to be doomed by starvation, overpopulation, unchecked disease, resource depletion, nuclear war, pestilence, and suffocating pollution. More than a few falsely cry wolf; an entire industry flourishes dedicated to fabricating cries about ever-newly constructed wolves.

Personally, this has been an enjoyable, reassuring tour though a few discoveries are unsettling. That thousands of groups, sects, sentiments, and organizations persist advertises the immense liberties we enjoy. Equally important, this robustness contradicts calls for further government meddling into the "hearts and minds" of its citizens. Scholars wishing to enlist in the *thoughtcrime* police can seek other duties. Though some predilections still fearfully remain "underground," and surely a handful believe themselves objects of debilitating hatred, it is hard to imagine any legal—or even semi-legal—propensity being lonely. The most radical, revolutionary citizen has plentiful choices in magazines, bookstores, websites, college courses, affinity clubs, and leagues of fellow-travelers. If an effort does exist to squelch dissent, and there are always those who faithfully insist, our review comes up empty. To be sure, government may still monitor and infiltrate potentially disruptive groups, but to imply that such assaults have cleansed the landscape of anti-status quo diversity is a wholly unwarranted accusation. The evidence is overwhelming: Such "anti-diversity" efforts hardly rise to a level of a nuisance.

Our canvass has likewise brought unease. The emerging view that the *very idea* of admission standards is illegitimate is especially troubling. Measured tolerance is the hallmark of a free society, but to embrace tolerance—individual or collective—is not to asseverate that everything, "as is," is uncritically welcome. Tolerance requires drawing distinctions and defining boundaries. There can be no convenient flight from moral judgment.[1] Lexiconically, regardless of growing contrary assertions, tolerance is not a synonym for unqualified acceptance. Even allowing for generous variability in precise denotation, tolerance as a concept implies that some things are preferable and others are absolutely *verboten*. A tolerant person, for example, might conclude that open homosexuality might be admitted *provided* specified conditions are satisfied—this behavior occurs in demarcated out-of-the-way localities, it does not undermine public health, or it excludes minors. U.S. courts have long imposed comparable restrictions on advocating revolutionary ideas, for example, protesters cannot disrupt traffic. Being tolerant is hardly simple—choices are perplexing and contentious, and all this endlessly shifts with time.

Though the standards a tolerant person imposes might be exceedingly generous, they nevertheless still, irreducibly, constitute standards. They are negotiable, but this means that some negotiation is required; unilateral settlement is not permitted. Though criteria of acceptability may be ill defined at the edges, this does not proclaim boundarylessness. That codes evolve expansively does not mean everything will eventually be permitted, so why not now. The lessons we drew from the Amish and the Mormons are especially relevant here—tolerance is not unilaterally decided by those seeking it. Tolerance and discrimination within a community are intimately bound together. To deny this connection is to wholly refurbish the intrinsic meaning of tolerance. The path toward "improved" tolerance is not to subvert the act of discrimination. The debate must occur within the framework of discrimination; it must not be a contest of discrimination versus nondiscrimination. In principle, a discriminating person could well be exceedingly generous in accepting nonconformity, but the right to exclude *always* is retained. To be discriminating is not, despite what some teachers might tell children, unequivocally evil and harmful to democracy.

In our rush to advance ever-wider tolerance, this concomitant discrimination component remains neglected. At times, choosing and ranking are judged antiquated, an unfortunate remnant of a soon-to-be-abolished, hierarchy-obsessed oppressive society. Nevertheless, soliciting tolerance, like a mortgage application, must entail serious inquiries into civic worthiness. It is not enough to say "Democracy requires differences be fully accepted, therefore, because I am different, I must be thoroughly accepted." If this were society's guiding dictum, why have laws? Why have moral codes if all is equally "good"? This is a fatuous and ultimately corrosive argument that survives by endless repetition, not worthy reasoning. In the case of tolerating open homosexuality, for example, one might assess its effect on decency more generally or its consequences for upholding public order. These are not inappropriate questions with transparent answers, and raising them scarcely condemns the interlocutor to hateful homophobia. Surely a civil society is capable of serious debate regarding what is to be tolerated and what deserves banishment.

Of course, what we advance—this reasoned debate over the intricacies of tolerance—is currently the norm. Ours is a defense of the status quo under siege of a long, once self-evident tradition, not a call for change. For some, this contention is too well-established, too correct on its face, to reiterate. Perhaps not as banal as defending intact families, at least before the days when soaring illegitimacy grew more acceptable. Nevertheless, as Chapter 8 demonstrated, a growing segment of the political spectrum *does* wish to convert tolerance into a promiscuous enticement. And, as witnessed, they daily achieve measures of success, often under the guise of worthy motives and alluring rhetoric. Our rejoinder is that much is to be lost and little gained by this transformation. Virtually their entire agenda of practices to be welcomed more vigorously—including homosexuality—is *already* tolerated. From fat children to those speaking nonconventional English, from proud, open lesbian teachers to militant Marxist professors of philosophy, all flourish unbothered by dreaded government intrusion. McCarthyism lives only in history books despite the fears of immediate resurrection. Nor is there any need to rescue these nonconformists from angry mobs of hateful citizens.

The battle over the standing of these off-center practices instigates the conflict. What is being sought is taking something *merely* tolerated—for example, obesity or transsexuality—and elevating it to a "perfectly 'normal' though different" status. One might call this ennoblement process "super-tolerance." The recipe for remaking the once devious into the perfectly normal is made up of equal parts of affirmative tolerance, moral relativism and group-based multiculturalism, with the removal of all right-wing sentiments such as the Klan or Nazis. At core, "tolerance battles " have become disputes over hierarchy of values, lifestyles, sexual preferences, ideology, or whatever else divides human beings. To depict the conflict as acceptance versus banishment is a canard. To accept this counterfeit version of tolerance as the genuine article is akin to believing that Lake Wobegon's schoolchildren *really* are all above average.

This is a doomed campaign—no society is willing to confer "esteemed normality" on everything that might be believed, practiced or advocated. The quest is mindlessly Utopian. Witness the howls of derision when the Oakland, California School Board suggested that "Ebonics" (black street slang) be equated to conventional English. Traditional parents are not going to acquiesce when confronted with demands that their children venerate homosexuality. Replacing acceptance of the disliked (tolerance) to graciously welcoming this once-loathed object multiplies political costs exponentially. Witness the endless impassioned conflicts in schools over matters of slight educational importance. And the last few increments may require investments of colossal treasure, including the costs of backlash. It is just not worth it—there are better battles to fight, including teaching children how to write.

Finally, to reinvoke a metaphor from Chapter 1, do we wish to build a society whose resistance to danger resembles laboratory rats bred sans immunity systems? This worrisome vision is not as grotesque as it might initially appear. The juvenile delinquent lacking moral sensibilities who commits heinous crimes has become all too familiar. For these sociopaths, stealing money is indistinguishable from earning it: Both involve getting money, no more, no less. Nor is this deficiency limited to children. A few corporations seem unwilling to discriminate between selling useful and unsafe products: Both satisfy popular appetites, no more, no less. Such inability to judge between right and wrong has many roots, and some of it is well beyond civic instruction. Nevertheless, to conscript "tolerance" into the cause of weakening the definitions of public life is to commit a horrendous disservice for what makes civilization possible. Tolerance is too valuable to be rendered an empty cliché in the service of heightened self-esteem.

NOTE

1. This connection between moral judgment and tolerance is a much neglected, but essential, topic in the "tolerance industry." It is typically assumed that tolerance survives—indeed, flourishes—where nonjudgmentalism is the norm. It may well be the opposite: To be tolerant requires that one first stand on firm moral ground. He or she who rejects the superiority of anything cannot be tolerance. This complex set of issues is addressed in detail by Budziszewski (1992).

References

Aberbach, J. D., & Walker, J. L. (1970). The meaning of Black Power: A comparison of White and black interpretations of a political slogan. *American Political Science Review, 64,* 367-388.

Abrahamson, M.(1996). *Urban enclaves: Identity and place in America.* New York: St. Martin's.

Adler, L. K. (1991). *The Red image: American attitudes towards communism in the Cold War.* New York: Garland.

Adorno, T., Franke-Brunswik, E., Levinson, D. J., & Nevitt S. R. (1950). *The authoritarian personality.* New York: Harper.

Ahlstrom, S. E. (1972). *A religious history of the American people.* New Haven: Yale University Press.

An American answer to intolerance. (1939). Council Against Intolerance in America.

America Online (August 13, 1996). Embattled gay teacher resigns Byron Center.

The appeal to vigilance by fourty intellectuals (D. Cook, Trans.)(1994). *Telos, 98-99,* 135-136. (Originally appearing in *Le Monde,* July 13, 1993).

Aronson, D. (1994). Why tolerance? *Phi Kappa Phi Journal, 74* 28-30.

Avery, P. A., Bird, K., Johnstone, S., Sullivan, J. L., & Thalhammer, K. (1992). Exploring political tolerance with adolescence. *Theory and Research in Social Education, 20,* 386-420.

Balch, S. H., & London, H. I. (1986). The tenured left. *Commentary.*

Baldwin, T. (1985). Toleration and the right to freedom. In J. Horton & S. Mendus (Eds.), *Aspects of toleration.* London: Methuen.

Banks, J. A. (1994). *An introduction to multicultural education.* Boston: Allyn & Bacon.

Barnum, D. G., & Sullivan, J. L. (1989). Attitudinal tolerance and political freedom in Britain. *British Journal of Political Science, 19,* 136-146.

Barnum, D. G., & Sullivan, J. L. (1990). The elusive foundations of political freedom in Britain and the United States. *Journal of Politics, 52,* 719-739.

Barson, M. (1992). *"Better dead than Red!" A nostalgic look at the golden years of Russiaphobia, Red-baiting, and other Commie madness.* New York: Hyperion.

Barta, J., & Winn, T. (1966). Involving parents in creating anti-bias classroom. *Children Today, 24,* 28-30.

Bawer, B. (Ed.). (1996). *Beyond queer: Challenging gay left orthodoxy.* New York: Free Press.

Bawer, B. (1996). Truth in advertising. In B. Bawer (Ed.), *Beyond queer: Challenging gay Left orthodoxy.* New York: Free Press.

Beatty, K. M., & Oliver, W. (1984). Religious preference and practice: Reevaluating their impact on political tolerance. *Public Opinion Quarterly, 48*, 318-329.

Belknap, M. R. (1977). *Cold War political justice: The Smith Act, the Communist Party and American civil liberties.* Westport, CT: Greenwood.

Berrill, K. T. (1992). Anti-gay violence and victimization in the United States: An overview. In G. M. Herek & K. Berrill (Eds.), *Hate crimes: Confronting violence against lesbians and gay men.* Newbury Park, CA: Sage.

Billingsley, K. L. (1997). Afrocentric curriculum. In P. Collier & D. Horowitz (Eds.), *The race card.* Rocklin, CA: Prima Publishing.

Bird, K., Sullivan, J. L., Avery, P., Thalhammer, K., & Wood, S. (1994). Not just lip-synching anymore: Education and tolerance revisited. *The Review of Education/Pedagogy/Cultural Studies, 16*, 373-386.

Blumenthal, M. D., Kahn, R. L., Andrews, F. M., & Head, K. B. (1972). *Justifying violence: Attitudes of American men.* Ann Arbor, MI: Institute for Social Research.

Boulard, G. (November 1, 1994). If words could kill. *The Advocate.*

Braden, C. S. (1950). *These also believe: A study of American cults and minority religious movements.* New York: Macmillan.

Braude, B., & Lewis, B. (1982). Introduction. In B. Braude & B. Lewis (Eds.). *Christians and Jews in the Ottoman Empire* (Vol. I). New York: Holmes & Mier.

Brown, B. A. (1992). Mad about multiculturalism. *Diversity and Division, 2*, 30-32.

Budziszewski, J. (1992). *True tolerance: Liberalism and the necessity of judgment.* New Brunswick: Transaction Publishers.

Budziszewski, J. (1993). The illusion of moral neutrality. *First Things,* August/September.

Bullard, S. (1991). Sorting through the multicultural rhetoric. *Educational Leadership, 49*, 4-7.

Button, J. (1995). *The radicalism handbook.* Santa Barbara, CA: ABC-CLIO.

Byrd, M. L. (1995, April). *Cultural diversity and tolerance.* Paper presented at the Western Social Science Association Annual Conference, Oakland, CA.

Cantril, H. (Ed.). (1951). *Public opinion 1935-1946.* Princeton, NJ: Princeton University Press.

Carnegie Foundation. (1989). *The condition of the professoriate: Attitudes and trends.* Princeton, NJ: The Carnegie Foundation for the Advancement of Teaching.

Caute, D. (1978). *The great fear: The anti-Communist purge under Truman and Eisenhower.* New York: Simon & Shuster.

CBS News/*New York Times* (February 1993). *CBS News/New York Times State of the Union and Call-Back, February 1993.* New York: CBS News. Data supplied by the Inter-university consortium for Political and Social Research.

Cecil, A. R. (1990). *Equality, tolerance and loyalty: Virtues serving the common purpose of democracy.* Austin: University of Texas.

Center, B. (March 19, 1996). Gay teacher set up for firing, union says. *The Grand Rapids Press.*

CLAGS News (Vol. VI, no. 1) The Center for Lesbian and Gay Studies, The Graduate School and University Center of the City University of New York, Summer 1996.

Code of Federal Regulations: National Defense. (1996). Vol. 32, part I to 190. Revised July 1, 1996. Office of Federal Register, National Archives and Records Administration.

Cohen, R. (1993). *When the old left was young: Student radicals and America's first mass student movement, 1929-1941.* New York: Oxford University Press.

Comstock, G. D. (1991). *Violence against lesbians and gay men.* New York: Columbia University Press.

Conley, J. J. S. J. (1994). Another tolerance: A reading of *Summa Theologica, I-II, Q.96.* Paper presented at the ACPA (Roundtable), Fairfield University, December 3, 1994.

Converse, P. E. (1970). Attitudes and nonattitudes: A continuation of a dialogue. In E. R. Tufte (Ed.), *The Quantitative Analysis Social Problems.* Reading, MA: Addison-Wesley.

Conway, M. M. (1991). *Political participation in the United States* (2nd ed.). Washington, DC: Congressional Quarterly Press.

Corbett, M. (1982). *Political tolerance in America.* New York: Longman.

Coser, L. (1964). *The functions of social conflict.* New York: The Free Press.

Cover, M. R. (1995). Focus on tolerance. *Update on Law-Related Education, 19,* 16-17.

Cowling, M. (1990). *Mill and liberalism* (2nd ed.). Cambridge, England: Cambridge University Press.

Crespi, I. (1971). What kinds of attitude measures are predictive of behavior? *Public Opinion Quarterly, 35,* 327-334.

Crick, B. (1971). *Political theory and practice.* London: Allen Lane/The Penguin Press.

Cutler, S., & Kaufman, R. L. (1975). Cohort changes in political attitudes: Tolerance of religious nonconformity. *Public Opinion Quarterly, 39,* 63-81.

Davis, J. A. (1975). Communism, conformity, cohorts and categories: American tolerance in 1954 and 1972-1973. *American Journal of Sociology, 81,* 491-513.

DeBold, K. (Ed.). 1994. *Out for office: Campaigning in the gay nineties.* Washington, DC: Gay and Lesbian Victory Fund.

Delli Carpini, M. X., & Keeter, S. (1996). *What Americans know about politics and why it matters.* New Haven, CT: Yale University Press.

D'Entreves, M. P. (1990). Communitarianism and the question of tolerance. *Journal of Social Philosophy, 21,* 77-91.

Deutscher, I. (1975). Words and deeds: Social science and social policy. In A. E. Liska (Ed.), *The Consistency Controversy.* New York: John Wiley.

D'Souza, D. (1995). *The end of racism.* New York: Free Press.

Eberstadt, M. (1996, June 17). Pedophilia chic. *The Weekly Standard.*

Ellis-Stoess, L. (1996). Tolerating tolerance in the classroom. *Journal of Law and Education, 25,* 181-189.

Erikson, K. T. (1968). *Wayward Puritans: A study in the sociology of deviance.* New York: John Wiley.

Erskine, H. (1970). The polls: Freedom of speech. *Public Opinion Quarterly, 34,* 483-496.

Faber, M. (1994). A story about size. *NEA Today, 13,* 6.

FactSheet5. #51. March 1994.

Federal Bureau of Investigation (1995). *Uniform crime report for the United States 1995.* Washington, DC: US Government Printing Office.

Ferrar, J. W. (1976). The dimensions of tolerance. *Pacific Sociological Review, 19,* 63-81.

Fishbein, M., & Ajzen, I. (1975). *Belief, attitude, intention and behavior.* Reading, MA: Addison-Wesley.

Flacks, R. (1992). Marxism and sociology. In B. Ollman & E. Verhoff (Eds.), *The Left Academy: Marxist Scholarship on American Campuses.* New York: McGraw-Hill.

Fletcher, G. P. (1996). The instability of tolerance. In D. Heyd (Ed.), *Toleration: An elusive virtue.* Princeton, NJ: Princeton University Press.

Fotion, N., & Elfstrom, G. (1992). *Toleration.* Tuscaloosa: University of Alabama Press.

Fuller, L. (Ed.). *The international directory of little magazines and small presses, 1995-1996.* Paradise, CA: Dustbooks.

Fulton, L. (1996). *Directory of small presses/magazine editors and publishers.* Paradise, CA: Dustbooks.

Fumento, M. (1996). Politics and church burning. *Commentary.*

Gans, H. J. (1995). Urbanism and suburbanism as ways of life: A reevaluation of definitions. In P. Kasinitz (Ed.), *Metropolis: Center and symbol of our times.* New York: New York University Press.

Gay and lesbian professional groups. (1992). Atlanta, GA: Gay and Lesbian Task Force, American Library Association.

General Social Surveys 1972-1994: Cumulative Codebook (1994). Chicago: National Opinion Research Center.

Gibson, J. L. (1987). Homosexuals and the Ku Klux Klan: A contextual analysis of political tolerance. *The Western Political Quarterly, 40,* 427-448.

Gibson, J. L. (1988). Political intolerance and political repression during the McCarthy red scare. *The American Political Science Review, 82,* 511-529.

Gibson, J. L. (1989). The policy consequences of political intolerance: Political repression during the Vietnam War era. *Journal of Politics, 51,* 13-35.

Gibson, J. L. (1987). The political consequences of intolerance: Cultural conformity and political freedom. *The American Political Science Review, 86,* 338-356.

Gibson, J. L. (1992a). The political consequences of intolerance: Cultural Conformity and Political Freedom. *American Political Science Review, 86,* 338-356.

Gibson, J. L. (1992b). Perceived political freedom in the Soviet Union: A comparative analysis. Paper presented at the 1992 Annual Meeting of the Western Political Science Association, San Francisco, CA, March 19-21.

Gibson, J. L., & Anderson, A. J. (1985). The political implications of elite and mass tolerance. *Political Behavior 7,* 118-146.

Gibson, J. L., & Bingham, D. (1985). *Civil liberties and Nazis: The Skokie free speech controversy.* New York: Praeger.

Ginsberg, B. (1986). *The captive public: How mass opinion promotes state power.* New York: Basic Books.

Gintis, H. (1992). The reemergence of Marxian economics in America. In B. Ollman & E. Verhoff (Eds.), *The Left academy: Marxist scholarship on American campuses.* 1982. New York: McGraw-Hill.

Goldstein, R. J. (1978). *Political repression in modern America.* Cambridge, MA: Schenkman.

Grabb, E. G. (1979). Working-class authoritarianism and tolerance of outgroups: A reassessment. *Public Opinion Quarterly, 43,* 36-47.

Grant, C. A., & Sleeter, C. E. (1993). Race, class, gender, and disability in the classroom. In J. A. Banks & C. A. McGee Banks (Eds.), *Multicultural Education: Issues and Perspectives(* 2nd ed.).Needham Heights: Allyn & Bacon.

Gray, J. (1992). The virtues of toleration. *The National Review.*

Gray, J. (1993). The failings of neutrality. *The Responsive Community, 3,* 21-31.

Greenawalt, K. (1989). *Speech, crime, & the uses of language.* New York: Oxford University Press.

Halberstam, J. (1982-1983). The paradox of tolerance. *The Philosophical Forum, 14,* 190-207.

Heller, C., & Hawkins, J. A. (1994). Teaching tolerance: Notes from the front line. *Teachers College Record, 95,* 337-368.

Herbert, M. R. (1984). Marxism and biology. In B. Ollman & E. Verhoff (Eds.), *The Left academy: Marxist scholarship on American campuses* (Vol. II). New York: Praeger.

Herek, G. M. (1992). The social context of hate crimes: Notes on cultural heterosexism. In G. M. Herek & K. Berrill (Eds.), *Hate crimes: Confronting violence against lesbians and gay men.* Newbury Park, CA: Sage.

Herman, D. (1997). *The antigay agenda.* Chicago: University of Chicago Press.

Heyd, D. (1996). Introduction. In D. Heyd (Ed.), *Toleration: An elusive virtue. Princeton, NJ: Princeton University Press.*

Himmelfarb, G. (1990). *On liberty & liberalism: The case of John Stuart Mill.* San Francisco: Institute for Contemporary Studies.

Himmelfarb, G. (1994). A de-moralized society. *The Public Interest, 117,* 57-80.

Hofstadter, R. (1964). *The paranoid style in American politics.* Chicago: University of Chicago Press.

Hollander, E. P. (1975). Independence, conformity and civil liberties: Some implications from social science research. *Journal of Social Issues, 31,* 55-68.

Human Rights Campaign 96. (1996). *A manual for candidates*. Washington, DC: Human Rights Campaign.

Huntington, L. (1997). *The floodgates are open: How the Internet unleashes purveyors of strange politics*. Independent Study Project. Urbana: The University of Illinois.

Janzen, W. (1990). *Limits on liberty: The experience of Mennonites, Hutterites and Doukhobor communities in Canada*. Toronto: University of Toronto Press.

Jennings, K. (Ed.). (1994). *One teacher in Ten*. Boston: Alyson.

Jones, R. S. (1980). Democratic values and pre-adult virtues: Tolerance, knowledge and participation. *Youth and Society, 12*, 198-220.

Kamen, H. (1967). *The rise of toleration*. New York: McGraw-Hill.

Karpat, K. (1982). *Millets* and nationality: The roots of the incongruity of nation and state in the post-Ottoman Empire. In B. Braude (Ed.), *Christians and Jews in the Ottoman Empire* (Vol. I). New York: Holmes & Mier.

Kelling, G., & Coles, C. (1996). *Fixing broken windows*. New York: Free Press.

Kennedy, R. (1995, August 17). Jews and Muslims share a piece of Brooklyn. *New York Times*.

King, P. (1976). *Toleration*. New York: St. Martin's.

Klehr, H. (1984). *The heyday of American Communism: The Depression decade*. New York: Basic Books.

Klehr, H., Haynes, J. E., & Firsov, F. I. (1995). *The secret world of American Communism*. New Haven, CT.: Yale University Press.

Koch, S. (1994). *Double lives: Spies and writers in the secret Soviet war of ideas against the West*. New York: Free Press.

Kraybill, D. B. (1993). Negotiating with Caesar. In D. B. Kraybill (Ed.), *The Amish and the State*. Baltimore: Johns Hopkins University Press.

Kymlicka, W. (1996). Two models of tolerance and pluralism. In D. Heyd (Ed.), *Toleration: An Illusive Virtue*. Princeton, NJ: Princeton University Press.

Ladd, E. C., & Lipset, S. M. (1973). *Professors, unions and American higher education*. Washington, DC: American Enterprise Institute for Public Policy Research.

LaNoue, G. R. (1993). Social science and minority set-asides. *The Public Interest, 110*, 49-62.

LaPiere, R. T. (1934). Attitudes vs. actions. *Social Forces, 13*, 230-237.

Lawrence, D. (1976). Procedural norms and tolerance: A reassessment. *American Political Science Review, 70*, 80-100.

Lefkowitz, M. (1996). *Not out of Africa*. New York: Basic Books.

Lefton, T. (1992). Building bridges in the Big Apple. *Teaching Tolerance, 1*, 8-13.

Legutko, R. (1994). The trouble with toleration. *Partisan Review, 61*, 610-624.

Levin, M. B. (1971). *Political hysteria in America*. New York: Basic Books.

Lindholm, W. C. (1993). The National Committee for Amish Religious Freedom. In D. B. Kraybill (Ed.), *The Amish and the State*. Baltimore: Johns Hopkins University Press.

Lipset, S. M., & Raab, E. (1973). *The politics of unreason: Right-wing extremism in America, 1790-1970*. New York: Harper.

Locke, J. (1963). *A letter concerning toleration*. Mario Montuori (Ed.). The Hague: Martinus Nijhoff.

Lockhead, C. (1996). The third way. In B. Bawer (Ed.), *Beyond queer: Challenging gay Left orthodoxy*. New York: Free Press.

Manatt, R. P., & Drips, J. (1994). Hate crimes: Bigotry, harassment, vandalism and violence on campus *International Journal of Education Reform, 3*, 481-490.

Marcus, G. E., Sullivan, J. L., Theiss-Morse, E., & Wood, S. L. (1995). *With malice towards some: How people make civil liberties judgments*. New York: Cambridge University Press.

Marcuse, H. (1968). Repressive tolerance. *A critique of pure tolerance*. Boston: Beacon Press.

McClosky, H. (1964). Consensus and ideology in American politics. *The American Poilitical Science Review, 58*, 361-382.

McClosky, H., & Brill, A. (1983). *Dimensions of tolerance: What Americans believe about civil liberties.* New York: Russell Sage Foundation.

Mendus, S. (1989). *Toleration and the limits of liberalism.* Atlantic Highlands, NJ: Humanities Press International.

Meyers, T. J. (1993). Education and schooling. In D. B. Kraybill (Ed.), *The Amish and the State.* Baltimore: Johns Hopkins University Press.

Mickens, E. (1994, July 12) Is there a lavender class ceiling? *The Advocate.*

Mill, J. S. (1947). *On liberty.* In A. Castel (Ed.). Arlington Heights, IL: AHM Publishing.

Miller, J. A. (1992). Radical economics. In M. Buhle, P. Buhle, & D. Georrgakas, *Encyclopedia of the American Left.* Chicago and Urbana: University of Illinois Press.

Moskos, C. C., & Butler, J. S. (1996). *All that we can be: Black leadership and racial integration the army way.* New York: Basic Books.

Mueller, J. (1988). Trends in political tolerance. *Public Opinion Quarterly, 52,* 1-25.

Muller, J. Z. (1993, August-September). Coming out ahead: The homosexual movement in the academy. *First Things.*

Murray, C. (1994). *In pursuit of happiness and good government.* San Francisco: Institute for Contemporary Studies.

NGLFT Policy Institute. (1992). Anti-gay/lesbian violence & defamation in 1992. Washington, DC: National Gay & Lesbian Task Force Policy Institute.

National Coalition of anti-violence programs & New York gay and lesbian anti-violence project. (1995). Anti-lesbian/gay violence in 1995 (2nd ed.). New York: National Coalition of Anti-Violence Programs & New York Gay and Lesbian Anti-Violence Project.

National Union catalogue pre-1956 imprints (Vol. 366). London: Mansell Information.

Nestle, J. (1992). Flamboyance and fortitude: An introduction. In J. Nestle (Ed.), *The persistent desire: A femme-butch reader.* Boston: Alyson.

Nie, N., Junn, J., & Stehlik-Barry, K. (1996). *Education and democratic citizenship in America.* Chicago: University of Chicago Press.

Nieto, S. (1994). Moving beyond tolerance in multicultural education *Multicultural Education, 1,* 9-12, 35-38.

Noël, L. (1994). *Intolerance: A general survey.* (Trans. A. Bennett). Montreal: McGill-Queen's University Press.

Nunn, C. Z., Crockett, H. J., Jr., & Allen Williams, J., Jr. (1978). *Tolerance for nonconformity.* San Francisco: Jossey-Bass.

Nuyan. A. T. (1997). The trouble with tolerance. *American Catholic Philosophical Quaterly, 71,* 1-12.

O'Dea, T. F. (1957). *The Mormons.* Chicago: University of Chicago Press.

Ollman, B., & Verhoff, E. (Eds.). (1982). *The left academy: Marxist scholarship on American campuses (Vol. I).* New York: McGraw-Hill.

Ollman, B., & Verhoff, E. (Eds.). (1984). *The left academy: Marxist scholarship on American campuses (Vol. II).* New York: Praeger.

Olshan, M. A. (1993). The National Amish Steering Committee. In D. B. Kraybill (Ed.), *The Amish and the State.* Baltimore: Johns Hopkins University Press.

Oskamp, S. (1977). *Attitudes and opinions.* Englewood Cliffs, NJ: Prentice Hall.

Overstreet, H. A. (1964). *The strange tactics of extremism.* New York: Norton.

Page, B. I., & Shapiro, R. Y. (1992). *The rational public.* Chicago: University of Chicago Press.

NGLFT Policy Institute. (1992). *Anti-gay/lesbian violence & defamation in 1992.* Washington, DC: National Gay & Lesbian Task Force Policy Institute.

People for the American Way. (1995). *Hostile climate 1995.* Washington, DC: People for the American Way.

Podhoretz, N. (1996). How the gay-rights movement won. *Commentary.*

Place, E. (1993). Appendix: Significant legal issues. In D. B. Kraybill (Ed.), *The Amish and the State*. Baltimore: Johns Hopkins University Press.

Posner, R. A., & Silbaugh, K. B. (1996). *A guide to America's sex laws*. Chicago: University of Chicago Press.

Powers, R. G. (1995). *Not without honor: The history of American anticommunism*. New York: Free Press.

Pritchett, C. H. (1977). *The American constitution*. New York: McGraw-Hill.

Prothro, J. W., & Grigg, C. W. (1960). Fundamental principles of democracy: Bases of agreement and disagreement. *Journal of Politics, 22*, 276-294.

Rieder, J. (1985). *Carnarsie: The Jews and Italians of Brooklyn against liberalism*. Cambridge: Harvard University Press.

Rips, G. (1981). *The campaign against the underground press*. San Francisco: City Lights Press.

Roche, J. P. (1958). American liberty: An examination of the 'tradition' of freedom. In M. R. Konvitz & C. Rossiter (Eds.), *Aspects of liberty : Essays presented to Robert E. Cushman*. Ithaca, NY: Cornell University Press.

Roche, J. P. (1989). Was everyone terrified? The mythology of 'McCarthyism.' *Academic Questions, 2*, 64-79.

Rosenstone, S. J., Kinder, D. R., Miller, W. F., & the National Elections Studies. (1994). *American National Election Study; 1992-1993 Panel study on securing electoral success*. Ann Arbor: Inter-university Consortium for Political and Social Research.

Scanlon, T. M. (1996). The difficulty of tolerance. In D. Heyd (Ed.), *Toleration: An elusive virtue*. Princeton, NJ: Princeton University Press.

Lord Scarman (1987). Toleration and the law. In S. Mendus & D. Edwards (Eds.), *On Toleration*. Oxford, England: Clarendon Press.

Schrecker, E. (1986). *No ivory tower: McCarthyism and the universities*. New York: Oxford University Press.

Schrecker, E. (1994). *The age of McCarthyism: A brief history with documents*. Boston: Bedford Books.

Schreier, B. A. (1995). Moving beyond tolerance: A new paradigm for programming about homophobia/biphobia and heterosexism. *Journal of College Student Development, 36*, 19-26.

Schuman, H. (1972). Attitudes vs. actions *versus* attitudes vs. attitudes. *Public Opinion Quarterly, 36*, 347-354.

Schur, E. M. (1980). *The politics of deviance: Stigma contests and the uses of power*. Englewood Cliffs, NJ: Prentice Hall.

Scott, R. M. (1995). Helping teacher education students develop positive attitudes towards ethnic minorities. *Equity and Excellence in Education, 28*, 69-73.

Shalit, W. (1995). A lady's room of one's own. *Commentary*.

Shore, E. (1992). Radical professionals and academic journals. In M. Buhle, P. Buhle, & D. Georrgakas, *Encyclopedia of the American Left*. Chicago and Urbana: University of Illinois Press.

Smith, T. W. (1990). Report: The sexual revolution. *Public Opinion Quarterly, 54*, 415-435.

Smolowe, J. (1996, April 29). The unmarrying kind. *Time*.

Sorrells, J. (1993). *The directory of gay, lesbian and bisexual community publications in the United States and Canada*. nd ed.). Guerneville, CA: James Sorrells.

Sowell, T. (1993). *Inside American education*. New York: Free Press.

Stamouli, A. A. (1912). In J. Hastings (Ed.), *Encyclopedia of religion and ethics (Vol. 12)*. New York: Scribner.

Stephens, J. F. (1991). *Liberty, equality and fraternity*. Chicago: University of Chicago Press.

Stouffer, S. A. (1955). *Communism, conformity and civil liberties*. New York: Doubleday.

Suall, I. (1962). *The American ultras: The extreme right and the military-industrial complex*. New York: New America.

Sullivan, J. L., Piereson, J., & Marcus, G. E. (1982). *Political tolerance and American democracy.* Chicago: University of Chicago Press.

Sunstein, C. R. (1993). *Democracy and the problem of free speech.* New York: The Free Press.

Suris, O. (1995, August 22). Saugatuck attracts many gay tourists, but there is friction. *The Wall Street Journal,* P.1, A4.

Swearingen, J. A. (1996). Promoting tolerance in preservice teachers. *Social Education, 60,* 152-154.

Terry, P. (1993). Language diversity in a complex classroom: Teaching teachers linguistic tolerance. Paper presented at the Annual Meeting of the Modern Language Association, Toronto, Canada, December 27-30.

Tooley, M. (1996, October). Burn, baby, burn. *Chronicles: A Journal of American Culture.*

Triandis, H. C. (1975). Research directions suggested by the ACLU. *Journal of Social Issues, 31,* 165-182.

Tussman, J. (1977). *Government and the mind.* New York: Oxford University Press.

von Schultress, B. (1992). Violence in the streets: Anti-lesbian assault and harassment in San Francisco. In G. M. Herek & K. Berrill, *Hate crimes: Confronting violence against lesbians and gay men.* Newbury Park, CA: Sage.

Walsh, W. B. (1944). What the American people think of Russia. *Public Opinion Quarterly, 4,* 513-522.

Washington Post. (1991). *Washington Post Soviet attitude poll, August 1991.* Radnor, PA: Chilton Research Services. Data made available through the Inter-University Consortium for Political and Social Research, Ann Arbor, MI.

Weir, J. (1994, August 23). Mad about boys, *The Advocate.*

Weissberg, R. (1996). The Real Marketplace of Ideas. *Critical Review, 10,* 107-122.

West, R. B. (1957). *Kingdom of the saints: The story of Brigham Young and the Mormons.* New York: Viking.

Whalen, W. J. (1979). Doukhobors. In P. K. Meagher et al., *Encyclopedic Dictionary of Religion (vols. A-E).* Washington, DC: Corpus Publications.

Wilcox, L. (1988). *Guide to the American left: Directory and bibliography.* Olathe, KA: Laird Wilcox Editorial Research Service.

Wilson, W. C. (1975). Belief in freedom of speech and press. *Journal of Social Issues, 31,* 69-78.

Wolfson, A. (1996). Toleration: Locke versus Mill. *Perspectives on Political Science, 25,* 192-197.

Woog, D. (1995). *School's out.* Boston: Alyson.

Yoder, P. (1993). The Amish view of the state. In D. B. Kraybill (Ed.), *The Amish and the State.* Baltimore: Johns Hopkins University Press.

Zalkind, S., Gaugler, E., & Schwartz, R. (1975). Civil liberties, attitudes and personality measures: Some exploratory research. *Journal of Social Issues, 31,* 31-53.

Zaller, J. R. (1992). *The Nature and Origins of Mass Opinion.* New York: Cambridge University Press.

Zaragoza, F. M. (1995). Tolerance—Indispensable requirement for global security. *UN Chronicle, 32,* 73-74.

Zellman, A. (1965). *Teaching 'about Communism.'* New York: Humanities Press.

Zellman, G. (1975). Antidemocratic beliefs: A survey and some explanations. *Journal of Social Issues, 31,* 31-54.

Index

About the Author

Robert Weissberg, PhD, was born and raised in New York City. He graduated with a BA from Bard College and a PhD from the University of Wisconsin-Madison. He has taught at Cornell University, and is currently teaching political science at the University of Illinois-Urbana. Dr. Weissberg has published books about political socialization and public opinion as well as numerous articles in professional journals on political behavior. In addition to his scholarly work, he regularly contributes serious and humorous essays to popular publications.